Derrida and Lacan

Properly speaking, the *nœud bo* [Borromean knot] in question completely changes the meaning of writing. It gives to the aforementioned writing an autonomy, which is all the more remarkable in that there is another writing [*une autre écriture*], which results from that which one could call a precipitation of the signifier. Derrida has laid emphasis on this, but it is quite clear that I showed him the way.

(Jacques Lacan, *Seminar XXIII*, 144)

[T]he motif of divisibility is perhaps the argument of last resort in '*Le facteur de la vérité*' [...]. It is formally, in the chain of consequences, that on which everything depends. The affirmation of the indivisibility of the letter [...]

(Jacques Derrida, *The Postcard*, 512)

DERRIDA AND LACAN

Another Writing

Michael Lewis

Edinburgh University Press

For Zöe Sutherland

Edinburgh University Press Ltd
22 George Square, Edinburgh

Typeset in Sabon
by Servis Filmsetting Ltd, Stockport, Cheshire, and
printed and bound in Great Britain by
Biddles Ltd, King's Lynn, Norfolk

A CIP record for this book is available from the British Library

ISBN 978 0 7486 3603 7 (hardback)

Contents

Acknowledgements

The necessary conditions: Lorenzo Chiesa and his work, without which hardly any of this book would have been possible; Simon Fuller for his discourse on deconstruction, which he perhaps hoped would have become dialogues; Damian Veal for an unbending critical vigilance and the use of a computer; Siobhan McKeown and Darren Ambrose for their support in the Autumn of 2005, the Winter of 2005–6 and the Spring of 2006; Anna Johnson for Luke Thurston's wonderfully helpful translation of Seminar XXIII; Stephen Barrell and Marjorie Gracieuse (along with the noble Cormac Gallagher) for assistance with translation; Michael Kolkman for the continued use of computers; Mum and Dad for a place to go and for providing emotional support in the Summer of 2006, as well as their joy and assistance during my move to Sussex in 2007.

Darren, Siobhan and Emily, for their support in 2006–7; Stephen Houlgate, who encouraged me to feel at home at Warwick and provided financial and Hegelian support; conversations with Nick Butler and Eleni Karamali (who also lent me her office and library in the Summer of 2007); Grandma for her strength in enduring and infinite patience, in memoriam of Nana; Mogfish, the Summer of 2006 and the sun for which I did what I could to be grateful; *Test Match Special*; Ricky Gervais, Stephen Merchant, and Karl Pilkington, for their company through the necessarily solitary times of reading and writing in the summer, autumn and winter of 2006, when this book was composed (and when it was revised during the spring, summer, and autumn of 2007), although their company had begun the previous winter.

Carol Macdonald, copy editor Tim Clark, and two anonymous readers at EUP for granting me an extension and for their help and generosity.

Lisa Barnett, Olivia Case, Soomi Do, Caroline Bass, Raphaelle Moor, Ed Greig, Briony Coates-Rees, Verena Kroth, Gal Levin.

For those friends who remain: first of all, Nick Butler, Alex Hartland, Kelly Beard, Hilary Chapman, Siân Smith, Bronia Evers,

Charmaine Coyle, Martin Burley, Barry Phipps, Darren Ambrose, Siobhan McKeown, Eleni Karamali, Tom Greaves, Simon Hill, Havi Carel, Daniel Jones, Emily Harding, Stephen Houlgate, Greg Hunt, Paul Davies, Miguel de Beistegui, Chris Ellis, Jim Graham, Nina Power, Jenny Bunker, Ben Smith, Nick Joll, Alexandra le Bolloch, Christa Percival, Becky Mahay, Chris Branson, Pete Wolfendale, Ioannis Trisokkas, Jo Kuzma, Rafael Winkler, Gerald Moore, Barnaby Hutchins, Stephen Dunne, Marjorie Gracieuse.

And to all at Sussex University, for saving me, and for such hospitality. In particular, Tanja Staehler, Sarah Sawyer, Michael Morris, Murali Ramachandran, Gordon Finlayson, Joe Ward, Dylan Trigg, and all my students, particularly Cara, Andres, Carly, Joe, and Debbie.

(Scholars should note with amusement the disparity in length between this list and that from my first book. . .)

This book was finished for the first time in November 2007; the last revision was made in March and April of 2008. Everything happened in the intervening time, which allowed me to write its dedication.

Michael Lewis
Sussex
Friday, 18 August 2006 – Friday, 18 April 2008

Abbreviations

Works by Jacques Derrida

D	(1981) *Dissemination* [1972]
EW	(1991) ' "Eating Well", or the Calculation of the Subject: An Interview with Jacques Derrida' [1988]
FL	(2001) 'Force of Law: The "Mystical Foundation of Authority" ' [1989–90]
MP	(1982) *Margins: of Philosophy* [1972]
OG	(1974) *Of Grammatology* [1967]
P	(2002) *Positions* [1972]
PC	(1987) *The Postcard: From Socrates to Freud and Beyond* [1980]
R	(1998) *Resistances: Of Psychoanalysis* [1996]
S	(1979) *Spurs: Nietzsche's Styles* [1978]
SM	(1994) *Spectres of Marx: The State of the Debt, the Work of Mourning, and the New International* [1993]
SP	(1973) *Speech and Phenomena and Other Essays on Husserl's Theory of Signs* [1967]
W	(1998) 'I'll have to wander all alone' [1995]
WD	(2001) *Writing and Difference* [1967]

Works by Jacques Lacan

AE	(2001) *Autres Écrits*
E	(2006) *Écrits* [1966]
SI	(1988) *Seminar Book I: Freud's Papers on Technique, 1953–1954*
SII	(1988) *Seminar Book II: The Ego in Freud's Theory and in the Technique of Psychoanalysis, 1954–1955*
SIII	(1993) *Seminar Book III: The Psychoses, 1955–1956*
SIV	(1994) *Le Séminaire livre IV: La Relation d'Objet, 1956–1957*

SV	(1998) *Le Séminaire livre V: Les Formations de l'Inconscient, 1957–1958*
SVI	(1958–9) 'Le Séminaire livre VI. Désir et son interprétation, 1958–1959'. Unpublished manuscript [References to unpublished seminars are given by the date of the session]
SVII	(1992) *Seminar Book VII: The Ethics of Psychoanalysis, 1959–1960*
SVIII	(1991) *Le Séminaire livre VIII: Le Transfert, 1960–1961*
SIX	(1961–2) 'Le Séminaire livre IX. L'Identification, 1961–1962'. Unpublished manuscript
SX	(2004) *Le Séminaire livre X: L'Angoisse, 1962–1963*
SXI	(1998) [*Seminar Book XI:*] *The Four Fundamental Concepts of Psychoanalysis* [1964]
SXIII	(1965–6), 'Le Séminaire livre XIII. L'Objet du psychanalyse, 1965–1966'. Unpublished manuscript
SXIV	(1966–7), 'Le Séminaire livre XIV. Logique du fantasme, 1966–1967'. Unpublished manuscript
SXVII	(2007) *Seminar Book XVII: The Other Side of Psychoanalysis* [1969–1970]
SXX	(1999) *Seminar Book XX: Encore, 1972–1973*
SXXIII	(2005) *Le Séminaire livre XXIII: Le Sinthome, 1975–1976*

Preface

> In comparison with a genius, that is to say with a being which either *begets* or *bears*, both words taken in their most comprehensive sense – the scholar, the average man of science, always has something of the old maid about him. [. . .] The worst and most dangerous thing of which a scholar is capable comes from the instinct of mediocrity which characterises his species.
>
> (Nietzsche, *Beyond Good and Evil*, ¶206)

The concern of contemporary philosophy, philosophy that stands in the wake of the travails of the transcendental problematic, is to understand the difference between a (present) being and the (absent, transcendental) event that produced it. An attempt to understand contemporary philosophy may thus legitimately take the form of a comparative study of the various ways in which the one unique difference has been understood. To superimpose these explanations of the nature of this difference will bring to light the idiosyncrasies of each explanation and perhaps throw into relief the deficiencies of one account relative to another.

If contemporary thought is an attempt to discern an event and to deal with the potentially distorting effects of *naming* this event in language, is the comparative study, as a superimposition of two or more thoughts of the event, not a productive course for philosophy as it muses on its own end? Is it not a way in which philosophy can be *almost* as vibrant as in its metaphysical pomp and splendour? Is this not what the true adult does, to look back on his younger self with ever more unclouded eyes, forever repeating childhood in its exuberance, and gradually eliminating the mistakes that accompany every 'first time'?

What are texts of philosophy if not explicit considerations, which now stand as signs, of the way in which beings as a whole present themselves at a certain epoch, and an attempt to understand how that could be so, signposts of the moment at which the absent event crystallised itself into a present entity? Do they not constitute moments of reflection in human life where, rather than being blithely lived through, the conditions of this existence are scrutinised? Moments in which the human being turns towards the transcendental event and tries to think it.

And now at the end of history, the injunction to read these and other signs is more shrill than ever, when it is impossible to strike out on one's own and write another metaphysical text. One is compelled rather to explain how the transcendental could have been given, how being could have been 'sent' to thinkers and named by them in so many diverse ways.

By striving upstream in the river of Heraclitus, which is permanently creating and destroying the determinations of beings we see as present, we attempt to reach back before the fully constituted being, to the event which produces it; we attempt actively to move with the flow of the river, instead of merely gazing at one of its stretches. We attempt to eradicate as far as possible those determinations which are imported from the actual being which the event produces. To do otherwise would be to limit the event to our own actuality, which is posterior to and always a restriction of the virtual event. It is to reduce the virtual to the potential, to the possibility modelled upon the actuality that has eventuated from it. It is to make the traditional mistake of transcendental thinkers, in understanding the prior on the basis of the posterior, the origin on the basis of the originated, and thus to explain nothing.

The question we shall ask in the following study is this: must we not do all we can to achieve a proper understanding of our current *actuality*, in order to ensure that we know precisely *what* we might be imputing to the event, to prevent determinations that we do not recognise as such from creeping into our understanding of the event that is meant to explain this determination? And in order to do this, should we not utilise those discourses, perhaps scientific, which elucidate the *genesis* of this actuality?

One way in which one might understand thinkers of the transcendental to set themselves apart from each other is in terms of how much they see their peers or subjects as determining the transcendental on the basis of that which it makes possible. It seems to me, then, particularly in the case of the two thinkers to whose work we shall devote ourselves, that one may fruitfully interpret the divergence between them in terms of their respective understandings of *what precisely* one's explanation is compelled to import into the origins of our current state and the strategies that are required in order to reach the real source in defiance of this current.

When we are operating at the level of the transcendental, today, at the end of history, there is, I believe, a certain justification – if not a necessity – for operating at both a textual and a comparative level. And one can carry out one's *own* original erasure precisely by means of comparison, superimposing one thinker's text upon another, to produce a new palimpsest, bringing to light something that has genuinely not been seen before.

It is this that I am attempting to achieve by superimposing Lacan's text on Derrida's. The peculiarity which this reveals in *Derrida's* text relates to the question of the animal, which, it seems to me, Derrida cannot properly acknowledge us to be. Here we are following a trope of Agamben's in suggesting that, for Derrida, we, *zōon logon ekhon*, are exhaustively determined by *logos*. To the exclusion of all *zōē*. Lacan avoids this mistake by beginning with a *genetic* approach to the human being, an examination of the modification of the non-human animal or the animalic human which results in the novel creation of language (*logos*). It is this genetic approach that allows Lacan to perhaps more fully understand man's actuality, and thus more competently to approach his transcendental.

Thus, by means of such a superposition, a comparative study can open up a *new* vision of an 'old' philosophy. It can cast new light on an old thinker, shed from a different perspective, setting the other's work into a hitherto concealed relief. In the difference, a revelation can split open.

Perhaps it is hubristic to claim that in this way the comparative study can be *creative*, but in any case it can have an important critical role, a vigil against potentially dogmatic slumber. It can remind *any one perspective* that it cannot be the ultimate, any finite reading that it is not infinitely comprehensive, and precisely by confronting one thinker with another, particularly one with whom they have not themselves engaged, or, as is the case here, with whom they have been able to engage only in a way that is tellingly unsatisfactory. For, as Heidegger has it, great thinkers think but one thought. And those who are not great thinkers have the privilege of being able to envision *more than one*, to open the blinkered and therefore tenaciously unfolded system of one thinker to another. To view the battle of the giants (*gigantomachia peri tēs ousias*) from the position of an ivory tower, from whose vantage one looks on from afar without as yet entering the strife.

Thus, in deference to Nietzsche, this comparative study of Jacques Derrida and Jacques Lacan *is* the work of a 'scholar', but perhaps we have a different estimation of scholarship. We do not say that it is a substitute for true creativity, but neither is it – today – as sterile as Nietzsche thought.

Introduction

Derrida presents deconstruction as if it were not a thesis.

Perhaps deconstruction is almost nothing more than the most extreme consequence of Saussure's linguistics. Following Saussure, Derrida understands a 'text' as a system in which a plurality of differences precedes any presence and makes it possible; and conversely, any system of differences may be deemed a 'text'. The significance of each element of a text is determined by its differences from all of the other elements of the same system. A text is thus a system in the literal sense that no one element can act as a textual element or 'signifier' without 'standing together with' (*syn-stema*) others.

Deconstruction demonstrates that in fact no finite system can be isolated from other systems in which its elements partake. These systems would for this reason be spatially understood as those which 'surround' it. And naturally, the same would apply to these systems, and so on *ad infinitum*. The result would be that each element of a textual system is defined by its differences from an infinite number of elements, and thus by an infinite number of differences.

This infinity is beyond the comprehension of a finite consciousness, and hence if the significance of any one signifier depended upon its references to an infinite number of signifiers, then this significance would be indeterminable for such finite intelligences. Therefore, any finite text which attempts to exist in a self-contained fashion must cut itself off from this infinity of other signifiers in order to achieve a semblance of determinate meaningfulness. It must set a limit to the reference of signs from one to the other and thus manufacture a finite whole. It must posit something absolutely outside of the text which sets a clear limit to its textuality. That which is 'outside the text' (*hors-texte*) is the 'transcendental signified'.

The system of textuality extends infinitely and thus any belief in a moment of presence that would remain outside, precedent to, and governing this text is illusory.

There is no final presence outside of difference, nor would such a presence be reached by subdividing signifiers to reach some atomic presence that would stop the differences becoming infinitesimal. This presence would be a substance, something that exists and maintains its identity without reference to anything else. It is an immediate self-presence which takes as its model God's relation to himself, or the subject's immediate auto-affection which is figured in the voice of the interior monologue. Divine substance or human subject makes little difference: both are to be submitted to a 'deconstruction' which demonstrates that individual identity cannot be formed if that identity is not differentiated from an infinity of other signifiers which that individual could be. How can one be unique if one has not differentiated oneself from everything else?

Deconstruction demonstrates this reference of any one signifier or text to an infinity of others. This reference is necessary in order for that signifier or text to form its identity and at the same time, since the extent of language is infinite, it results in the impossibility of ever fully forming this identity. The identity of any signifying element will always be in process, an event that is unfolding, as one realises more and more of one's references. One is constituted by this process of signification from one element to another, and from here to yet another. One never finishes finding out who one is, or what it is. The event of differentiating oneself is an event that is never over and done with. This infinity means that one's identity, and the meaning of what one says, or what one's text says, is never entirely within one's control. The text is not governed by a meaning or intention-to-say (*vouloir-dire*) that would be outside of it. It is this that deconstruction demonstrates: that one's meaning cannot be entirely determined independently of the signifiers one is compelled – contingently – to use. It demonstrates not only the dependence of meaning upon the text or context but also that since this text is infinite there are an infinite number of contexts in which a signifier can be used. Thus the meaning of a signifier is never determinable independently of the text and its meaning is simply never fully determinable, or indeed determinate.

In order to mean something, it is necessary to set a limit to one's textuality. But at the same time it is impossible to do so. Deconstruction is the attempt to acknowledge this necessity and its impossibility. Therefore it shows that signifiers cannot mean just what they are *intended* to mean since they *retain* their references to an infinity of other signifiers. Thus any text is susceptible of a double reading: one according to the authorial attempt to suture it, to isolate a finite text within an infinite one, and the other (which is always an infinity of others) which is opened up by this situation of any finite text within an infinite one.

Deconstruction, therefore, involves no thesis of its own, it merely draws the most extreme consequences from the most penetrating discourses of its day, including, most importantly for our purposes, Saussure's understanding of the signifier. This issues in the notion of an infinite textuality, upon which every supposed instance of presence depends.

The only act which a deconstructive author performs is to show that any finite text depends for its meaning upon an infinite textuality which exceeds it, and at the same time upon its own excision from this infinite context. It finds a moment at which both this dependence and this attempt at independence become visible: in the signifier whose significance is in a technical sense 'undecidable'. Something akin to the 'navel', as Freud deployed the term, which marks at one and the same time one's dependence and independence (Freud 1953 [1900]: 525).

'Deconstruction' is meant to be nothing beyond a series of readings. It is not some thesis or procedure that can exist independently of the texts *which* it reads. Indeed it attempts to be the most faithful reading possible, more so than those which simply reconstruct the author's intention *or* simply ignore it. The decision to mean something (the belief in an intuitive access to a transcendental signified) and the ultimate undecidability of meaning are both *inherent* in the finite system, for we are finite subjects immersed in a textual system that can only be infinite.

If there is nothing outside of the determinate languages and discourses we find ourselves in at any point in history, clearly deconstruction cannot do otherwise than occupy the languages and discourses it has been given, but it does so in a way that admits their contingent placement within an infinity, which philosophical texts at least do not admit to be finally determinant of their meaning.

Deconstruction insists that one's access to an outside of language – 'reference' – is not so simple as is often believed. This is crucial in order to prevent any signifier from believing that it is the ultimate, that it has finally spoken the truth about the real. It is necessary to demonstrate the continuous impossibility of biunivocal reference, by situating texts within an infinite con-text, in order to show that no one word can ever name the real. And yet, by means of a strategic use of signifiers – which precisely involves a continuous deconstruction, a continual identification of undecidables, proving the manufactured status of the transcendental signified – one can at least negatively indicate this beyond of language, this unnameable 'other'.

Deconstruction thus proposes itself as innocent of all idiosyncratic theses, about either the nature of language or the nature of the real that is otherwise than language and the manner whereby the one can or cannot reach the other.

But what if this were not the case? What if this were merely how things appeared? What if, in deconstruction's demonstration of the production of signification through differential textuality, there *was* a certain idiosyncrasy that amounted to a substantive thesis on the nature of language and its relation to the real? To demonstrate this would be to open deconstruction to the possibility of *criticism*.

It is not with the aim of criticising deconstruction that we open this book, but in order to ask the question of whether it is *possible* to criticise it, because it appears *prima facie* to be of a kind that is not *susceptible* to criticism. If we can demonstrate that deconstruction does in fact involve some idiosyncratic, thetic content in the form of a disavowed proposition, then we may be able to show that it can indeed be criticised.

The best way we have found to bring this purported idiosyncrasy to light is by exposing the existence of an *alternative* approach to the same problematic. That of Lacan. This will allow us to show that deconstruction's idiosyncrasy relates to its attitude to the transcendental. To believe that we must adopt a transcendental approach and a transcendental approach *alone* might itself be deconstruction's presupposition – although, as we shall come to suggest at the very end, perhaps this is merely philosophy's presupposition, which Derrida, as much as Lacan, wishes to demonstrate. The difference will then perhaps be that while Derrida does not appear to believe in an alternative, Lacan – the non-philosopher? – does.

In any case, the transcendental attitude would be deconstruction's most basic attitude to the other of the text. We shall come to specify just what 'transcendental' means for Derrida. In truth, the meaning he finds in the word, the direction in which it signals, will have been imparted to it by every major turning point in the word's history: Aristotle, the Scholastics, Kant and Husserl. Preliminarily, and very simply, it will be a concern with the conditions of possibility of meaning, that which is generally thought to be a presence or self-presence *without* conditions.

This will also amount to asking the question of the conditions of possibility of language. It will therefore be to ask the question of what is *other than* linguistic, but it insists that we can address this other of language only by *means* of language. Language cannot leave itself, and so one can only gesture towards its other by using language in a certain way. Deconstruction amounts to the destruction of the metaphysical pretension of language simply to leave itself and refer to the real, the 'thing in itself'.

If we can say anything about the real this must be derived transcendentally from the standpoint of language, or the signifier (*le signifiant*). We can begin nowhere else in our attempt to reach the real.

If the signifier is actual, deconstruction asks, if there really are signifiers, 'in the real', what must necessarily characterise the real? What must necessarily and continuously characterise the real in order that the signifier be possible? The answer is that the real must *write*. It must contain a heterogeneity or two orders, one of which is capable of leaving a trace in the other. From our standpoint, within the signifier, one way in which we may speak of the capacity to trace is in terms of a 'primitive' form of *writing*. And there are many other words one could use, and which Derrida indeed does use. The crucial point is that the other of language can be spoken about – by definition one might say – only *with* language. It must be figured on the basis of some feature which language can pick out, or rather, which characterises language itself.

And yet, one might ask: might there not be another way in which man as the speaking animal could reach the real? Might it be the case that Derrida understands man to be *entirely* 'imprisoned' within language, and to have no features which might themselves be otherwise than language? It is as if man were trapped within language and had to find some cunning way with words that would provide the password *out* of language, or the linguistic strategy with which to indicate that language is *not* everything, that there is another to it, but another that can only be reached by means of language.

But might there not be another way to approach the real? If man has language, is he not, according to the Aristotelian definition, also an animal? Might this animality not remain a feature of man and provide him with another access to the real than that provided by language? The psychoanalytic theory of Lacan argues for the proposition that the linguistic animal is incapable of leaving this animality behind, and that thereby the real that is other than language continues to feature in his existence, at least in the form of the object of his *desire*.

By juxtaposing Lacan with Derrida we are attempting to determine whether there is an alternative to Derrida's 'quasi-transcendentalism'. But this will not simply be the abstract hanging together of two independent positions; the fixation on the genesis of the human being in Lacan will be shown to affect the way in which we understand the transcendental deduction of the beyond of language. Thus, the Lacanian approach will issue in *another* understanding of the 'writing' which the real must carry out in order for language to exist. The genetic and the transcendental approaches to the signifier meet in the heart of a letter, the Greek letter *khi* (χ), which the current work, by superimposing the two trajectories of Lacan and Derrida, inscribes.

But why the need to criticise? Why should we ever have wished to ask about deconstruction's very susceptibility to criticism? And why initially turn to Lacan in this search? At least in part, this was determined by Derrida's own relationship with Lacan's texts, and the peculiar differences between this relationship and those which Derrida maintains with others of his contemporaries. It is noticeable that there is a certain haste and at the same time an incompleteness about Derrida's relations with Lacan. It is as if he engaged with *this* contemporary earlier than anyone else and persistently throughout his *œuvre*, but without ever getting to grips with his work. This haste and this lack do not characterise his relations with others, such as Habermas and Nancy, which came much later, and others that often occurred only posthumously.

Given the similarity of Lacan's project, the nature of this engagement has made us wonder about deconstruction's ability to enter genuine *dialogues* with discourses that present an alternative way of approaching the problems that deconstruction itself addresses. Is it perhaps the case that the texts which deconstruction reads are either deconstructible (which always means being susceptible to a non-metaphysical reading), such as those of Rousseau, or are themselves close approximations, to be made exact, of a deconstructive reading, such as those of Bataille? Thus one is either unconsciously both deconstructible and deconstructive, or one consciously attempts to be deconstructive. There is no other way in which texts are for Derrida.

But what of those texts which can*not* be deconstructed? What of those other writings which presuppose neither a metaphysical relation between a text and its outside *nor* a deconstructive re-writing of this relation? Derrida honestly admits that there are some thinkers whom he does not know how to address. Looming large on this horizon is Deleuze, and for a long time it was Marx.

For us, the same seems to be the case with Lacan, and yet here there is a difference. From the very beginning, Derrida spoke of Lacan. Marginally, subliminally, but nevertheless tangibly; and, uniquely, Derrida admits to forming an opinion of Lacan *before* he had ever or could ever have read his complete *œuvre*. In this case then, he seems to apply deconstruction as a purely formal *framework* which he elsewhere resolutely claims that it is not. We might even say, without the caution of quotation marks, that he *criticises* Lacan. Is this because Derrida perceives Lacan as a *rival*?

In its fundamental characteristics, deconstruction does not change from one end of Derrida's work to the other. That this is so testifies to the extraordinary rigour of his thought from the start, but this persistence risks a certain rigidity which rules out in advance a genuine debate and a properly hospitable relation to its *rivals*. This would explain why Derrida rarely engaged with his contemporaries to the same extent as he did with figures from the past. But this reluctance makes Derrida's attitude to Lacan all the more surprising, and illuminating. It is as if Derrida sensed that Lacan, and Lacan alone, represented a genuine alternative to deconstruction, irreconcilable with it. And the fact that Derrida – surely one of the most intellectually honest men who has ever lived – never left Lacan behind, testifies to his continuing unease.

What does Derrida himself say about his precipitant entry into the fray? Without doubt, he saw Lacan as an aggressor, and the force of Lacanian discourse in France at the time was such that it had to be engaged with by a discourse, like deconstruction, which understood so well its inevitable situation within its contemporary discursive configuration.

Derrida's early impression of Lacan, formed on the basis of a small number of his earlier texts, before they were collected in *Écrits*, was that it contained 'motifs' that were pre-deconstructive. And yet at the same time Derrida saw that psychoanalysis was from the start an ally of deconstruction – and particularly insofar as language is central to an understanding of the unconscious. The paradox which Derrida never seems to be able to explain fully is that Lacan, the Freudian who most insisted upon the linguistic nature of the unconscious, was also the 'most deconstructible'. We shall understand this to result from the fact that Lacan was asking the same questions as Derrida but providing answers that were different to his own.

If something about Lacan disturbed Derrida, we suggest that it was his proximity. Lacan shared Derrida's terrain, his own problematic, but he approached it from a quite different angle, one which Derrida perhaps could never quite measure. It was perhaps the uncanniness of this doubling, which Derrida could not control, that spurred his premature action. Towards the very end of their long, sporadic, joust, Derrida came to think of Lacan and himself as 'lovers', and what are lovers if not two subjects who actively strive, not for each other, but for a common object beyond both of them, accidentally almost, in reaching for this forbidden fruit, clutching each other's hand? This in any case was Lacan's understanding (cf. SVIII: 66–7).

Derrida's failure properly to encounter Lacan indicates one thing: that *deconstruction can only deconstruct* – it can only be itself, and cannot become other than it is, and thus respond within a genuine dialogue. This after all is the limit of any great thought: it can be just one thing. It can only be itself. Mediocre thinkers can be many things, while great thinkers are consumed by a single thought and their task is to remain true to the fullest expression of that insight. That 'deconstruction can only deconstruct' means that deconstruction *is* idiosyncratic, and hence vulnerable to criticism.

The Lacanian alternative

Let us look ahead to what Lacan's alternative comprises. It concerns the animal, and the generation of the human being from animal nature.

What initially suggested to us that Lacan might be attempting something both akin to deconstruction and different from it, was his famous triad of imaginary, symbolic and real. Derrida often rails against this tri-partition, but it seems to us that his attention is confined to the symbolic and the real. Now while he is naturally concerned to find an 'excluded middle' (*tertium datur*) between the inside and the outside of the text as metaphysics understands it, a relationship of opposition, we shall contend that this third is simply the real, but the real as properly understood. The notion of an autonomous realm, with a nature heterogeneous to both, is something that we believe Derrida does not allow himself. Lacan, on the other hand, does. This suggests both that Lacan is addressing Derrida's question, and that he reaches a different conclusion. And, as we shall see, it shows that he goes about this by way of a different method.

We shall argue that Derrida's limiting himself, and man, to just two terms, the symbolic and the real, evinces his belief that we are fundamentally trapped within our cultural symbolic system and all that can be attempted is a strategic manner of indicating its beyond, basically *per negativum*. This would be to approach the real transcendentally, but to acknowledge that the conditions of one's own possibility are only relatively other and not absolutely other. In other words, that the other extends beyond that otherness which is relative to ourselves, we creatures of language.

This is evinced in Derrida's belief that we can only speak of the outside of the opposition between symbolic and real in terms of oppositions and the deconstruction *of* these oppositions. Opposition is a relation which characterises *language*. We are condemned to an oppositional relation to the outside, all we can do is work strategically within the opposition, and indicate what it eclipses.

On the other hand, from the very start, Lacan attends to the imaginary. A third realm that obeys the rules neither of the text nor its outside. It is a realm which was revealed to Lacan by his initial travails as a psychiatrist, in the region of science. This attention to science was part of his study of the *chronological* genesis of the human being, from infant to adult. This extended later on into a psychoanalytic and quasi-anthropological interest in the emergence of language and the cultural system, together forming the order of the 'symbolic'. Both of these (ontogenesis and phylogenesis) seem to us to be either ignored by Derrida or restricted in the importance bestowed upon them.

For Lacan, the human being is characterised not by an oppositional understanding of the relation between symbolic and real, but by a triplex binding of symbolic, real and imaginary. Thus from the very beginning, despite his stress on language and culture – a crucial part of psychoanalysis generally – Lacan did not characterise the human being in terms of language alone. For after all, the 'animal that has language' (*zōon logon ekhon*) is also the *animal* that has language. We are not merely entrapped by language, we are also caged in by our *bestial* nature.

Thus, with respect to Derrida, we alter our understanding of the present state in which we find ourselves, and this must in turn alter the manner in which we go about extracting ourselves from this state. We must know from what to abstract before we begin our abstraction. It is not just the symbolic that entraps us but the imaginary as well. But at the same time, the imaginary may provide us with another opening onto the genuinely real, outside of its oppositional determination by language. In fact, this is the ambiguity of the imaginary as Lacan understands it.

The imaginary is the realm of Gestaltic images which, when perceived, trigger instincts. It is only due to a malfunctioning of the imaginary in the human animal that the symbolic order is produced. Man needs the crutch of the symbolic in order to compensate for his inability *naturally* to satisfy his vital needs. (These needs are then minimally satisfied but at the cost of their infinitisation into desire.) If one does not attend to evolution – or rather, since Lacan is not a Darwinian, to 'genesis' – and the sciences which speak of the animal and its characteristics, one will perhaps miss something of the nature of language. It is perhaps an essential feature of the word that it is the answer to a need that arises in a realm which precedes it. For Lacan, its present nature forever bears the scar of its genesis. Language yields up traces of a *chronological*, pre-historic past, in which our inhuman, animal nature can be read.

That language never truly eradicates the beast is foundational for psychoanalytic thought. The *zōon*'s primal cries resound in the *logos* of the *zōon logon ekhon*. We are simply not consumed by language without remainder. The animal persists.

The imaginary is the animal within us. If Derrida ignores this imaginary, it is because he ignores the genesis of the human being and believes that we must ignore it, now that we are firmly enmeshed in a network of oppositions, of dualities. Does he thereby understand the human being in a way that is *too* human? Does this not leave Derrida unable to take into account the insights of any natural and human sciences which do *not* understand the world in a way that conforms to the laws of the signifier or the nature of the trace? Does Derrida display too much belief in the philosopher when he understands man as the animal who has language and then proceeds to investigate only the *logos*?

By failing to envisage the full repercussions of this animal genesis, does Derrida miss the fact that the human remains a product of pre-human and inhuman tendencies, animal tendencies, material tendencies, which have conglomerated in one only apparently stable species, which we perceive as such only as a result of our selective and limited perceptual systems? What if the human were rather a site which of itself involved an inhuman otherness, and one which set a definite limit to the infinite differentiation of the signifier? Perhaps we are not only human, but also animals, and even minerals, and as such able in some way to access these elements which existed long before this conglomerate 'man' came about?

If the present is constituted by something other than language, if the symbolic is joined and limited by the *imaginary*, then this must lead us to understand the real in a different way. The real is differentiated not merely oppositionally, from the symbolic, but from *both* the symbolic and the imaginary. This real will not simply be the real as it is accessed from the standpoint of the symbolic, which Derrida calls 'archi-writing' – among other things – but also the real of the *imaginary*.

Lacan's thought provides philosophy with a new way to relate to the *non*-philosophical, and to the sciences in particular. For do these sciences not at times genuinely reveal an inhuman or pre-human world, elements which are utterly distinct from those categories which our perspectival perception attributes to the world? At least one name for the jointure of philosophy and science is 'psychoanalysis'.

Thus, while we agree with Derrida's assertion of the necessity of transcendentalism, we shall propose that the way in which we transcend determination towards the indeterminate – the 'other', the 'real' – should be modified by an attention to genesis, to scientific insight, to the animal. This is the method that will lead Lacan towards an alternative to Derridean deconstruction.

The chiasm of the two paths

The course of this work may be mapped by the miniscule form of the letter *khi*. I insist on this diagram partly in tribute to Lacan's diagrams and the way in which they present a different form of writing to Derrida's. At the same time, it will be remembered that it is on the topic of the *letter* that Derrida distances himself from Lacan. The latter's diagrams are deliberately overloaded with signification; they are meant to transport us sublimely beyond the limits of meaning towards the real, and they must, I believe, always be understood as a form of *letter*. Every diagrammatic image is a letter, and every letter a diagram. Writing for Lacan always involves an imaginary dimension, the trace that lies at the basis of language constituting an indivisible imaginary unity, which amounts to the pre-symbolic real as it is preserved in the symbol. This imaginary dimension is precisely what distinguishes his writing from Derrida's.

Thus the letter as diagram and the diagram as letter is the perfect model for our own approach, our own writing, which imprints Lacan's *œuvre* on Derrida's:

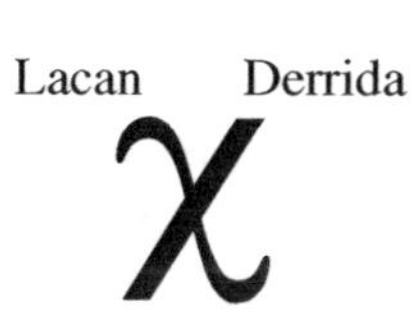

Our journey begins from the top left, and descends. Lacan's path is different to Derrida's, although they do intersect, and initially appear to be aiming for the same place. What distinguishes Lacan's path is first of all that it changes: there is a twist, from the very start, which Derrida does not fully see, and which remains in a different way at the end. This will be the notion of the imaginary, and its development will explain the crucial changes in Lacan's thought that cause him to diverge from Derrida and evade him. Lacan's later work is not the same as that work which Derrida encounters and, with justification, deconstructs. While admitting that some things change in Lacan's later work, Derrida cannot see that the basis for this later difference lies in the imaginary twist that was already present in the early work.

Perhaps this is unfair. At the very least it goes beyond what deconstruction proposes itself as capable of achieving. Perhaps Derrida can only isolate a certain moment, a certain text of Lacan's, and cannot envision the entire trajectory. Deconstruction restricts itself to a finite text. It is precisely the indication that any one finite text remains dependent upon an infinity of other texts and yet is required to imperfectly separate itself therefrom in order to present itself as meaningful. Does it not risk thereby failing to bring together the different *periods* of a thinker's work in an appropriate way? This is exceptionally important in the case of Lacan, whose divergence from the deconstructive project can, in its most basic thrust, be indicated only if we follow the very unfolding of his work.

Perhaps deconstruction is still too philosophical. The beginning of Lacan's path, which explains his later development, is characterised by a serif, depicting a twist that philosophy in itself cannot encompass whilst it remains *purely philosophy*. Derrida leaves the encounter with Lacan – and by extension with science, and the non-philosophical – quite unperturbed, his trajectory never seriously deviating from first to last. He ploughs on through the texts, furrowing a necessarily endless series of trenches. His path continues straight to the very end, where it peters out with his untimely death.

Lacan's course, on the other hand, does change, but not as a result of Derrida's interception. In fact, it was already on course to differ, thanks precisely to the twist from which it began, the crook that hooks it onto science, which was used to dissect human genesis and reveal the imaginary dimension, a dimension that remained concealed to Derrida. Lacan did indeed see the need for a *certain* deconstruction of the work of his middle period, which is why it was *possible* for

Derrida to intervene here. But crucially, Lacan's deconstruction does not lead him in the same direction as Derrida's leads him.

To summarise the four individual chapters this work comprises:

In Chapter 1 we expose Lacan's early psychoanalytic theory in such a way as to demonstrate where and how it is vulnerable to deconstruction.

In Chapter 2, this deconstruction is carried out. In this way we exhibit the nature of Derridean deconstruction as it understands itself, by giving credence to its claim to be exhausted by the in each case singular readings which it constructs. Here we show that Lacan does indeed understand the relation between the text and its other – the symbolic and the real – as a relation of opposition, where the real is defined as what is *not* symbolic, not differential, and hence as composed of things that are fully and originally present, and immediately self-identical. Thus his position is vulnerable to deconstruction.

Chapter 2 is the only chapter we devote to Derrida since his path is at all points the same. We choose the moment at which it intersects with Lacan's to show that, while it is possible to render Lacan vulnerable to its incision, Derrida is in fact indifferent to the development of Lacan's line of thought, to the twists that characterise both of its extremities. In the remainder of the book, we unfurl this line before and after the moment of intersection, and thus we address the question of whether Derrida's procedure is adequate to a text such as Lacan's.

Chapter 2 indicates the encounter between the two thinkers from Derrida's point of view; Chapter 3 explicates the same moment from Lacan's. Lacan himself realised that his understanding of the relation between the symbolic and the real was inadequate; his approach had been too transcendental and had not fully lived up to the possibilities of a more genetic account implied in his early attention to the *imaginary*, which had faded into the background to some extent during his more structuralist period. He had become too much a philosopher, and too little a psychoanalyst. However, he did *not* find himself obliged to divert from his path and join Derrida's path to the end, for the simple reason that Derrida's inattention to the beginning of his path missed a crucial feature, the specificity of Lacan's non-philosophical character. This provided Lacan with other resources to cope with his thought's deconstructibility. Lacan casts a long look in both directions, towards his origin and his future. In light of this, he deconstructs *differently*.

In short, Lacan responds to the problems which Derridean deconstruction rightly identifies, and yet his thought contains resources other than those which Derrida had at his disposal, and these centre around the imaginary.

Thus Chapter 3 may be located at the centre of the *khi*, in the same place as Chapter 2, but while Chapter 2 envisaged the centre from the perspective of Derrida's upper right-hand corner, Chapter 3 should rather be understood to stretch outwards *from* the point of intersection and include both the upper left-hand corner and the bottom right – for it is an account of Lacan's *development*, which actualises a potential that was not perhaps fully operative in the work which Derrida skewers with his quill. This potential is that of the imaginary, which indicates the opening of the symbolic onto the real, and which ameliorates the oppositional relation between the two. That the real has emerged as a result of an occurrence within the imaginary realm means that it enjoys a different relation to the real. This alternative relation is brought out in striking contrast to Derrida's quasi-transcendentalism in the guise of Lacan's notion of the *fantasy* (*le fantasme*), which is the way in which the imaginary *continues* to bind the symbolic to the real; the fantasy is the transcendental relation which the symbolic enjoys with the real.

Derrida meanwhile, has left Lacan behind, although his conscience continues to prick him, and he will cast continual backward glances in Lacan's direction as if expecting him to follow, or at least concerned as to the divergence of their paths. The two were like lovers between whom harsh words had been spoken, but who cannot find the gesture that would reconcile them.

Lacan's divergence is rightly troubling, for his forking path will offer an alternative way of answering Derrida's questions. The moment of bifurcation that follows the central convergence depicts what we intend to show: that there is an alternative to deconstruction, another writing.

At the heart of the letter *khi*, the two distinct strokes of the pen cross, and it is in and as this crossing that our superposition occurs, our own scholarly writing of the one upon the other. We construct the (imaginary and symbolic) letter, a renewed understanding of the transcendental by means of this reinscription of Lacan and Derrida, of the marks they have left behind, the clinamens they have imparted to the trajectories of contemporary thought.

In Chapter 4 we examine the distinct positions in which Lacan and Derrida end up, with respect to the notion of writing. For Lacan, as a result of his originally wholly genetic account of the human being, the 'archi-writing' that constitutes the signifier is not understood merely on the basis of the symbolic; it is also understood on the basis of the imaginary. Thus it is not just a transcendental matter, however refined, it is also the trace of a prehistoric genesis of the symbolic order itself.

Lacan calls the archi-written trace, the 'letter'. This is the real-of-the-symbolic. And yet, the real is not determined just with respect to the symbolic, but also with respect to the *imaginary*: it is an originally pictorial written mark that was evacuated of all its imaginary qualities in the prehistoric institution of the signifier. In this way the letter is also the very first letter of the alphabet, the very first moment in the phoneticisation of language which the alphabet expresses: the letter 'a' of the *objet petit a*, which is the real-of-the-imaginary, the real insofar as it is part of and yet distinguished from the imaginary. The real is not just the real of the symbolic but also the real of the imaginary.

For the later Lacan, the real must be understood as the deficiency afflicting both the imaginary and the symbolic, the impossibility of their ever constituting a totality, homogeneously self-same, without reference to another. This failure, and subsequent involvement with the real, necessitates for each their involvement with the other, their overlapping, as depicted in the famous diagram of the Borromean knot, which Lacan explicitly describes as a form of 'writing'.

In this way, ultimately, an attention to the genetic and the imaginary must alter the way in which we understand our transcendental method, the manner in which we transcend our current determinations and stretch out towards the indeterminate, the infinite, the real other.

The transcendental should still be understood as 'writing', but the letters of this writing will be related not just to the symbolic but also to the imaginary, thus constituting the moment at which the transcendental and the genetic overlap. The writing of Lacan will thus constitute *another writing*.

1

Lacan: the name-of-the-father and the phallus

In this chapter, we shall expose Lacan's thought in such a way as to demonstrate its vulnerability to deconstruction. The period of Lacan's thought which is most susceptible to deconstruction is his 'structuralist' period, the time of his most 'philosophical' work, which may be dated to the 1950s. Neither Derrida himself, nor any of his heirs, reconstructs Lacan's work in precisely this way but it presents Lacan's thought at its strongest and still shows it to be vulnerable to deconstruction.[1]

Deconstruction concerns the relation between the text and the other of the text, the symbolic and the real. Lacan's own understanding of this relation may be reconstructed around two notions: the 'name-of-the-father' and the 'phallus'. We shall show that Lacan's initial understanding of the notion of the name-of-the-father, heavily influenced by structuralist anthropology, compels him to understand the relation between the symbolic and the real as an *opposition*. It is this oppositional understanding that must be deconstructed. Deconstruction demonstrates that an opposition is not a co-belonging of two equal halves, but is always governed by one of these halves. The opposition of text and non-text always implies that a moment of full presence precedes and conditions the differentiality of the text. Deconstruction shows this understanding of the relation to be conditioned by the text itself and hence that the moment of presence does *not* precede textuality.

This understanding of the relation is most characteristic of *philosophy*. Since we are concerned here with the possibility of deconstructing Lacan, we shall consider, as far as possible, only the 'philosophical' elements of Lacan's work, those which concern more or less directly the relation between the real and the symbolic.[2] Indeed, this is precisely what Derrida does, excluding the imaginary, and everything that is unique about it. This means that within Lacan's psychoanalytic work we must isolate his understanding of the human subject, which exists on the border between human culture and inhuman nature. Culture may be identified with 'the symbolic' and nature with 'the real'.

But we shall delineate the philosophical character of Lacan's work along with its deconstructibility only because we shall be interested in its *non*-philosophical elements, including the origin of Lacan's thought in the medical, the scientific. It is only insofar as Lacan does not remain entirely true to this origin in his middle period that he becomes 'philosophical' in the Derridean sense of positing an opposition between the real and the symbolic, understood in terms of the opposition between presence and absence, the matrix of all oppositions. We shall ultimately be concerned to demonstrate the way in which this non-philosophical origin impacts on philosophy itself, including deconstruction.[3] In light of this, despite our attempt to deconstruct Lacan, we shall also indicate that element of his work which already resists deconstruction, and which will be allowed to unfold to its full breadth in Chapter 3, after we have followed through with the deconstruction of Lacan in Chapter 2.

Lacan's resistance to deconstruction is largely a result of his notion of the phallus. The phallus and the name-of-the-father act against one another here, for while the phallus helps Lacan to elude Derrida, the name-of-the-father delivers him up to deconstruction's clutches.

The phallus has a double aspect, it is both symbolic and imaginary. But the imaginary aspect is at this point in Lacan's development overpowered by the name-of-the-father. Nevertheless, the imaginary phallus will always already have added a third element to the symbolic and the real, and this will eventually allow Lacan to surpass his earlier understanding of the relation between the symbolic and the real. But for the moment, the imaginary remains in abeyance and Lacan is vulnerable to Derrida. We shall devote the greater part of this chapter to showing how this is the case.

I. THE REAL AND THE SYMBOLIC OPPOSED

Psychoanalysis

Psychoanalysis is the study of those problems which beset human beings as a result of their aporetic position on the border of nature and culture. In man's case, an already corrupt and needful natural body has to be supplemented by a symbolic system that allows the organism to survive but at the price of alienation and an infinite desire unknown to the animal. We need the symbolic order to supplement our deficient animality, but this prosthesis introduces a further estrangement that is expressed in the constant 'discontent' of the civilised animal, the infinitely unsatisfied nature of his perverse desire. We human animals need the symbolic order and yet suffer from it: this is the aporia which psychoanalysis confronts.

Trained in medicine, Lacan was initially a psychiatrist. The properly psychoanalytic period of his thought, within which we may, with Lacan's endorsement, isolate the 'philosophical', can be delimited by his Seminars.[4] These began in earnest at Saint Anne's Hospital in Paris in 1953. In 1964, the Seminar moved to the *École Normale Supérieure*, under the auspices of the *École des Hautes Études en Sciences Sociales*, following Lacan's expulsion from the International Psychoanalytic Association, the psychoanalytic 'Establishment' instituted by Freud himself. Then, from 1969 onwards, it took up residence in the Law Faculty of the *Université de Paris I* (*Panthéon-Sorbonne*) (cf. SXVII: 17–18). With these Seminars, Lacan undertook an explicitly psychoanalytic endeavour: the training of psychoanalysts. He also dealt explicitly with a psychoanalytic text: from the very beginning until the early 1960s, Lacan's seminars were described quite simply as 'commentaries on the texts of Freud' (SI: vii).

Lacan's own psychoanalytic theory might be understood to be entirely consumed by a reading of Freud. It seeks to provide a firmer theoretical ground for Freud's thought than Freud himself was able to provide. Indeed, Lacan suggests that his work was 'to express the conditions thanks to which what Freud says is possible' (SII: 320).

How does one improve on Freud? Simply by existing at a later point in history and having at one's disposal certain scientific discourses which Freud himself did not. For Lacan, these rendered obsolete Freud's desire to provide a purely neuro-physiological, biological foundation for the unconscious. The most essential of these discourses were contemporary linguistics, anthropology, and philosophy.[5] Not that Lacan ignored the natural and 'exact' sciences: from the beginning he appealed to mathematics – particularly probability theory, set theory and topology. But it was the human sciences that Freud had neglected, with some notable exceptions (*Totem and Taboo* prominent among them). But his encounter with these sciences had preceded the structuralist revolution in their foundations, which was to provide them with the exactitude of their natural counterparts.[6]

Lacan identified a strand in Freud's thought which could not be accommodated to the master's naturalistic, reductionist urges. For Lacan, the unconscious could be explained only by the fact that the human being was a creature immersed in *language* and the realm of symbols in general. The broadly speaking semiological human sciences were for Lacan equipped to explain the aporias which were in fact the *result* of Freud's attempt to ground his thought solely in the *natural* sciences.[7]

The human sciences after structural linguistics attempted to do justice to the almost ubiquitous *significance* of the human world by understanding the nature and interaction of its elements according to the laws of the linguistic *signifier*. Almost all phenomena which enter man's experience are *significant* for him, which is to say *meaningful* in a way that is articulated into *concepts*, which are themselves individuated according to the system of language at a certain culture's disposal. This attention to the signifier and its significance allowed the human sciences to understand phenomena which the natural sciences, particularly in their positivistic guise, could not. These included the phenomenon of the unconscious.

It is as if in Freud's method there is a primal conflict between the sciences of nature and the sciences of the human being, as perhaps befits a thought that scrutinises the limit separating the two. However, for Lacan, Freud's immediate successors had elided the latter in favour of the former. His task was then to restore the linguistic basis of Freud's thought, a task for which certain of Freud's earliest works proved essential.[8]

In order to bring this primal discord to the fore, Lacan returns to the very foundations of Freudian psychoanalysis, and here finds it necessary to make his great threefold distinction between the imaginary, the symbolic and the real.[9] The 'return to Freud'[10] is a return to the *ontological* foundations of Freud's thought.[11]

The inadequate grounding of Freud's thought had led not only to aporias, but also to the misinterpretation known – aptly – as 'ego-psychology'.[12] For Lacan, ego-psychology had effectively regressed to a pre-Freudian and quasi-Cartesian notion of the ego as the governing principle of man's psychic life. In Lacan's eyes, this reduced psychoanalysis to a mere psychology, a science of the conscious ego (E: 350),[13] while the entire point of psychoanalysis was to resituate the ego in a wider psychic economy which preceded it and within which it was generated. Ego-psychology, in contrast, set itself the task of restoring the ego to a position of sovereignty within the psychic economy.

The first three of Lacan's published seminars may be read as a reclamation of Freud's notion of the ego from ego-psychology. To this end, Lacan re-examines precisely that moment in Freud's text which had been taken to license the ego-psychological approach, and demonstrates the misappropriation involved. This was the institution of Freud's second topology, the rethinking of the psychic apparatus as id (*Es*), ego (*Ich*) and superego (*Überich*), superseding the first topology of unconscious, preconscious, and conscious: 'the metapsychological work of Freud after 1920 has been misread, interpreted in a crazy way by the first and second generations following Freud' (SII: 10); 'far from being understood as it should have been [. . .] [t]here was satisfaction in being once again able to believe the ego to be central' (SII: 11; cf. SI: 15).

Ego-psychology precisely forgets that the ego is not the governing centre of the psyche, but is in fact a secondary product *of* this impersonal economy, a realm in which the only appropriate pronoun is not 'I' but 'it'.[14] Ego-psychology forgets that, far from being a substantial entity, 'the *ego* is an imaginary function' (SI: 193, my italics). The ego is the image the subject has of himself, his sense of his own, consciously controlled totality.

This ego is a mere *image* constructed within the experience of the subject, beginning at the moment that Lacan calls the 'mirror stage' (*le stade du miroir*).[15] In other words, the ego is patently *not* the 'subject' in the sense of the controlling agent, since it is an *object*. The ego is 'a particular object within the experience of the subject. Literally, the ego is an object' (SII: 44; cf. SI: 193).[16] It is an object that is presented to the perception of the human subject in the form of an *image*. This perception is not originally metaphorical, it involves a literal sensory perception of another human being's *body* in its totality. Thus, in a certain sense, one's ego is not one's (subjective) soul but one's (objective) body, one's body understood as a *totality* on the basis of a visual perception of the whole body of *another*. The fact that the ego is constructed in this way demonstrates it to be a derived and not an original principle of the psyche.

It is as if ego-psychology were uncritically advocating the cause of the ego itself, adopting its perspective and trying to bolster its own illusory perception of itself. For Lacan, 'this constitutes a repudiation of psychoanalysis [. . .] what is at work here is the mechanism of systematic *misrecognition* [*méconnaissance*]' (E: 346, my italics). 'Misrecognition' is Lacan's precise technical term for the ego's mistaking the wholeness of another entity for its own.

For ego-psychology, the unconscious was the un*known* (*das Unerkannt*) (cf. SXXIII: 149). It was that portion of the psyche which had not yet been brought under the ego's conscious control. The unconscious was thus understood to be the *opposite* of the ego, it *is* what the ego is *not*. The purpose of psychoanalysis was 'the enlarging of the field of the *ego*, it is [. . .] the reconquest by the *ego* of its margin of the unknown [*l'inconnu*]' (SI: 232). The unconscious *id* was to be conquered by the *ego*. The unconscious was responsible for the patient's harmful behaviour, so a successful analysis would leave the subject in full conscious control of every one of his actions, effectively without an unconscious.

This was the interpretation of psychoanalysis that Lacan encountered at first hand: Lacan's own analyst was Rudolf Loewenstein, one of the chief exponents of ego-psychology. For Lacan, the two fundamental problems with this approach were that it ignored the radical heterogeneity of unconscious and conscious, and it ignored the crucial relation between speech and language in the understanding of the unconscious. The two problems are logically joined, for a genuinely heterogeneous unconscious can be understood only on the basis of language and its relationship with the subject's speech, his signifying behaviour. The symbolic order itself is understood by Lacan to be 'the big Other' (*le grand Autre*), the truly heterogeneous. Thus Lacan's return to Freud returns to that other strand of his work which had been sidelined by ego-psychology, its concern with language and speech: psychoanalysis as the 'talking cure' (E: 211).

The ego is not the subject

That of which the subject is conscious is always an *object* for consciousness: that of which we cannot become conscious is therefore a 'subject'. 'What do we call a subject? Quite precisely, what, in the development of objectivation, is outside of the object' (SI: 193–4). The only genuine subject is one that has not been objectified, it is a subject that is acting, an agent, and if one is speaking of a subject that is involved with language this means a speaking subject. 'Speech' here would mean any emission of signifiers, any behaviour, verbal or otherwise, that would be 'significant'.[17] Insofar as it is speaking the subject can never be spoken (about). Once it is so objectified it is evacuated of its active 'speaking', the verb is reduced to a noun.

If the unconscious subject is fundamentally and always unconscious – subjectal – it can enter conscious awareness – objectality – only in a form that distorts its true nature: 'the unconscious is not expressed, except by deformation' (SI: 48–9). The subject can become an object for consciousness only in the form of 'symptoms'. A symptom is, in vulgar usage, an indirect manifestation in one order of something from another, often something which cannot directly manifest itself at all. In physical nosology the symptoms of a disease are the only form in which that disease can be seen and diagnosed. In psychological illness, the symptom *speaks* of the unconscious subject, but indirectly, necessarily so given the objectifying nature of language. It is a pure act of wordless speaking put into words, into language. It is the form the undetermined (infinite) act of speaking takes when it is understood to express itself in a determinate *language*.

The symptom is a *trace*, it is the presence of the *absence* of the unconscious, the mark left in presence of something which simply cannot *be* present. It is precisely this presentation of absence that must be acknowledged in the psychoanalytic treatment. The symptoms speak, and one must thus engage them in some sort of conversation, in an attempt to recognise what they are attempting to say. This is why psychoanalysis is a talking cure, a cure by means of speech and nothing besides.

The unconscious speaks, it is nothing besides the subject's speech, and it expresses itself by means of deformations in the ego's conscious use of language and the patient's experience and behaviour. Treatment attempts to allow the patient to recognise his symptoms *as* symptoms (of the unconscious), as a pure speaking trapped in a language that is inadequate to express it. '[I]f this speech is muzzled and is to be found latent in the subject's symptoms, do we, or do we not, have to release it?' (SI: 185). One bestows 'recognition' upon the symptom in the formal, ethical sense, which means to recognise the fact that it has and indeed is a voice, and not to treat it as a mere mistake to be eliminated.

Lacan shows that Freud's very distinction between conscious and unconscious can be explained by a thesis on the nature of *language*, or of *la langue* and *la parole*, 'language' and 'speech', in Saussure's technical sense. *Langue* is the system of signifiers from which every instance of speaking draws its resources, while *parole* is an act of actual enunciation. Speech and the supposedly purely idiosyncratic meaning we intend to convey must draw upon a common language in order to be understood by *others*. Language is the third party that must intervene between two human beings in order for them to communicate successfully, for each individual not to be enclosed within an entirely private world of signs that signify something to him alone. A common medium which does not originate in or belong uniquely to either person is required in order to avert this. The third must be an 'other' with respect to those who use it to communicate their intentions. This third is 'the big Other', not the other who is involved in the communication, but the third which is genuinely heterogeneous to both.

Crucially, the system of language is infinite. We shall come to understand this point better when we examine Derrida's use of Saussure. For now, it is enough to accept it as a hypothesis. Since language must precede any individual speaker,[18] it cannot be *encompassed* by that finite individual. It is precisely the infinite extension of language that makes it fundamentally other to the individual speaker, other as the infinite is to the finite. The entire infinite system of language cannot be comprehended in finite consciousness, and cannot even be traversed sequentially, by apprehension. Therefore, it is not possible to be conscious of the entire system of references which determine the value and hence the meaning of the signifiers with which one speaks. The infinity of the system of language must remain *unconscious*: 'the unconscious is language [*l'inconscient est langage*]' (E: 736).

The subject which *speaks*, insofar as it is always fundamentally repressed by this system of language, through being objectified, deprived of its subjecthood, is the subject *of* the unconscious, the subject subjected *to* language and thus rendered forever unconscious. The very first repression, the a priori repression which will always already have happened, is that of the speaking subject; all subsequent, 'secondary repressions' involve other elements of language, which are closely associated with the primarily repressed subject.

This whole infinite system of language, in its present state (synchrony) and in its entire history (diachrony), *determines* the signification of any one of its signifiers. Thus the signification of any signifier we consciously invoke is *not* the result of a meaning which we consciously intend to convey. 'This language [*langage*] system, within which our discourse makes its way, isn't it something which goes *infinitely* beyond every intention [*dépasse infiniment toute intention*] that we might put into it [. . .]?' (SI: 54, my italics). Our meaning, which we believed to be fully formed and fully present in advance of its (secondary) expression in language, is in truth determined by the infinite system of language into which we are thrown at birth, the ultimate signification of our words is in the hands of the Other, the unconscious.

Meaning, signification and the infinite system of language

What is language? Simply speaking, every element of language, everything 'symbolic', *stands for* something else. It is not simply itself but is constituted by its reference to something other than itself. This is what distinguishes the symbolic from the real. A word refers to a thing, a concept, or it refers to other words. Indeed, each individual is defined in its individuality by its differences from all of the other signifiers in the same system of reference. This is the primal insight of structural linguistics which is so called because it understands the signifier to be defined by nothing besides its place in a structure, a network of *other* signifiers to which it refers, irrespective of the actual positive content of the signifier, which is 'arbitrary'.[19] The form logically precedes the substance when it comes to the signifier. The value of the signifier, its individual significance, is determined only by its differences from other signifiers in terms of their relative positions within a structure.

These signifiers which individuate and thus decide upon the significance of the conscious signifier – our meaningful experience – are *synchronous* with the conscious signifier. 'It is in the dimension of a synchrony that you must situate the unconscious' (SXI: 26). As Chiesa puts it, '*Lacan transforms the logical necessity of the vertical axis* [. . .] – the existence of a linguistic *structure* which, according to Saussure and Jakobson, concrete discourse continuously presupposes – *into the actual reality of the unconscious*' (Chiesa 2007: 52–3). This structure presupposed by our speech is infinitely extensive and so the exact significance of the signifiers we use can *never* be absolutely determined by us. Because the ego is finite, it cannot encompass all of the signifiers which determine the meaning of any signifier that is conscious to it.

When one signifier is uttered, emitted, or impinges upon consciousness – in other words, when it is presented to another – it refers to an infinity of *other* signifiers. These other signifiers *in their infinity* constitute the unconscious. 'The unconscious is that part of concrete discourse qua transindividual which is not at the subject's disposal in re-establishing the continuity of his conscious discourse' (E: 214). Lacan asks, 'Why is it unconscious at this time? Because it infinitely surpasses [*déborde infiniment*] what both of them, as individuals, can at this time consciously apprehend of it' (SII: 122).

Signifiers as such are nothing besides their references to other signifiers. This means that signifiers are nothing besides the differences *between* signifiers. Each signifier is composed of traces which mark the absence of *other* signifiers. These traces are real, material things. If the infinite references of the signifier constitute a material mesh, then what occurs in consciousness is the *idealisation* of this mesh, the forgetting of the signifier's material nature. This is necessary in order to render present to consciousness the *signified* of the signifiers one is using, and this signified is precisely not material but ideal, present in consciousness rather than body. What is elided in consciousness is thus the signifier as such, in favour of the signified. The *dependence* of this precise signified on the material differences between signifiers is forgotten. We have seen that these material differences are infinite in number, commensurate with the extension of language. It is the elision of this infinity of differences which *constitutes* repression. Due to its finite nature, consciousness represses the dependence of meaning upon an infinity of material signifiers, and so it represses the signifier itself, in favour of the conscious signified, the meaningfulness of its own experience.

At the (imaginary) level of the ego, signifiers are experienced as signifieds, as exhausted by and fully transparent to their meaning, and thus as lacking any senseless density of their own. But it is just this unconscious density of signifiers which is *presupposed by* the very production of meaning. The production process must be elided in the product: that is the meaning of repression, the 'secondary' repression consequent upon the original or 'primary' repression of the subject itself, which is to say the repression caused by our being forced to use language in the first place, a language which is antithetical in nature to our speech.

This determination of the signified by signifiers, and by more signifiers than the ego can consciously comprehend, means that signifiers can always mean more than one thing. This means that the *meaning* which the subject believed himself to possess within consciousness was in fact always already *signification*. 'The discovery of the unconscious [. . .] is that the bearing of *meaning* infinitely overflows the signs [*la portée du sens déborde infiniment les signes*] manipulated by the individual. Man is always cultivating a great many more signs than he thinks' (SII: 122). This is a signified's 'overdetermination' by signifiers. There is always more than one thing that a signifier could signify. Inherent to the signifier is a dimension of *ambiguity*: 'Language entirely operates within ambiguity, and most of the time you know absolutely nothing about what you are saying' (SIII: 115–16).[20]

Thus one's behaviour and one's words, by means of this ambiguity, mean *more* than one thinks, they are not just determined but overdetermined: 'he always says more than he means to, always more than he thinks he says' (SI: 266). It is by means of this ambiguity that *symptoms* can present themselves, that something we did not intend can nevertheless find a way to express itself in our speech.

Overdetermination and the symptom

It is by means of this overdetermination that the repressed can *return*, that the unconscious can make its *absence felt* within language. And it does so by making visible the fact that meaning is determined by something other than the conscious ego. An other is clearly at work if we mean more than we thought we meant. A symptom occurs when the linguistic overdetermination of meaning breaks through its usual concealment, or rather becomes manifest *in* its very repression. The signifier breaks through the signified and acts according to its own logic, contrary to that of meaning.

It is not as if the unconscious reveals itself; rather it is revealed that there *is* an unconscious. The repressed returns in the symptom, but it returns *as* repressed. 'What comes under the effect of repression returns, for repression and the return of the repressed are just the two sides of the same coin. The repressed is always there, expressed in a perfectly articulate manner in symptoms and a host of other phenomena' (SIII: 12). What returns is not *that* which is repressed, but the very event of repression itself, the very fact that speech is determined and hence overdetermined by an infinite linguistic context, which we finite agents cannot control.

The fact that any one signifier can be used in multiple contexts – an infinite number – allows a signifier used in one context to recall these other contexts, and thus allow a signifier from another, traumatic context, to insinuate itself upon consciousness. Secondary repressions (*Verdrängungen*) always act upon signifiers, that materiality which overdetermines every conscious signifier and renders its signified ambiguous.[21] Once a plurality of signifiers reveals itself to be constituting the signification of a certain signifier, it is as if that signifier can no longer pretend to be transparent and nothing more than a mere representative of a prior signified; the signifier now appears to possess a density of its own.

No one signifier can be understood by consciousness to have two signifieds *at once*. Hence it must appear to oscillate between the two. Or perhaps one must appear to be *entirely* ruled out by the context in which it appears, when that context is properly understood. What is precisely unconscious is the materiality of the one signifier insofar as it inherently contains both meanings at one and the same time, synchronously.

Consciousness is inhabited only by signifiers which do *not* have contradictory meanings. Those elements of language which cannot be present to consciousness due to the laws which constrain experience, form the unconscious. Consciousness, governed by the law of non-contradiction, cannot experience two contradictory meanings of the same signifier at any one time. In a symptomatic formation, the two signifying contexts of a single word create an absolute oscillation in the word's meaning, which is felt by the individual as painful, as troubling, or indeed as the tickling sensation of laughter, at the double entendre. It is a moment at which one feels uncertain and out of control. It is because in the symptom contradictory signifieds attempt to gain access to consciousness by means of the overdetermination of signifiers that Lacan so frequently expresses the nature of symptoms by way of contradiction: the successful and the bungled, the truth appearing in the least true: 'one's *bungled* actions are the most *successful* and [. . .] one's failures fulfil one's most secret wishes' (E: 341, my italics). 'I [the *truth*] wander about in what you regard as *least* true by its very nature: in dreams, in the way the most far-fetched witticisms and the most grotesque nonsense of jokes *defy meaning*, and in chance – not in its law, but rather in its contingency' (E: 342, my italics; cf. SI: 247, 266).

The symptom is the appearance of two incompatible contexts in which the same signifier can function, and thus the indirect manifestation of the signifier's material differentiality:

> for a symptom [. . .] to be considered to come under psychoanalytic psychopathology, Freud insists on the minimum of overdetermination constituted by a double meaning – symbol of a defunct conflict beyond its function in a *no less symbolic* present conflict – and if he teaches us to follow the ascending ramification of the symbolic lineage in the text of the patient's free associations, in order to detect the nodal points of its structure at the places where its verbal forms intersect, then it is already quite clear that symptoms can be entirely resolved in an analysis of language, because a symptom is itself structured like a language. (E: 222–3)

This overdetermination *manifests* itself in an ambiguity of the *signification* of the conscious signifier, which causes us to worry, to sense a lack of control, a miscommunication of our intention, or in the case of a double entendre, to laugh.

A symptom is a distortion in the smooth running of a meaningful life, of words or deeds as they acquire signification in conscious experience. They are moments at which our intention to convey a meaning or carry out a conscious purpose miscarries. The signifier is repeated, forgotten, replaced, rushed. One returns to the same signifier again and again, without realising it, in tics and obsessional rituals.

The determination of conscious objects by the *unconscious* here becomes manifest. What appears is the density of the signifier itself. This is one reason why Lacan represents the subject – the primally repressed, the unconscious subject – with the mark, '$'. It is to show that the subject has no signifier that can properly express it, and is always betrayed by the signifier as such; it is crossed through, *written over* by the differential traces that go to make up the signifier. The '$' should then be understood as the *symptom*. It is the appearance of the subject under erasure, in its absence. The bar that writes over the S is precisely the bar which joins together any one signifier with the infinite system of others that differentially define it. It is the material mark which ideal consciousness cannot contain. The symptom, $, is a word that is always inadequate and hence crossed out, the meaningless or hyper-meaningful signifier that consciousness cannot abide.

How can speech find a place within language? How can the real speaking subject find a place within the signifier which alienates it? He can perch, and express himself symptomatically, in the gaps *between* signifiers, in the way in which they are joined together. The subject is compelled by language to differ from himself, cut off from himself, barred from accessing and freely controlling his own meaning. Hence he can appear *as* difference *in* the differences that run between signifiers, in referential relations. The subject inhabits the 'holes in discourse' (E: 253),[22] those gaps that exist between signifiers and constitute them, rather than the signifiers in their fully constituted positivity: 'the subject resides in this very division which in its time I have represented for you by the relation of one signifier to another signifier' (SXXIII: 148).

The finite ego and the infinite unconscious

It is precisely the immersion of the human subject in language that accounts for his being split into a conscious ego[23] and an unconscious subject: 'the unconscious is the *fact* that man is inhabited by the signifier' (E: 25, my italics). The ego is that which *resists* the unconscious's acceding to consciousness. This is to say that the ego makes the unconscious unconscious. Why? Because the ego is finite, and thus incompatible with the infinite. It is this resistance, this continuous force of repression, that allows the unconscious to persist in its nature *as* unconscious. If the ego is nothing besides this resistance, ego and subject need one another in order to exist. 'Thus Freud's intention [. . .] was to restore, in all its rigour, the separation [. . .] between the field of the ego and that of the unconscious he discovered first, by showing that the former is in a "blocking" position in relation to the latter, the former resisting recognition of the latter' (E: 360). The unconscious is unconscious because it is infinite and consciousness is finite. The ego's finite individuality is derived from the perceived form of the physical body of an other. The fact of bodily finitude, the imaginary individuation of the body identified as our own, is ultimately responsible for our having an unconscious.

The ego is our individuality. Because we are individuated, and individuated spatio-temporally as ego, we have only a perspectival and hence limited access to the system of language. We can access it only at a certain point in its historical development and we can use only those systems which our particular culture has at its disposal. It is as if the speaking subject were, in itself, the ahistorical instance of speaking as such, forced to express itself in a *determinate* historical language, which necessarily distorts pure speech in a certain way. And it is precisely the situatedness of the *ego* which brings this about. This is why the ego constitutes 'resistance' to the passage of the pure speaking of the unconscious subject and why Lacan refers to the '*wall* of language': 'it is the wall of language that blocks speech' (E: 233). Pure speech would be the pure intention to express ourselves, to express a meaning which is originally a need, a need to communicate something to someone who might provide for our needs when we are at sea in a primeval helplessness. It is the signification of the absolute singularity that we are.

The very fact that we have bodies, and thus egoity, situates us in language in which our speech must be expressed, in a necessarily inadequate way. By condemning us to the use of language *as such*, the ego necessitates the speaking subject's primal repression into the unconscious. The speaking subject in itself is speech *undetermined* by any particular historical language – and language is always particular. The (unconscious) subject is *pure* speech, outside of all language.

The unconscious infinity of language and the unconscious subject

The unconscious takes two forms: the entire system of language in its infinity subjacent to any act of speaking, and the speaking subject itself, repressed by the need to use language at all.

Thus we may distinguish unconscious *language* from the unconscious *subject*. Since we are always already, as conscious egos, part of a symbolic order we did not choose, the repression of the speaking subject is *a priori*, it is *primal* repression. Lacan names this repression with the Freudian word, *Verwerfung*, which he translates as '*forclusion*', foreclosure.[24] This is to be distinguished from the usual Freudian word for (secondary) repression, *Verdrängung*.

Thus we can see that the speaking subject is in truth our *singularity*, that absolutely unique intention which we originally wished to convey. It is the *real* aside from any symbolic or imaginary determination that would alienate it from itself.[25] And since the subject is distinct from the individual ego, we must distinguish between this singularity and our individuality. The subject is *singularity*, the ego is *individuality*; the subject is real, the ego imaginary.

Individuality is subordinate to a genus that many individuals share, while our singularity is subordinated to nothing more general than itself, it is absolute, *kat'hauto*. This singularity is distorted by our individuality, and appears there only as a symptom, $, the singular subject crushed under erasure. Our individuation represses our singularity, primally.

The two alienations, imaginary and symbolic

One can also speak of this repression of singularity in terms of 'alienation' (cf. SIV: 12). The ego's individuality is derived from the image of *another* at the mirror stage of the child's development. That which one really is is alienated by being understood in the image of another, and indeed in terms of individuality. But this is only the first of two alienations that the subject must undergo. The ego is the 'little other' or 'imaginary other', in that it is fundamentally a '*semblable*', it is our spitting image. The ultimate deficiency of the ego necessitates a second alienation in the *big* Other. An imaginary lack necessitates the crutch of the symbolic and thus precipitates us into language, which betrays yet again our real singularity. The small alienation of the imaginary is redoubled by the big alienation of the symbolic. In both cases, it is the subject as real or singular that is alienated.

This twofold alienation is at the same time the formation of a reflexive self. The alienations are necessary, they form an 'orthopaedics' for a real entity which did not of itself suffice, which ultimately could not have survived (E: 78).

First of all one achieves a certain finite and unified ipseity by means of the mirror stage, our identification with the little other, which gives us a sense of our individuality as a body and then as an ego; secondly, the loop of selfhood is more firmly tied by the signifiers with which one identifies in the big Other, the signifiers to which one finds oneself pinned and which one uses to describe oneself. Originally, this signifier is quite simply the first-person singular pronoun.

At the imaginary level we acquire a 'who' and at the symbolic level we acquire a 'what'. Thus our self-relation, our understanding of who and what we are, is fully determined, at the level of both the imaginary (which is to say the signified) and the symbolic (which is to say the signifier). These are both alienations because our real singularity is neither a 'who' nor a 'what'. It *precedes* the determination of the individual subject (ipseity, whoness) and the determination of an essence (quiddity, whatness).

The subject's (re)flexing back on itself implies that it must first of all have left itself. Self-relation implies an initial difference from one's self. How can I relate to myself if I have not already been duplicated, split from myself? Thus there is no selfhood, no 'subjectivation', without alienation. This is the double meaning of the barred subject in Lacan, written '$'. Language scores a line through the singularity of the subject. This subject is not an I (*ego*) but an 'it' (*id*), in Freud's German, *Es*, which Lacan writes as the single letter, 'S'. It is that pre-individual impersonality which precedes any nominated entity that would be able to use the *personal* pronoun, 'I'. S before I: Singularity before Individuality. Singularity must leave itself, become alienated, in order to form our individuality. The ego represses the subject.

The alienating individuation at the imaginary level is cemented at the symbolic level. Language joins the loop of the graphic 'S' to itself, as if it were a knot of string, and at the same time splits it in two, preventing a smooth relation of continuity between its two halves, which we spend our entire lives trying to reunite, like the lovers of Aristophanes'. 'If anything constitutes the originality of the analytic treatment, it is [. . .] to have perceived at the beginning, right from the start, the problematical relation of the subject to himself. The real find, the discovery [. . .] is to have conjoined this relation with the meaning of symptoms [$]' (SI: 29). We shall later argue for this position logically, but for now let us simply state that this singularity, that of the speaking unconscious subject, since it is alienated by both the imaginary and the symbolic, must be *real*.

Not only is language infinite and so incomprehensible to the ego, language as such *objectifies*. Language objectifies by transforming events into substances, freezing their free unfolding with *nouns*. The alienation of the real is the *determination* of an as yet indeterminate moment. That which has not yet been determined should be understood as an *event*, which remains indeterminate as long as it is still *occurring* or eventuating. Language turns a singular event into a determinate individual, freezing its unfolding and subsuming it under a more general category. However, in the real, the process of individuation is always incomplete, and it is only language which constructs the illusion that it is complete, that the river has stopped flowing and is now identical with itself. We thus describe the real as singular since it remains other than all imaginary and symbolic determination, all comparable traits which might allow us to situate it in one class of things or another.

The speaking subject, insofar as it is undefined, is without limit, it is infinite. And it only becomes finite by being tied to the individuated body and its image, the ego.[26]

The real of the subject cannot be expressed in language. This would require a 'biunivocal' or 'binary signifier', a sign, where a real entity is unambiguously referred to by an element of language. This is impossible, for the essential reasons we have expounded, not least because this individuation of an element of the real by language *produces* the individuality of that thing in the very first place. It does not exist in the real itself. This is why Lacan describes the real as 'the impossible' – impossible to refer to by means of the signifier. The real can only be alienated or 'murdered' by the symbolic: when we refer to it with a signifier we turn an event into a substance and at the same time subordinate it to a general determination. The real is alienated from itself, snatched from its absolute proximity with itself, its very life is mortified: 'the symbol first manifests itself as the killing of the thing' (E: 262).

The real as immediate presence is rendered impossible by the symbolic as difference.

The speaking of the subject

So what is this purely idiosyncratic speaking that is thrust into and betrayed by a common language? We may begin to get an idea of this speaking by considering it in a purely empirical sense, as when one tries to express to an other precisely what it is that one wants. A human infant *has* no words for what it wants, and indeed its purely singular needs are simply not individuated in a way that could accord with the signifiers of a language-system. It just lacks, in a way utterly peculiar to itself.

One learns to speak as one finds that the emission of sounds – and then *particular* sounds – seems to have certain effects on the human beings that surround one, issuing in the presence or absence of something which causes the stirrings of need to cease or arise. All the infant knows initially is that it is in a certain state, and wishes to be otherwise. This primal difference in states would be the origin of our acquisition of language. Language presupposes the opposition between presence and absence, for the sign just is the referral of a presence *to* an absence: 'the oppositional couple presence-absence, the connotation plus-minus, which gives us the first element of a symbolic order' (SIV: 67–8).

Lacan understands the origin to consist in the baby's perception of the mother, the mother as the agent who can frustrate the child of the breast, and who can thus be present *and* absent: 'the agent of frustration, which is originally the mother' (SIV: 67). She introduces the child to the symbolic order in the moment of frustration (SIV: 56). The maternal object is what the child calls for when she is absent, and it proves to be an absence that a certain signifier succeeds in summoning to presence. 'It is this which offers the subject the possibility of joining the real relation to a symbolic relation' (SIV: 67). Thus it is not the breast itself that constitutes the first symbol given to the baby. Before the frustration of the actual withholding of the breast, the mother is herself 'symbolic'.[27] The (proto-)symbol is already present at this stage, precisely as the alternation in the child's state of need which the mother's presence and absence brings about: one is either satisfied or not satisfied. Is the very first symbol for the child the presence and absence of the mother as bearer of the breast?

In any case, if there is *no* (quasi-)oppositional alternation of states, there can be no language.

Following frustration, the cry becomes duplicitous, it becomes ambiguous: it calls not just for the object of need but for that which the donation of this object *expresses*, and that is that the donor loves the child enough to give it. Thus a symbolic dimension accrues to both word and object. The objects of need, from the moment of frustration onwards, also act as symbols of the mother's love: 'it satisfies a need, but also it symbolises a favourable power' (SIV: 69). Once the child's demands become unchained from its natural needs and demand love for its own sake, a demand which unlike need can never be satisfied, the need becomes a *desire*: 'Desire begins to take shape in the margin in which demand rips away from need, this margin being the one that demand [. . .] opens up in the guise of the possible gap need may give rise to here, because it has no universal satisfaction' (E: 689). It is the opening of the symbolic dimension that allows an object to stand for something other than itself. And this means that it will never be certain that any object is a definite sign of love. Hence the demand becomes infinite, because it always involves a margin of dissatisfaction. Thanks to the symbolic, need becomes demand, and demand becomes desire.

One's language becomes ever more determined and ever more generic, as one learns to approximate the pre-existing linguistic system more closely, and to communicate more effectively with others, and a wider circle of others. Whenever an adult – no longer *in-fans*, wordless – speaks, he is unable to make his words correspond precisely to the meaning he intends to communicate, which is ultimately the need to be without need that provoked within him his first babbling cries. One can never reach back to this wordless stage and simply communicate the fact of needfulness: one must always communicate a specific object *desired*.

As a result, the speaking subject is ever more definitively split from the 'subject' who ends up in the linguistic utterance, the subject whose needs (now become desires) are differentiated according to a pre-given language and symbolic culture. This subject is the subject of the sentence in the grammatical sense: the 'I' in the phrase 'I want this. . .'. The first person nominative singular in Latin and Greek is '*ego*' (ἐγώ). Following the French linguist Benveniste, Lacan baptised these two 'subjects', speaking and spoken, stating and stated, *la sujet de l'énonciation*, and *la sujet de l'énoncé* (cf. Benveniste 1971 [1966]: 223–30).[28] The best translations of these terms, in light of my interpretation, are 'the speaking subject' and 'the subject *in* the statement'. The speaking subject is the real subject that *makes* the statement and the subject in the statement is the grammatical subject as it *appears* in the statement made, determined by its language. This captures the difference between the indeterminate *act* of speaking – the verb – and the actuality that is spoken – the noun; between the infinite act of desiring and the definite object given to desire.

The subject as it appears in the statement is the '*ego*', the 'I', the linguistic representative of the *imaginary* ego, the word which the *subject* uses to describe himself: 'analytic experience is deeply bound up with this *discursive* double of the subject, his discordant and ridiculous ego' (SIII: 134, my italics).

The unconscious subject is the subject *strictly speaking*, since it is that which is truly not an object. When it is objectified, it loses itself as a subject but refinds itself as (the signifier) 'ego': 'at the level of the subject of the enunciation, [. . .] it loses itself as much as it finds itself again' (SXI: 26). This is the movement which Lacan calls, adapting a term of Ernest Jones', '*aphanisis*' (cf. SIX: 4/4/62). This is used to describe the subject's characteristic of vanishing the moment it expresses itself, the moment it would attain any form of presence whatsoever. It describes the way in which the real is 'present' within the symbolic order: it is the instantaneous flickering, the scintillation that indicates the impossibility of full presence, but which does not amount to a *complete* absence. The real subject twinkles a moment before being snuffed out, in the coruscation of the symptom, the presence of that which is absent and cannot be made properly present, which is the unconscious subject itself. Speaking is determined by language the moment it is emitted, the proper name of the subject rendered unpronounceable: 'in the enunciation [*l'énonciation*], he elides something which is properly speaking what he cannot know [*savoir*], namely the name of what he is qua speaking subject [*sujet de l'énonciation*]' (SIX: 10/1/62).

'[T]he [speaking] subject in his reality, [is] *foreclosed* as such in the system and enter[s] into the play of signifiers only in the form of the dummy [*mort*[29]], but becom[es] the true subject [of the statement] as this play of signifiers makes him signify' (E: 461). The subject is 'foreclosed' from the system of the signifier since it is impossible to capture it with a statement that would not betray it: the subject is *real*: 'The subject partakes of the real precisely in that it is impossible, apparently' (SXVII: 103). He exists there as a corpse (*mort*). In the form of a corpse the living being is both present and absent. The absent presence of the subject's cadaver is his 'symptomatic' presence. The symptom is the linguistic knot in which the subject's speech is entangled and indeed garbled.

It is with reference to the more usual meaning of the word 'dummy' that Lacan will come to associate the subject of the enunciation with 'idiocy' in its original Greek sense, which still resounds in the English word, 'idiosyncrasy'.[30] Lacan speaks of, 'the subject, who is naturally an idiot [*un idiot*]' (SXIV: 10/5/67). This idiocy is precisely something that cannot be encompassed by the general order of language. This absolute singularity amounts to my bare facticity, the *fact* of this peculiar existence, its '*that*ness', as opposed to any linguistic predicates or imaginary features which might differentiate it. The *position* from which speaking occurs cannot be placed within language, and is thus, from that perspective, idiotic. Lacan states explicitly that for him, relative to the meaningful ego, the subject is to be understood as 'his *ineffable* and *stupid* existence' (E: 459, my italics).

'There is, in effect, something radically inassimilable to the signifier. It's quite simply the subject's singular existence' (SIII: 179).[31] We always already find ourselves *within* a determinate language, whose borders we cannot even see.

The ego is that about our situation which is conscious or potentially conscious to us, that about ourselves which we can understand, however mistaken this understanding is. It is our individuality as we know it. What cannot be understood is the *fact* that we are individuated, the very event which we are.

One uses a system of signifiers in order to communicate one's meaning to others. One's intending to mean would be the trace of the simple motive force of need, wanting to be satisfied, but one's meaning cannot be made *significant* unless one uses a language shared by those with whom one wishes to communicate. When one needs to *communicate* one's purely idiosyncratic intention to others, then it must be expressed according to the jointure of signifiers. One needs to communicate because one cannot satisfy one's needs by oneself. It is thus a moment of deficit in the natural or real human animal that necessitates the symbolic order's intervention.

It is precisely the illusion that communication can be successful in this sense that a psychoanalytic session reveals to the patient. The analyst, by remaining silent, refuses to confirm that the words spoken by the analysand are indeed conveying the truth about his desire.

Indeed such communication is discouraged by the rule of free association, in which one is not compelled to communicate a meaning, but remains free to emit signifiers without concern for meaningfulness.[32] In this way, the overdetermination of each signifier by its many contexts can be brought forth, the fact that words are connected in ways and for reasons that are otherwise than logical. In this way, the psychoanalytic session is the constant generation of symptoms, those signifiers to which one constantly returns because they have a signification determined by a context of which one is not conscious. It is only by being unconcerned for consciously controlled communication, which requires of us that we convey an unequivocal meaning, that the signifier can be brought to reveal itself.

That one's real subjectivity is constantly repressed by language causes us to constantly desire its expression: 'the symbol first manifests itself as the killing of the thing, and this death results in the endless perpetuation of the subject's desire' (E: 262). A symptom is a failed attempt on the part of the speaking subject to express itself in language. Thus the symptom is a symptom of our *desire*. 'Freud shows us how *speech*, that is *the transmission of desire*, can get itself recognised through anything, provided that this anything be organised in a symbolic system' (SI: 244, my italics). Desire is the striving for wholeness, for a situation in which the words spoken coincide with the position from which they are enunciated, that the subject and the ego overcome the division between them instituted by the stroke of the signifier, $: 'it is in relation to this *Spaltung* that the functioning of desire as such is to be articulated' (SVII: 209).

But desire never achieves any more than a symptomatic failure, which reveals the unconscious only *as* unconscious: 'the unconscious is always manifested as that which vacillates in a split in the subject, from which emerges [. . .] desire' (SXI: 28). We as human beings are precisely this aporetic situation between conscious and unconscious: '*desire is the essence of man*' (SXI: 275; cf. SIX: 21/2/62). Psychoanalysis is to reveal to us the truth of our singular desire, which amounts to the repression of our singularity behind the individual masks that we have been given to wear.

Why does the subject not simply die? Why does its corpse persist in the symbolic order? Why is singularity only incompletely stifled by individuality? This is to ask why the real appears in the symbolic *at all*, if only in its absence. Why is there desire?

Desire: to fully speak

Desire is the desire for real singularity, for that which is 'killed' by the symbolic order. It is in fact the desire to 'fully speak', to allow the speaking subject fully to express itself in or in spite of the language it is forced to speak. To fully attain one's desire would be to find a way within *language* to express *speech*. This would perhaps amount to achieving 'full speech' (*la parole pleine*), which was originally thought by Lacan to constitute the very aim of psychoanalytic treatment.

According to its name, 'full speech' seems to oscillate between two possibilities: a speech entirely *without* language and a speech which *uses* language but is not alienated by it. Desire would then be either the attempt to leave the symbolic altogether or the desire to find a place for the real *within* language. The implication of Lacan's thought at this stage is that full speech should mean the latter, but his theoretical commitments with regard to the nature of the real and the symbolic compel him to mean the former. The ultimate reason for this is that he understands the relation between the real and the symbolic as an *opposition*. And yet, the fact that there *is* an oscillation between two understandings of full speech indicates a resource as yet unexploited which might allow Lacan to explain how speech might be able to inhabit language, and how the real might occupy a place *within* the symbolic, and not require its eradication in order to express itself.

The first interpretation of full speech

Is the first interpretation of full speech, speech *without* language, a return to that mythical moment before language arose, when we were animals or babies?[33] And is psychoanalysis, in the babble that it encourages, an attempt to return to this state? This would be to recognise one's singularity before and apart from the determinate language and cultural system which have diverted one's need into an endless series of desires for culturally specific objects. Full speech would be *antithetical* to the symbolic order, an attempt actually to destroy it altogether for the sake of a direct presentation of the real.

If this is truly what full speech means, then it can surely exist only as a regulative ideal, impossible to attain, for one always needs others and one needs *language* in order to communicate one's needs to them. Lacan is certainly aware of the problem: 'at the end of analysis, [. . .] will a part of the subject still remain on the level of this sticking-point which we call his *ego*?' (SI: 193). We have after all insisted that the unconscious *is* unconscious only because the ego in its finitude resists its infinity. One of Lacan's seminar participants, Colette Audry, insists on just this point: 'analysis amounts to being a demystification of what was previously imaginary. So we get to the following point – once demystification has been accomplished, we find ourselves in the presence of death. All that is left is to wait and contemplate death' (SII: 214).

Death would amount to the disintegration of imaginary unity, the eradication of the ego, and psychoanalysis would amount to a quasi-Bataillean eradication of the conscious ego that would free the uninhibited expression of unconscious desire, without a conscious ego to govern it, a return to some sort of natural animality, or pure will. Lacan answers by saying, 'Why not? In *Oedipus at Colonus*, Oedipus says the following: *Am I made man in the hour when I cease to be?* That is the end of Oedipus's psychoanalysis' (SII: 214). But, '[t]here is no reason why the subject should end up without an ego, except in an extreme case such as that of Oedipus at the end of his life' (SII: 217).

Full speech, then, is only ever an ideal: 'Speech can express the being of the subject, *but, up to a certain point, it never succeeds in so doing*' (SI: 107, my italics). Lacan describes the goal as 'virtual' (SII: 246). And the reason for this is that one is never without ego, because one is always *embodied* (so long as one is alive, at least). Even in the one situation in which pure speech without language might have been possible, the psychoanalytic session, the analyst, despite being hidden behind the couch, is himself embodied. 'One trains analysts so that there are *subjects* in whom the *ego* is absent. That is the ideal of analysis, which, of course, remains virtual. *There is never a subject without an ego*, a fully realised subject, but that in fact is what one must *aim* to obtain from the subject in analysis' (SII: 246, my italics). The possession of a body cannot wholly be ignored: 'the ego becomes what it wasn't, [. . .] it gets to the point where the subject is. [. . .] Don't, however, get the idea that the ego volatilises after an analysis [. . .] one doesn't go to heaven, disembodied and pure symbol' (SII: 325, my italics).

Thus Lacan suggests that *embodiment* is the reason why the goal of full speech must always remain virtual: '*Between* the two [subject and ego], there is this structuring given, namely that the subjects are *embodied*' (SII: 324, my italics). The analyst can never entirely eradicate his own ego and thus in the analytic scenario demolish the wall of language that was deforming the subject's speech thanks to the presumed necessity for intersubjective communication:[34] 'the analyst is never fully an analyst, for the simple reason that he is a man, and that he, too, partakes of the imaginary mechanisms that are obstacles to the passage of speech' (SIII: 162, my italics).

> They are on the other side of the wall of language, there where *in principle* I never reach them. [. . .]
>
> If speech is founded in the existence of the Other, the true one, language is so made as to return us to the objectified other [. . .] language is as much there to found us in the Other as to drastically prevent us from understanding him. And that is indeed what is at stake in the analytic experience. (SII: 244, my italics)

Embodiment, egoity, and the consequent necessity to use language and communicate make full speech impossible, a mere ideal. Lacan is committed to this by an understanding of the relation between real and symbolic which renders them absolutely incompatible. This commits him to an understanding of full speech under the first interpretation we have just laid out, and amounts to a pessimistic view that one's desire can be freed only by destroying language altogether, and since this is impossible it remains permanently thwarted. There is simply no way either to express speech in language or to eradicate this language altogether and allow the free passage of speech to another that would be able to sate one's desire.

However, already present in this period of Lacan's work is a *second* interpretation of full speech, and here it becomes clear that Lacan is attempting to think *beyond* an oppositional relation of real and symbolic. This would mean that the goal of psychoanalysis was no longer virtual but actually attainable. This second interpretation will be overpowered by the first, but at the same time it opens up a space that the later Lacan will have the resources to fill.

The second interpretation of full speech

The second possible meaning of 'full speech' is that it constitutes a certain manner of using language which allows speech properly to express itself within it. This would mean that the real could find some way to exist within the symbolic, and thus the two realms could *not* be entirely opposed in nature.

In this case, full speech would occupy the same ambivalent position as the symptom, and perhaps therefore it will be with this interpretation of full speech that we can understand precisely *how* the symptom is possible, *why* the real subject leaves its corpse behind as some sort of absent presence in the symbolic order.

The symptom speaks of the subject. But it does not know it. Full speech would be something akin to a symptom that *did* know it. Is full speech precisely the free production of symptoms that we are conscious of as such? Would this free associative process have the aim of full speech in the sense of the patient's coming to realise that his symptoms are in fact speaking, that his meaningless meanderings in fact wend ever nearer to the truth in a way his consciously meaningful speech does not? Full speech would be the speech *of* the symptom, a speech now *recognised* by the patient to be such. This would mean that the subject *recognises* his symptoms to express his own singular desire – his 'truth' – rather than being accidental and *meaningless* glitches.

Full speech would be to recognise *everything*, even those idiotic acts which seem dumb or mute, to *bespeak* a desire that is ours. Free association would lead us to view in another way the *value* of meaningless things. It would ultimately allow us to recognise in certain of the meaningless symptoms which we brought to the doctor's in the first place the *incommunicable* singularity of the subject who speaks. Full speech would then mean that everything which speaks, which signifies, is recognised as such, including, above all, those elements which speak irrespective of meaning. 'Full speech' would mean to recognise that 'everything is full of speech'. This would be the 'full realisation of speech' (SI: 247).

Full speech would be 'performative'; it would be a certain manner of speaking in which the recognition is *performed*. In Lacan's examples of performative speech one merely bestows a meaningless title upon someone: master, wife, and so on, but the title of itself changes everything. One hereby recognises the power of the word *alone* irrespective of its meaning. One thus sees that words can do more than just mean, and that those words which are meaningless can nevertheless have an effect. We are thus brought into a position from which we can recognise the meaningless symptom as expressing our proper truth. Full speech is 'speech which aims at, which forms, the truth such as it becomes established in the recognition of one person by another. Full speech is speech which performs' (SI: 107).

The analyst reflects back the real message the analysand as speaking subject is trying to convey, without knowing it. Hence Lacan speaks of 'that essential form of the human message whereby one receives one's own message from the other in an inverted form' (SII: 51; cf. SIV: 120 *et al.*). The message is in 'inverted form' in that the message is not a signified but a signifier. The 'inversion' at stake here is Lacan's inversion of Saussure's diagram of the sign: S/s for s/S.

The real as meaningless can be spoken only in language that has no concern for meaning, or which recognises meaning's determination by signifiers, by context. Would full speech be speech that did not elide or ignore the material density of language, something like poetry? We have stated that it is the signifier as such in its infinite totality that constitutes the unconscious. Full speech would then be speech that recognised its dependence *on* this unconscious: 'this full speech in which its base in the unconscious should be revealed' (SI: 52).

A speech that does not believe itself governed by a single transcendent meaning would be one that is open to its own ambiguity. And perhaps it is the oscillation of this ambiguity that Lacan is describing in the following passage: 'The fundamental speech which goes from *A* to *S* here encounters a *harmonic vibration* [*une vibration harmonique*], something which, far from interfering, allows its passage' (SII: 325, my italics).[35] The 'harmonic vibration' would then mean the resonance of an individual signifier over a plurality of different contexts and hence the uncontrollable plurality of its meanings. But this ambiguity, while it would be ruinous for communication, is ideal for the expression of one's real singularity. 'When the space of a lapsus no longer carries any meaning [*sens*] (or interpretation), then only is one sure that one is in the unconscious' (SXI: xxxix).

The subject exists, it secretly presents itself in the discrepancy between word and deed, between word and intention, in those words which present themselves without our knowing *why*. This is how the unconscious presents itself. It is the way in which the density of the signifier *refuses* to be elided before the ideality of its signified, and, because it is this phonic or graphic material that is shared between contexts, this opens the signifier's signified to its contextual ambiguity. The signifier presents itself in the guise of the uncontrollable ambiguity of meaning which infects any instance of speech *as a result of meaning's dependence on language*. It is the revelation of the dependency of meaning on a prior instance of meaninglessness that allows the signifier itself to come to the fore. Thus, full speech would be a symptomatic use of language that did not attempt to elide this dependence upon language itself. The usual use of speech precisely denies language, it believes itself to be transparent to an unequivocal meaning. Ironically, full *speech* would then be a speech which did *not* deny *language*. This is indeed a 'paradox': 'This paradoxical path consists in extracting speech from language' (SI: 175).

This interpretation is bolstered by Lacan's statement that we must discern speech in the language of the symptom: 'a symptom is *language* from which *speech* must be delivered' (E: 223, my italics). This is why Lacan says that we must free the subject's *speech* by 'introducing' him to the *language* in which his symptoms are speaking, and speaking to us of a desire, where he sees only chance and mishap.

> In order to free the subject's *speech*, we introduce him to the *language* of his desire, that is, to the *primary language* [Lacan's emphasis] in which – beyond what he tells us of himself – he is already speaking to us unbeknown to himself, first and foremost, in the symbols of his symptom. (E: 243, my italics)

Thus full speech is not speech unfettered by language but speech which recognises that it can speak *only* in language, that pure desire is always forced to take the form of determinate desires. '[W]e must be attentive to the unsaid that dwells in the holes in discourse, *but the unsaid is not to be understood like knocking coming from the other side of the wall* [of language]' (E: 253, my italics). Here Lacan is explicit that this second interpretation of full speech is incompatible with the first interpretation where the real was opposed to the symbolic, on 'the other side of the wall'.

And yet, the symptom as it is understood by the early Lacan is a sign of the subject *in its absolute impossibility*. The real (subject) is impossible. This is why Lacan describes the subject as appearing in its *trace*, which is to say, present *in* its absence, and *vice versa*: 'But the truth can be refound; most often it has already been written elsewhere. Namely [. . .] in its *traces* that are inevitably preserved in the distortions necessitated by the insertion of the adulterated chapter into the chapters surrounding it' (E: 215, my italics).

The symptom is nothing but a sign that *anything* of another order to language simply cannot exist within language. It is a sign of death, of the amortisation of desire in language. There is simply no room for singularity in the symbolic order, and if one comes to hear the silent call of the symptom in 'full speech' one will hear only the voice of doom. One will understand only that one's desire will *never* be expressed and that one's real singularity will forever remain stifled by the symbolic. The subject is always the *missing* signifier, the *lack* of a signifier, 'the subject is literally at his beginning the elision of a signifier as such, the missing signifier in the chain' (SVII: 224).

The barred subject, the essence of the human being as desire, can then exist only in the bar. Full speech is the expression of desire in that desire is never satisfied by one object, but precisely by the transition between objects, by ever new objects of desire. It is this constant metonymy[36] of objects which acknowledges that desire is precisely to be understood as a verb, as desiring, and desiring nothing other than itself. Thus if it relates to an object at all it is only to the nullity of this object, to nothing. 'Desire [. . .] is lack. [. . .] [T]here is no object that desire is satisfied with' (SXIV: 21/6/67). It is 'the desire to desire' (SVII: 309). It merely desires ways in which to continue to *be* desire. Hence the imperative delivered to the analysand is, 'do not give way on your desire!' (SVII: 319), which is to say, do not believe that any object will satisfy it! Do not be fixated on any one object, in the belief that it will satisfy your desire! Keep desiring!

Desire then, in the absence of any final object, would be infinite. It is precisely this infinity which renders it unconscious, due to the finitude of consciousness. The aim of psychoanalysis would be to ensure that desire never became fixated on one object, and so 'blocked'. With respect to any one signifier, desire desires *nothing*. This is what has to be acknowledged, that there is no final object that will stop us desiring, and this is precisely due to the oppositional exclusion of real and symbolic.

It is crucial to distinguish cognition (*connaissance*), rendering conscious, from *re*cognition (*reconnaissance*). 'To recognise' is here used in the sense of to respect the distinctness of the other. What is recognised is the desire of another – the real subject – within me, who will always *remain* other.

> But for this desire itself to be satisfied in man requires that it be recognised through the accord of speech or the struggle for prestige, in the symbol or the imaginary.
>
> What is at stake in an analysis is the advent in the subject of the scant reality [*peu de réalité*] that this desire sustains in him, with respect to symbolic conflicts and imaginary fixations, as the means of their accord, and our path is the intersubjective experience by which this desire gains recognition [*se fait reconnaître*].
>
> Thus we see that the problem is that of the relations between speech and language in the subject. (E: 231)

Thus, (unconscious) desire does not ultimately desire whatever object it causes us consciously to pursue, but merely desires recognition.

The struggle between the two interpretations

May we mediate between the two interpretations of full speech by saying that they share the common presumption that it is impossible for the real to enter the symbolic? In neither case is it assumed that there is any place in the signifier for the subject.

Perhaps in the end, however, the very syntagm 'full speech' tends too much towards the first interpretation, the ideal situation of speech without language. That Lacan tended towards this interpretation is also suggested by his prevalent indications that the situation is only an 'ideal'. This would seem to speak against the second interpretation in which full speech *is* attainable.

The fact that Lacan eventually eradicates the notion of full speech (along with this talk of 'ideals'), and, as we shall see, replaces it with his notion of '*la*langue', indicates a shift towards the second interpretation of full speech, which would outgrow its very name. The later notion of *lalangue* relinquishes Lacan's early pessimism in believing that the subject can be present in the signifier only as absent. Taking the relationship between the real and the symbolic to be an opposition compelled Lacan to understand it in this way, and this finally told against the more promising second interpretation of full speech. Later, however, the first interpretation would be ruled out, as the real and the symbolic would no longer be opposed.

The future of full speech: the real between signifiers

Language is not composed solely of signifiers. There are also the differences *between* signifiers. *Signifiers themselves* are not signifiers. They are not themselves, they are not the same as themselves, they *are* difference, they differ even from themselves and lack the self-identity that would characterise a present-substance. The presence of a signifier is composed of the absence of others, the fact that one is different from those absent others constituting the presence of that signifier. But these others are not themselves anything positive, they are made of traces as well. This is why, as Derrida has it, signifiers are nothing but 'traces *of* traces' (P: 26, my italics). Each absent signifier differentiates itself from every other signifier by leaving within it a mark of its absence. The sum total of these marks constitutes that particular signifier in its individuality.

Language itself is constituted of elements that are non-linguistic. We shall eventually show why we are entitled to describe these non-linguistic marks as 'real'. But if this is the case, then it *should be* possible for Lacan, even in his middle period, which we are currently considering, to say something other than that the subject has no place in the symbolic. This is to say that the relation between the real and the symbolic need not be understood as an abstract opposition, in terms of a pre-linguistic real that is killed stone dead, once and for all by the emergence of the symbolic, leaving only the corpse of the real in its place. Rather the real could be the very traces which *constitute* these signifiers in the first place, the material of the signifier when considered apart from its signifying qualities. It is just this 'real-*within*-the-symbolic' that Lacan has not yet fully learnt to see. The real is as yet impossible for him.

II. THE NAME-OF-THE-FATHER AND THE PHALLUS

In the first part of this chapter, we have seen that the overwhelming tendency of Lacan's thought is to understand the relation between the real and the symbolic as an opposition. We now need to examine precisely *why* a more 'deconstructive' notion of the relation is overwhelmed in this way. This overpowering amounts to the triumph of the *name-of-the-father*, which is in truth the suppression of the inherent geneticism of psychoanalytic thought by the structuralism of Lacan's middle period, which amounts to a certain transcendentalism. The 'transcendental signifier', which makes the entire symbolic order possible, amounts to that order's mythical understanding of its own origin.[37] This signifier is the 'name-of-the-father', the prohibition of incest that characterises all human culture and appears to distinguish it absolutely from nature.[38]

To demonstrate the way in which the name-of-the-father reigns supreme in Lacan's thought at this stage we shall examine Lacan's explicit discourse on the real and the symbolic at both the phylogenetic and the ontogenetic levels. We shall identify a discrepancy between Lacan's two accounts of the development of and accession to the symbolic order. The phylogenetic is a chronological account of the development of the human race as such, the emergence of culture from nature. The principal notion here is the *name-of-the-father*. The ontogenetic is an account of the manner in which the infant enters into a pre-existing system of language (or how it becomes manifest to him that he is always already there). The central notion here is the *phallus*.

One can see already that the question is too abstractly posed in *both* cases, and that Lacan *begins* with a rigid oppositional separation of real and symbolic and then asks how this gulf is to be bridged.

However, it is curious that it should be the phylogenetic account that is at fault, since it would seem that here we have a more properly genetic way of posing the problem, while at the ontogenetic level the question is posed with regard to a language that always already exists – 'always already' being the distinguishing mark of a transcendental discourse and approach. And yet, at this stage, it is the phylogenetic approach that strays closer to transcendentalism, insofar as it understands the incest taboo as the condition of *every* instance of human culture, and as instituting an absolute break between nature and culture, something so novel that it simply cannot be explained by an evolutionary account. Given this absolute difference, it is clear that the relation between symbolic and real must ultimately be understood as an opposition. And while the ontogenetic account seems the more transcendental, in truth it is in the latter that the possibilities of a non-transcendental, genetic thinking are broached. Then again, this is not to deny that there are *elements* of Lacan's thinking of phylogenesis which trouble a purely transcendental approach and the oppositional determination it involves.

To simplify matters in advance, while the name-of-the-father lets us understand the signifier as a finite whole, bounded by nature, the phallus, by allowing us to think in terms of a continuity between the natural and the cultural, opens up the possibility of a truly infinite textuality, and thus a deconstructive understanding of the relation between the symbolic and the real.

And yet, ultimately the transcendental approach embodied in structuralism's name-of-the-father will prevail over the genetic account. It is precisely this vanquishing that will leave Lacan open to deconstruction. Thus we shall establish that, despite every attempt at charity, there *is* a problem with Lacan's earlier position. The problem is the relation between the symbolic and the real and it is precisely the construal of this relation as an opposition which deconstruction takes issue with.

But, if this is deconstruction's *problem*, this does not mean that we have to adopt deconstruction's *solution*.

The entrance of man into the symbolic order

If we may identify the real with nature and the symbolic with culture, we can see that our earlier exposition of the mutual presupposition of the subject and the ego implies that the aim of psychoanalysis is not a return to nature: even in the first interpretation of full speech, this was only an asymptotic ideal. The unconscious depends on the difference between conscious and unconscious. It is maintained by the gap. Without culture there is no such thing as the unconscious, and so psychoanalysis could not mean a return of the discontents of culture to their uninhibited animal selves. Rather what is required is an acknowledgement that the natural is and must always be repressed by the emergence of the cultural, and perhaps even that the idea of the purely natural is a mythic projection carried out by culture itself.

Lacan describes the interpretation of psychoanalysis as the removal of prohibitions imposed by the law of culture as the illusion of the 'pastoral', the sentimental way in which civilisation views that from which it is irremediably alienated but to which it dreams of returning (SVII: 88–9; cf. SXIV: 18/1/67). Psychoanalysis attempts to reawaken both the animal underside of our symbolic identities *and* the prohibition that makes pure animality impossible for us – it indicates the fact that our desire is both created and rendered unsatisfiable by the symbolic order of culture.

But this already commits us to a transcendental approach. We are trapped in the symbolic and any inferences to what lies beyond it must make this leap by asking after the conditions of possibility of the symbolic, to transcend the symbolic order by asking after its essence, the more or less generic characteristics which apply to every culture, and thus make its distinct character possible.

Lacan believes this transcendentalism is necessary in order to oppose the notion of an *evolution* of the symbolic and of the human species. Any such continuous notion of development is for him irrevocably teleological and non-explanatory, for it presupposes a certain continuum between the various stages in the evolution of a certain entity. This very continuity implies that something like the human was already there *in embryo* at the beginning of the process and therefore acted as some sort of guiding force in its unfolding. Thus, by presupposing these entities, one simply defers an explanation of how they originally came to be. Evolutionism looks back from its own standpoint, discerns earlier forms of itself, and thus views itself as the highpoint of a development composed of inchoate versions of itself.

> Implicitly, modern man thinks that everything which has happened in the universe since its origin came about so as to converge on this thing which thinks, creation of life, unique, precious being, pinnacle of creation, which is himself, with this privileged vantage-point called consciousness.
>
> This perspective leads to an anthropomorphism which is so deluded that one has to start by shedding the scales from one's eyes. [. . .] This is a newcomer for humanity, this idiocy of scientistic atheism. (SII: 48)

For Lacan, if we are not to evade the burden of explanation, consciousness must be understood to result from some form of contingent event. He continues: 'consciousness is linked to something entirely contingent, just as contingent as the surface of a lake in an uninhabited world' (SII: 48).

Paradoxically, it is precisely Darwin's situating man in a non-teleological nature, as one evolving subject among others, with no special privilege, that is at fault here. Evolutionism intended to remove the idea of a *telos* from the development of species, to eliminate any anticipation of the later by the earlier. The problem for Lacan is that the very definition of 'evolution' implies a *continuous* development. This continuity prohibits the emergence of anything new, and thus in no way can evolutionary theory be used to explain the contingent emergence of a wholly novel trait, such as that which will be understood to characterise *culture*. 'An evolution that insists on deducing from a continuous process the ascending movement which reaches the summit of consciousness and thought necessarily implies that that consciousness and that thought were there at the beginning' (SVII: 213).

The only way to avoid this continuist evolutionary position, which ends up retrieving precisely the non-explanatory teleology it was intended to refute, is to think of the human being as *unique*, as a pure *novelty* with respect to the rest of nature. What is unique about man is the signifier. Far from thinking this to be the product of a gradual evolution, we are compelled to think of it as the result of a sudden, absolute beginning, a *creation*:

> It is only from the point of view of an *absolute beginning* [*un commencement absolu*], which marks the origin of the signifying chain as a distinct order, and which isolates in their own specific dimension the memorable and the memorised [*le mémorable et le mémorisé*], that we do not find being [*être*, culture] implied in beings [*étant*, nature] in perpetuity, the implication that is at the basis of evolutionist thought. (SVII: 213–4, my italics)

The paradox is that creationism does away with god, in the sense of designing intelligence, while evolution retains it:[39] 'The idea of creation is consubstantial with your thought. You cannot think, no one can think, except in creationist terms. What you take to be the most familiar model of your thought, namely evolutionism, is with you, as with all your contemporaries, a form of defence, of clinging to religious ideals' (SVII: 126).[40] But how can one believe in creation without believing in God? Lacan differentiates his position from that of pure faith by suggesting that a believer must be able to locate the moment of creation in *chronological* time, as a cause. The psychoanalyst on the other hand, understands this creation *retrospectively*, as a condition of possibility, a *transcendental* moment rather than a causal one. Thus, as the arch-debunker of such 'illusions' as religion, psychoanalysis treats creation as a '*myth*', but accepts the necessity of myths in human existence. A myth is a symbolic or imaginary retelling of a beginning. A myth is something that the symbolic order finds it necessary to invoke in order to explain itself. The myth of creation, an event of absolute novelty, is the only way that the signifier can explain its own origin.

First among these myths of the creation of the super-natural symbolic order is the myth of the *prohibition of incest*. The prohibition of consanguineous sexual relations does not exist in nature, save in a few cases at the level of real instincts, which are precisely *not* what is at stake in the case of man. The prohibition in the human species is not a physical prevention, but a symbolic one.

The prohibition of incest is one with the formation of the human family, that collectivity which is united by the inherited patronym, the surname or 'name of the father'. By forming a family, the name-of-the-father makes incest possible and at exactly the same moment prohibits it. This however is a purely symbolic prohibition, a prohibition in name only, deriving its force from the word alone, from the surname itself.[41] In the animal realm there is only instinctual tug and aversion, *Drang*. The prohibition of incest is for modern man 'the law' as such in the sense of a constraint independent of the physical, which is to say the natural (*physikōs*). 'There is no biological reason, and in particular no genetic one, to account for exogamy' (SII: 29)

The Law characterising and constituting culture is that sexual relations shall not take place within the same bloodline or kinship group. Lévi-Strauss established that the most fundamental prohibition in every particular set of kinship laws was the interdiction of sexual relations between father and daughter. Since mating could not take place within the immediate family, the incest taboo was understood to necessitate the exchange of women between families, in order for this intercourse to take place (cf. SII: 261ff.). Exchange, involving the equivalence of two heterogeneous entities, indicates that the structure of the sign, in which one thing stands *for* something else, has already arisen. The very possibility of exchange is thus premised upon the arising of the symbol. The name for the very first symbol is therefore, 'the name of the father' (*le nom du père*). That a certain consanguineous group has acquired a family name makes it possible to exchange women *between* families. Thus the origin of the symbolic order, the 'transcendental signifier', is the 'name-of-the-father'.

Men would refrain from congress with their daughters and (in some cultures) their sisters, and they would do so *in the name of the father*. This restraint led to the marriage between women and men from non-consanguineous groups, and this in turn meant that the name-of-the-father would be inherited by those who were *not* naturally related to its original bearer. Thus the name-of-the-father begins to enjoy an existence independent of the biological filiation of the natural father. The name, the signifier, would come to signify people (signifieds) who were not naturally related. The surname is the precursor of the arbitrary sign, which is to say the non-natural, non-iconic relation between signifier and signified.

The symbol is precisely an entity which stands for something other than itself, it can refer to something that bears no relation to its *natural* properties. The symbolic is the place where a gap opens up between word and thing, name and named. Thus the name-of-the-father constituted the beginning of a super-natural order.

Exchange is commonly understood to characterise the beginning of human society. The anthropological tradition considers the object exchanged to be the woman. This exchange is possible thanks to the name of the father, and at the same time it allows this name properly to exist. If the name remained solely within the biological father's blood line it would have no reason to exist.

Some 'created' (indeed 'creative') surplus in the father must have instituted his lineage as a non-natural tradition unified solely by the signifier of his *surname*. The name cannot extend itself to the non-natural without exchange, and hence its very existence prohibits consanguineous marriage, which opposes this exchange. The name *is* the prohibition. The surname constitutes the transcendental signifier that makes the human 'race' as such possible, a cultural totality strictly opposed to nature.

The religious connotations of the name-of-the-father suggest that the irruption of the surname, of the prohibition, simply cannot be understood evolutionarily, but rather the whole race must be understood as the product of divine creation. The original father who *created* the surname – and thus the very notion of 'fatherhood' – *created* the human race. The human race *as a whole* can be unified only by the name-of-the-father understood as the name of *God*: 'there is no other father but God' (SIX: 17/1/62). '[T]he attribution of procreation to the father can only be the effect of a pure signifier, of a recognition, not of the real father, but of what religion has taught us to invoke as the Name-of-the-father' (E: 464).

There is simply no genetic or, at least, no *evolutionary* way for Lacan, in his middle period, to explain how such a thing as a symbol could have arisen.

This at least is how things seem to the symbolic: it is unable to conceive of a time when it did not exist, and hence to trace its true origins in the non-symbolic. Why? Because difference can only be infinite. No end to difference is in sight, and we cannot see beyond the borders of language. The symbolic order's attitude can only be transcendental in relation to its own origin, which is to say mythopoietic, myth-producing. The question is how much Lacan thinks this mythic projection on the part of the symbolic order is the perspective *he* must adopt, to what extent he believes that nothing of the *real* genesis of the symbolic can be addressed.

How are we to understand Lacan's creationism? Does it fall victim to that which it was meant to criticise and presuppose what it was meant to explain, just as evolutionary thought does? Does it evade the necessity for explanation by recourse to myth? My hypothesis is that by *explicitly* presupposing what it was meant to explain, by its clear transcendentalism, Lacan's discontinuist creationism attempts to avow what evolution presupposes and yet denies. The idea of creation is ridiculous, it explains precisely nothing, but it points towards that which must be explained: the *appearance* of a radical discontinuity that is brought about by the infinitising of the signifier. If one is an actual creationist then one is no better than an idealist or mythicist: one presupposes the existence of the signifier without explaining it. To be materialist one must begin from the pre-symbolic real and explain its genesis. One can only begin to explain something properly when one does *not* presuppose it, and Lacan avoids this by taking the extreme step of positing a moment of creation. Creation is a way to indicate the absolute novelty of the signifier's functioning in the case of man, which is then precisely what needs to be explained or at least acknowledged to be insusceptible of explanation.[42]

Thus, adopting a creationist position is a strategy designed to show that evolutionism does not explain the emergence of the human. Creationism posits the arrival of something genuinely new, and thus presents in the starkest fashion the challenge with which explanation is confronted. The arising of something new, the absolute opposition of the cultural and the natural, the irruption of infinity, is what needs to be explained. Darwinism merely assimilates culture to nature and thus denies the *explanandum*.

Lacan is keen to point out that the structuralist notion of the incest taboo is not an explanation, nor perhaps was it designed to be one. The prohibition merely *describes* what culture is, and it does so in such a way as to absolutely oppose it to nature. It is the opening up of a non-natural form of tradition or transmission, information and signifiers of all kinds that are transmitted in a way that differs from the transmission of genetic material. This is precisely the constitution of the very notions of tradition and history.

Thus the prohibition explains nothing because it does not form part of a logical sequence of events which result in the human race, it just describes an absolute beginning. Lacan could not be more explicit that a genetic explanation of the taboo is impossible: 'There is no possible means, starting from the natural plane, of deducing the formation of this elementary structure called the preferential order' (SII: 29). It is precisely this novelty – the symbolic order itself – that cannot be explained naturalistically.

Something becomes unhinged, unlimited, when the signifier arises: need is infinitised to become desire. This is the moment at which nature becomes unnatural. Somehow, man becomes capable of the destruction of the entirety of nature and of himself. He becomes unfitted to survive.

If in the beginning, 'signifiers' or 'fundamental symbols' are few and far between, they cannot form a systematic totality, and hence cannot properly be called signifiers. So the proto-signifiers which might have been identified as the precursors of the signifier in *nature* cannot be called 'signifiers' *stricto sensu*. Indeed, this totality of signifiers is precisely what we wished to explain by reference to these things which were taken to *precede* it.

> [I]n the human order, we are dealing with the complete emergence of a new function, encompassing the whole order in its entirety. The symbolic function is *not new* as a function, *it has its beginnings elsewhere than in the human order*, but they are only beginnings.
>
> [. . .] we must start with the idea that this order constitutes a totality. In the symbolic order the totality is called a universe. The symbolic order from the first takes on its universal character.
>
> It isn't constituted bit by bit. As soon as the symbolic arrives, there is a universe of symbols. (SII: 29, my italics)

It is this notion of totality, the fact that a signifier can only come into being as part of a system, that renders a naturalistic explanation impossible, or at least presents a demand to which evolutionary theory does not respond. It is this curious moment of infinitisation. Lacan describes this infinitisation as the consumption of the real by the symbolic: 'One can only think of language as a network, a net over the entirety of things, over the totality of the real. It inscribes on the plane of the real this other plane' (SI: 262). If language extends over every inch of the real, however far our vision extends, then there will be no way *from our standpoint* to envisage the moment at which this language *began*.

This is the transcendental standpoint of structuralism. And yet, insofar as the myth of the incest taboo understands itself as a myth and so presents a challenge to explanation it opens up the *space* for a genetic explanation. As part of this genetic explanation, to which we shall return in Chapter 3, Lacan will demonstrate that the real is not an inert immanence but can produce something of another order to itself: the real can produce images. Lacan is quite clear about this. Although this imaginary capacity reaches a higher stage of development in the organic world, it is present even in the non-organic, as we can see from Lacan's example of the reflection in a lake on an *uninhabited* planet (SII: 48, *et al.*).

The natural deficiency and the symbolic prosthesis

Lacanian psychoanalysis involves two theses which are often taken to be outdated: that man is unique with respect to all other animals, and that man is a *corrupted* form of animal, *un*fitted to survive. It is the second of these theses which makes room for a *genetic* explanation of the emergence of the symbolic order in man. We shall mention it here only in passing since in truth it is structurally impossible for Lacan in his middle period properly to accommodate it. Our purpose here is to demonstrate that this side of Lacan's thought is fundamentally overpowered by the transcendental. This is what renders it vulnerable to deconstruction.

This corruption does have to be understood as a biological fact, and thus provides psychoanalysis with a basis in the extra-philosophical *sciences*.[43]

For Lacan, man is an animal *un*fitted to survive. What makes him unique is the fact that he is the *only* animal which *is* so unfitted *and yet survives*. He survives by invention, *technē*, by a crafting of supplements that constitute another, non-natural order. The animal's instinct is that which allows the animal to fit in with its natural surroundings, and it is this aspect of animality which malfunctions in man. Man does not fit with his environment. Lacan understands animal instincts as those impulses which control the biological features of the animal necessary to its survival and reproduction (its nutrition, maturation, self-defence, and reproduction). Lacan understands these instincts to function according to *images*.

Why images? Because what elicits the animal's instinctual response is the *form*, the pictorial form, of an element of the real world. The primal image, that concerned with mating and the avoidance of predators, is the image one has of *oneself*, one's own species. Images act as mediating schemata which allow the animal to recognise certain elements of its environment as relevant for its inner needs. Thus the objects which 'fit' these images cause an automatic response on the part of the animal, an instinctual act. Schematic images allow animals to institute a one-to-one correspondence between inner needs and those elements of the outer world which 'answer' these needs. Animals thus 'fit' into their surroundings, they are fitted to survive in that particular environment.

Man, on the other hand, does not fit. In man, it is precisely this reliability of the imaginary that is lacking. He does not have natural instincts which are sufficiently infallible to allow him to survive. As a result, he needs prosthetic support, extra guidance in how to relate to his world. Indeed he has to create a world that is fitted to himself, or rather he has to create some third realm between himself and the world, in which the two can come to some sort of agreement. This will be the realm of the symbolic.

It is not simply the case that the big Other, the symbolic, is alienating for man's singularity, it is also an essential crutch to mankind. Without the symbolic supplement, mankind as a species would have withered away. 'The symbolic order has to be conceived as something superimposed, without which no animal life would be possible for this misshapen subject that man is' (SIII: 96).

To compensate for a natural lack of self-sufficiency, and a failure of the imaginary mediation between inner and outer, man, thanks to the chance arrival of the thumb and upright stance, began to build. Only thus did he manage to survive his natural deficit, by means of a technical supplement. Man builds his own hollow and protection to enable him to survive long enough to mate and raise his children from their unusually long tutelage.

Man builds because there is a gap between himself and nature, caused by an inadequacy in his schematising imagination, which hinders his ability to discern which elements of the environment are harmful or helpful. The necessity for the schematisation of the imagination, the matching of non-conceptual sensation with conceptual categories of the understanding, arises contemporaneously with something like the signifier, while the analogous form of 'schematisation' that exists in animals is non-symbolic.

The most crucial inability that man suffers from is the inability to achieve the coupling that is most likely to produce offspring who will survive and propagate. Even though man may be able, by means of technical prosthesis, to survive until his reproductive capacities have developed, his instinctual, imaginary deficit would doom his chances of successfully finding an appropriate mate. This is partly what Lacan means when he speaks of the 'impossibility of the sexual relation [*rapport*[44]]'.[45] In order to fill the gap of a fully functioning imaginary, man uses the symbolic order: 'in man, no truly effective and complete imaginary regulation can be set up without the intervention of another dimension' (SI: 141).

This is Lévi-Strauss's insight into the 'elementary structures of kinship [*parenté*]', the insight that *structure* intervenes in the sexual life of man. Sexual preferences are founded upon the preference of the father, which is most basically expressed as an absolute prohibition of whom *not* to mate with: our mother or father. The symbolic is the order of the traditional, the moral, the normative, the conventional. It is the order of 'preference' with regard to man's sexual partners, it comprises the guidelines for what we *ought* to desire.

On an ontogenetic level, Freud addressed this with the notion of the Oedipus complex, wherein the prohibition of incest is inculcated by the individual,[46] as well as in the complementary phylogenetic myth of the murder of the father in *Totem and Taboo*, where the prohibition is revealed to be a consequence of the father's *name*. 'The subject finds his place in a preformed symbolic apparatus that institutes the law in sexuality. And this law no longer allows the subject to realise his sexuality except on the symbolic plane. This is what the Oedipus complex means' (SIII: 170).

Since the imaginary does not guide us towards our proper partner, there is the danger – which Freud described as the infant's 'polymorphous perversity'[47] – that we will mate with *anything*, even those things with which a coupling can produce no offspring. This is precisely the arbitrariness of the sign in Saussure's sense; there is no longer a natural or biunivocal relation between signifier and signified, desiring (*desirant*) and desired (*desiré*). But this danger is not immediately biological, our instincts are perhaps not *so* corrupted that the majority of mankind would mate with things that are not human. What is endangered is the supplement to the biological, the symbolic order itself, *without which* man could not survive. In the case of man, acting as if we were pure animals would result in the obliteration of the symbolic order, and since man's instincts *need* this symbolic guidance in order to function, this would result in the extinction of the human species. For all Lacan's anti-Darwinism, there is a trace of survivalism in the symbolic order. In the following passage, Lacan describes the ruin of mankind that would ensue if he attempted to return to an animal state of imaginary duality:

> The ambiguity and the gap in the imaginary relation require something that maintains a relation, a function, and a distance. This is the very meaning of the Oedipus complex.

> The Oedipus complex means that the imaginary, in itself an incestuous and conflictual relation, is doomed to conflict and ruin. In order for the human being to be able to establish the most natural of relations, that between male and female, a third party has to intervene [. . .]. The order that prevents the collision and explosion of the situation as a whole is founded on the existence of this name-of-the-father. (SIII: 96)

In this way the incestuous lack of distance from the mother, a 'natural' relation, is split asunder and a regulated distance is maintained, the distance between man and the real – or the real and itself – introduced by the signifier; mediation becomes the law, the laws of the symbolic intervene as a third party in all human relationships. Lacan describes the intervention of the symbol as 'speech', in the sense that it involves a pact between human beings, and this involves first of all giving one's *word*: 'It is *speech*, the symbolic relation, which determines the greater or lesser degree of perfection, of completeness, of approximation, of the imaginary' (SI: 141).

The symbolic order represented by the name-of-the-father, the symbolic father, outlaws an absolutely free choice of sexual object. We must submit to a normative order to achieve what nature achieves without assistance. In truth, while the animal is constrained by the limits of its instincts, and the compulsion they exert, it is man's freedom that must be constrained if he is to survive. This amounts to a 'structuring' of man's instinctual life and the imagination which governs it. It supplies his disordered imagination with *structure*.

The name-of-the-father as a sign

The surname enmeshes the individual man in the differential fabric of the symbolic order. It is the manner in which our imaginary bodies and egos find a place within an alien, linguistically structured order.

The name-of-the-father is the moment at which subjects are stitched into a wider *inter*subjective textile, language and linguistically structured legality, the realm of culture. It is by virtue of language that a plurality of human beings can co-exist. For this reason, Lacan describes the name-of-the-father by means of an analogy from the realm of fabrics: *le point de capiton*, the upholstery button or quilting point.[48] This sews the subject into the symbolic order and thus redoubles him as both an imaginary individual and a subject of legal responsibility and social expectation: 'the notion of father [. . .] gives [Freud] the most palpable element in experience of what I've called the quilting point [*point de capiton*] between the signifier and the signified' (SIII: 268).

The quilting point is what links a signifier and a signified, the symbolic and the imaginary.[49] It is a *sign* in the strict Saussurean sense. But this is precisely what the notion of the signifier, taken to its logical conclusion, was supposed to rule out, a one-to-one correlation of signifier with signified. This is why the name-of-the-father is not just any old signifier, but a *name*. A name is a label linking one entity uniquely to a single word.

The name-of-the-father as the signifier of signifiers

If the name-of-the-father is a *signifier*, what does it signify? For the one who is to assume the name, and thus enter the order of tradition which it represents, it signifies the symbolic order, the signifier, the order to which one is to accede. Thus, the name-of-the-father may be said to be 'the signifier *of* the signifier': 'the Name-of-the-Father [. . .] being the signifier which, in the Other, qua locus of the signifier, is the signifier of the Other qua locus of the law' (E: 485). 'The Name-of-the-Father redoubles in the Other's place the very signifier of the symbolic ternary, insofar as it constitutes the law of the signifier' (E: 481, cf. 345).

The name is unique among signifiers because it alone is capable of referring to just one signified, without ambiguity. How can a name be possible in a symbolic order which precisely rules out such unequivocal reference? A name, a sign, can exist in just one case: when it signifies *every signifier there is*. Since there is only one realm of culture, a signifier that signifies or names this culture in its entirety *can* be understood as a name or a sign.

The name-of-the-father signifies the whole of the signifier *without* being caught up in its ambiguating effects. As a name, the signifier 'name-of-the-father' is not defined by its differences from any determinate, historical set of signifiers. It stands on the threshold of culture and indicates it as such and as a whole. It is in some way outside of history and language, it is a 'meta-language', a language beside or beyond every determinate system of language, it signifies it without being a part of it. The name enjoys a different relation to its object than a mere signifier: it signifies not simply by signifying, but by naming.

If the name-of-the-father is indeed a name, then there can be only one symbolic order. At least insofar as there is just *one* name of the father. This means that there is no choice but to accept the one dominant cultural code that one is thrown into. There is no choice but to be a human being and all human beings are at root the same. The one god-the-father unites us all or the one symbolic father exists as his name in the taboo on incest that characterises *every* human culture.

This is what Chiesa means when he identifies Lacan as locating the name-of-the-father *outside* the circle of the symbolic order (Chiesa 2007: 107–8). '[T]he father is, in the Other, the signifier that represents the existence of the place of the signifying chain as law. It is situated, if I may say so, above it [*au-dessus de celle-ci*]' (SV: 196). Thus the postulation of the name-of-the-father not only implies that the symbolic order is unique, but also, by occupying a point external to it, allows it to form a totality. If the surname – the taboo – characterises every human culture as such, it allows this culture to form a totality absolutely *opposed* to nature.

If there is a point of exception, an absolute outside, the signifier, the inside relative to this outside, can form a totality. Culture is definitively separated from nature, the symbolic from the real. This exteriority explains why Lacan describes the name as 'the other *of* the Other'. 'Experience demonstrates to us at which point the backdrop [*l'arrière-plan*] of an Other with respect to the Other [*un Autre par rapport à l'Autre*] is indispensable, without which the universe of language [*langage*] would not know how to articulate itself' (SV: 463); 'the Other of this Other, if I may say so, is that which allows the subject to perceive this Other, the locus of speech, as itself symbolised' (SV: 463).

The question is whether this name is a myth or whether such a thing really exists. Can we ever ask questions about the genesis of this name, or must we as creatures of language simply presuppose it. In 1959, on the cusp of his later thought, we find Lacan already questioning its reality, and we should recall that from the start 'the *point de capiton* is nothing but a mythical affair, since nobody has ever been able to pin a signification to a signifier' (SV: 196). 'The other of the Other exists only as a place. It finds its place even if we cannot find it anywhere in the real, even if all we can find to occupy this place in the real is simply valid insofar as it occupies this place, but cannot give it any other guarantee than that it is in its place' (SVII: 66).

The name-of-the-father is a sign, and the sign is the biunivocal or 'binary' signifier. The binary signifier is to be identified with the *Vorstellungsrepräsentanz*, the 'ideational representative' or the signifier which is repressed into the unconscious in repression: 'The *Vorstellungsrepräsentanz* is the binary signifier' (SXI: 218). This is the signifier whose repression institutes the unconscious. The sign as such, the name is ruled out with the arising of the infinite system of the signifier proper, the unconscious. The signifier of the signifier would be precisely that which is rendered impossible as soon as the infinite system of the signifier comes into being. Hence its primal repression.

We have already seen that primal repression operates on the singularity of the speaking subject thanks to the existence of determinate language. It is the primal repression of the real by the symbolic, the suppression of the natural, the impossibility of ever *finding* our name. Thus that which is primally repressed is precisely that signifier which would link the signifier and the real, the name.

The *Vorstellungsrepräsentanz* as a sign would be that which represented *representation* itself, it would be the signifier of the signifier as a whole: 'It is a matter of that which in the unconscious represents, in the form of a sign, representation' (SVII: 71). Now, if this representative is rendered primally impossible by the signifier's infinity, then the name-of-the-father as the unique signifier of the signifier necessitates transcendentalism, since it makes it impossible for the symbolic to do anything other than see itself extending infinitely into the past and the future.

We should thus identify this binary signifier, this representative of representation itself, with the name-of-the-father, the signifier of signifiers. Indeed, Lacan describes the name-of-the-father as itself 'primally repressed' (*urverdrängt*): 'This signifier constitutes the central point of the *Urverdrängung*' (SXI: 218).

In this way, as representative of representation, signifier of signifiers, other of the Other, the name-of-the-father is distinguished from all signifiers as what makes them possible. It would be the very first signifier, governing the creation of the signifier in its totality, a true novelty with respect to nature. The name would be the signifier of the very moment of creation itself, the creation of 'god the father'. As long as one believes that this mythical signifier is a necessary presupposition, and as long as one does not attempt to address the question of its natural genesis, one remains a transcendental thinker, for one posits a transcendent moment of conditioning that makes possible every single signifier there is.

Thus the symbolic realm of culture is utterly closed off to the realm of nature, thanks to the name-of-the-father: real and symbolic are *opposed*.

This is precisely the question upon which everything hangs: whether Lacan believes in this god, in this moment of creation, and is hence a transcendental philosopher, genuinely believing in the one transcendental condition for the entirety of the symbolic, the one name. The question is whether this avowed myth is the *only* access we have to the real, in other words, whether we must adopt the standpoint of the symbolic order which creates this myth and this mythical relation to its own outside. Is Lacan merely exposing a necessary misunderstanding on the part of the symbolic order which he does not from his own standpoint endorse, or is he himself compelled to be complicit in this transcendentalism?

This question is crucial because, as we have already intimated, the problem with something like the prohibition of incest characterising and uniting the whole of human culture is that it sets up an *oppositional* relationship between nature and culture, real and symbolic. And this is just the notion that deconstruction shows to be untenable. Is the relation between nature and culture not in truth more complicated, and is the name-of-the-father, the unique feature of human culture, not itself the product of some natural development that can be subject to a genetic explanation?

As if to indicate that there was a part of Lacan which always resisted the transcendental standpoint, there is another element to his earlier thought, and, ironically, one on which Derrida himself insists in order to *deconstruct* Lacan, as if it were identical with the name-of-the-father, which it is not. It is the notion of the *phallus*. The phallus forms part of an attempted explanation of the *genesis* of the symbolic order.

We must now attend to this phallus in order to open up the ambiguity in Lacan's understanding of the relation between the real and the symbolic, since it is this ambiguity which he will later develop, and which already problematises any unified understanding of his earlier work as straightforwardly transcendental. Rather, despite being overpowered by the transcendentalism inherent in the name-of-the-father, it contains a potential which will later be mobilised against this transcendental approach.

The phallus

The name-of-the-father was evoked by Lacan to solve a problem that the phallus had opened up. To proceed quickly, the phallus, by its very nature, opens up precisely that infinity of the signifier which deconstruction is interested in promoting. At the same time, the phallus partakes of and opens the symbolic onto a *genetic* explanation of its origins, which transcendental thought rules out. It manages to relate the symbolic and the real in a way that does not simply swallow up the real in signification. It can do this as a consequence of its *imaginary* aspect. The phallus will be that which does not signify the symbolic, but *resembles* it.

The name-of-the-father renders the infinity of the signifier a *totality* and so ensures that there *is* something outside of and heterogeneous to the text: the real, which is *defined* as that which is not symbolic.

Without the name-of-the-father, Lacan, in his middle period, saw only the autism of psychosis, and since, empirically, so many were not even vulnerable to psychosis, let alone actual psychotics, it was necessary to explain the 'suture' of the symbolic, the limitation of the signifier by its anchoring in a point external to it.[50] It was necessary to unify the entirety of the cultural world in order to ensure intersubjective and indeed intercultural communication. This unity and totality was provided by the name-of-the-father (cf. Chiesa 2007: 109–11). The aim of psychoanalysis was more or less to bring the patient to accept his placement in the symbolic order, to accept the necessity for speaking of one's singularity in language, and to therefore accept as one's own the name-of-the-father in the general sense of one's cultural humanity.

Thus, to avoid rendering everyone a potential psychotic, Lacan needed the name-of-the-father.

But the phallus ensures that we are all slightly mad.

There are two reasons for the name 'phallus': the Oedipus complex itself, and the place of the phallus in the emergence of human culture, as an actual organ of the generative process and as a symbol, seen in phallic structures such as monoliths or the actual Greek *phallōs* which symbolised the power of nature to regenerate itself cyclically, but only by means of erection. It should be remembered that the *phallōs* was a *symbol* of the *real* penis in its erect *imaginary* form. It is the symbol of potency, and particularly the natural potency of sex, which is the power to reproduce the species and thus perform a natural cycle; the ability of the male of the species to propagate itself and the ability of nature to perpetuate its own circularity as a result of erection.

The phallus impregnates the mother and allows her to fulfil her 'natural' function. Through her, nature itself can achieve its own reproduction in the most general sense. Thus, in the case of the human, a sexed entity requiring sex for reproduction, the phallus is the supplement of the female. The phallus signifies the 'artificial' completeness of nature. Nature *in itself* enjoys this completeness. But in the case of the human being, this capacity is lacking. The phallus is both the symbolic crutch and the mirage of the impossible natural perfection of mother-Nature. It is one in nature but split in two for man. It is the image of natural fullness, a harmony of two opposed halves. In truth, this image of nature is a myth projected from the standpoint of something sundered from the start, the sign.

Since it is the man who is in charge of the structures of symbolic exchange, he is the possessor of the phallus, a fact perhaps ultimately contingent upon his anatomical possession of the penis.[51]

The human being as such is a little phallus, in that he begins recumbent and has the ability to erect himself. *Homo erectus* as such, in his total form, embodies this quasi-oppositional capacity: recumbent–erect. He himself, along with several of his attributes (including the nipple), even the opposable thumb, seems capable of figuring the opposition as such. The technical ability to build is the ability to erect, and thus to create an opposition, a presence where there was once an absence. Perhaps this is the uniqueness of man, that in himself he *is* the image of the symbolic. Perhaps the symbolic was fashioned 'in his image'.

The (symbolic) phallus is thus what the woman desires in order to find a place in the symbolic, where she is and can be understood solely as the partner of a male, as his complement or opposite: opposites arise only in the symbolic order, so outside of this androcentric order, sexual difference cannot be understood as an opposition, if it can be understood at all.[52] The woman's pursuit of a man is thus the pursuit of the phallus which will bind her to a point in the symbolic order. This is required by the symbolic order as well, since woman and nature are absolutely crucial to its continuation: the woman incubates a new human being who will bear the symbolic, a new generation to inherit it. The woman can generate children, naturally.[53]

She is afflicted with 'penis envy' (*Penisneid*) only insofar as she is left out of the phallocentric symbolic because she lacks the physical organ, the penis, which confers upon man the power to impregnate and so reproduce the human being as support of the symbolic order, which thus acts as a support for the phallic *signifier*.

The woman is always an object, exchanged, a signifier passed from man to man, the true subject of the action. But by bearing a child, the woman becomes a subject, an actor in the symbolic in her own right. Thus the child is a phallus for the mother, a symbol of the power of which she is frustrated, but at the same time the symbol of a power she potentially has. The child is the form of production specific to the woman. While the man has the real erection of the penis (though this is caused by the woman), the woman has the imaginary erection of the small child who will one day walk erect and indeed perhaps possess a penis of his own. In any case, he or she is the specific power of the woman as opposed to the man.

The phallus desired by the woman is thus a child. The child will give her a certain power over the man which the man in himself lacks. The child is the mother's imaginary phallus (SIV: 47). The child qua imaginary phallus is a substitute for the *penis* she lacks (cf. SIV: 70), which is to say that he is a *symbol* of what she lacks in terms of her imaginary, bodily form, which is smooth where the man's is protrusive: 'the phallus [. . .] is defined as imaginary, it is not possible in any way to confound it with the penis in its reality, it is properly speaking the form, the erected image' (SIV: 70).

And yet the child is more than just an image. He is real and so cannot be a genuine replacement of the penis. Thus he can only be a *symbol* of what the woman lacks in her imaginary form: 'the child inasmuch as it is *real*, *symbolises* the *image*' (SIV: 71, my italics). The Oedipus complex is the process whereby the mother realises the realness of the child and hence the impossibility of her union with the child, the impossibility of her truly *owning* a phallus. The child will grow to become his own man and cannot be hers.

In Seminar IV, Lacan persistently describes the sequence of the three lacks – privation, frustration and castration – from both perspectives, that of the child and that of the mother. The perspective of the child at the moment of castration is illuminating. The castration is the moment at which mother and child are revealed to have always already been separate individuals, even in the womb. They will have been separated by the signifier. The child must be separated from the mother in order to disseminate the father's name, which he already legally possesses. It is the surname which fundamentally rules out the imaginary union of mother and child. The fact that the parents already had such a name indicates the necessary intervention of the symbolic into human sexual life and therefore the impossibility of any imaginary harmony such as the mother imagines could exist between her and her baby.

Before the moment of castration however, the child himself wishes for this absolute union with the mother. And yet already at this level, the presence of the father threatens this unique bond.

Before the child has any true knowledge of the nature of the symbolic, he is able to compare himself with the father only at the imaginary level, which is to say in terms of his likeness. He considers himself solely as the object of his mother's desire and the father intrudes on the scene as a rival for her attention. At the pre-linguistic level, the child has only his individuality, his bare ideal ego, and so the only thing he has to compare himself with both the mother and the father is the size of this imaginary form or 'Gestalt', his awareness of his own physical size. The rivalry with the father is an imaginary rivalry between the child as the mother's imaginary phallus and the father's actual penis. Or rather, since the child may never actually see this penis, he must compare the size of his own body and the father's larger, more upright body (cf. Borch-Jacobsen 1991: 216).[54]

At this stage the child may not connect the phallus with the actual penis. The child is merely attempting to embody in his totality everything the mother desires. To speak of the child's understanding himself as a phallus is to speak, as we must, of the pre-linguistic from the perspective of the symbolic, where we understand the true nature of desire and sexuality: 'The pregenital relation cannot be apprehended save by beginning from the signifying [*signifiant*] articulation of the Oedipus complex' (SIV: 53; cf. SIV: 65).

In the castration of the incestuous couple, the child is forced to accept his determination by the signifier, initially in the form of the name of the father, he is forced to accept his inheritance of and subordination to the father as symbol. The father's intervention amounts to the intervention of the signifier in the child's life, or the dawning awareness that a signifier will always already have governed his destiny. Thus he will never have been one with the mother, with the real. The intervention of the trace-structure of the signifier is depicted by the incision of a line between S and s in the diagram of the sign, 'S/s', in which the bar is re-interpreted as a barrier, the impossibility of pinning a signifier to a single signified, the deconstruction of the sign, the prohibition of a natural imaginary relationship between desire and its object, the impossibility of natural sexual relations, which are for human beings exclusively incestuous ones.

The two sides of the phallus

The phallus has two aspects: imaginary and symbolic. It functions as a representative of the imaginary forms of erectness and flaccidity; and as the symbolic mark of presence rather than absence. It embodies an alternation of imaginary forms which resembles a *symbolic* opposition. If the phallus is a part of the real, then anything that has a phallic form may be seen retrospectively to *anticipate* the oppositional nature of the signifier. The phallus thus forms part of the *genesis* of the symbolic order.

The phallus can thus be said to form both halves of the Saussurean sign. The imaginary phallus is the signified, the symbolic phallus is the signifier. The symbolic phallus *signifies* the imaginary phallus.

Signifier	symbolic phallus
———	———
Signified	imaginary phallus

This marks the way in which the child understands the superiority of the signifier over the signified, of the symbolic phallus which is in the father's possession, over the imaginary phallus, which is always sublated by the former. With the castration carried out by the symbolic order, the imaginary competition of 'mine is bigger than yours' has ended, and the child is forced to assume his position in the symbolic bloodline of the name-of-the-father, in expectation of inheriting the dead father's position as head of his own house. The slave waits for the master in order one day to repossess the enjoyment that he believes he has lost (SI: 286–7). He waits to inherit the symbolic phallus. He wants to *have* it since he has been prohibited from *being* it: 'it's by way of an *imaginary* conflict that *symbolic* integration takes place' (SIII: 212, my italics).

The phallus is something *real* which is an *image* of the *symbol*. Thus, unlike the name-of-the-father, it is not a signifier of the signifier but an *image* of the signifier. It *resembles* the signifier without naming or signifying it. It is *genuinely* the 'symbol' as that which enjoys a *natural* relation between 'signifier' and 'signified' and not a conventional one like the 'sign'.

The phallus *is* the power to span the two halves of an opposition. It is the potential of being in two opposed states, to move between absence and presence. In this way, the specific power of the phallus resembles the signifier itself which is ultimately founded on the opposition of presence and absence.[55] The phallus – or the phallic form – *is* the genetic origin of the signifier. It is that element of the real which explains how the signifier came about.

The name-of-the-father claims to signify every signifier there is. But it does so only from the point of view of the fully constituted sign. It does not address the 'proto-signifiers' which formed its genesis. These are absolutely excluded from the symbolic. Insofar as one writes and thinks solely under the auspices of the name-of-the-father, one will not attend to the actual genesis of the signifier which is to be found in the phallic form.

The phallus does not mythically erect a fully-fledged signifier at the origin of the signifier, with the inevitable circularity that this entails. It is the *image* of every signifier there is, but is *not* or *not yet* a signifier in the strict sense. The phallus is a rhythmic alternation in the real, which anticipates the opposition. In other words, if the name-of-the-father is impossible, mythical – it being impossible that a sign should stand at the origin of the sign – the phallus is *not* impossible.

The name-of-the-father claims to signify all signifiers, and that must include itself. But this is impossible, for the signifier can never signify itself, it can only differ from itself. On the other hand, since the phallus is *itself* both symbolic and imaginary, a signifier *and* a signified, it *can* signify itself, but as Lacan says, it is not *named*, unlike the name-of-the-father: 'even though it can signify itself, it is unnameable as such' (SIX: 9/5/62).

The phallus as joint of imaginary and symbolic

The phallus, as a symbol, symbolises *in virtue* of its *imaginary* nature: it has the shape of an upright stick or score-mark, something which of its very form embodies an oppositional or *proto*-oppositional relation: something is marked rather than not-marked. It is an imaginary entity, a pure image, which *resembles* the signifier. It is 'the *image* that is raised, elevated, in relation to the first, that of the *big Other*' (SIII: 209, my italics). The phallus does not just represent the origin of the signifier, it *is* the origin.

> The woman's access to the Oedipal complex, her imaginary identification, is accomplished via the father, exactly as in the boy's case, by virtue of the prevalence of the *imaginary form* of the phallus, but insofar as this form is itself taken as the *symbolic* element central to the Oedipus complex. (SIII: 176, my italics)

In the phallus, an image is used as a *symbol*. Therefore, the phallus can be used to explain *genetically* how the signifier arose: 'But what is new in man is that something is already sufficiently open, imperceptibly shifted within the imaginary coaptation, for *the symbolic use of the image* to be inserted into it' (SII: 322–3, my italics).

> That which serves as a support for the symbolic action, which is called castration, is an image, chosen in the imaginary system to be its support. The

> symbolic action of castration chooses its sign, which is borrowed from the imaginary domain. Something in the image of the other is chosen to carry the mark of a lack. (SV: 464)

It is a question of a certain *rhythm* or *schema* which lays the foundation for the symbolic order. It is an image which is not constant, which has two quasi-oppositional states, a 0 and a 1, a state which can either be there or not.

Without erectness, the penis is still there, but the phallus has completely vanished, although it remains in existence *as potential*. In what sense are presence and absence figured in the penis, the real ground of the phallus? Simply in the fact that the penis can become erect, but any erection is only temporary. The penis is the organ which manifests 'the thrust of life' (*la poussée de la vie*): 'This is why it is the phallus, in so far as it represents the rise of vital power [*la puissance vitale*], which takes its place in the order of signifiers' (SV: 465). This rise is contrasted with the phallus's 'caducity' (*caducité*), its capacity to *fall* (*caducere*) (SV: 465).

The signifier would not have existed without this original proto-opposition between presence and absence embodied in the phallic form. Thus the phallus is an image of what stands at the very origin of the signifier. Not a substance or a word, but a certain event, an alternation, which actually occurs in the real and provides the real support of this signifier, effectively 'producing' or 'creating' it.

The phallus as signifier of signifieds

The phallus signifies every signified there is, in the sense that it signifies the castration which is carried out when the signifier is produced as an infinite system, rendering any univocal signified impossible. Castration is the impossibility of a sign, the impossibility of one signifier ever signifying just one signified. The phallic signifier signifies the phallic signified, but this is always either absent or appears against the background of its own absence, always absence *in potentia*, and so, effectively, the symbolic phallus signifies the absence of the imaginary phallus. 'I designate Φ as the phallus insofar as I indicate that it is the signifier that has no signified' (SXX: 81). In an infinite differential order, with the arbitrariness this entails, no one signifier can have a univocal signified. For this reason, the phallus represents every signifier there is.

The phallus is what Lacan calls the 'unary signifier', the pure signifier without signified, because it is not yet a proper signifier, strictly speaking, and is still immersed in the imaginary relation of resemblance. It is the proto-signifier that in itself is rendered inaccessible when the signifier becomes a fully fledged system, when the name-of-the-father is established as its principle. The unary signifier is not the *binary* signifier which has a univocal relation to a signified. Simply speaking, it is not yet a 'signifier' at all.

Lacan describes the unary signifier, 'S1' (the first signifier, and the signifier '1', the mere mark), as a pure signifier, pure in the sense that it has no signified. It is an element of symbolicity, having the imaginary *form* of a signifier, which anticipates the symbolic order: 'the Φ that props [man] up as signifier and is also incarnated in S1, which, of all the signifiers is the signifier for which there is no signified, and which, with respect to meaning [*sens*], symbolises the failure thereof' (SXX: 80).

Lacan renders the nature of the phallus more precise as follows: 'But is that to say that what is at stake here is, as people all too quickly thought they could translate it, the signifier of what is lacking in the signifier? That is what this year ought to put an end to' (SXX: 39). The lack is not in the *signifier* but in the signif*ied*. Thus the symbolic phallus is not a lack of signifier, it is not a missing signifier in the sense that the subject occupies the symbolic order in the form of a lack of signifier, but a signifier *of lack*, the signif*ier* of a lack of signif*ied*.

So the phallus signifies not a lack of signifier, it signifies *nothing*, it signifies an absence of signified. If it does not signify anything, then the phallus is not yet fully a signifier. The phallus does not signify, it *just sticks up*. The phallus is *pure* signifying, it is the pure event of referral, which characterises all signifiers, but which is manifest as such here because it has no final term. It does not refer to anything, it merely refers. But this is the nature of all signifiers in the symbolic order, insofar as their references never cease in some moment that would not itself refer. The possibility of an unequivocal signified is castrated by the signifier.

For this reason, the *symbolic* phallus is thus understood as the signifier of *signification* as such, the signifier of the nature of signifying which is to exclude any one-to-one reference with a unique signified. The phallus is 'the signifier of the signified in general' (SV: 240; cf. Chiesa 2007: 119). This is because every signifier lacks a univocal signified, it is always castrated, cut off at the waist.

This is the deconstructive import of the phallus, it indicates that the chain of referrals can never find a reassuring end in any moment that would be outside of this referentiality or 'text'. It presents the law of castration, the absence of any exterior, transcendental signified.

The name-of-the-father, signifier of the signifier, attempts to be a *sign* of the symbolic, while the phallus is the *image* of the symbolic. In fact, the phallus represents the absence of that which has traditionally been considered transcendental with respect to the symbolic order: the transcendental *signified*, the meaning which only later comes to be conveyed by signifiers, and which stands outside the signifier and its referrals. The imaginary phallus is, when incorporated into the S/s diagram we invoked above, assimilated to the order of the sign, the representative of meaning. It would represent the one transcendental signified which anchored the entirety of the signifier and was not dependent on this signifier for its existence, and it would represent it as impossible from the standpoint of the signifier. The phallus represents its own castration, precisely because it contains in potential its own lack of erection.

Castration may be understood graphically as the scoring of the slash between S and s, which indicates the 'sliding of the signified[s] under the signifier' (SIV: 47), and 'the function of the bar is not unrelated to the phallus' (SXX: 39). This is not just the bar separating signifier and signified but the bar in the $ which is the subject's symptomatic presence in the symbolic order, the presence under erasure of the real. It is in other words by means of the imaginary phallic form that the real remains present *within* the symbolic order, and the symbolic order, despite the name-of-the-father, enjoys some access to its real beginning.

The overpowering of the phallus by the name-of-the-father

To understand the phallus as a *sign* is a symbolic appropriation of what it is in itself, which is an image of the symbolic that could be said to precede it. It is as if Lacan in his middle period, under the sway of structuralism, understands the phallus *primarily* in this appropriated form, where the rhythm of presence and absence has been 'grouped' into a genuinely symbolic sequence. It is as if he could only read it as a sign, and thus see it through no other eyes than those of the symbolic, which naturally understands the phallus in this way.

This is to close off the genetic possibilities of the phallus and to understand it once again as a purely transcendental condition of possibility. It is to perform a move analogous to the name-of-the-father's creationist myth, and that is to place at the origin of the signifier a (non-explanatory) *sign*.

The rhythmic alternation of states is always appropriated by the symbolic, looking back upon its own origins, as a proper *opposition*, the symbolic opposition between having and not having. Castration just *is* this institution of an opposition between presence and absence, a clear-cut opposition where one half is marked as the absence of the other.

The image of the origin of the symbolic order can be present *in the symbolic order itself* only as *absent*. The symbolic can only appropriate its own origin. It does not understand the accession to the symbolic in terms of a real genesis but merely attempts, by means of the name-of-the-father, to show the supposedly pre-symbolic, animalic child that they have always already been captured by this order and were *never once* outside of it. The *real* origin is signified only as a blank, an absence, the scar of castration or the umbilical cut from the real mother, now inscribed on the body only in the form of the senseless navel. The symbolic cannot incorporate the positivity of its origin. It can signify it only as a void: S/Ø.[56] The scar signifies *something* but it signifies nothing.

After the symbolic has been constituted, we might represent the phallus as S/Ø, and the name-of-the-father as S/S.

The name-of-the-father is the symbolic order's mythical (transcendental) re-telling of its own origin. The symbolic could not have originated in a signifier, but this is how the name-of-the-father represents it: that in the beginning of the word *was* the word. This is the illusion of the transcendental. It forces itself to believe that a chronological explanation for the moment of creation is impossible and takes refuge in myth. It believes that it has no access to the real genesis and that the only way to exceed itself is by means of transcendence on the basis of the properties which it knows itself to possess: from the differentiality of the signifier it infers that the nature of the non-symbolic real is *presence*, *non*-differentiality. It spurns the opportunity offered by the phallus that could have been understood as a *proto*-opposition, which could have explained the very generation of the symbolic itself.

It is as if Lacan believes that we cannot escape the signifier, that we can reach outside of the symbolic order only transcendentally. It is as if the only standpoint that psychoanalytic theory can adopt is that of the symbolic. In the work of Lacan's middle period, the transcendental overwhelms the genetic. It is as if the name-of-the-father springs fully formed from the creative mind of god and has no natural genesis. The signifier does not have a genesis that we can address 'naturalistically'.

All we can do is speak from the perspective of the symbolic and recount myths of how god the father must have moulded the raw clay of humankind.

But how in that case would we account for the nature of psychosis in which the name-of-the-father has been 'rejected' (*verwerft*, foreclosed).[57] In this case the name does not return in the form of symptoms but makes a direct approach from the real. It is to ward off this threat of a psychotic indetermination of meaning, an absorption of each individual in their own universe of imaginary meanings, that Lacan appeals to the name-of-the-father as a real sign. Lacan needs a way to unify a potentially infinite fragmentation of the symbolic, such that every individual or group of individuals would speak an entirely distinct language. In other words, Lacan believes that he needs to presuppose the reality of the signifier of signifiers, the name-of-the-father, in order to ensure that the vast majority of mankind can share a single symbolic order. It is as if the myth *should* be believed in, for the sake of one's 'mental health'. The name-of-the-father should be posited as *really* characterising the whole of human culture because it is arrived at by a transcendental argument, the only manner in which generality and 'otherness' may properly be posited.

The name-of-the-father implies an oppositional determination of the real and the symbolic, and thus it ensures that for everyone but psychotics the intrusion of the real into the symbolic is impossible.

But this *can* happen, and indeed, this is precisely what deconstruction shows: deconstruction, that maddening of the philosophical *logos*. It shows that the symbolic is always already real, and we can know the real only in the guise of that real which constitutes language itself, that real which is the material trace that makes difference possible.

Lacan *wants* to say that the name-of-the-father is a necessary consequence of the infinite nature of the symbolic, the way it can project its origin only mythically or transcendentally. By means of his avowal of creationism he wishes to point up the non-explanatory nature of the myth and at the same time the impossibility of providing an evolutionary explanation for it. He does not see that there are other genetic explanations *besides* the evolutionary. And already, the phallus will have opened the way for just such a genetic explanation of the signifier. It will have shown that the origin of the signifier need not be understood in the form of a signifier but can be understood more genetically as an *image* of the symbolic that anticipates its oppositional structure. The phallus could be employed to moderate strictly transcendental approach and address the origin of the signifier in terms of its real genesis. But at this stage Lacan is compelled to stifle the insight that the phallus offers him.

The name-of-the-father institutes an oppositional relation between the symbolic and the real, but the *opposition* as such is a characteristic of the symbolic order. In other words, the relation between originated and origin is understood *on the basis of* and in terms of the *originated*, the signifier. This can only be an appropriation, and it is one which characterises traditional transcendentalism.

If Lacan understands the origin of the symbolic in this way, positing the signifier 'the name-of-the-father' as the other of the Other, he is making what Derrida describes as a 'structuralist' move. The real is impossible, dead, irrelevant to the functioning of the independent symbolic machine. Thus, when the machine is required to ask after its own origin, it can only adopt a transcendental approach, which is to stand firmly in the present and look backwards towards its conditions, to begin from entrapment and ask after the possibility of escape or 'transcendence'.

Derrida perfectly captures the necessity and the paradox of any attempt to stabilise the structure of signifiers in this way, the paradox of an other of the Other, a metalanguage or name-of-the-father, the paradox of transcendental thought itself:

> The function of this centre was not only to orient, balance, and organise the structure [. . .] but above all to make sure that the organising principle of the structure would limit what we might call the *play* of the structure. By orienting and organising the coherence of the system, the centre of a structure permits the play of its elements inside the total form [. . .]. As centre, it is the point at which the substitution of contents, elements, or terms is no longer possible [. . .] is forbidden. [. . .] Thus it has always been thought that the centre, which is by definition unique, constituted that very thing within a structure which while governing the structure, escapes structurality. This is why classical thought concerning structure could say that the centre is, paradoxically, *within* the structure and *outside* it. (WD: 352)

The name-of-the-father forces – or allows – Lacan to adopt a transcendental rather than a genetic approach, and institutes a deconstructible relation between the real and the symbolic, at the expense of the phallic insight into the imaginary, on the border of the symbolic and the real, troubling their strict opposition, and allowing the signifier to be truly infinite in the quasi-Hegelian sense.

In the next chapter, we shall focus on Derrida's deconstruction of this oppositional relation, not at all unrelated to the Hegelian differentiation of the true and the bad infinite, along with his own positive response to the problem of understanding the origin of language, which amounts precisely to the problem of this overpowering of any other approach to the real than a transcendental one. We shall investigate just how he understands the 'transcendental illusion' of the prohibition of incest which makes those of us trapped within the symbolic believe that the real is our opposite.

But does Derrida himself do all that he can to avoid the transcendental gesture, or does he also ignore the real genesis that the phallus opens onto?

This real genesis is just what we have seen Lacanian psychoanalysis to open up, before closing it down under the pressure of its own 'philosophical' influences. We shall – for now – set aside this other possibility which we have seen to emerge with the notion of the phallus, and the possible role of the imaginary in troubling the complacent and transcendental assertion of an opposition between symbolic and real, in the name of a genetic account of the development of the symbolic itself. For this will bring before us a domain into which even Derrida, for all his critique of transcendental philosophy, will not venture. But we shall return to it.

Notes

1. These heirs include Lacoue-Labarthe and Nancy (1992 [1973]) and Borch-Jacobsen (1991). Strictly speaking, the only *deconstruction* of Lacan that Derrida ever carried out is 'The *facteur* of truth' in *The Postcard*, his other engagements being more informal. It will be verified in Chapter 4 that Derrida's deconstruction does not run along the same lines as ours.
2. '[I]in the end, forgive my infatuation, what I am trying to do with my Borromean knot [*nœud bo*] is nothing less than the first philosophy which, it seems to me, has support' (SXXIII: 145).
3. '[T]he statement [*dit*] which results from what is called philosophy is not without a certain lack [*manque*], a lack which I am trying to supplement [*suppléer*] with this recourse to what can only be written – the Borromean knot [*le nœud bo*] – for something to be taken from it' (SXXIII: 144–5).
4. '[F]rom a certain moment on, and precisely that of the birth of these seminars, I believed I had to bring into play this triad of the symbolic, the imaginary, and the real' (SIX: 13/12/61).
5. '[Psychoanalysis] owes its scientific value solely to the theoretical concepts Freud hammered out as his experience progressed [. . .]. But it seems to me that these terms can only be made clearer if we establish

their equivalence to the current language of anthropology, or even to the latest problems in philosophy' (E: 199).

6. '[T]here is a problem, an impasse, that Freud himself emphasises and that can be explained by the state of linguistics in his time' (SVII: 44–5); 'when the *Traumdeutung* was published it was way ahead of the formalisations of linguistics' (E: 426).
7. Lacan refers to 'the aporia this great mind encountered in the most profound attempt to date to formulate one of man's experiences in the *biological* register' (E: 82, my italics). This is why a dogmatic retelling of Freud's thought would be incoherent: 'contrary to the dogmatism with which we are taxed, we know that this system remains open as regards both its completion and a number of its articulations. [. . .] These hiatuses seem to come together in the enigmatic signification Freud expressed with the term "death instinct"' (E: 82; cf. AE: 35; cf. Safouan 2004: 1–3).
8. Lacan continually identifies '[t]he three books that one might call canonical with regard to the unconscious' (E: 434): *The Interpretation of Dreams*, *The Psychopathology of Everyday Life*, and *Jokes* [Witz] *and their Relation to the Unconscious* (cf. SI: 280; cf. SI: 244).
9. 'Without these three systems to guide ourselves by, it would be impossible to understand anything of the Freudian technique and experience. Many difficulties are vindicated and clarified when one brings these distinctions to bear on them' (SI: 73). This distinction is there already in Freud, but needs to be brought out: 'that is what can be immediately translated, almost algebraically, from any Freudian text' (SI: 89; cf. SII: 123).
10. 'If psychoanalysis can become a science (for it is not yet one) and if it is not to degenerate in its technique (and perhaps this has already happened), we must rediscover the meaning of its experience. [. . .] To this end, we can do no better than return to Freud's work' (E: 221ff). 'Our step forward in psychoanalysis, is at the same time a return to the aspirations of its origin' (SI: 275).
11. Lacan denies this – 'it is not a matter of an ontological definition, it is not fields of being that I am separating out here' (SIX: 13/12/61) – but given that Lacan hardly thematises 'being' anywhere in his work, we may set this objection aside. Two years later, he is prepared to admit that, 'I have my ontology – why not? – like everyone else, however naive or elaborate it may be' (SXI: 72).
12. '*Zurück zu Freud*, return to Freud, I said first of all, at a moment when this took on its sense from the confused manifestations of a colossal deviation in analysis' (SXIII: 1/6/66).
13. Crucial in this regard is Lacan's scintillating critique of associationism and psychology (E: 58–74).
14. 'That primacy of the *Es* is now completely forgotten' (SVII: 137).
15. A proper consideration of the mirror stage, and the imaginary as a whole, will be deferred until Chapter 3, for essential reasons.

16. Lacan avows his task to be 'to maintain the fundamental distinction between the true subject of the unconscious and the ego' (E: 347).
17. 'What the subject does makes sense, his behaviour speaks just as his symptoms do' (SII: 136). 'I speak without knowing it. I speak with my body and I do so unbeknownst to myself. Thus I always say more than I know' (SXX: 119).
18. 'And the subject, while he may appear to be the slave of language, is still more the slave of a discourse in the universal movement of which his place is already inscribed at his birth' (E: 414).
19. Lacan defines structure as follows: 'A structure is in the first place a group of elements forming a covariant set. [. . .] [T]he notion of structure is by itself already a manifestation of the signifier. [. . .] [T]he notion of structure and that of signifier appear inseparable' (SIII: 183–4).
20. 'It is precisely on these ambiguities, on these riches already involved in the symbolic system as it has been constituted by the tradition in which we as individuals take up our places, far more than we can spell out or learn of it, it is on these functions that the analytic experience plays. At every moment this experience consists in showing the subject that he is saying more than he thinks he is' (SI: 54).
21. '*Verdrängung* operates on nothing other than signifiers' (SVII: 44).
22. '[W]e can effectively find thought – not in an idealist sense, but thought in its presentification [*présentification*] in the world – only in the intervals of the signifier [*intervalles du signifiant*]' (SVII: 214).
23. To say 'conscious ego' does not mean to give the same extension to 'consciousness' and 'ego'. The ego may be conscious but it is alienated by its reference to the other, and there is thus an element which it lacks (which will eventually be named by Lacan 'the object *a*'), an element of itself which remains unknown to itself. It is only the *illusion* of a full and immediate self-transparency or self-consciousness.
24. 'Prior to all symbolisation – *this priority is not temporal but logical* – there is, as the psychoses demonstrate, a stage at which it is possible for a portion of symbolisation not to take place. [. . .] It can thus happen that something primordial regarding the subject's being does not enter into symbolisation and is not repressed but rejected [*verwirft*]' (SIII: 81, my italics). '[A] function of the unconscious that is distinct from the repressed [*Verdrängt*]. [. . .] *Verwerfung*' (E: 465; cf. SIII: 12–13, 149–51, 321; cf. E: 445–88).
25. Although we shall establish this logically later on, Lacan hints at it when he describes as 'real' the needs which our cries bespeak prior to our mastery of the symbol: 'real need' (*le besoin réel*) (SIV: 141).
26. Lacan stresses that the movement from enunciation to enunciated is the movement from a verb to a noun, a substantivisation, at both the imaginary and the symbolic level, where this pre-verbal ego becomes the signifier '*ego*' or 'I' (cf. SI: 166). 'Who, if not us, will call back into question

the objective status of this "I", which a historical evolution peculiar to our culture tends to confuse with the subject?' (E: 96).

27. Since it is only at the moment of frustration that 'she becomes real, which is to say that she becomes a power [*puissance*]' (SIV: 68), in other words, an agent who appears to the child as distinct from the breast, as one who has the power to withhold it as a (now symbolic) object.
28. Lacan is quite explicit that the *Spaltung*, the splitting of the ego and the subject, relates to these two subjects: it is 'the *Spaltung* between the enunciation and the enunciated' (SVII: 306; cf. SVII: 273–4).
29. A corpse, an empty place, an absence that remains present; in Bridge, *le mort* is the player who has put all his cards on the table, everything about himself that can be displayed symbolically is so displayed, he has nothing hidden any more: he is an idiot. We shall return to this in Chapter 4.
30. Lacan himself makes the connection: 'the idiotic character – if I take up the Greek reference [. . .] – the very *idiotic character* of the proper name' (SIX: 20/12/61; cf. SXIV: 14/12/66).
31. Perhaps this is the aleatory nature of the event: Lacan identifies the real as the element of *chance* (cf. SXIII: 2/2/66). See his discussion of Aristotle's '*tychē*', 'chance' (*hasard*) as an 'encounter with the real' (SXI: 52–64). The real is contingency, the unpredictable.
32. Lacan describes the law of free association (described by him as subsuming the law of non-omission and non-systematisation) with exceptional clarity in 'Beyond the "Reality Principle"' (E: 65–8).
33. Lacan does admit that such a thing might be possible, and connects it with inhuman animality, in the guise of the domestic animal which he understands to have *speech*, without the human relation to *language* (SIX: 29/11/61).
34. In Lacan's 'L schema', the imaginary relation blocks the transit of speech between S and A, subject and Other, analysand qua subject and analyst (E: 40).
35. Lacan uses this term to describe the imaginative writing of a *novel*: 'A novel, which is made of a load of small sensible traits of the real which mean nothing [*ne veulent rien dire*], not having any value unless it makes a sense beyond it harmonically vibrate [*vibrer harmoniquement un sens au-delà*]' (SIV: 145).
36. Lacan uses 'metonymy' primarily in the sense of two words that are contiguous, rather than the more specific meaning of a part standing for a whole.
37. '[T]here's a mirage whereby language, namely all your little 0s and 1s, is there from all eternity, independently of us. [. . .] [W]ithin a certain perspective, we can only see them as being there since the beginning of time' (SII: 292).
38. 'How is one to return, if not on the basis of a peculiar discourse, to a prediscursive reality? That is the dream – the dream behind every conception

of knowledge. But it is also what must be considered mythical. There's no such thing as a prediscursive reality. Every reality is founded and defined by a discourse' (SXX: 32). 'What I'm recounting to you is also a myth, for I in no way believe that there is anywhere at all a moment, a stage, at which the subject first acquires the primitive signifier' (SIII: 151).

39. Lacan admits that the notion is a 'paradox': 'It is paradoxically only from a creationist point of view that one can envisage the elimination of the always recurring notion of creative intention as supported by a person' (SVII: 213). And this creationism also explains why Lacan explicitly invokes the *religious* overtones of his term for the incest prohibition, the 'name of the father' (E: 464).
40. 'Lots of things have been made to fit within the political myth of the "struggle for life". [. . .] [. . .] In fact, everything tells against this thesis of the survival of the fittest species' (SI: 177; cf. E: 98)
41. 'The primordial Law is therefore the Law which, in regulating marriage ties, superimposes the reign of culture over the reign of nature, the latter being subject to the law of mating. The prohibition of incest is merely the subjective pivot of that Law [. . .]. This law, then, reveals itself clearly enough as identical to a language order. For without names for kinship relations, no power can institute the order of preferences and taboos that knot and braid the thread of lineage through the generations' (E: 229–30).
42. 'All myth is related to that which is *inexplicable* in the real' (SVIII: 67–8; cf. SVII: 143).
43. Chiesa identifies this as the 'only explicit biological reference' in Lacan's thought (Chiesa 2007: 32).
44. '*Rapport*' also means 'ratio', hence the English connotation of 'rapport' as a *successful* relation, a certain symmetry or opposition between the sexes, one providing what the other lacks.
45. '[A]nalytic discourse is premised solely on the statement that there is no such thing, that it is impossible to found a sexual relationship' (SXX: 9).
46. 'The very normalisation of this maturation is henceforth dependent in man on cultural intervention, as is exemplified by the fact that sexual object choice is dependent upon the Oedipus complex' (E: 79).
47. 'Perversity' being the pursuit of sex for aims other than reproduction (Freud 1977: 62–7).
48. '[T]his is the point at which the signified and the signifier are knotted together, between the still floating mass of meanings that are actually circulating [. . .]. Everything radiates out from and is organised around this signifier, similar to these little lines of force that an upholstery button forms on the surface of material. It's the point of convergence that enables everything that happens in this discourse to be situated retroactively and prospectively' (SIII: 267–8).

49. 'The register of the symbolic and the imaginary recur in [. . .] the structure of language, [. . .] the signifier and the signified' (SIII: 53). Meaning finds its inchoate form in the animal kingdom in the guise of whatever is 'meaningful' for the animal, whatever ensnares its interest, which is to say that to which it has a pre-programmed instinctual response, that which makes it prick up its ears: 'There's no doubt that meaning is by nature imaginary. Meaning is, like the imaginary, always in the end evanescent, for it is tightly bound to what interests you, that is, to that in which you are ensnared' (SIII: 54).
50. This is just what Lacan will later contradict: 'there is a certain degree [. . .] a structural one, at the level of which desires are properly speaking mad, if for us the subject does not include in its definition [. . .] the possibility of psychotic structure, we will never be anything but alienists' (SIX: 2/5/62).
51. I believe this can be inferred from a close reading of Seminar IV. Lacan refers to the 'penis' as that which the woman lacks. As a result of this the child comes to symbolise the phallus for her (SIV: 70). The child is 'symbolic of her lack of object', her lack of a penis necessitating a symbolic supplement in the form of the child as phallus (SIV: 82). We shall adduce more compelling evidence to this effect in Chapter 3.
52. '[L]anguage reduces sexual polarity [to] having or not having the phallic connotation [. . .] language is, by its very status, "antipathetic", if I may say so, to sexual reality' (SXIV: 18/1/67). One cannot for instance say that the woman 'lacks' a penis outside of the symbolic order since it is only in the symbolic order that lack exists, that lack 'has a place'.
53. The woman 'introduces in the symbolic, patrocentric genealogy, in itself sterile, natural fecundity' (SIV: 154). The woman receives the phallus symbolically in exchange for giving a child, 'which takes on for her the function of *Ersatz*, substitute, equivalent of the phallus' (SIV: 154).
54. Lacan hints at the relevance of the size of the phallus in distinguishing the symbolic phallus, at which level one either has it or lacks it, and the imaginary phallus, where size matters, where for instance the clitoris can be understood as a '*little*' phallus (SIV: 153). This must be the reason why in the Oedipal struggle with the father the child always loses. . .
55. '[T]he couple of presence-absence, the connotation more-less, which gives us the first element of a symbolic order [. . .] [is] already virtually the origin, birth, possibility, fundamental condition of a symbolic order' (SIV: 67–8).
56. The big O is barred, there is no signifier that would signify it. Lacan himself suggests this symbolisation, in French, the '*A barré*' (SV: 466).
57. 'Let's suppose that the [psychotic's] situation entails for the subject the impossibility of assuming the realisation of the signifier *father* at the symbolic level. What's he left with? He's left with the image the paternal function is reduced to' (SIII: 204, cf. 12–13).

2

Deconstructing Lacan

The 'thesis' of deconstruction

What is the thesis of deconstruction?

Derrida encloses the word in quotation marks, to draw attention to the signifier itself and to indicate a caution with respect to its etymological sense. He speaks, with respect to Deleuze, of 'a nearly total affinity concerning the "theses" ' (W: 192).[1] He insists that his works are almost nothing in themselves, but are 'entirely consumed by the reading of other texts' (P: 3). Deconstruction merely repeats what the text itself says, even if the latter does not always *mean* to.

An author always interprets his own text in a certain way. But this interpretation will not exhaust all possible meanings of the text. Deconstruction will demonstrate this, that every purported whole is incomplete, and can be supplemented. It is this logic of the whole that deconstructive theory addresses, the incompleteness of any finite totality, the dependence of any totality on something that it must exclude in order to institute a clear border between itself and its outside and thus constitute itself *as* a totality. If anything is to constitute an individual identity it must differentiate itself from everything else, and so at the same time as it wishes to be an absolute, independent entity, it must depend entirely on others. This is due to the nature of the signifier, wherein the identity of any one element is constituted by traces of the absence of every other one.

Since the signification of any one signifier depends on its differences from other signifiers, and since a finite human being cannot comprehend an infinity of differences, a finite totality *must* be isolated from the infinity of signifiers in order for any signifier to be fully determined. However, in fact, the system of differences cannot so easily be sutured, for this always depends on the positing of a moment which is *not* a signifier: an outside of the text which allows the borders of the finite totality to be definitively established. However, deconstruction demonstrates that any purported moment of presence must by its very nature depend upon a prior system of signifying differences.

Thus deconstruction establishes that a finite totality of signifiers is necessary in order for the text to have meaning, but is at the same time impossible. The meaning of a signifier can never be decisively established.

According to the double imperative which governs textuality, deconstruction admits the necessity of isolating a *finite* totality in order to form a meaningful text at all, but it also exposes the impossibility of a finite totality's ever fully controlling its meaning given its dependence upon an infinite context or series of contexts in which the finite text is embedded.

> The absolute *parousia*[2] of the literal meaning, as the presence to the self of the *logos* within its voice, in the absolute hearing and understanding-itself-speak [*s'entendre-parler*], should be *situated* [Derrida's italics] as a function responding to an indestructible but relative *necessity*, within a system that encompasses it. (OG: 89, my italics)

Deconstruction demonstrates that a finite text is able to believe in its own determinate meaning by referring to a moment which exceeds it, to something which is *not* a signifier, but a 'meaning' or 'transcendental signified' outside of it. This would be the final moment of all the references belonging to the text's signifiers, a moment at which these references would stop since it would itself refer to nothing further, but would gather all of these manifold threads within itself. It would be entirely present and self-present in what it was, and would not need to refer to anything else to achieve its identity.

This moment of absolute presence to itself, or presence to consciousness, would mark an absolute limit to the signifying system it governs and so allow this system to constitute a finite totality. This would in turn allow each signifier within the totality to attain a definite signification, since its references to other signifiers would not carry on indefinitely. Thus, in order to believe that it means something definite, the finite text is compelled to posit a mythical moment of presence that would precede and govern it.

Derrida, however, shows that textuality is by definition *infinite*, and as a result one cannot presuppose a moment of presence prior to or simply outside of the system of differentiality. The notion of such an absolute outside must in fact be *derived* from the infinity of textuality. Deconstruction thus implies a thesis on meaning and signification, *Sinn* and *Bedeutung*,[3] in Frege's terms, reinterpreted by Husserl and Heidegger, and thence by Derrida, in the founding work of his *œuvre*, *Speech and Phenomena*.[4]

There is no meaning that could exist outside of signification. Meaning is a moment of immediate self-presence that consciousness can simply understand without reference to anything else, while signification is the form which meaning assumes when it forms part of a referential network and is individuated solely by its differences from other meanings. Significations are thus defined by the differences between the signifiers which signify them and all the other elements in the same structure.

The prime example of such a system of signification is language (*langue*). When considered in linguistic terms, nothing is immediately present to itself, defined solely with reference to itself, but is individuated only by being differentiated from *other* things: 'the properness [*propre*] of presence has no longer a place: no one is there for anyone, not even for himself; one can no longer dispose of meaning [*sens*]; one can no longer stop it, it is carried into an endless movement of signification [*signification*]. The system of the sign has no outside [*dehors*]' (OG: 233–4).

Deconstruction demonstrates that the very idea of such a pre-linguistic meaning is a myth, a retroactive projection on the part of beings who were always already immersed in language as a system of differential significations, and whose very entrapment within this infinity caused them to project something beyond its horizon. There is no meaning that can be immediately accessed in consciousness and that would be expressed in language only *later*; meaning *as such* is dependent upon the signifiers we inherit. Meaning is always already signification. This is to say that meaning, or presence, cannot be presupposed as the origin of anything, but must itself be explained. Derrida's writing thus traces the event of the origination of sense itself, which is always relative to a particular, determinate (con)text. 'I try to write the question: (what is) meaning [*vouloir-dire*]?' (P: 14).

This theory of language and its relation to meaning, a certain construal of the relation between the symbolic and the real (the non-symbolic), we might say, is deconstruction's thesis.

Deconstructing Lacan

Derrida – or rather Derridean deconstruction – wishes to deconstruct the notion that the relation between the symbolic and the real is a simple opposition between absence and presence, or between differentiality, where the thing in itself is never present in person, and non-differentiality or self-identity. The work of Lacan's middle period as we have expounded it in the previous chapter is, at least in one dominant respect, deconstructible for precisely this reason.

In the present chapter, we shall merely go along with deconstruction and allow it to present itself in its purportedly non-thetic character, by demonstrating how it would deconstruct the Lacanian position and any 'metaphysical' discourse which understands its meaning or referent to be completely heterogeneous to the text, 'outside' of it. We shall demonstrate the theoretical grounds of this 'critique',[5] which we take to be the Saussurean understanding of the signifier taken to its logical conclusion – the demonstration of the infinite extension of the differentiality that characterises the signifier. This extension shows why the traditional understanding of the relation between a text and its outside as an *opposition*, in which one half is understood solely as what the other is *not*, is false and needs to be revised. We shall then present Derrida's understanding of the true relation between a text and its outside, the manner in which he exhorts us properly to address the other of language. This will be a certain non-differentiality which characterises textuality itself, in the guise of the traces which go to make up the signifier and make possible its very differentiality. The trace of 'archi-writing' is the non-differential – undifferentiable – mark that allows two things to be differentiated from each other, a 'distinguishing mark'. This non-differential trace is that part of the signifier which is *not* a signifier, and for this reason may be understood as the 'real within language', the only aspect of the real to which we creatures of language have access.

By allowing deconstruction to be presented as a reading of *Lacan* we are giving as much credence as we can to its claim to be exhausted in its own readings. But we have chosen Lacan because, even after submitting to deconstruction at a certain point, his work will prove to *resist* this deconstruction and the position it results in. It will thus eventually allow us to demonstrate that deconstruction is compelled to think that its own particular form of deconstruction is the only one there is, and it is wrong to think this.

In fact, we have already indicated an ambiguity in the early Lacan with respect to the imaginary, which we shall prise open in Chapter 3 to show that in truth it will always have eluded deconstruction and as a result can be used to criticise the very procedure and conclusions of deconstruction itself.

With respect to the *khi* diagram which describes our trajectory, this chapter describes the moment at which Derrida and Lacan appear to converge, when Derrida ploughs into Lacan's trajectory at its midway point. Lacan is forced to agree with Derrida that he has mistaken the relation between the real and the symbolic and must accept a deconstructive notion of the relation. But this is to view the path and the encounter solely from *Derrida*'s point of view. Later on, we shall view things differently.

To summarise briefly the deconstructive reproach to Lacan: if we are entirely trapped within language and can see nothing beyond it, our only relation to the outside of the text can be by means of a transcendental approach. Deconstruction would thus expose the *myth* of the name-of-the-father, which Lacan believes in despite himself. It would show that this transcendental access to the real origin of the signifier can only appropriate the real unto language. At the same time, a certain transcendental approach *is* the only way for us to reach a real, but it is important not to understand this real in terms of the signifier (as occurred with the name-of-the-father) but in a way that would not *transcend* the signifier (as was attempted with the name-of-the-father). This '*quasi*-transcendental' is the real *trace* that is the condition of possibility of the signifier, the real from which every signifier is made.

The opposition and difference of language

Linguistics in the Saussurean tradition presupposes an opposition. It is the opposition between presence and absence. This is the matrix for all possible oppositions since an opposition is defined by mutual exclusion, the very presence of one half being constituted by the absence of the other. For Derrida, linguistics *presupposes* this opposition without explaining its origin. In this regard, linguistics is 'metaphysical': 'the form of the opposition and the oppositional structure are themselves metaphysical' (S: 117). What is ultimately presupposed here is presence, in relation to which absence is considered to be derived. It is this presupposition of a full and immediate presence that characterises metaphysical thought.

That linguistics does not think beyond the opposition towards its origin is not some theoretical flaw of Saussurean linguistics but reflects an inherent tendency of language itself. Language is ultimately composed of oppositions, or rather it is composed of what this opposedness *presupposes*, the difference between the presence of a mark and the absence of a mark. Thus, when it is compelled to address that to which it refers or that from which it originated, it can think of it only as its *opposite*. Thus it understands the real as what is *not* symbolic. The symbolic is differential and therefore the real will be the self-same, requiring no differential reference to otherness in order to constitute its self-sameness, which will thus be *im*mediate. The real is what is in itself *present* and does not depend on anything that is absent. There does not need to be absence in order for this presence to exist. Thus the real is understood as *presence*, and a presence that is prior to and presupposed by any absence.

According to a principle which metaphysics has always presupposed, that which is endowed with more presence must precede that which has less, and as a result the differential signifier is understood to derive from a real that is more primordial. The origin is thus a moment of (self-)presence which is only later split off from itself by the necessity of using language. The illusion that Derrida deconstructs is that of an opposition presupposed between the textual and the non-textual. This opposition is a feature of language, and thus, in order to understand the construction of the problem and deconstruction's solution to it, we must understand the nature of language. The problem and the solution are both contained here. We must show that linguistics' insight into the differentiality of the signifier demonstrates the impossibility of anything 'outside the text'. This amounts to saying that human beings *have* no access to anything non-textual, since the system of language can not be given strict limits and is hence infinite. It is impossible for something to be signified without itself being involved in the system of differences that is language. We must not be deluded into thinking that we can experience anything fully present, in the form of the real thing in itself or a meaning within our consciousness.[6] Mediation is the law and there is no access to the immediate – to that which is present without requiring the medium of something else – from which it would differentiate itself. And yet at the same time, this infinite system of the signifier cannot but create the illusion that it is finite and bounded by a moment of full presence which makes it possible and unambiguously significant.

The opposition of real and symbolic

From Saussure, Derrida accepts the thesis that language, and more generally the 'symbolic order', are distinguished from other orders by their differentiality. It is not just that they contain fully present terms that would differ from one another; each term is *constituted* of nothing besides these differences. Presences are mere effects *of* prior differences, signifiers acquire their identity only by being differentiated from all other signifiers in the same system. This means that no signifier can be defined solely on the basis of and with reference to itself. It must refer to others. The absence of these other signifiers is marked in and as the presence of any one signifier. This mark may be deemed a 'trace':

> The play of differences presupposes, in effect, syntheses and referrals which forbid at any moment, or in any sense, that a simple element be *present* in and of itself, referring only to itself [. . .] no element can function as a sign without referring to another element which itself is not simply present. This interweaving results in each 'element' – phoneme or grapheme – being constituted on the basis of the trace within it of the other elements of the chain or system. (P: 26)
>
> [S]ignification is possible only if each so-called 'present' element [. . .] is related to something other than itself, thereby keeping within itself the mark of the past element, and already letting itself be vitiated by the mark of its relation to the future element [. . .] and constituting what is called the present by means of this very relation to what it is not. (MP: 13)

That which is present within the signifier is constituted only by traces of that which is *absent*.

The differentiality of the signifier is for Derrida one of 'the least contestable findings of Saussurean doctrine' (OG: 55). Deconstruction can perhaps be exhaustively described as a sterling attempt to draw the most extreme consequences of this insight. This ultimately means that the entire system of differences is infinite and so cannot be grounded in any moment of presence, thus rendering every *purported* presence subordinate to the differentiality of the signifier. Anything that one places in relation to difference is automatically *differentiated from* that to which it relates, and thus it is consumed by the system of the signifier. Since the signifier continually devours its boundaries in this way, it can only extend to infinity.

The real is considered by language and metaphysics, paradoxically, to be different from the signifier – *different* to *differentiality*. It is the non-differential. In the real, it is supposed, entities do not depend on other things for their identity. The real is the opposite of the symbolic. Language comes along later, secondarily and always inadequately to serve the real by signifying it, which means to open it to experience, to render it apparent, significant. It is precisely this opposition between the real and the symbolic which deconstruction takes apart.

The transcendental signified

The value of a certain signifier is given only by its differences from *all* of the other signifiers in its system. If this system is infinite then there is no way that a finite consciousness will be able to apprehend or comprehend the signification of *any* signifier in the system, since this would involve comprehending an infinity of traces. This is why a moment absolutely outside of the signifier must be assumed. It sets a limit to the previously infinite number of differences and thus renders the value of each signifier within a certain finite realm comprehensible. In this way, the real that is posited outside of the signifier allows each signifier to enjoy a determinate signified.

Thus the signifier posits its own opposite, and this opposite acts as its own condition of possibility. The system has to presuppose it in order to be possible. This is precisely the transcendental gesture. The real is thus understood as 'transcendental' with regard to language. Derrida's name for this real is the 'transcendental signified' (*le signifié transcendental*):[7] 'the transcendental signified, which, at one time or another, would place a reassuring end to the reference from sign to sign' (OG: 49).

For Derrida, *anything* which acts to stop the infinite series of references between signifiers should be deemed a transcendental signified.

> There is a point in the system where the signifier can no longer be replaced by its signified, so that in consequence no signifier can be so replaced, purely and simply. For that point of nonreplacement is also the point of orientation for the entire system of signification, the point where the fundamental signified is promised as the terminal point of all references. (OG: 266)

And deconstruction sets itself precisely to show that this external positioning of the signified is a mirage brought about by our position *within* language, '[t]hat the signified is originarily and essentially [. . .] trace, that it is *always already in the position of the signifier*' (OG: 73).

Derrida makes it clear that his goal is to make us question the received notion that language originates in a moment of *presence*: 'To make enigmatic what one thinks one understands by the words "proximity", "immediacy", "presence" [. . .] is my final intention in this book' (OG: 70). Derrida demonstrates that this supposedly original moment of presence is understood to *precede* all differentiation: 'unblemished by the work of difference, [. . .] not to be corrupted by interval, discontinuity, alterity [. . .] this experience of a continual present [. . .] is not inscribed with a system of differences' (OG: 249). And this for the reason that it is thought not to refer to anything *other* than itself for its identity. This presence has a *subjectal* structure, it must support *itself*, 'referring only to itself' (P: 26).

To refute the very possibility of such a notion, Derrida demonstrates that this structure of self-presupposing self-identity requires what is identical with itself to *differ* from itself. How after all could one *refer* to oneself if one had not first been separated from oneself, unless one were *not* originally self-identical? The very phrase gives itself away: presence '*re*-fers' to itself, it is borne away from itself and borne back. This is to say that it is *differentiated* from itself *before* being identical with itself. And since there is no 'itself' prior to this differentiation, we cannot even say that it is first differentiated *from* itself. It must be differentiated from *another*.

Contrary to what it intended, then, the present is related to itself in the manner of the *signifier*. This is the meaning of reflexivity, the meaning of a 'self'. The reflexive notion of 'self' in the 'itself' of any supposedly present entity is simply a mediation, a detour through something else, as the reflexive loop leaves 'itself' in order to rejoin itself. If presence has to be understood as immediate or infinite self-proximity – '*proper* [propre], that is to say absolutely *proximate* to itself' (OG: 50) – then *difference* is always inherent in the very constitution of presence. Difference stands at the origin of self-sameness or identity and so at the origin of any 'transcendental signified'. 'The fundamental signified, the meaning of the being represented, even less the thing itself, will never be given to us in person, outside the sign or outside play' (OG: 266).

This is why the very notion of the 'proper', of uninterrupted and immediate self-presence is the target of deconstruction. It has to be shown that presence in its very notion implies difference and hence textuality, that the immediate is of itself mediated by the structure of the signifier. Thus the mirage of presence outside of the signifier can only be something that is created *by* the signifier:

> Through this sequence of supplements a necessity is announced: that of an infinite chain, ineluctably multiplying the supplementary mediations *that produce the sense of the very thing they defer*: the *mirage* of the thing itself, of immediate presence, of originary perception. Immediacy is derived. (OG: 157, my italics)

Thus Derrida is attempting to show that language cannot originate in a moment of presence that is opposed to language since this moment of presence, meaning, *itself originates* in the linguistic: 'one must ask the question of meaning and of its origin in difference' (OG: 70).

Deconstruction demonstrates that, if the relation between the text and the outside is understood as an opposition, then this very opposition is *made possible* by textuality itself:

> if one got to thinking that something like the *pharmakon* – or writing – *far from being governed by these oppositions, opens up their very possibility* without letting itself be comprehended by them; if one got to thinking that it can only be out of something like writing – or the *pharmakon* – that the strange difference between inside and outside can spring; [. . .] one would then have to *bend* [Derrida's italics] into strange contortions what could no longer even simply be called logic or discourse. (D: 103, my italics)

The understanding of the relation between text and non-text as an *opposition* must be derived from the nature of language itself since it is only within language that oppositions *can* exist. To understand the relation in this way is thus to appropriate it to one *half* of the opposition and to understand the other on the basis of the same, merely as its inverted 'mirror image'. This is the reason for describing linguistic thought (*logos*) as 'speculative' or 'specular'. The problem with this way of understanding things is that it does not allow them to present themselves in the way that they are in themselves, in their 'absolute otherness', but merely as derived or seen from the standpoint of the other half of an opposition.

A genuine relation of *otherness* is thus rendered an *opposition*.[8] The other is posed or posited by me as *my* other. The absolute becomes *relative*. One half of an opposition thus posits itself as the standard according to which the nature of the other is determined. One understands the other of an opposition by negation: what I am, you are not.

Thought and language *reflect* the world as they believe that it is in itself, but they do so *in their own mirror*, which is to say according to their own measure, looking outwards but seeing only themselves *in reverse*: 'this is an effect of the specular nature of philosophical reflection, philosophy being incapable of inscribing (comprehending) what is outside [*dehors*] it otherwise than through the *appropriating assimilation of a negative image of it* [*qu'à s'en assimiler l'image négative*]' (D: 33, my italics). To op-pose an other – something that is its 'own', a 'propriety', an absolute singularity – to oneself is to understand its nature solely by abstracting from one's own, with the relata thus constituting two symmetrical halves of a mutually exclusive relation.

The place which Derrida wants to delineate is precisely a space *beyond* the opposition. The other of language.

Affirming the other of the opposition

Since one half of an opposition is merely the mirror image of the other, that which is *genuinely* other to the opposition can be *neither* half of the opposition: 'Beyond these borders, what I will call the philosophical *mirage* [Derrida's italics] would consist as much in perceiving philosophy [. . .] as in perceiving the desert. For this other space is *neither* philosophical *nor* desert-like, that is, barren' (MP: 113, my italics). The truth of this other is that it is *neither* half of an opposition, it cannot be defined by this linguistic structure. It is an absolute other with respect to the opposition. This is why Derrida often speaks of it by negating the oppositional structure itself, refusing the very terms of the opposition: 'neither the one nor the other', and thus as far as possible negating language *itself*, with its inherent tendency to understand things oppositionally, speculatively.

It is precisely this absolute other that deconstruction wishes to protect from appropriation by language and thought. Deconstruction concerns 'the *absolute outside of the opposition*, [. . .] that absolute otherness which was marked – once again – in the exposé of *différance*' (D: 25, my italics). As Derrida says, '*différance* is the displacement of this oppositional logic' (FL: 235).

Derrida's own thought attempts to think otherness *beyond* the structure of opposition, beyond *relative* otherness, and this means that it attempts to go beyond metaphysics or philosophy. And yet this cannot mean to oppose oneself to metaphysics, since oppositions are themselves metaphysical: 'the relation of metaphysics to its other can no longer be one of opposition' (S: 117–9). This is to say that the step beyond metaphysics cannot produce something that is *not* metaphysics; rather it must be metaphysical *in a certain way*, it must use language *in a certain way*. And the otherness it reaches must be an otherness that is somehow inherent to language, without actually being linguistic.

Derrida is quite clear that it is this realm of absolute otherness beyond the opposition, beyond relative otherness, that he is concerned with: 'in question will be, but according to a movement unheard of by philosophy, an other which is no longer *its other*' (MP: xiv). Thus, by no means does deconstruction amount to an indifference to that which is otherwise than textual. This is not what is to be inferred from Derrida's very precise phrase 'there is nothing outside the text' (*il n'y a pas de hors-texte*). Derrida could not be more vehement about this:

> It is totally false to suggest that deconstruction is a suspension of reference. Deconstruction is always deeply concerned with the 'other' of language. I never cease to be surprised by critics who see my work as a declaration that there is nothing beyond language, that we are imprisoned in language; it is, in fact, saying the exact opposite. The critique of logocentrism is above all else the search for the 'other' and the 'other of language'. Every week I receive critical commentaries and studies on deconstruction which operate on the assumption that what they call 'post-structuralism' amounts to saying that there is nothing beyond language, that we are submerged in words – and other stupidities of that sort. Certainly, deconstruction tries to show that the question of reference is much more complex and problematic than traditional theories supposed. [. . .] But to distance oneself thus from the habitual structure of reference, to challenge or complicate our common assumptions about it, does not amount to saying that there is *nothing* beyond language. (Derrida in Kearney 1995 [1981]: 172–3)

Deconstruction's insistence, its imperative, is that one allow the other to be other, and not reduce it to its relation to the same, to op-pose it.

> If, instead of engaging our steps toward *the fundamental* debate in its classical form [. . .] we appear to be limiting ourselves to 'textual' indications, it is because we have now arrived at the point where the relation between the 'text' – in the narrow, classical sense of the term – and the 'real' is being played out, and because the very concepts of text and of outside(of the)text [*hors-texte*], the very transformation of the relation between them and of the preface we are engaged in, the practical and theoretical problematic of that transformation, are at stake. (D: 32–3)

Derrida here indicates a certain homology between this 'outside(of the)text' and the 'real', a word which is comparatively rare in Derrida's work.[9] By transforming and generalising the notion of what counts as a 'text', by rendering this system of language infinite, Derrida will attempt to show that the phrase 'there is nothing outside the text' does not mean that we are trapped in a suffocating immanence. Rather, precisely this infinity will amount to a genuine 'otherness'.

> To allege that there is no absolute outside of the text is not to postulate some ideal immanence [. . .]. The text *affirms* the outside, marks the limits of this speculative operation [. . .]. If there is nothing outside the text, this implies, with the transformation of the concept of text in general, that the text is no longer the snug airtight inside of an interiority or an identity-to-itself [. . .], but rather a different placement of the effects of opening and closing. (D: 35–6)

Thus Derrida makes it quite clear that the purpose of deconstruction is to examine the appropriation of the outside but at the same time not to go beyond the text in any way, since this outside can be indicated only *through* the text. The text itself 'affirms the outside'. It must bear the scar of its suturing itself against this outside, the mark of the finitisation of an infinite realm. Deconstruction confines itself to indicating these marks, which tell of the finite totality's distinction from and dependence upon the infinite other of which it is a part.

If the text is infinite, then it is *impossible* to get out of in the way of a simple leap outside: 'Is there an "outside-the-archive"? Impossible, but the impossible is deconstruction's affair' (R: 48).[10] Deconstruction is concerned precisely to understand what it means that it is impossible to get 'outside' of the signifier, and the way in which this does *not* in fact prevent us from acknowledging the non-textual real. We just have to understand this real in an appropriate way, which is not to oppose it to language as its 'outside': 'outside', as Derrida often indicates, is a spatial locution imposed by language.

It is only by remaining *within* the text that one can ever hope to mark the other of language: '*within discourse*, to mark that which separates discourse from its excess' (WD: 345, my italics). In other words, we shall use language, use oppositions, in such a way as to indicate that which they eclipse, that which is truly other than the linguistic, the oppositional.

Derrida links the deferral of the real to its affirmation. Deconstruction suspends a text's pretensions to directly refer to a real that is opposed to and outside of it for this does not do 'justice' to that other: 'deferring not what it affirms but deferring just *so as to* affirm, to affirm *justly*' (SM: 17).

The real other as event and singularity

One crucial way in which Derrida describes the real is as an 'event' (*évenément*, an event*uating* or occurrence).

The absolute outside of the text was named by Derrida from the very start as 'the unnameable' (OG: 14). The unnameable is what always remains impossible to name. It may be inferred that the unnameable is that which Derrida refers to later with his only apparently innovative notion of 'the messianic', the Jewish Messiah being precisely that which refuses a name and prohibits its own representation.

The true other is not to be understood as a being, for if being (*Sein*, *être*) is understood as presence then an entity must be understood as something present. And Derrida describes the other as futural and past precisely in order to keep it distinct from the present. The only true other is an other of another order to the substance, the being, and that means – from our perspective – that it must be an event. It is the event of the very *constitution* of the present. If what is present is differentiated in the way of the signifier, then this event will be the *differentiation* of differentiated signifiers, and at the most basic level the positing of an opposition. Derrida dubs this differentiation '*différance*': 'Retaining at least the framework, if not the content, of this requirement formulated by Saussure, we will designate as *différance* the movement according to which language, or any code, any system of referral in general, is constituted "historically" as a weave of differences' (MP: 12). 'Differences, thus, are "produced" [. . .] by *différance*' (MP: 14). The real to which we have access is the event of the differentiation of the differentiality in which we always already find ourselves entrapped.

Derrida is absolutely clear that in his understanding of the trace he is describing the very origin of opposition, that which is *other* than the opposition: 'one thinks of its possibility *short* of the derived opposition between nature and convention, symbol and sign, etc. These oppositions have meaning only after the possibility of the trace' (OG: 47); 'the *thought of the trace* [. . .] escapes binarism and makes binarism possible on the basis of *nothing* [*à partir de* rien]' (WD: 289).[11] 'The *pharmakon* has no ideal identity [. . .]. It is rather the prior medium in which differentiation in general is produced, along with the opposition between the *eidos* and its other' (D: 126). 'The *pharmakon* is [. . .] (the production of) difference' (D: 127). 'If the *pharmakon* is "ambivalent", it is because it constitutes the medium in which opposites are opposed' (D: 127).

Once the differentiation has taken place, we have fully fledged signifiers, and these are then used to individuate beings in the world. So language, by naming an entity with a signifier, always implicitly takes it to be a substance. And yet beings in the world are developing all the time, or at least passing through time, becoming individuals and losing their individuality, and in this sense should also be understood as *events*. We shall see that when attempting to shield the real from appropriation Derrida will utilise a linguistic strategy which uses linguistic substantives in such a way as to indicate an *event* that is always elided by language, 'to affirm the coming of the event' (SM: 17).

Because the event, this peculiar and ever changing unfolding, eludes the genericity of language, Derrida also names this event, 'the singularity of the other': 'the relation of deconstruction [. . .] to what must (without debt and without duty) be rendered to the singularity of the other, to his or her absolute *pre*cedence or to his or her absolute *pre*viousness [. . .] [which] comes from the future or as future: as the very coming of the event' (SM: 27–8). Singularity is both past and future for creatures who inhabit language. In the past because language has always already betrayed it, and in the future since the possibility of attaining it will always be deferred by our inhabitation of language. With regard to language, singularity, event, remains an absolute past and an absolute future.

In speaking of the absolute outside of the opposition, deconstruction is concerned with an other that would not be subordinated to any universal, any genus, but would rather be *unique*. This would be a singularity that was not yet or was no longer self-identical, since the signifying relation of reference has precisely not infiltrated here. This singularity then, can be understood only as the singularity of an event, that is either tying the knot of self-reference or untying it (or perhaps neither). As long as it is truly an event it will never be able to achieve the proximity of self-presence, since it will at every moment be developing, either becoming identical with itself or becoming different from itself. 'The other' would then be the *in*determinate, the infinite, that which has not yet entered or is leaving behind the limiting boundaries of a substance.

This real singular event is thus what Derrida calls the 'unnameable'. It *cannot* be named *as such*, precisely because in being named it ceases by definition to be unname*able*. Naming the event betrays its nature as event. Linguistics, describing language only after the fact of its constitution, can therefore never reach this event: 'the positive *sciences* of signification can only describe the *work* and the *fact* of *différance*, the determined differences and the determined presences that they make possible' (OG: 63).

Let us now examine in more detail the process whereby the event is named and transformed into a substance or entity, this is to say how the event of differentiation or op-position takes place, how language comes to exist. This will demonstrate precisely how it comes about that the absolute other of the text comes to be understood as its opposite. It will answer the question: why is the real (the *non-present* event) confused with *presence*? How is the non-self-identical mistaken for immediate self-identity? How does the illusion of presence beyond the differential text come about? Why does the signifier project a precedent meaning as the origin of its differentiated significations?

The origin of presence in infinite difference

The very notion of opposition presupposes a minimal notion of language. An opposite is opposed simply insofar as it can be present only when its opposite is not. Thus, in an opposition the absence of the other must be *marked* in and as the presence of the one. The opposition requires a certain 'marking' that allows a presence to indicate an absence, to *refer* to an absence. This distinguishing mark, discriminating the present entity from an absent one, is the *trace* of an absence within presence, and the trace is a characteristic which we know to belong to empirical *language*.

The differentiation of two entities produces the opposition. But differentiality *itself* requires something in order to be possible, and that is the *trace* (*la trace*).[12]

Opposition is a *relation*. Rather than simply remaining indifferent to each other, the two halves are defined by mutual exclusion: what the one is, the other is not. If the two halves of an opposition are differentiated by one half's being whatever the other is *not*, then in order to constitute itself the *other* half must have inscribed within it the *absence* of the other half. Thus, the *absence* of the other in the place of the same must be marked in the same. And since the same is *nothing besides* this absence of the other, the *marks* of this absence will *constitute* the same. The same, the present signifier, is *nothing besides* the absence of all the other signifiers that might be used in its place: 'the trace is the relation of the intimacy of the living present with its outside [*dehors*], the opening onto exteriority in general, upon what is not one's own [*non-propre*]' (SP: 86).

The trace does not simply render present what is absent, but renders it present *in its absence*. When we see an animal's tracks on the woodland path, that animal's existence and *absence* is presented to us thereby. The trace is 'the nonpresence of the other inscribed within the sense of the present' (OG: 71). The trace is the presence of absence, which is at the same time the absence of (full) presence.

We can already see that language's other is *not* the full presence of a transcendental signified, but a mere *trace*. This is all that we can know of the real, for it is clear that we thus have access to very little real, stranded as we are in a boundless forest of signifiers.

What is the trace? It is simply a mark. Something whose sole quality is to be present rather than absent. It simply marks something out as different from something else, something which does *not* carry the mark.

But a mark must differ from the surface on which it is inscribed. Even if it were to inscribe on itself, the trace marks itself as different than it was before, as different from itself. The trace is the mark of the *other* in the *same*. 'The trace, where the relationship with the other is marked' (OG: 47). The trace allows two identical things to be differentiated from one another and thus makes difference itself possible: 'difference cannot be thought without the *trace*' (OG: 57). There is something that logically precedes difference, that precedes the signifier, and that is the trace.

The trace, then, makes difference as such possible, it makes the signifier possible, and the identity of individuals within the symbolic order as differentially defined with respect to each other. Because it unifies the same and the other, presence and absence, the trace is described by Derrida as an 'originary synthesis':

> the appearing and functioning of difference presupposes an originary synthesis not preceded by any absolute simplicity. Such would be the originary trace. Without [. . .] a trace retaining the other in the same, no difference would do its work and no meaning would appear. It is not the question of a constituted difference here, but rather, before all determination of the content, of the *pure* movement which produces difference. (OG: 62)

The present is constituted of traces, and all oppositions, all differences, depend on the trace, which must therefore be considered originary: 'one must indeed speak of an originary trace or archi-trace' (OG: 61). Not that this origin is the ultimate, for there is in fact something 'more original' than the origin, the 'origin of the origin' (OG: 61). The trace requires the distinction between the inscription itself and the surface upon which it is inscribed, the other and the same, joined together by the actual process of inscribing.

The trace is itself the product of a process of originary inscription or 'writing'. Derrida's word for the inscribing of the trace is 'archi-writing' (*archi-écriture*), original writing, writing taken as *archē* or governing principle. Archi-writing is the inscription of a trace that allows differences to arise and so first allows individuation to occur and fully present individuals to appear. 'It does not depend on any sensible plenitude [. . .]. It is, on the contrary, the condition of such a plenitude [. . .] it permits the articulation of signs among themselves' (OG: 62).

Derrida at one point connects the following: 'archi-writing, movement of *différance*, irreducible archi-synthesis, opening in one and the same possibility' (OG: 60). This is to say that writing is the very *movement* of difference, *écrit*ure as the motion of inscribing traces, those stable and distributed 'things written' or 'writs' (*écrits*). Thus, if we refuse to place the trace at the origin, but instead understand the ultimate origin to be a synthesis of same and other in the archi-writing *of* this trace, we can see that Derrida in fact resists, or tries to resist placing a simplicity at the origin, which is for him always complex or plural.[13]

Presence thus involves a whole series of presuppositions, when it was presumed by metaphysics to be originary. The trace itself does not appear, become present, it is always dissimulated by the presence that it makes possible: 'the movement of the trace is necessarily occulted, it produces itself as self-occultation. When the other announces itself as such, it presents itself in the dissimulation of itself' (OG: 47).

The question is: how could such an illusion of full presence be produced by the trace? Why does the trace occult itself?

The answer lies in the *infinity* of the trace.

An infinity of traces mistaken for presence

Since the signifier has no limits, and since each signifier individuates itself by referring to *every* other signifier in the system, each signifier must be composed of an *infinite number* of traces. Since human beings are finite, embedded within this signifier system at a certain place and time with only a finite capacity, they cannot comprehend (or even apprehend) the infinite number of traces which constitute any one signifier. We are as finite subjects *situated* within a particular, determinate language and symbolic order, we *cannot see* the infinity of traces which determine the nature of any signifier we might use or experience. Empirically speaking, the entire history of signifiers, the sum total of contexts which have bestowed meaning upon it, and the infinite synchrony of signifiers subtending any particular signifier, are simply not available to us in their totality.

We cannot perceive an infinity and retain the distinctness of each trace as discontinuous with every other trace, and so we are deceived into perceiving in the *place* of the signifier a smooth continuity of presence, a space which is in fact differentially *fissured*: 'always different [*toujours différentes*] faults, [. . .] fissures [*partages*]' (P: 57).

But, given the infinite number of traces, these fissures become *infinitesimal* and thus, to a finite intuition such as ours, too small to be discerned. As Derrida says: 'presence as *différance ad infinitum* [*la présence comme différance à l'infini*]' (SP: 101). Our perception causes us to perceive a multiplicity as a continuous unity. We take a differential weave for a full presence without fissure. We mistake the infinity of differences for a presence *outside* of difference.

In order to make significance possible we posit the presence for which we have mistaken an infinity of traces as the transcendental signified which eludes and precedes all tracery. By remaining wholly outside of textuality, this signified would allow there to be a strict border to the signifier, an absolute limit. Thus the trace, by its very infinity, institutes the opposition of (present) signified and (absent) signifier, the Saussurean sign. It creates language. It is its condition of possibility.

But once this presence has been posited, everything is reversed, and the trace must then appear to be *derivative*, because the trace has *less* being, less presence than the transcendental signified: this is 'the classical scheme, which would derive it from a presence or from an originary nontrace' (OG: 61). The very purpose of the signifier, the differential, becomes to efface itself before the signified, to subordinate and erase itself before the presence which now appears to have made it possible.[14]

> This immediate presence results from the fact that the phenomenological 'body' of the signifier seems to fade away at the very moment it is produced [. . .], transforming the worldly opacity of its body into pure diaphaneity. This effacement of the sensible body and its exteriority is *for consciousness* the very form of the immediate presence of the signified. (SP: 77)

This diaphaneity is to be contrasted with the ineffaceable 'opacity of the signifier [*l'opacité du signifiant*]' on which Derrida insists (OG: 166). This opacity of the empirical signifier is the appearance of its material construction, an infinity of real traces with a density of their own. It is precisely this infinity, this material 'other', which deconstruction takes it upon itself to recall.

> Immediacy is here the myth of consciousness. Speech and the consciousness of speech – that is to say consciousness simply as self-presence – are the phenomenon of a lived [*vécue*] auto-affection as suppression of *différance*. That *phenomenon*, that presumed suppression of *différance*, that lived reduction of the opacity of the signifier, are the origin of what is called presence. (OG: 166)

What is really at the origin of presence, of meaning, is an infinity of traces, an 'other'. It is 'other' to us precisely because it is *infinite*. This can be seen with particular clarity in 'Violence and Metaphysics' where Derrida speaks of the exceeding of the finite totality in Levinas's notion of infinity. 'Infinity (as infinitely other) cannot be violent as is totality (which is thus always *defined* by Levinas [. . .] as *finite totality* [totalité finie]: totality, for Levinas, means a finite totality. This functions as a silent axiom)' (WD: 133).

Thus, presence itself is a construction of the signifier, but it is understood to be the origin of the signifier, occupying the *transcendental* position, in the guise of the transcendental signified. We might call this gesture the 'transcendental election' or 'selection', since it selects an element from a certain system and promotes it to the position of the transcendental condition of that system.

It is necessary that from the mass of contingency and potentiality which precedes an actual formation, the formation can comprehend only those elements relevant to *itself* and its own formation. This is the meaning of Derrida's opposing the 'semantic' to 'dissemination', a reference to the scattering and loss of seeds of which only a few take root and grow into arborescent plants. There are many more seeds than plants, many more acorns than oaks, but what does the tree know of these others? It does not understand its origin in this *wider* process of dissemination, but only in the one seed that finally took root. This is the selection carried out by the myth of the simple origin or of 'paternity': 'the preface, as *semen*, is just as likely to be left out, to well up and get lost as a seminal difference, as it is to be reappropriated into the sublimity of the father' (D: 44). This scattering has historically been understood to characterise *writing* as the 'dissemination' of one's thoughts and words.

The real in itself is indeterminate. If it is to receive a determination, where could this come from? Only from the *determinate* systems and entities which the real has become (in the particular perspective of we finite humans). Thus one can see that any understanding of the real as presence and as a transcendental signified will *import* a determination *from* something that has resulted from the real *into* the real itself. This is what it means to understand something as transcendental: it is to restrict it, to determine it in a certain way, to understand it as the condition of possibility *of* a certain order that is supposed to have issued from it alone. But this is always a *selection*, a denial of the preceding process of dissemination, which in truth was part of the process of its construction.

The myth of the real

The transcendental signified, presence, is understood to be the *origin* of the symbolic order, the latter having only a derived importance and being used to record and communicate, to disseminate thoughts and deeds beyond those who enjoy a privileged intuitive proximity to them.

The paradox of recounting one's own origin, of rendering it present, is the very definition of myth: 'the myth of the simplicity of origin. This myth is linked to the very concept of origin; to speech reciting the origin, to the myth of the origin and not only to myths of origin' (OG: 92).

The transcendental signified is a myth. Myth is the image of full presence projected by the differential, 'the dream of a life without difference' (WD: 226). It is the establishment of a centre to the structure which would limit the ambiguity caused by the infinity of the signifier: 'this [mythopoietic] function makes the philosophical or epistemological requirement of a centre appear as mythological, that is to say, as a historical illusion' (WD: 363). One such myth is the myth of the prohibition of incest. The myth understands the relation between culture and nature as an *opposition*. The name-of-the-father is precisely the myth of the signifier, paradoxically supplying a signifier for the origin of the signifier, a signifier of signifiers.

Deconstruction demonstrates that this myth is just that, a construction on the part of the signifier, a 'transcendental (s)election' and *not* the depiction of a real (genetic) origin, as it might risk claiming to be. For metaphysics *believes* in this myth, in language's ability to name and capture its origin. Metaphysics believes it possible to assign *one* signifier to the origin, for the origin to be simple. The postulate of metaphysics is that there is one 'name of the name', one signifier of the whole of language, which exhaustively defines its nature and sutures it into a finite totality. This would be the sign that is of such a nature that it can utterly efface itself before the real presence of the origin, an absolutely diaphanous signifier.

But for Derrida, 'an account or reason cannot be given of what *logos* (account or reason: *ratio*) is accountable or owing *to*' (D: 83). The name itself does not have a name, the event of the production of language will only be betrayed by its naming. And yet the illusion is a necessary one. Deconstruction confines itself to pointing this out.

The philosophical text and the theory of writing

One especial manner in which the signifier is brought to the fore and *not* effaced before the signified is to be found in those places where the text itself *speaks* of the signifier. One of these places is where the text speaks of that signifier which has always been understood to signify *another* signifier: writing. Writing is the signifier *of* the signifier, in other words, a secondary and rightfully unnecessary transcription of something that is already a signifier, speech. Thus one composes the traditional chain: Signified (meaning) – signifier of the signified (speech) – signifier of the signifier (writing).

At each level, presence becomes more and more disparate from itself and difference more firmly entrenched, the possibility of ambiguity and the dissemination of meaning ever more acute.

Derrida describes his own writing as follows:

> a writing interested in itself which also enables us to read philosophemes – and consequently all the texts of our culture – as kinds of symptoms [. . .] of something that *could not be presented* [Derrida's italics] in the history of philosophy [. . .]. Now, one can follow the treatment accorded to writing as a *particularly* revelatory symptom. (P: 7, my italics)

Why exactly is writing *particularly* revelatory?

There are two particularly important ways in which a text relates to itself, explicitly signifying its own signifiers: philosophical texts, and descriptions of writing ('grammatologies').

Philosophical texts relate to themselves but only in order to *erase* the signifier most thoroughly and allow language to refer to a presence beyond language. Thus philosophers reflect on language only in order to thoroughly *efface* it before its signified. Philosophy addresses language solely in order to undo the damage that it is perceived to inflict.[15]

On the other hand, theories of writing and literary texts which dwell on their own written character reflect on the signifier *without* attempting to efface it. Grammatologies in particular simply cannot do so because the very signified of their discourse *is* the signifier itself (indeed the signifier *of* the signifier, the signifier redoubled and hence yet more dense and ineffaceable).

In the case of philosophy however, the effacement is never entirely successful, and this is what deconstruction will demonstrate. There are remnants of the signifier and its density even in the most *extreme* attempt at effacement. And indeed these remainders often include the appending of a theory of writing to a philosophical text. It is precisely because their attempt at effacement is so extreme that philosophical texts are the most important for Derrida:

> Even if there is never a pure signified, there are different relationships as to that which, from the signifier, *is presented* [Derrida's italics] as the irreducible stratum of the signified. For example, the philosophical text, although it is in fact always written, includes, precisely as its *philosophical specificity*, the project of effacing itself in the face of the signified content which it transports and in general teaches. [. . .] The entire history of texts, and within it the history of literary forms in the West, should be studied from this point of view. (OG: 160, my italics)

The philosophical text is the extreme privileging of the signified, and the theory of writing is the extreme privileging of the signifier. The two discourses are equally necessary to deconstruction, and to each other, if only they knew it. They demonstrate the necessity for the effacement of the signifier and its ultimate impossibility.

Writing

Writing has always been understood as 'the signifier of the signifier', a merely secondary transcription of a speech that will always have been spoken in advance, and which is closer than writing to the self-presence of the intended meaning and thus to the presence of the referent. Indeed, historically speaking, in most human cultures, speech developed long before writing was engineered. Writing signifies the voice, another signifier, and is understood from the point of view of this signifier to be *dispensable*, contingent upon the need to communicate with those who are not present or too distant to be within earshot of the speech itself, or to preserve the import of the speech when the living voice has died away:

> the immediate and privileged unity which founds significance and the acts of language is the articulated unity of sound and sense [*du son et du sens*] within the phonie [*phonie*]. With regard to this unity, writing would always be derivative, accidental, particular, exterior, doubling [*redoublant*] the signifier: phonetic. 'Sign of a sign' [*Signe de signe*], said Aristotle, Rousseau, and Hegel. (OG: 29)

And yet, theories of writing keep reappearing, albeit as appendices, as if it were somehow *necessary* to redouble the signifier, or to admit its density, as if the signifier *could not* be rendered entirely transparent to the signified.

There is a curious *re*doubling at work in any theory of writing, an extra doubling beyond the fact that writing itself is the signifier *of* the signifier, for any theory of writing *is itself writing*. The written theory is a *signifier* of the signifier of the signifier. Here, too many layers are folded on top of one another for the signifier to be transparent. Here, and here alone, the signified is *avowedly* nothing outside the text: 'one cannot abstract from the written text to rush to the signified it *would mean*, since the signified is here the text itself' (OG: 150); 'the theme of supplementarity is certainly no more than one theme among others. [. . .] *But it happens that this theme describes the chain itself* [. . .]. It tells us in a text what a text is, it tells us in writing what writing is' (OG: 163, my italics); 'the concept of the supplement and the theory of writing designate textuality itself in Rousseau's text [. . .]. Thus Rousseau inscribes textuality in the text' (OG: 163).[16]

The description of writing is just one small part of a text, an aside, inessential to the real meaning of the text, and yet, the *whole* of the text is written. Thus, in these moments, the text inscribes the whole into one of its parts. This constitutes a '*mise en abyme*', an heraldic term for the inscription on a shield or coat of arms of the entirety of an image in one of the parts of that image, generally a quarter.[17]

Curiously, theories of writing have always *criticised* writing, berated it for its tendency to disseminate meaning; for the dissemination of meaning at the same time risks its irrevocable loss. Writing is 'that dangerous supplement' (OG: 141ff). Hence we find a curious state of affairs in which one *uses* writing to *condemn* writing: 'writing in the literal and strict sense, is condemned' (OG: 17). In this context, Derrida recalls the very first philosopher in the strict sense, he who transcribed the living speech of Socrates, who never wrote himself: 'what has always been considered so baffling: why Plato, while subordinating or condemning writing and play, should have written so much [. . .] *indicting* writing in writing' (D: 158).[18]

This structure is repeated wherever writing is spoken of *in philosophy*, and philosophy's concern is that the signifier fulfil its purpose and efface itself before meaning. Thus writing is condemned *from the perspective of meaning*, condemned for being too material and thus incapable of becoming sufficiently ideal to act as an appropriate vehicle for meaning.

Writing and meaning

It is in the theory of writing that the text begins to reflect upon itself in its materiality, as a series of marks made on a sheet of paper or tablet of stone or some other surface. In this doubling alone, the signifier's own qualities and density come to the fore. 'If supplementarity is a necessarily indefinite process, writing is the supplement *par excellence* since it marks the point where the supplement *proposes itself* as supplement of supplement, sign of sign [. . .]. It marks the place of the initial doubling' (OG: 281, my italics).

Precisely by *not* rendering itself transparent, but presenting its own materiality as such, the signifier here shows up just how *dangerous* it is to meaning. Thus, in the theory of writing, the signifier is exposed as having properties which are characteristically its own and which have an *effect* on meaning. The *philosophical* attempt to render the signifier diaphanous is thus put in question by the theory of writing's depiction of its peculiar opacity.

The signifiers used to describe writing have a different relation to the signified than those 'philosophical' signifiers which usually efface themselves: it is one of refraction. Refraction occurs when light hits a prism and is split into more than one line, ambivalence being created by the material density of a foreign medium. If sufficient words are written on a page, its surface becomes so dense that it turns black, and no light, no meaning, can be discerned through its interstices. Sufficient scribbling can blot out meaning altogether.

If the theory of writing is one moment at which the signifier signifies the signifier, it is (perhaps) acceptable to call these words 'signs' in the strict sense, biunivocal unities of signifier and signified, 'sound and sense', *son et sens*, as the near homophone has it, indicating the traditional proximity of ethereal sound and wholly ideal sense. One might have thought that Derrida's radicalisation of Saussure would have ruled out any such thing: 'It is thus the idea of the sign that must be deconstructed through a meditation upon writing' (OG: 73). And yet it is possible, in one instance only, for a signifier to refer to a univocal signified, and that is when that signified is *the signifier as such*. Every signifier is constituted by 'written' marks, and so every signifier that signifies the nature of writing will signify every signifier there is.

Derrida does at times describe these signifiers as 'signs' or 'words' in the strict linguistic sense: 'We expressly said the *sign pharmakon*, intending thereby to mark that what is in question is *indissociably* a signifier and a concept signified' (D: 100). Derrida is quite explicit that, given the nature of the signifier, this is the *only* way a sign can exist. Hence his description of one such sign, *hymen*, as 'the *only* word': '"Hymen" (a word, indeed the only word [. . .])' (D: 209). He then explicitly generalises this: 'What holds for "*hymen*" also holds, *mutatis mutandis*, for all other signs [. . .], like *pharmakon*, *supplément*, *différance*' (D: 221).[19]

These signifiers are signs, but they do not efface themselves before their signified, subordinating themselves thereto, as a sign has long been understood to do. Rather, the only signs there are for Derrida are those which indicate *textuality* itself.[20] Thus the signifier does not efface itself in the sign, since its purpose is precisely to refer to the *signifier itself*.[21] Derrida explicitly shifts the meaning of the word 'sign' from the most transparent signifier of the transcendental signified, to the signifier which signifies nothing but the signifier itself.

Undecidables in the text of philosophy

Thus the theory of writing demonstrates the dependence of the very notions of presence and the signified upon the opacity of the signifier itself. And yet *every* philosophical text, whether it considers writing or not, contains elements which demonstrate the dependence of any supposed transcendental signified upon the signifier. These elements are words which are in effect *implicitly* descriptions of writing. They are moments at which the text refers to the signifier in order to determine its own meaning. They are signifiers which signify signifiers. Thus, once again, the weave of textuality becomes threadbare, and deconstruction seizes upon a thread.

Why do these words refer to the signifier? Because without this reference their meaning remains indeterminate. Derrida shows that when one ignores their particular context, these 'undecidables' oscillate between opposed or contradictory meanings. They depend upon their context, the text in which they occur, to decide which of two potential meanings they have in that particular case.[22]

Thus, taken by themselves, or rather, taken across a plurality of different contexts which together ascribe contradictory meanings to the same words, the meaning of these words is 'undecidable'. If one refers them *outside* of the text, they will not have an unequivocal meaning. This *proves* that there is no transcendental signified, which would have allowed each and every word to enjoy such a meaning. The absence of such a signified implies that *no* signifier can have its signified determined in this way, and so the nature of *every* signifier is condensed in this one sign, the undecidable. The undecided nature of the meaning remains apparent, ineffaceably so, even when the signifiers of one context attempt to obliterate it: 'this double play, marked in certain decisive places by an erasure which allows what it obliterates to be read' (P: 6).

Thus deconstruction's activity is to demonstrate certain moments in a text where the lie of the originality of the transcendental signified is exposed, where it is irrefutable that the *signified* of a certain signifier is decided only by the signifiers which provide it with its context. This amounts to 'violently inscribing within the text that which attempted to govern it from without' (P: 6).

The undecidability of meaning

What is crucial is that the metaphysician believes that any particular context *entirely obliterates* any reference to other contexts in which a word can have a different signification. In other words, he believes that an absolutely conclusive decision is possible. Deconstruction shows that, according to the nature of the signifier as determined in its value by *all* of the contexts in which it can occur, the signifier retains a reference *to* these other contexts, and this *cannot* absolutely be effaced. The only link between these contexts is the material quality of the signifier itself – the fact that it is 'the same word' – but given that significations are individuated solely by the signifier which signifies them, the primacy of the signifier, this reference to other contexts can *not* be erased: the reference to every other of its possible contexts is irreducible. In each particular context, the other possible contexts are erased, but precisely this erasure is a necessary part of the definition of the signifier in that context. Thus these other contexts are and must be referred to in defining the particular signification that that signifier has in that context. Reference to these contexts, far from being obliterated, must be retained; these other contexts must be, literally, 'ruled out', erased but legible beneath this erasure. Again, it is a question of textuality, in which one is defined by that which one is not. One must remain attached to the other parts of the fabric that are at the same time *not* oneself.

The other meanings of the same signifier remain *virtually* present in any of its uses. Derrida describes this reference of the undecidable signifier to its other meanings as 'citation' or 'anagram' (after Saussure):

> *Remedy* is the rendition [of *pharmakon*] that, more than 'medicine' or 'drug' would have done, obliterates the virtual, dynamic references to the other uses of the same word in the Greek language [as 'poison', although there are other references]. The effect of such a translation is most

> importantly to destroy what we will later call Plato's anagrammatic writing, to destroy it by interrupting the relations interwoven [*s'y tissent*] among different functions of the same word in different places, relations that are virtually but necessarily 'citational'. [. . .] [*P*]*harmakon*, even while it means remedy, cites, re-cites, and makes legible that which *in the same word* signifies, in another spot and on a different level of the stage, *poison* [. . .], the choice of only one of these renditions by the translator has as its first effect the neutralisation of the citational play, of the 'anagram', and, in the end, quite simply of the very textuality of the translated text. (D: 98)[23]

Deconstruction, far from effacing it, precisely attempts to make evident 'the very *textuality*' of the text, *as it is evinced by the text itself*. The text cannot help but show itself as a text at certain points, and it is these that deconstructive readings pick up on.

It can be purely by chance that two significations share the same signifier. This would be the case with puns and 'mere' plays on words. Derrida describes the undecidables as 'simulacra'. Naturally, the valuation of the image, as a secondary and inferior copy of the idea, will not hold for Derrida. It is precisely the repeatability of a certain signifier across different contexts, and the elision of these contexts in any one context, that constitute the very identity of the signifier.

> [I]t has been necessary to analyse, to set to work, *within* the text of the history of philosophy, as well as *within* the so-called literary text [. . .] certain marks [. . .] I have called undecidables, that is, unities of simulacrum, 'false' verbal properties (nominal or semantic) that can no longer be included within philosophical (binary) opposition, but which, however, inhabit philosophical opposition, resisting and disorganising it. (P: 42–3)

Undecidables upset oppositions because they cannot simply be distributed on either side of the opposition. They embody two, opposed meanings: they mean neither exclusively, because they mean both, they are '[n]either/nor, that is, *simultaneously* either *or*' (P: 42–3).

If a single material signifier can accrue *absolutely* opposed meanings, this suggests that signifiers are not expressions of unequivocal signifieds that would occupy a realm entirely beyond them. A contradictory pair of meanings belonging to the same signifier forces us to disengage the word from its subordination to meaning, to recognise that signification accrues only contextually, and that there are always more contexts.

To deconstruct the transcendental signified is to free language from the 'teleology of meaning', to demonstrate that syntax should not be understood to be subservient to the semantic. The undecidable word 'disrupts the opposition of the semantic and the syntactic, and especially the philosophical hierarchy that submits the latter to the former' (MP: 270). It thus brings out 'the irreducible excess of the syntactic over the semantic' (D: 221). The semantic is itself 'reinscribed' in a preceding 'syntax', the infinity of differential references, within a context and to other contexts: 'The generalisation of the grammatical or the textual hinges on the disappearance, or rather the reinscription, of the semantic horizon' (D: 21).

This is precisely to bring out the very textuality of the text, the fact of its being written and the way its meaning depends upon the signifiers it uses. As Derrida says, 'that excess of syntax over meaning [. . .]; that is, [. . .] the re-marking of textuality' (D: 231). Deconstruction confines itself to showing that the undecidable's meaning is determined solely by its context, its syntactical placement, and that this context is defined by referring to and ruling out the other possible contexts of the same signifier:

> What holds for '*hymen*' also holds, *mutatis mutandis*, for all other signs which, like *pharmakon*, *supplément*, *différance*, and others, have a *double contradictory, undecidable value that always derives from their syntax*, whether the latter is in a sense 'internal', articulating and combining under the same yoke, *hyph'hen*, two incompatible meanings, or 'external', dependent on the code in which the word is made to function. (D: 221, my italics)

It is not as if, had Plato done without the word '*hymen*', the text would not have been infected with undecidability, since this undecidability is structural, and *some* word would have to have occupied the 'syntactical' place in which any apparently closed and consistent system opens onto another, refers to another context or another part of the same context.

> What counts here [at least in this case] is not the lexical richness, the semantic infiniteness of a word or concept, its depth or breadth, the sedimentation that has produced inside it two contradictory layers of signification [. . .]. What counts here is the formal or syntactical *praxis* that composes and decomposes it. We have indeed been making believe that everything could be traced to the word *hymen*. But the irreplaceable character of this signifier, which everything seemed to grant it, was laid out like a trap. [. . .] It produces its effect first and foremost through the syntax, which disposes the '*entre*' ['between'] in such a way that the suspense is due only to the placement and not to the content of words. (D: 220)

Every signifier ultimately suffers from undecidability, it is just that those signifiers in which the undecidability becomes so extreme as to allow *contradictory* meanings to the same word are particularly 'exemplary': 'In its polysemia this word ['*différance*'], of course, *like any signification*, must defer [*à être soutenu*] to a discourse or an interpretive context, and yet to defer to it in a certain way, or at least *more readily than any other word* [*plus facilement par lui-même que tout autre mot*]' (MP: 8, my italics).

Every signifier acquires its meaning *not* from a transcendental signified but from its differential position with respect to the other words around it, its 'interpretive context'. And yet, these undecidables admit their dependence on the context 'more readily', precisely because *in another context* they have a meaning that is quite *opposed* to the meaning they are supposed to have in the *present* context. This is why deconstruction picks on them. They defer absolutely to their context because if they did *not* do so, it is not as if their meaning would be less precise, their meaning could be *opposed* to that which they were intended to mean.

All signifiers can be placed in contexts in which they mean the opposite of what they are intended to mean, but undecidable words have opposed meanings across contexts *within the same text*.

In undecidables the very nature of the text comes to the surface. The undecidables can be made to demonstrate the nature of *every* signifier. Because these words represent the text itself, if they are infected with contextual dependence so must every signifier: 'what must be found, no less than the word, is the point, the *place in a pattern* [lieu dans un tracé, Derrida's italics] at which a word drawn from the old language will start [. . .] to slide [as the signified slides under the signifier, to *oscillate* between two opposed meanings] and *to make the entire discourse slide*' (WD: 333–4, my italics).[24]

Once the sign of the transcendental signified has been unmoored – 'the earth unchained from its sun', Plato's sun, as Nietzsche has it – the univocal reference of every signifier to a signified is endangered.

The undecidable as the threadbare stitch

These undecidable signifiers thus provide the leverage or 'foothold' for the deconstructive reading (OG: 314). They can be picked on as places where the very specific materiality of the signifier becomes *apparent* within the text itself, which claims to subordinate *every* instance of textuality to a fully present *meaning* that would be outside of all textuality. They are places at which the weave of the text has become *threadbare*. When picked at they cause the entire fabric to unravel, thus exposing its material threads – differences, the differentiality of the text – at *every* point.

The text then, presents us with the 'resources' for its own deconstruction.[25] Thus, even if the text 'wants' to make it impossible for us not to follow the author's decision as to the meaning of a certain word, each signifier's signified will involve a margin of indeterminacy or ambiguity (under- and overdetermination) that eludes the author's conscious control. Thus there is always a disparity between what the writer wants to say, his *intended meaning* (*vouloir-dire*) and what he is able to say, given language and its nature. A writer always '*declares* what he *wishes to say* [*Il* déclare *ce qu'il* veut dire] [. . .]; he says or *describes* that which he *does not wish to say* [*il dit ou* décrit *ce qu'il* ne veut pas dire]' (OG: 229).

It is this other, unintended meaning that Derrida describes as the text's 'blind-spot' or 'scotoma', physiologically speaking a result of the optic nerve's impinging upon the retina, and thus the mark of a vessel which makes sight *possible* and at the same time makes a complete visual field *im*possible. 'The concept of the supplement is a sort of blind spot [*tache aveugle*][26] in Rousseau's text, the not-seen that opens and limits visibility' (OG: 163–4).

This failure to say exactly and in every case what we mean is due to our situation within language, this infinitely extensive system which *governs* the possibility and impossibility of meaning, by constraining us, contingently, in the signifiers we can use to *express* this intention, and indeed constraining our very 'meaning' (*sens*). 'His declared intention is not annulled by this but rather *inscribed* within a system which it no longer dominates. The desire for the origin becomes an indispensable and indestructible function situated within a syntax without origin' (OG: 243). The undecidables indicate the event of determination, the situation of the writer within a linguistic system that exceeds him in every direction.[27] Undecidability demonstrates that each finite text depends on an infinite text, which prevents the finite text and the finite author from fully controlling its meaning.

Deconstruction's procedure

Deconstruction exposes undecidability by laying out a twofold reading of a single text in which the two readings can be shown to contradict one another. These readings are centred around the two meanings of the undecidable word. Thus deconstruction presents itself as being 'exhausted' in its reading of other works; all it adds is a second reading, a double reading.

The undecidable is the bridge that links the two readings. The deconstructive text acts as a hyphen running between the two, allowing them to communicate, and thus demonstrating their virtual citation of one another. Deconstruction thus demonstrates that the text can be subjected to two equally justifiable readings, and that there is no way (*a-poria*) to decide between them, an aporia marked by the undecidable signifier itself. One thus exits from the apparent completeness of the system under consideration. Derrida, following Hegel, understands a system to be represented by a circle, the most perfect of all shapes, the repetition of an entirely regular trajectory, eternally returning on itself, to form a finite whole.[28] Deconstructive reading repeats the circle but institutes another centre, thus adding another circle to the author's own, forming a shape that is defined by *two* 'origins' in the geometrical sense: the ellipse. The lack of a single centre – an 'ellipsis' or elision[29] – allows the system's centre to play out of true and each of its points to stray from its original position: ambiguity is thus generalised, beginning with the absolutely ambiguous 'undecidable' (cf. WD: 373; MP: 173).

We should understand the circle that surrounds the second origin to be the 'minor' reading (cf. WD: 336), which reconstructs the text around the alternative signification of the undecidable signifier, the meaning *not* intended by the text's author. Derrida describes this repetition as 'the addition of some new thread' (D: 63). Derrida's repetition of the author's system is thus marked out as *different*. This thread is the hyphen that draws a connection, hitherto unnoticed but already virtually present in the language of the text, between certain self-effacing moments which a conventional reading would have relegated to the margin. The thread weaves together certain scattered passages of the text. If these passages had not been linked together, the undecidable word would have appeared to be comfortably distributed between two opposed meanings in each case. The signifier is thus shown, in itself, to have an undecidable signification: 'writing both marks and goes back over its mark with an *undecidable stroke*' (D: 193, my italics).

Metaphysics, philosophy, has always attempted to deny the signifier, remaining oblivious to its undecidability. Deconstruction distinguishes itself from metaphysics by writing an entire text that is one long *re-marking* or *re-scoring* of the signifiers of the original text, to bring to the *fore* the infinity of the signifier which overdetermines signification. Every stroke written by deconstruction goes over the same words as the original, but precisely thereby it crosses them through, and with this extra layer of ink it makes their textual materiality *palpable*.

This is the meaning of Derrida's suggestion that the difference in the repetition is 'imperceptible' or 'invisible'. The difference between the metaphysical text and the deconstructive rewriting is simply the (avowal of the) very opacity of writing, the unintelligible fact that another way of writing the same text can be essayed. This extra layer brings to the fore the very impenetrability of the signifier – its construction from real traces – disrupting every signifier's 'identity' with itself, but leaving them just the 'same', *le même*, as opposed to *l'autre*, the other. Repetition 'permits us efficaciously, rigorously, that is, discreetly, to exit from closure [. . .] from the identical into the same [*hors de l'identique dans le même*]' (WD: 373).

Deconstruction's ink is drawn from the *tain* of the mirror reflecting on the text, and it refuses to reflect the text back to itself exactly as it sees itself.[30] It contaminates the text with the meaning that its writing was designed to occlude, precisely by showing that its text *is* a cover, a density rather than the absolute translucency it purports to be. The fact that a text is composed of material, differential traces shows that any unit of textuality depends on an infinite textuality and a determinate language, which *constrains* the meaning that the author supposed himself to freely 'intend'. Deconstruction demonstrates this by linking together the various contexts in which a certain undecidable word accrues two opposed significations.

Deconstruction does not propose its doubled, minor reading as the correct one but has to maintain the absolute possibility of *both* readings simultaneously, to show that the text is structurally ambiguous, dependent upon its *language* for the actual meaning which it claims to express, each context dependent upon the exclusion of all other contexts. By exposing an alternative meaning that can be read into the same signifier, deconstruction demonstrates that meaning is not something that lies at the origin of a text, but that the original authorial intention itself depended upon something *beyond* intention, a system of language and a symbolic tradition which cannot be chosen, but which infinitely overflows the finite capacity of any human subject. Signifiers are not employed secondarily to serve a meaning better or worse, but actually determine what that meaning is. Meaning does not become signification, it is always already signification, dependent upon the contingent signifiers of a language in order to mean *anything*. Derrida speaks of 'writing that philosophy in which the philosopher has long believed, not knowing what he was doing, and not knowing that a most convenient writing permitted him to do it' (OG: 287).

Overturning-reversal and displacement-generalisation: from philosophy to grammatology

Revealing the differential syntax that underlies a text's meaning is a twofold operation which Derrida describes as 'overturning' and 'displacement', and similarly as 'reversal' and 'generalisation'. Metaphysics believed meaning to stand at the origin: reverse that! The origin is a text. But then displace the meaning of 'text'! This is necessary in order to understand *how* a text, a differentiality and not an abundant presence, *can* be 'originary'. One needs to understand 'text' as the entirely indeterminate trace or pure mark which the *real* must be capable of in order for the differentiality of the signifier in the empirical sense to be possible. We must displace the ordinary sense of 'signifier' and *generalise* differentiality until every moment of presence is shown to presuppose it. That half of a hierarchy which was once subordinated is now seen to occupy a *transcendental* position, at the *origin* of the opposition that language presupposes.

It is because the subordinate is placed in the position of the origin that it does not function as an origin in the sense that this word has always possessed. Thus the very reversal forces us to renew our thinking of the origin, to dislodge it from its traditional position. For metaphysics, the origin was always more present, possessed of more being than that of which it was the origin. Here we are passing from a reading of the undecidables of a *philosophical text* to the positive possibilities offered by a *theory of writing*, and thus moving between the two kinds of text which concern the deconstructive procedure: the two poles of *metaphysics* and *grammatology*, the erasure and rescoring of the signifier.

It is as if the first phase of overturning were the inversion of the Saussurean diagram of the sign, putting the signifier in the place of the origin, as if grammatology could replace metaphysics, and the signifier could ground the signified in just the same way as the signified was formerly understood to ground the signifier. But this overturning *as such* is insufficient. '[W]e must traverse a phase of *overturning*. To do justice to this necessity is to recognise that in a classical philosophical opposition we are not dealing with the peaceful coexistence of a face-to-face, but rather with a violent hierarchy. One of the two terms governs the other' (P: 41; cf. MP: 329). The governing *archē* is precisely the term that has more *presence*, which it can hence bestow, in smaller quantities, on the other half. This other half would then be derived from it, and thus secondary and inferior.

This explains why reversing the order will not allow one to understand that which the opposition excludes, the genuine singularity of the other. For this approach would fundamentally preserve the oppositional relationship, in which one half defines the other solely in terms of itself. It would still understand the other *in relation to* something else, as a relative and not an absolute other, understood on its own terms, and it would still presuppose a defining moment as prior to that which it defines and not fundamentally affected by its relation with the other. The defining principle would remain absolute despite the fact that it gives rise to an other: thus, the self-positing of a substantial ground would remain in place, a different term that was still understood to ground itself. This overturning would not fundamentally elude the hierarchy that characterises the oppositional structure as such, along with the substantial grounding it implies: 'the hierarchy of dual oppositions always re-establishes itself' (P: 42).[31] Switching around the terms of an opposition does not rethink the notion of substantial grounding itself and the transcendence of the ground over the grounded which is structurally akin to the grounding of differentiality (relative *absence*) in presence: despite the appearance of difference and a genuine explanation of how something can originate in something *else*, origination is always understood as a mere fall or diminution in a quality which is *shared* by both ground and grounded. No genuine novelty is introduced or explained by this mode of grounding, the same issues from the same, with only a difference in quantity. Therefore one must do more than just reverse: 'To remain content with reversal is, of course, to operate within the immanence of the system to be destroyed' (D: 6; cf. P: 12).

One *does* reverse. But this reversal changes the very sense of that which one places at the top of the hierarchy and indeed undoes the hierarchical structure itself. What is usually considered to be transcendent or 'outside' is now understood to be immanent to that which it 'grounds'. And, strangely, this immanence allows the origin to be genuinely *other* than the originated, infinitely other.

Thus by overturning the classical opposition between presence and difference (presence and absence), one displaces this difference and 'generalises' it, one renders it infinite: 'Deconstruction [. . .] must, by means of a double gesture, a double science, a double writing, practise an *overturning* of the classical opposition *and* a general *displacement* of the system' (MP: 329).

The subordinated half of an opposition, promoted to the position of origin by the phase of reversal, makes a formerly substantial, present ground into an *event*. It begins to indicate that *every* substance, every presence, originates in a non-present *event*. This will be the ever ongoing and hence infinite event of differentiation which distinguishes signifiers from one another. Thus we fundamentally change the way in which we understand 'grounding'. Overturning forces us to displace the ground and to scatter it, to realise that it is infinite, an ongoing event whose end is never reached, as the reference of sign to sign never comes to rest in a transcendental signified.

If this displacement occurs *by means of* overturning, then overturning just *is* displacement, displacement is not something that one would have to carry out *after* the overturning: 'It is not a question of a chronological phase' (P: 41–2).

The undecidable demonstrates the fallacy of the transcendental signified, and thus draws attention to the fact that presence has a ground and requires explanation; with his theory of 'archi-writing' (one outcome of the procedure of overturning and displacement), Derrida is attempting to explain just what this 'grounding' is, how the illusion of full presence comes about.

What is so ludicrous about placing something differential, contingent and secondary at the origin is that it means that the *more* must issue from the *less*. It changes the very meaning of origination, which in the Platonic and Christian traditions of philosophy has been understood as a fall from a full presence to a lesser presence. *Eidos*, the *ontōs on*, is copied degeneratively by something that is less in being, the *mē on*.

> [T]o wrench the concept of the trace from the classical scheme, which would derive it from a presence or from an originary nontrace and which would make of it an empirical mark, one must indeed speak of an originary trace or archi-trace. Yet we know that that concept destroys its name and that, if all begins with the trace, there is above all no originary trace. (OG: 61)

The secondarity must *retain* its reference to the system from which it has been taken *in order to retain its secondarity* in the sense of a *lack of full presence*. It was this metaphysical system that *ranked* it as secondary according to the *standard* of presence. The signifier which is promoted to the transcendental position must nevertheless remain the same signifier that was subordinated by the opposition. After all, no context can be obliterated entirely, the signifier's reference to this context remains, under erasure:

> Such a *rupture of symmetry* [of the opposition] must propagate its effects throughout the entire chain of discourse. The concepts of general writing can be *read* only on the condition that they be deported, shifted outside the symmetrical alternatives from which, however, they seem to be taken, and in which, after a fashion, they must also remain. (WD: 344)

One must not invent a new word, beyond the text under consideration, to speak of this new form of ground. It must be promoted to the position of ground *as* a subordinate, as *less* than present, less in being. The signifier remains '*caught* – both seized and entangled – in a binary opposition, one of the terms retains its old name so as to destroy the opposition to which it no longer quite belongs, to which in *any* event it has *never* quite yielded' (D: 4). Derrida often insists on his quasi-transcendental signifiers retaining a reference to their old sense: 'Not that the word "writing" has ceased to designate the signifier of the signifier, but it appears, strange as it may seem, that "signifier of the signifier" no longer defines accidental doubling and fallen secondarity' (OG: 7). It only 'appears' so because a closer look reveals that writing *remains* locked within a system of oppositions: as a signifier defined by difference and opposition it cannot *not* be.

It is necessary to proceed here by 'simulacrum' (WD: 332), by appearances, to use the old language in order to 'communicate' with the old system, to retain one's reference to it. 'Archi-writing' is something 'which I continue to call writing only because it *essentially communicates* with the vulgar concept of writing' (OG: 56, my italics; cf. MP: 330). This is the communication of content along the conduit of the hyphen which deconstructive writings construct, the same words meaning different things across different contexts, forming 'unities of simulacrum' (P: 43).

At the same time, the notion of 'communication' retains its more vulgar sense in that Derrida's writing needs to communicate with readers who are of necessity locked within a metaphysical system of language – for all language is metaphysical, being composed of oppositions – and deconstruction's very purpose is to lead the reader to look beyond that. Indeed, language as such is necessary in order to avoid the appearance of mystical communion, the attempt to access and communicate the real through silence or inarticulate sound, the fallacious belief in a meaning individuated prior to language. It is necessary to speak 'paleonymically' in order to become intelligible to those others who share our system(s) of language.

In order to retain the signifier's ambiguity, one leaves it as it is, and assigns it a new meaning on the basis of the role it plays in the deconstructive discourse, or one attaches a new mark to it, one which indicates that it has been displaced to the senseless position of the origin. Sometimes this mark is simply the Greek word for 'origin' (*archē*), attached by a hyphen to that which was once thought to be the originated: 'archi-'. Thus one 'marks' the difference of the repetition and generalisation of the subordinated traits *graphically*, with the addition of a prefix or a slight *written* change: 'quasi-', for instance, or the '*a*' of '*différance*' which cannot be spoken or heard.[32] The prefix indicates that something has been put in an unaccustomed place, thus changing the meaning of both halves of the newly minted signifier. This indicates that the hyphen is that which is *really* worthy of thought, since it joins together two things which should not be conjoined, by rights. The hyphen is the mark of writing, the trace of the signifier that is responsible for signification and yet a bar to the signifier's passage into the signified, its reference to a transcendental signified. It is this hyphen that deconstructive writings inscribe, bringing textual difference itself to the fore, and blocking a finite text's attempt to refer to a transcendental signified.

The hyphen is precisely the barrier that separates two halves of an opposition, for instance, Saussure's sign, S/s, but here it is rotated, played with, flattening two levels onto a single immanent plane, lowering the transcendental signified, presumed to hover outside of the text, to the level of the signifier. The dash no longer represents the barrier of transcendence but the immanent process of differentiation, the traces that constitute the body of the signifier, infinite in number.

Derrida is quite explicit that this process of displacement is the *only possible way* to mark within language that which is *otherwise* than language: by placing the secondary half of an opposition at the origin and thus rethinking the present origin as a differential event, as infinite and therefore truly *other*, '*in excess*' of the system that it actualises: 'Tradition's names are maintained, but they are struck with the differences between the *major* and the *minor* [. . .]. This is the only way, within discourse, to mark that which separates discourse from its excess [*son excédent*]' (WD: 345). 'Excess' does not mean 'outside', but that which forms the heart of the signifier and yet is not a signifier, that infinite textuality *in which* any individual signifier finds its place, that general economy of which any finite meaningful text is a *restricted* economy. That which is not yet a signifier is the signifier in the process of its *emergence*, the event-like *differentiation* of the signifiers which compose a certain language. Since there are infinitely many signifiers, infinitely many traces distinguishing one signifier from another, this process of differentiation will never be complete, and there will always be more signifiers from which any individual signifier has to be differentiated in order to achieve a fully determinate value.

This process of differentiating is the inscription of traces of the absence of one signifier in and as the presence of another. It is the process of archi-writing or archi-tracing. This will turn out to be all that we can know of that which is beyond language, that which is 'real': a mere (ability to) trace. Derrida is quite explicit that the 'trace' is the 'remnant', the slightest vestige of the real, which is (potentially) a much greater and stranger entity, with many more capacities. But this is all that we can know of it *looking at it, as we always must, from our linguistic perspective*.

We are not justified in saying that the real is *presence* in the sense of a transcendental signified, as metaphysics presupposes; but all we *are* licensed in saying about the real *is* derived from the nature of the empirical signifier as we know it, in the form of its condition of possibility. All that we can say of the real is that a certain vestige of it can be used as a trace and actually carries out this tracing function. This means that it must contain two heterogeneous orders, 'the same' and 'the other', one of which can make a mark in the other, which in turn must be susceptible of receiving a trace. A pure immanence – 'the same' alone – could not explain how language came about. We must presuppose this heterogeneity – which Derrida sometimes understands as a difference of 'forces' – in order to explain how empirical language could have come to exist. This real understood as architrace is thus the conclusion of a 'transcendental argument' on Derrida's part. We begin from the fact of empirical language and deduce that which must characterise the real in order for this language to be possible.

Derrida is acutely aware that he is thus treating the real in formally the same way that metaphysics does, by means of a transcendental selection, addressing it solely insofar as it makes something of our acquaintance possible. The difference is that deconstruction *acknowledges* the broader process of dissemination from which linguistic thought picks only a single seed, the otherness of the transcendental, its infinity. Derrida seems to regard *this* transcendental selection as inevitable: our situation within an infinite linguistic system necessitates the transcendental attitude, it limits our vision to that which is itself 'linguistic' or constitutive of it (the archi-trace).

At the same time, by refusing to posit the real as presence, and instead accepting that creatures of language understand only a *trace* of it, we admit that the real is much richer in possibilities, which actualise themselves in many divergent lines only some of which reach human awareness. In truth, the displacement inherent in placing a differential signifier at the origin of presence *infinitises* the origin. This of itself renders the real origin *genuinely other* to us, given our finite capacities, and at the same time, since we are creatures of language, it does not make the (perhaps Levinasian) mistake of addressing the other in the way of the 'bad infinite', which is simply opposed to the finite and thus limited (finitised) by it.

Metaphysics understands the origin to be *essentially the same* as the originated. The origin is understood as a self-founding, self-presupposing *substance*, which does not require or is perhaps insusceptible to explanation. However, by placing something at the origin that is *less* present than that to which it gives rise, one replaces the traditional origin with something which does *not* presuppose itself. The origin is not a substance, it *explains* substance. Formerly the origin had been understood as a substance, now it is understood as an *event*. It is the event of differentiation, the splitting apart of differences, that is the very opening up of the signifier within the real, the opening up of absence, the space across which referral takes place.

Thus deconstruction's reversal of the traditional order of foundation *is* a displacement. Placing something unlike the origin of old in *place* of the origin, in the transcendental *position*, changes the way we think about origination. It displaces the origin from one substantial half of the opposition to the very relation of oppositionality and the process of op-posing, the production of (the opposition of) presence and absence. The origin now precedes all determinate substances. It is the event of differing or the event of *différance*.

The real that writes

If the real is not present but rather the event of the production of the present, or at least the production of what makes it possible to believe that there is such a thing as presence, it must '*write*' in some way. Writing in its most basic form, and that is to say the trait which it must retain when displaced to the origin, is the capacity to leave a mark:

'we say "writing" for all that gives rise to an inscription in general' (OG: 9).

Thus we may understand the real as '[a]n element without simplicity [. . .] of what one must forbid oneself to define within metaphysics' system of oppositions' (OG: 9). The trace is a groove that inscribes something other in what should then, relatively speaking, be called 'the same'. Crucially, the mark must endure, but endure finitely. 'It creates meaning by enregistering it, by entrusting it to an engraving, a groove, a relief, to a surface whose essential characteristic is to be infinitely transmissible' (WD: 13). Once it is separated from the act which inscribed it, it is susceptible of effacement: 'An unerasable trace is not a trace' (WD: 289; cf. WD: 336). The trace is inscribed by something that must be called 'writing': 'the trace, writing in general' (OG: 74).

The trace is not simply some mental abstraction or creature of reason but should actually be taken to characterise 'the real': this is implied in Derrida's reference to the natural sciences. For Derrida, in 1964, the sciences had 'all'[33] come to discern some form of trace in nature: 'the trace (*Spur*), as it appears [. . .] in all scientific fields, notably in biology, this notion seems currently to be dominant and irreducible' (OG: 70). Derrida does not explain here how any science other than biology addresses the trace. Indeed, he later refers to biology alone, where the trace, and even the letter, are clearly invoked in genetic theory: 'It is also in this sense that the contemporary biologist speaks of writing and *pro-gram* in relation to the most elementary processes of information within the living cell' (OG: 9). The trace in biology would refer at once to (genetic) codes, the 'memory' of traits that are transmitted across generations,[34] and even to the perceptual and memory systems belonging to all organisms, the reception and retaining of an impression.[35] Perhaps we might extend this to the objects of the non-biological sciences by stating that the trace is present even in pre-organic 'memory' in the guise of the capacity of substances to retain imprints, or surfaces to retain reflections. The nature of the trace is that it implies a material that is capable of relating to something of a heterogeneous nature which impinges upon it. This is the minimal notion of 'writing' which Derrida believes can be presupposed of the real. But does this mean that every area of nature should be conceived as capable of inscribing the trace? Rather, I think we must infer here that this amounts to a transcendental appropriation of which all sciences are themselves guilty, perhaps unbeknownst to themselves, understanding characteristics of non-linguistic nature as akin to the empirical signifier (cf. P: 35).

What is crucial is that at least in some part of nature we can infer that there must be the capacity to trace. If this had not been the case then the human species could never have arisen. But the real other may be vastly richer in possibilities, exceeding the very order of tracing or the discursive. Deconstruction is modesty itself: we must acknowledge precisely that *the trace* is *just* a trace.

The real and the transcendental

This is the transcendental as deconstruction understands it. It is, strictly speaking, only 'quasi-transcendental'[36] because it is not fully in presence, not external (transcendent) to the system it governs, and not *named* in the same way by every system, so neither universal nor ahistorical – nor is it a 'subject' in the sense of Kant or Husserl. Each system understands its transcendental condition in a different way, and it must: this is deconstruction's thesis. The transcendental is the word a system uses to explain its origin by totalising the infinity within which it takes shape. The finite system takes an element of itself and displaces it into the spaces that run *between* the signifiers of the system, the traces which proliferate to infinity. It uses a word to describe the origin of words. But crucially, it believes itself to have found the unique word with which to do this, a word which can be utterly transparent to its signified, which would then be transcendental. Deconstruction points out that one word is after all just one word. Each word is just one attempt to indicate an event that precedes all words and is hence 'unnameable', an event that erupts between signifiers and constitutes them, an infinity, an other, the origin of what is called 'the same'.

This use of one part of a system to describe its origin is what we have called the transcendental (s)election. By making it explicit that each system selects a part of itself to represent the whole, by 'generalisation' or 'displacement', promoting one of its own signifiers to the transcendental position, Derrida makes clear the falsity of metaphysics' thesis. Derrida's writings form a chain, a plurality of words, each of which claims to be the one word that is absolutely transparent to the real, a portal onto the outside of language. Derrida thus indicates that these words are many, by showing that in each case a philosopher uses a word taken from his own system to refer to what is supposed to be independent of it. Deconstruction is an attempt to admit the appropriation of the origin, the necessity of naming the transcendental by means of a signifier. It is an attempt to admit the necessary appropriation of transcendental thinking, describing the origin as akin to the originated.

The infinity of traces which the real must be capable of producing is *named* by a fully constituted finite signifier. The event of the production of names is thus elided by the name itself. Deconstruction insists on the ludicrousness of believing that any one word will effectively do this, and indirectly indicates it to be an appropriation of the other. Thus deconstruction, unlike metaphysics, acknowledges the existence of this infinite other.

Perhaps the message of deconstruction is ultimately that the transcendental approach is necessary but that it explains nothing and involves a finite textual system speaking only of itself, oblivious to the infinity of the real other, the tracery which is our only access to a genuine other. Metaphysics seeks the other in the bad infinity that would be outside of the text, not realising that the only genuine other is the infinity of the trace, which the real must be capable of producing.

This infinity of traces is the only thing that we can know of the real, but the real in itself could well be *so* other that it can do much more than trace. We deduce its ability to trace by means of a transcendental argument, when the transcendental is properly, post-metaphysically understood. By taking the transcendental approach to its absolute extreme, Derrida means to gesture beyond it, beyond the linguistic understanding of the real as (archi/transcendental-)trace, without suggesting that we can ever *know* such a beyond. We can at least *think* it, negatively.

The explicit displacement of a signifier that does not claim to be fully present (and to exhaust the potentiality of what is *outside* the system, the real) does not conceal its own miraginary nature as the transcendental signified does. By taking something that is avowedly secondary it admits that what it knows of the *real*, what it takes to be its own transcendental origin, is only *a meagre part of it*, a remnant, a mere trace, the smallest possible vestige. What we can know of the real is rigorously limited by man's finite and specialised perception. And yet on the basis of these limitations all of man's grand metaphysical systems have been formed. Thus metaphysics elides genuine otherness, by assuming that it can comprehend it.

What had been understood as *symmetrical*, origin and originated, positivity and negation of positivity, is thus rethought by deconstruction as potentially *asymmetrical*. The origin is allowed to have *other* potentialities that are *not reflected* in the actuality it has *for us*. The origin is the infinity of traces which of themselves constitute signifiers and are *immanent* to them. And yet there is an essential difference, an *otherness*, between origin and originated, which is not to be found in the traditional scheme. For metaphysics there is no difference in kind between presence and difference, difference merely being understood to enjoy *less* presence than its origin. The true relation of the originated to its origin is the relation between the same and the *other*, the seed to the winds of dissemination.

Deconstruction is a means of pointing out the genuine other while accepting the necessity of remaining within the same. It accepts the necessity for transcendental philosophy, but refuses to posit the transcendental as *outside* the text, 'transcendent'. The transcendental is immanent to that of which it is the condition. It is the infinite and singular process of differentiation which creates individual signifiers as constituted and determinate differences. But this is still an appropriation of the real. Even the other of language which is immanent *to* it can only be appropriated, since the only means we have to think and speak of it are fully constituted signifiers. We can only use signifiers to name (and thus betray) the non-signifying origin of the signifier. Even the word 'trace' is an appropriation of the real. It is a 'representative' or simply a 'representation' of the real, not its original presentation, which is always in process, below the threshold of fully constituted signifiers and hence insusceptible of naming.

> The movement of the effacement of the trace has been, from Plato to Rousseau to Hegel, imposed upon writing in the narrow sense; the necessity of such a displacement may now be apparent. *Writing is one of the representatives of the trace in general*, it is not the trace itself. *The trace itself does not exist* [Derrida's italics]. (To exist is to be, to be an entity, a being-present, *to on*.) (OG: 167, my italics)

So, one's (linguistic) understanding of the real cannot exhaust its potentialities; one can understand it only insofar as it traces; and one can refer to the trace only with fully *constituted* signifiers that betray the real, even when these signifiers are as modest as the 'trace', 'writing': the most minimal appropriation there is, but an appropriation still.

And yet, deconstruction has a strategy to overcome this last betrayal and thus effectively demonstrate that *any* signifier which it uses to indicate the non-linguistic real is inadequate to it. It strategically uses and displaces a signifier to mean something that any signifier will efface by its very nature. Signifiers such as 'writing' – or any undecidable signifier, anything which oscillates or moves – are the only ones which effectively indicate an *event* of differentiation. The signifier is present, determinate, and yet it is capable of at least indicating an indeterminate event. The real is that which is without determination, but which gets determined as soon as it is addressed from *within* the signifier. But there are signifiers which betray it more and less, and there are strategies for using language that acknowledge this betrayal more and less.

The most differential, least present products of differentiation, the most meagre and secondary from the metaphysical standpoint of presence, are the ones most apt to represent that which precedes the full determinateness of the definite signifier.

It is clear that, for Derrida, it is necessary that we determine. This is what the transcendental selection amounts to. One has always to understand one's other in terms of a part of oneself, oppositionally, the other as relative. The only thing one can do to mitigate this appropriation is to be careful *which* signifier one selects for the task and to ensure that one does not believe one has ever discovered the *ultimate* word, a word which could not be replaced by anything and hence constituted a genuine 'sign' of the real.

One must not assert that the real other is present – present in language thanks to a transparent sign – for this makes it seem as if that which one knows of the other is the *whole truth*, rather than just the merest tip of a mightier multiplicity of forces of which we know only a little. It is necessary that the undetermined origin, the real, be determined in a way that is symbolic, that appropriates it unto the signifier, as its condition of possibility. All deconstruction can do is pick those (subordinated) signifiers that appropriate it the *least*, by refusing to understand the real as *presence*. Then it must acknowledge that no word it uses will ever be appropriate *even to this minimal capacity which we know the real must possess*. To do this, it carries on producing words, or rather it carries on reading and picking words out, inscribing each one in a longer and ever longer chain of references.

The quasi-transcendental

The real is not the opposite of the textual but is itself in a certain sense textual: all we can say about it is not that it is *not* textual but that it *is* textual *in a certain way*. It *traces*, and it traces in a way that does not reach anything like presence, but extends its tracery to infinity. Derrida therefore thinks that the only way to resist the appropriation of the relation between the symbolic and the real is to steadily cross out everything that metaphysics says, and thereby indicate that which lies beyond the opposition *in and as* the very marks which do the erasing. Repeating the marks composing the original signifiers indicates these signifiers themselves to be 'real', to be composed of traces.

Derrida does not see another way of countering the metaphysical understanding of the opposition between the text and its outside. He sees only the transcendental way, but a quasi-transcendental way which understands the transcendental as such to be an illusion – a *necessary* illusion, and one to be inhabited and subverted *from within*, immanently. The *only* way in which to understand the real is in the form of one's condition of possibility. Even though this condition is other than the system it originates, the only way to name it is to extract an element from within the conditioned system and elevate it to the 'transcendental position'.

> The *transcendental* position of the phallus (in the chain of signifiers to which it belongs, while simultaneously making it possible) [Derrida's footnote: 'This is the strict definition of the *transcendental position*: the privilege of one term within a series of terms that it makes possible and which presupposes it. Thus a category is called transcendental (transcategorial) when it "transcends every genus" (*transcendit omne genus*), i.e. the list of categories of which it is nevertheless a part while accounting for it']. (PC: 477 [n 56])

Derrida invokes a metaphor for this element within a series which sustains that series, an *immanent* transcendental: the *keystone* of the arch: 'the keystone of an institution, the stone which encapsulates both the possibility and the fragility of its existence' (WD: 4). The keystone is just another stone in the series of stones, but without it, the whole edifice collapses.

The condition of possibility is also the condition of impossibility (cf. SP: 101): 'the principle of a series also transcends it and, withdrawn from the meaning that it confers, it comes to deprive of meaning the very thing to which it gives meaning' (R: 23). This is one reason why the transcendental is only quasi-transcendental, because it makes meaning possible *and* endangers it. The infinity of marks is necessary for the value of any signifier to be determined, but at the same time it makes it impossible for us to determine it. The only way in which we can name the transcendental is inadequate. Whatever word we use will ultimately have no final right to be called transcendental. 'This surplus mark, this margin of meaning, is not one valence among others in the series, even though it is *inserted* [Derrida's italics] in there, too. It has to be inserted there *to the extent that it does not exist outside the text and* [therefore] *has no transcendental privilege*' (D: 251–2, my italics; cf. D: 103). This is why Derrida says, 'the labour of writing *erases* the transcendental distinction between the origin of the world and Being-in-the-world. Erases it while producing it' (WD: 267, my italics).

In this regard, Derrida refers to 'the transcendentality – *under erasure* – of the archi-trace' (OG: 88, my italics). This is why Derrida adds a prefix, to indicate a displacement of the old term: 'a quasi-transcendental law of seriality that could be illustrated in an analogous way by so many other examples, each time, in fact, that *the transcendental condition of a series is also, paradoxically, a part of that series*, creating aporias for the constitution of any set or whole [*ensemble*]' (R: 79, my italics). Only a certain strategic use of language can present the apparent avowal of the one unique transcendental in the appropriate way, as a mere simulacrum, for it is *not* the only word: 'only a conceptual strategy of some sort can temporarily privilege them as *determinate* signifiers or even as *signifiers* at all, which strictly speaking they *no longer are*' (D: 252).

The privilege is only temporary, no one text can adequately determine, without appropriation, the conditions of possibility of all language, for in each case they use a signifier to describe what precedes the signifier. Thus, each transcendental signifier is specific to the text under consideration. And in order to demonstrate its inadequacy to the other of the text, one must quite simply consider more than one text. This is the reason for the *plurality* of Derrida's writings, and even the fact that he initiated the project of deconstruction in two stages, each of which involved the simultaneous publication of more than one monograph, in 1967 and 1972.

In the case of each metaphysical, finite textual system read by Derrida, the transcendental position is occupied by a *different* signifier. The very fact that there was *from the very beginning* more than one such reading was intended to indicate the impossibility of ever finding the *one name* that would adequately capture the transcendental of language as such. It is to indicate that *nothing* from the originated system of signifiers could ever be appropriate to the real from which it – among other things – originated. 'There will be no unique name, even if it were the name of Being. And we must think this without *nostalgia*' (MP: 27), Derrida warns Heidegger, countering any notion that a more ancient (Greek) language had such a word. It is only in the continual *substitution* of words that language indicates its own inadequacy to capture that which is otherwise than language. Derrida is concerned that no one of the words he picks out from the texts in whose reading deconstruction *exhausts* itself should be taken to describe absolutely *what the transcendental is*, or be taken to understand the real as nothing besides that part of it which makes language possible. Each of 'Derrida's' famous words (archi-writing, *différance*, *pharmakon* . . .) is only the imitation of the transcendental, merely the semblance of such a thing, *quasi*-transcendental.

To show that none of these words is the 'master-word' or 'finally proper name' (MP: 27), Derrida writes a plurality of texts, each with a *different* word in the place of the sign, or the signifier of the signifier, in the sense of the signifier of the transcendental signified *or* the deconstructed 'sign', the signifier of all signifiers, the undecidable which resembles every signifier in its textuality, that signifier which has the characteristics of 'writing' (cf. P: 4).

There is no name (for the name, for signifiers as a whole), no way to capture the event of differentiation once the signifiers one is compelled to use have already been differentiated to form a determinate language.[37] What Lacan understood as the only possible sign, that which signifies the signifier itself, is impossible.[38] The signifier is simply incapable of unambiguously signifying itself once and for all. This is what the plurality of deconstructive readings performatively insists on. The undecidable is what fills this gap in the signifier in each particular text, it takes the place of the one signifier that is always missing and that is the proper name as such, the unique signifier *of* the signifier, which is really the signifier that entirely effaces itself before the transcendental signified: 'the concept of the supplement which, of course, *signifies* nothing, simply replaces a lack' (OG: 208).

There is no signifier of the signifier. As the circularity of the phrase itself indicates, this amounts to a non-explanatory self-foundation, the structure of the substance or subject, characteristic of metaphysics. If one assumes that such a signifier is any more than a myth, peculiar to one particular symbolic system, then one errs.

The beyond of language, the real, is the 'nameless' or the 'unnameable', that to which we can apply no name. This trope of namelessness was present in Derrida's work from the very start.[39]

The plurality of the 'names of the name'

The only way to indicate that the name of the name is unnameable, without renouncing language and naming altogether, is never to rest content with any name that might occupy this 'transcendental position', whether this be a sign that signifies the transcendental signified or the signifier as a whole, as in the case of the undecidables.

Derrida frequently stresses that no one of the signifiers that he highlights in the texts of others should be understood as *properly* transcendental, universally so:

> it is out of the question that we should erect such a representative [. . .] into the fundamental signified or signifier in the series. Every signifier in the series is folded along the angle of this remark [in other words, it acquires two faces, undecidability of meaning]. The signifiers 'writing', '*hymen*', 'fold', 'tissue', 'text', etc. do not escape this common law. (D: 252)

Thus Derrida does not claim to endorse transcendental philosophy, but rather to show that it is both inevitable and an appropriation. We have no choice but to use a determinate signifier to signify the origin of signification itself. Even the real as we can know it transcendentally, in its ability to trace, is infinite, and we can know only that context which is closest to us. This is as much of the genuine other – the infinity of the signifier – as we can know, and we shall always appropriate it unto ourselves to this extent. But it always goes beyond what we can know of it. Thus we cannot even fully know our own transcendental, which is, once again, why it may be deemed merely 'quasi-transcendental'.

Thus, what Derrida is attempting to indicate with his work is *not* – as would be impossible – the nature of the indeterminate or as yet undetermined real in itself. Rather, because we are always 'downstream' of this, always approaching it after the fact, posterior to having been 'thrown' into language, Derrida is attempting to indicate the *event* of determination, that moment at which a signifying system is born, when the real gets determined in a particular, limited way. This is all we can hope to reach from within our determined linguistic system.

It is by indicating the different *determinations* in their very plurality, and the way in which they are always taken *from* the text itself, that Derrida attempts to make his readers see that in each case what is being covered over by these substantives is the *event* of determination itself, the fact that in each case something indeterminate is being determined *by* the text that claims to be able properly to *name* this indeterminacy, which is in truth unnameable.

What is indeterminate? The real; but all that we can know of the real is the infinity of traces which go to constitute signifiers. How is this infinity to be understood as an event? This infinity is a *process* of infinitisation, the constant opening of differences, which constitute and determine each individual signifier. 'It is not the question of a constituted difference here, but rather, before all determination of the content, of the *pure* movement which produces difference' (OG: 62). The event issues from the nameless real, and from our perspective within the apparently *fully formed* signifier the event can only be *determined* by a name, taken inevitably from the system of language in question:[40]

> all the determinations of such a trace – all the names it is given – belong as such to the text of metaphysics that shelters the trace, and not to the trace itself. There is no trace *itself*, no *proper* trace [. . .] the determinations which name difference always come from the metaphysical order. (MP: 66)[41]

From the determinate to the indeterminate, for the sake of a futural event

If we believed that any one determination of the indeterminate event of differentiation were final, we would betray it. Thus it is necessary constantly to move on to a new text, to find a new determination, in order that one never rest content with any one (inadequate) determination. One deconstructs the transcendental signified in each case by showing that it depends on the particular signifiers one has at one's disposal, and one does this for the sake of the future. To show that, if any form of transcendental is dependent upon the contingent references of the signifiers one has inherited, then there will always be other ways, at other times and in other discourses, to determine the transcendental. This will amount to the formation of a chain of quasi-transcendental signifiers, the chain which will define deconstruction itself, deconstruction's product. Only in this way will it become clear that no determination is adequate to the event itself, no signifier is ever adequate to the real.

This is why Derrida understands deconstruction's purpose as making room for or providing hospitality to the other, the new or the messiah, that which is *always* yet to come and which thus amounts to the future itself. It is necessary that there always be another signifier, another text to be read, in order that no one is ever elevated to the status of *the* Book, expressing absolutely adequately a revealed truth, and thus supplying the finally proper name for the name. The messiah *has* no name, or he has more than one.

This is the reason Derrida comes to stress more and more the notion of the ever impending 'event' of pure novelty, the promise of a future utterly unlike the present, one which is not even made possible and so anticipated in its content *by* the present. Hence the future is described as the '*im*possible'. 'Ascesis strips the messianic hope of all biblical *forms*, and even all *determinable* figures of the wait or expectation [. . .] the future that *cannot be anticipated* [. . .] a waiting without horizon of expectation' (SM: 168, my italics). Hence the attitude to the future is a 'desert-like messianism (without content and without identifiable messiah)' (SM: 28). Any particular messiah would determine the indeterminable by importing content from a particular religious discourse, when one cannot even understand the messiah as a *being*, hence Derrida's use of such locutions as 'a mess*ianic* without messianism' (SM: 59, my italics).

From the very start, in *Of Grammatology*, Derrida understands the future as danger or monstrosity.[42] The future 'anticipated' as an indeterminate danger is here translated into a purely *formal* attitude towards the future, since one is entitled to understand it formally as 'other', but any imputation of a content to this other will appropriate it to the present, or to some possibility that the present has made possible: 'this *epokhē* of the *content* [. . .] we hold it here to be essential to the messianic in general, as thinking of the other and of the event to come' (SM: 59, my italics; cf. SM: 73).[43]

It is this absolute difference between the present and the future that deconstruction is to protect. This is why Derrida ultimately comes to insist on a distinction that *should not* be deconstructed. The difference between same and other. Deconstruction is precisely concerned to use oppositions in a certain way to indicate the beyond of the opposition. The other is the other of the same, it is the relative other. Derrida inverts the hierarchy whereby the other is considered as other *only in relation to* the same, and then generalises otherness such that even the same would be absolutely other, which is to say absolutely itself, or rather – since this is perhaps too reminiscent of the Husserlian subject which it was nevertheless necessary to oppose to Levinas (cf. WD: 153–67) – absolutely singular. Every one would be absolutely other, absolutely unique. Why then should the difference of same and other not be deconstructed? To ensure that this other truly remain an absolute other, for that which would not be deconstructible would be the difference between the relative and the absolute, which separates the first and second stages of deconstruction. The difference would be between the present, in which we are fully immersed in language and its oppositions (ultimately the same and the other *of* the same), and the future, beyond language, where otherness could be absolute and free from oppositional determination, which renders it relative.

Naturally, we can never step outside of language. But it is crucial that this future exist to regulate our linguistic conduct, for it will act as a stimulus never to rest content with any one signifier that would claim to be the final word.

To reach any decision, any decisive cut, any epochal change, one must pass through the undecidable (FL: 252). 'This messianic hesitation [in undecidability] does not paralyse any decision, any affirmation, any responsibility. On the contrary, it grants them their elementary condition. It is their very experience' (SM: 169). One has no future if one does not deconstruct one's present. One will remain forever within the remit of the present if one comes to believe that one has said the last word.

The only way to indicate something radically new, *a new possible determination*, is by deconstructing. This is why one's future should be messianic without a *determinate* – 'determinable' or 'identifiable' – messiah: merely an 'idea' in the Kantian sense, remaining forever in the future, but contemporaneous in its guiding function. The messiah in Jewish theology is that which is promised and withheld, which exists *only* as a promise, a nameless other impending over mankind:

> what remains irreducible to any deconstruction, what remains as undeconstructible as the possibility of deconstruction is, perhaps, a certain experience of the emancipatory promise; it is perhaps even the formality of a structural messianism, a messianism without religion, even a messianic without messianism, an idea of justice. (SM: 59)

The relation to the future is simply '*opening*' as such, a questioning of the belief in the eternity of the present, the *finality* of whatever proper name we understand to condition us at present:

> *just* opening which renounces any right to property, any right in general, messianic opening to what is coming, that is, to the event that cannot be awaited *as such*, or recognised in advance therefore, to the event as the foreigner itself, to her or to him for whom one must leave an empty place, always, in memory of the hope. (SM: 65)

Deconstruction, dwelling on the undecidable, attempts the necessary but paradoxical task of delineating the conditions of possibility for something like an event, and so the conditions of possibility for that which *cannot have* conditions of possibility, which cannot be conditioned by and so reduced to the present:

> such a hospitality without reserve, which is nevertheless the condition of the event and thus of history [. . .] is the impossible itself, and [. . .] this *condition of possibility* of the event is also its *condition of impossibility*, like this strange concept of messianism without content, of the messianic without messianism, that guides us here like the blind [i.e. into a future that we cannot *see*]. But it would be just as easy to show that without this experience of the impossible, one might as well give up on both justice and the event. (SM: 65)

Deconstruction understands the event as an event of absolute novelty, of absolute otherness, as opposed to the relative otherness that arises from the actualisation of a potential that was already implicit in the present. The latter is not a true event at all, but merely an extension of the present and its domination:

> a thinking of the event that necessarily exceeds a binary or dialectical logic, the logic that distinguishes or opposes *effectivity or actuality* [effectivité] [. . .] and *ideality* [. . .]. It is also made more manifest by what inscribes the speed of a virtuality irreducible to the opposition of the act and the potential in the space of the event, in the event-ness of the event. (SM: 63)

One cannot avoid thinking of the future in relation to the present insofar as one opens up the conditions of possibility for an other *with respect to* the present, or at least insofar as the present, simply by being present, stands in the way of the coming of the genuine future. In other words, one must deconstruct, one must use the language of the relative other to speak of the absolute other.

This is perhaps what Derrida means by the following: 'The impossible [. . .] is, alas, always possible' (SM: 175; cf. WD: 98), which is to say that the indeterminate is always understood *with respect to* determination. The indeterminate is the in-*determinate*. It can be reached only negatively (oppositionally, relatively) *from the standpoint of determination*. One is still confined to a transcendental approach, to language, and one can only use it in a strategic way to indicate its limits. 'One must constantly remember that this absolute evil [. . .] can take place. One must constantly remember that it is even on the basis of the terrible possibility of this impossible that justice is desirable' (SM: 175).

Beyond the transcendental

Deconstruction's driving concern is never to rest content with any one symbolic system. It is impossible to approach the real save transcendentally, and the real is that which escapes all conditioning, that which all transcendentalising covers up by determining it: the concern of deconstruction is the absolute other, in itself, free of all perspectivality, which is to say, free of all limits, all determination.

Even if one were to rest content with the determination of the real as trace – which is to a certain extent correct, the real *does* trace – one would still have made a determination, and one would have restricted the real to the condition of possibility of the empirical signifier and one would have named it with a particular signifier that this trace is supposed to have engendered. This is why Derrida insists that *any* determination of the transcendental must not be maintained for long. There must be a future.

This is the secret of Derrida's works. What they appear to state is undercut by their very plurality. For instance, one might have thought that Derrida understood 'the trace' to be an adequate term to designate the real condition of possibility of everything we know. But in truth, by altering the way in which this quasi-transcendental is determined (with the sequence '*différance*', 'archi-writing', 'trace', '*pharmakon*', '*hymen*'. . .) he is demonstrating the inadequacy of *any signifier* that occupies the transcendental position or that tries to signify what does. He is attempting to indicate the absolute beyond of determination, the other (of the opposition [between the same and the other]) that is always appropriated by the textual. The secret of the slogan 'there is no outside of the text' is that it is the mask taken on by the desire to preserve precisely that which lies beyond *any* text, but to do so by forcing us to admit that we can speak of this other only deconstructively, *using* language, in a certain way.

Why else would Derrida describe the real other not as 'nameless' but as 'unname*able*'? '[S]uch a *différance* has no name in our language. But we "already know" that if it is unnameable, it is not provisionally so [. . .]. It is rather because there is no *name* for it at all' (MP: 26). The real is from the point of view of the signifier *quite undeterminable*, quite impervious to any form of capture by the signifier. And what alone is undeterminable? That which loses its very nature *by* being determined. Thus it is the indeterminate.

We can name the unnameable only as that which makes names possible and *by means of* names which must always be 'carried off', renamed: 'This unnameable is the play which makes possible nominal effects, the relatively unitary and atomic structures that are called names, the chains of substitutions of names in which, for example, the nominal effect *différance* is itself *enmeshed*, carried off, reinscribed' (MP: 26–7).

Thus one can see that the apparent transcendentals which Derrida might have been thought to erect, in the form of signifiers of the real, are even less 'transcendental' than we have suggested, they attempt to destroy the illusion of the transcendental altogether: they *mimic* the transcendental method, ironically assuming its guise, in order to show up its own masquerade (hence the prefix 'quasi', and the term 'simulacra'). Derrida repeatedly insists upon this, that one must remain dissatisfied with *any* name that appears to play the role of the transcendental:

> For us, *différance* remains a metaphysical name, and *all the names* that it receives in our language are still, as names, metaphysical. And this is particularly the case when these names state the *determination* of *différance* as the difference between presence and the present (*Anwesen/Anwesend*), and above all, as is already the case when they state the determination of *différance* as the difference of Being and beings. (MP: 26, my italics)
>
> What we know [. . .] is that there has never been, never will be, a unique word, a master-name. [. . .] There is nothing kerygmatic about this 'word', provided that one perceives its decapita(lisa)tion. And that one puts into question the name of the name.
>
> [. . .] [W]e must *affirm* this [Derrida's italics].
>
> [. . .] Such is the question: the alliance of speech and Being in the unique word, in the finally proper name. And such is the question inscribed in the *simulated* affirmation [*l'affirmation jouée*] of *différance*. (MP: 27, my italics)

The affirmation of one word as the name of the transcendental event is only a '*simulated* affirmation', a playful one. Any word that Derrida elects will itself need to be erased.

The very large *number* of Derrida's texts is not irrelevant to that which they wish to convey. Indeed it is precisely this plurality which must be taken into account if one is to understand the secret heart of deconstruction, which undercuts some of what the individual texts appear – or *pretend* – to say, the affirmation which they 'simulate'. Even the quasi-transcendental is a deceptive appearance. Derrida is thinking the necessity of transcendentalisation in order to think beyond the transcendental condition of possibility to the *im*possible. Derrida does not *wish* to be even a *quasi*-transcendental thinker.

It is as if, once so many different words have been scribbled in the same place, we are to receive the impression that they mingle into something that is not a signifier, into a pure *mark* with no determinacy at all, pure ink, pure materiality, pure writing or event of determination, in which the signifier itself is lost. All we can see is the mere fact that writing has taken place.

Let us lay down such a palimpsest now, and leave this image to impress itself on the reader's mind, as the following statements on *overlaying* quasi-transcendentals are themselves overlaid:

> In the delineation of *différance* everything is strategic and adventurous. Strategic because no transcendent truth present outside the field of writing can govern theologically the totality of the field [. . .]. By means of this solely strategic justification, I wish to underline that the efficacity of the thematic of *différance* may very well, indeed must, one day be superseded, lending itself if not to its own replacement, at least to enmeshing itself in a chain that in truth it never will have governed. (MP: 7)
>
> Now if we consider the chain in which *différance* lends itself to a certain number of nonsynonymous substitutions, according to the necessity of the context, why have recourse to the 'reserve', to 'archi-writing', to the 'archi-trace', to 'spacing', that is, to the 'supplement', or to the *pharmakon*, and soon to the *hymen*, to the margin-mark-march [*la marge-marque-marche*], etc.? (MP: 12)
>
> [I]t is out of the question that we should erect such a representative – for example the whiteness of the page of writing – into the fundamental signified or signifier in the series. [. . .] The signifiers 'writing', '*hymen*' [. . .] etc. do not escape this common law, and only a conceptual strategy of some sort can temporarily privilege them as *determinate* signifiers or even as *signifiers* at all, which strictly speaking they *no longer are*. (D: 252)
>
> No more than can castration, dissemination [. . .] can never become an originary, central, or ultimate signified, the place proper to truth. On the contrary, dissemination represents the affirmation of this nonorigin, the remarkable empty locus of a hundred blanks no meaning can be ascribed to, in which mark supplements and substitution games are multiplied *ad infinitum*. (D: 268, n 67)

'None of the terms of this series can, being comprehended within it, dominate the economy of *différance* or supplementarity' (OG: 315).

Thus, while we may have implied that Derrida was *avowedly* a transcendental philosopher, we can now see that he was all along adopting the *mask* of the transcendentalism of the metaphysical tradition, in order to expose (the limitations of) its logic. He thus demonstrates the *necessity* of the transcendental approach and at the same time its inherent appropriation. *This applies to Derrida's own quasi-transcendentals as well.* There *is* no transcendental for Derrida, such a thing is a myth projected by each particular signifying system, but there *is* transcendentalisation, always and everywhere.

Lacan: the name – of the father

Now, on the basis of this exposition, it is clear that the question which deconstruction poses to Lacan is the following: *is there only one name-of-the-father*? If this is the case, then Lacan would have fallen victim to the metaphysical illusion of a signifier of all signifiers, a signifier which truly captured the origin and nature of every signifier there is, or a metalanguage with which to speak of language as a whole without being contaminated by its differentiality and the concomitant potential for substitution. Lacan would then be truly a transcendental philosopher, he would not have learnt the secret of deconstruction's plurality.

Is the name-of-the-father a 'finally proper name', the 'name of the name'? Does Lacan believe in this one god? Does he believe that there is just one factor that unites every aspect of human culture and really opposes it to nature? Even if the prohibition were mythical, it would still be a signifier ('*le Nom-du-père*') and it would still be a myth shared by *all* culture. Is the name-of-the-father unique or does it only seem so? That is to say, does Lacan's earlier thought imply an oppositional relation between the text and the non-textual, which could then be deconstructed?

The universalisation of a myth increases the likelihood that that myth will be *believed*. Lacan wants to say that the prohibition of incest is a myth, not an event that actually happened and which can be located chronologically, but an event which is created as a result of the infinitisation of the signifier and the consequent impossibility of thenceforth and from that point of view seeing beyond its boundary. The question is whether he believes too much in this myth, without realising it, whether he believes that the determination of the real from the point of view of the symbolic captures the real *in itself*. It seems to me that his pronouncements on the real from the first half of the 1950s prove that he does. We shall demonstrate this in the following chapter.

We have seen at the end of Chapter 1 that the phallus symbolises the castration of any signifier from its signified, and thus opens up the possibility of infinite dissemination, an infinite ambiguity of meaning. We have seen that the name-of-the-father overpowers the phallus in Lacan's discourse and totalises the signifier, rendering the infinity of the signifier a finite whole, and thereby rendering meaning *possible*.

Thus we might understand Lacan to be depicting *precisely* the process that Derrida himself recognises to be necessary: the isolating of a finite set of signifiers within an infinite set, in a way that is necessary in order to produce the illusion of meaning. The question is whether Lacan can follow Derrida in giving both moments equal weight (akin to Derrida's 'double reading'). We shall suggest that Lacan, at this stage of his thought, overstresses the name-of-the-father, and at the same time its uniqueness, refusing the substitution that would be allowed by a deconstructive approach to the other of the text.

The unique name would be the proper name. The proper name allows one to *translate* between different symbolic orders, it allows alien individuals and alien (sub-)cultures to communicate. It allows the meaning of the entire system of signifiers to be fixed as far as is necessary for reasonably successful communication to occur. It allows the instigation of a (more or less) common symbolic order within which we are sometimes able to communicate.

The name-of-the-father opens up an oppositional relation between the cultural and the natural. The prohibition of incest, represented by the name, distinguishes every element of culture by means of some trait which nature *lacks*. Thanks to the name-of-the-father, the real and the symbolic are *opposed*.[44]

If Lacan himself describes the real in a way that opposes it to the symbolic, this will prove that he has himself fallen victim to the myth of the one creative father, and has ignored the necessity for the twofold deconstructive strategy whereby language can indicate that which is absolutely and not just relatively other. We shall see in the next chapter that Lacan does indeed understand the real in this way: the only predicates he applies to the real are *negations* of qualities possessed by the *symbolic*. Lacan falls victim to the metaphysical mistake of understanding the relation between the symbolic and its outside in *symbolic terms*, as an opposition.

If Lacan believes in the prohibition of incest, Derrida, on the other hand, explicitly disavows anything that allows one to believe that there is a real opposition between nature and culture. In the context of Lévi-Strauss as a Rousseauian, Derrida explicitly deconstructs the name-of-the-father, the symbolic father who announces the prohibition of incest as the pure origin of human culture:

> Even that which we say, name, describe as the prohibition of incest does not escape play. There is a point in the system where the signifier can no longer be replaced by its signified, so that in consequence no signifier can be so replaced, purely and simply. For the point of nonreplacement is also the point of orientation for the entire system of signification [. . .]. That

> point does not exist, it is always elusive or, what comes to the same thing, always already inscribed in what it ought to escape or ought to have escaped, according to our indestructible and mortal desire. [. . .] The festival *itself* would be incest *itself* if some such thing – *itself* – could *take place*; if, by taking place, incest were not to confirm the prohibition: before the prohibition, it is not incest; forbidden, it cannot become incest except through the recognition of the prohibition. We are always short of or beyond the limit of the festival, of the origin of society, of that present with which simultaneously the interdict is (would be) given with the transgression. (OG: 266–7)

'This *birth of society* is therefore not a passage, it is a point, a pure, fictive and unstable, ungraspable limit. [. . .] [I]t is not possible to recognise any linear order, whether logical or chronological' (OG: 267).

Derrida later states that deconstruction *began* with the disturbance of such a clear-cut division between nature and culture:

> a deconstructive questioning that starts, as has been the case, by destabilising or complicating the opposition between *nomos* and *physis*, between *thesis* and *physis* – that is to say, the opposition between law [*loi*], convention, the institution on the one hand, and nature on the other, with all the oppositions that they condition. (FL: 235)[45]

Since there is no definable point of prohibition, logically or chronologically, transcendentally or genetically, any opposition between culture and nature will be a retroactive projection on the part of culture, a traditionally transcendental myth. The name-of-the-father as a transcendental signifier.

It is only the name, the name-of-the-father as the moment at which law is instituted, that can create such an opposition. And Derrida is quite explicit that within the signifier, whose dominion is absolute, names are ruled out. They are effaced the moment the signifier arises.[46] There is simply no way to halt the differentiality of the signifier. It swallows up in differentiality anything that would attempt to be non-differential. Any name must be open to substitution. To apply *one* name, *one* signifier to the origin of the signifier demonstrates that Lacan believes in his own myth. If he had used a plurality of names, he would have been a Derridean deconstructionist, or at least adequate to this, its least contestable insight. The real and the symbolic would not be understood as irremediably opposed. But for the early Lacan, it is necessary that the symbolic be absolutely closed off from the real, that the real be its opposite, entirely outside the text.

Derrida admits that Lacan does indeed make an advance on 'naïve semanticism', the belief that language is made possible by a transcendental signified entirely outside of the signifier (PC: 420). He does this by understanding the condition of possibility of a fixed order of signification to be a *name*, thereby supplanting the transcendental signi*fied* with a transcendental signi*fier*. This is the transformation that initiates structuralism, which understands the symbolic order to be a perfectly self-contained autonomous region, explicable without reference to the real in which it originates, synchrony entirely overwhelming diachrony.

The name-of-the-father binds Lacan to this structuralism. It is a transcendental instance in the traditional sense of the term. The name-of-the-father as a singular *name*, the distinctive trait of a *universal* symbolic order, cannot be taken up into a series of substitutes as Derrida himself demands that his own quasi-transcendentals must be.

Transition

Thus Lacan's earlier work remains vulnerable to deconstruction. The transcendental approach instituted by the name-of-the-father overpowers the deconstructive potential contained within the notion of the phallus.

But the phallus can do much more than that. The phallus also refers Lacan's understanding of the symbolic to its *chronological-genetic* origins, a question which deconstruction can *not* address. We shall suggest that this fact indicates a residual transcendentalism in Derrida's thought, or at least that he believes the transcendental approach to be more binding than it actually is. Therefore, a renewed attention to the phallus, in its deconstructive *and* genetic possibilities, might allow Lacan not only to attain to the level of deconstruction's insights, but to surpass Derridean deconstruction itself.

In the following chapter we shall traverse the unfolding of Lacan's work as the balance tilts between the two notions of the name-of-the-father and the phallus. This will involve the gradual reassertion of the *imaginary*. In light of this, the nature of the real must be rethought, since it was only the dominance of the name-of-the-father that allowed it to be understood as the *opposite* of the symbolic. We shall plot the parallel movements of these two interrelated developments: Lacan's developing understanding of the real, and the changing place and importance of the imaginary.

Notes

1. In other words, 'seminal *différance* does constitute itself into a program, but *it is a program that cannot be formalised*. For reasons that *can* be formalised' (D: 52, my italics). 'According to *a law that can be formalised*, philosophy always reappropriates for itself the discourse that de-limits it' (MP: 177, my italics). Thus the character of language which makes deconstruction possible and necessary *can* be formalised, which is to say, presented in a way independent of the content of any particular text. The deconstruction itself is supposed to be peculiar to each text. Deconstructibility can be understood formally, but not the individual deconstruction. And yet at times, Derrida comes close to formalising deconstructive theses: '[*I*]*f such a thing were justifiable*, we would have to assert right now that one of the theses – there is more than one – inscribed within dissemination is precisely the impossibility of reducing a text as such to its effects of meaning, content, thesis or theme' (D: 7, my italics; cf. P: 44–5; OG: lxxxix). We shall in fact argue that a formalism of deconstruction becomes apparent precisely in Derrida's early treatment of Lacan.
2. Metaphysics' understanding of being: being (*ousia*) as presence (*parousia*), being understood as a fully present substance or essence (*ousia*).
3. However, referring back to *Speech and Phenomena* (SP: 18), in *Of Grammatology*, Derrida translates '*Bedeutung*' with '*vouloir-dire*' (OG: 49). Derrida does admit that 'the traditional translation of *Bedeutung* by "signification" [is] time-honoured and practically inevitable' and resists the translation primarily because it 'risks confusing the whole text of Husserl' (SP: 17). Thus I think the discrepancy can be mitigated by taking seriously Derrida's insistence that his choice of terms is *always* governed by the (in this case, Husserlian) context of what he is reading. In the context of my reading, and particularly given the Lacanian context, it certainly makes sense to understand *Sinn* as the conscious fully-present meaning, which we intend to say, the conscious intention to mean (*vouloir-dire*), and then to understand *Bedeutung* as the form which this meaning must take given that it is determined by the signifiers at one's disposal. '*Be-deutung*' refers to '*deuten*' which is the German word for 'pointing' and that is to say 'signifying' or 'referring'. Thus, *vouloir-dire* could be used interchangeably with *sens* (*Sinn*, sense, meaning) on our reading, at least in this context.
4. Derrida regards this work as the *philosophical* foundation of his thought: 'in a classical philosophical architecture, *Speech* . . . would come first' (P: 5). And yet 'philosophy' understands 'origin' in too *axiomatic* a fashion, as a *simple*, present origin. Perhaps this is why Derrida feigns to 'forget' it (P: 4), since – being too philosophical – it contradicts his assertion of the necessity for a founding *plurality*. In the

current work we are countering this forgetfulness and reasserting the rights of this philosophical, perhaps too philosophical foundation.

5. Derrida encloses the word in apostrophes (MP: 60).
6. Meaning and referent are distinct, but not crucially so, since both are moments of presence that are taken to be oppositionally distinct from the differentiality that characterises language. Derrida is quite clear that he does not limit the term '[transcendental] signified' to a concept; it can also refer to the referent: 'the sign must be the unity of a heterogeneity, since the signified (*sense* or *thing*, *noeme* or *reality*) is not in itself a signifier, a trace: in any case is not constituted in its sense by its relationship with a possible trace. The formal essence of the signified is *presence* [Derrida's italics]' (OG: 18, my italics).
7. Derrida refers his use of the word 'transcendental' back to the first occurrence of the cognate word from the middle ages, although this refers back to Aristotle and for Derrida remains appropriate to the Kantian and Husserlian concepts: 'precisely as it was fixed in the course of the development of the Aristotelian problematic of the categories, including whatever remains beyond the categories. Transcendental means transcategorial. Literally: "that which *transcends* every genus". ([. . .] undoubtedly invented by the Chancellor Philip, 1128, [it] also suits the Kantian and Husserlian concepts of the transcendental)' (MP: 195; cf. PC: 477, n 56). The transcendental signified is the '"*primum signatum*": the "transcendental" signified ("transcendental" in a certain sense, as in the Middle Ages the transcendental – *ens*, *unum*, *verum*, *bonum* – was said to be the "*primum cognitum*") implied by all categories or all determined significations, by all lexicons and all syntax, and therefore by all linguistic signifiers, [. . .] irreducible to all the epochal determinations that it nonetheless makes possible, thus opening the history of the logos, yet itself being only through the logos' (OG: 20). In other words, Derrida understands the signification of the word 'transcendental' to refer back to every one of the major turning points in its history. His own use of the term naturally takes all of these into account.
8. As we shall try to demonstrate, otherness in the proper sense is not a relation at all, it simply has to be expressed in *language* in terms of the opposition between '*same* and other'. Since we are speaking of the other 'of' language any structure borrowed *from* language will be inadequate to it. 'Otherness' is really the non-relational singularity that can only be gestured at by the language of same and other. To place 'the other' in relation to 'the same' reduces the *absolute* other to the *relative* other once again. This is why Derrida will often refer later to the Levinasian trope of the '*totally* other' (*tout autre*) (cf. Derrida 1995 [1990]: 82).
9. Aside from the previous passage, one instance is the following: 'the "real" supervening, and being added only while taking on meaning from a trace and from an invocation of the supplement, etc.' (OG: 159).

Also, in a passage on the outside of the text as the 'impossible', '[the real] doesn't exist, since there is nothing outside the whole. It does exist, since there is an "exception to everything", an outside of the whole, that is, a sort of subtraction without lack. And since it exists, all alone, the all is nothing, the nothing' (D: 56).

10. '[W]herever deconstruction is at stake, it would be a matter of linking an *affirmation* (in particular a political one), *if there is any*, to the experience of the impossible, which can only be a radical experience of the *perhaps*' (SM: 35). The impossible is that future which cannot be conditioned – made *possible* – by the present moment. Recall Derrida's statement that, 'the impossible has *already* occurred', which impossibility he refers to the other as that which is not possible on the basis of the 'established totality of facts' (WD: 98), the other as the infinite, which we shall identify with the incomprehensible infinity of signifiers and their traces.
11. 'The *pharmakon*, without being anything in itself, always exceeds them [the philosophemes of dialectics] in constituting their fund without ground [*fonds sans fond*]' (D: 127).
12. Why 'trace'? 'If words and concepts receive meaning only in sequences of differences, one can justify one's language, and one's choice of terms, only within a topic and an historical strategy. [. . .] [A] certain number of givens belonging to the discourse of our time have progressively imposed this choice upon me' (OG: 70). Derrida lists Levinas's critique of ontology, though without accepting its anti-Heideggerian intent, Nietzschean and Freudian discourse, and finally, 'all scientific fields' (ibid.). We shall return to the last of these later.
13. As we shall come to see, this is why Derrida posits an *undeconstructible* difference at the basis of deconstruction. The full 'logical' order of constitution runs as follows: same and other – archi-writing (which produces the trace) – trace – difference (signifier) – presence (signified).
14. '[T]he sign is from its origin and to the core of its sense [*sens*] marked by this will to derivation or effacement' (SP: 51). 'Ideally, in the teleological essence of speech, it would then be possible for the signifier to be in absolute proximity to the signified aimed at in intuition and governing the meaning. The signifier would become perfectly diaphanous due to the absolute proximity to the signified' (SP: 80).
15. 'If language never escapes analogy, if it is indeed analogy through and through, it ought, having arrived at this point, at this stage, freely to assume its own destruction and cast metaphor against metaphor: all of which amounts to complying with *the most traditional of imperatives*' (SP: 13, my italics).
16. 'The screen, without which there would be no writing, is also a device described *in* writing. The writing process [*Le procédé d'écriture*] is reflected in what is written [*l'écrit*]' (D: 318).

17. 'The whole is treated then by a "part" bigger than itself' (D: 54). Derrida describes '*en abyme*' as 'the current phrase' (OG: 163) and later enjoins wariness: 'I do not believe in it very much, I am wary of the confidence that it inspires fundamentally, I believe it too representative either to go far enough or not to avoid the very thing toward which it allegedly rushes' (PC: 304).
18. '[W]riting appears to Plato (and after him to all of philosophy, which is as such constituted in this gesture) as that process of redoubling [*redoublement*] in which we are fatally *(en)trained* [entraînement]' (D: 109). A literary figure, a writer, raises philosophy from its slumber here: 'Valéry reminds the philosopher that philosophy is written. And that the philosopher is a philosopher to the extent that he forgets this' (MP: 291). Lacoue-Labarthe's supreme essay 'Typography' should be consulted on this question (Lacoue-Labarthe 1998 [1989]: 43–138).
19. And yet, in another sense, these would not be signs in the traditional sense because their signified would not be a presence *distinct* from language. It would be the signifier! For this reason, Derrida will at other times *deny* that '*différance*', for instance, is a word (MP: 7). '[S]trictly speaking, it [*hymen*] is not a true sign or "signifier"' (D: 261). In truth, the undecidable can be neither a sign nor a non-sign, neither signifier nor signified, since it makes possible every opposition as such, including these oppositions.
20. The signifier signifies the 'between', the reference from one signifier to another, signifying (*signifiant*) itself: 'One no longer even has the authority to say that "between" is a purely syntactic function. Through the re-marking of its semantic void, it in fact begins to signify. Its semantic void *signifies*, but it signifies spacing and articulation [the differentiality of the signifier]; it has as its meaning the possibility of syntax; it orders the play of meaning. *Neither purely syntactic nor purely semantic*, it marks the articulated opening of that opposition' (D: 222).
21. The very particular quality of these words, their opacity as signifiers, is revealed with particular clarity when one attempts to translate them. One needs a laborious commentary in order to explicate and qualify the translation, one needs to write around it. 'The materiality of a word cannot be translated or carried over into another language. Materiality is precisely that which translation relinquishes' (WD: 264). Given Derrida's insistence on precisely this materiality, one can understand the frequent recourse of Derrida's translators to leaving certain words *un*translated, and the need to leave Greek, for instance, in its original graphicality (ὕμεν, φάρμακον).
22. Derrida calls upon the technical word from Gödel's work on the 'undecidability' of theorems in elementary arithmetic (D: 219). The meaning of an undecidable signifier *cannot* be determined on the basis of the text's proposed transcendental signified. In analogy with Gödel's term,

meaning cannot be either deduced or ruled out by the axioms of the system, which in this case may be identified with the transcendental signified. Meaning is here to be determined, if it is determined, by something else, the context or contexts in which that signifier can be used.

23. 'Rousseau cannot utilise it at the same time in all the *virtualities* of its meaning. The way in which he determines the concept and, in so doing, lets himself be determined by that very thing that he excludes from it' (OG: 163, my italics).
24. '[The undecidables'] effects [. . .] spread out in a chain over the practical and theoretical entirety of a text' (P: 40).
25. '[E]very text of metaphysics carries within itself, for example, *both* the so-called "vulgar" concept of time *and* the resources that will be borrowed from the system of metaphysics in order to criticise that concept' (MP: 60). For similar statements, see D: 11; MP: 49, 56; OG: 26; P: 77–8; WD: 288, 328.
26. Derrida also refers to 'philosophy's blind spot' (WD: 325, cf. 327).
27. At times, Derrida relates the overdetermination to history, to which language in a very general sense, as the possibility of inscription and record, gives us access: 'the history to which he belongs thanks to the element of language' (OG: 158). '[A]cknowledging the autonomy of the signifier as the letter's historicity; before me, the signifier on its own says more than I believe that I mean to say [*vouloir dire*], and in relation to it, my meaning-to-say [*vouloir dire*] is submissive rather than active. My meaning-to-say finds itself lacking something in relation to the signifier, and is inscribed passively, we might say [. . .] the autonomy of the signifier as the stratification and historical potentialisation of meaning [*stratification et potentialisation historique du sens*], as a historical system, that is, a system that is open at some point' (WD: 224).
28. Critchley gives an excellent account of this, in a book whose interpretation is on many points close to my own (cf. Critchley 1992: 59).
29. '*Ellipse*' in French means both the ellipse and the ellipsis. . .
30. Speaking of Philippe Sollers' *Numbers*, Derrida writes, 'their ink is drawn from this tain, a sort of metal covered with liquid mercury [which is poisonous, or, at least, a *pharmakon*]' (D: 314). Scratching the reflective surface of the mirror with a stylus of sufficient penetration exposes this tain such that its words would actually be written in mercury: 'dissemination is written on the back – the *tain* – of that mirror. Not on its inverted spectre [which is to say the virtual image which the mirror reflects and contains]' (D: 33). 'The mercury, the tain of this ink, forms a screen. It shelters and conceals. Holds in reserve and exposes to view. The screen: at once the visible projection surface for images, and that which prevents one from seeing the other side' (D: 314).
31. 'As long as we ask if the concept of differing should be conceived on the basis of presence or antecedent to it, it remains one of these old signs,

enjoining us to continue indefinitely to question presence within the closure of knowledge. It must indeed be so understood, but also understood differently' (SP: 102–3).

32. Derrida describes these tiny marks of difference that notch up a second repetition as having a 'hair's breadth': 'the *designation* of that impossibility escapes the language of metaphysics only by a hairsbreadth [*par une pointe*]' (OG: 314). '*Pointe*' signifies the tip of a pen's nib and thus enjoys the breadth of a hyphen, a written mark.
33. This 'all' is crucial. It implies that the notion of trace is not confined to creatures of language, nor is it confined to the biological real, but extends to the objects of all sciences, including inorganic material. This is a problem that we shall pose to Derrida, that by demonstrating to his satisfaction the impossibility of any strict oppositional differentiations, he risks leaving himself bereft of the means to postulate *any* relevant differences between the various levels of material objects and life-forms.
34. At almost exactly the same time as Derrida published these thoughts in the form of a monograph, Lacan was also recognising 'DNA' (which is of course a string of letters) as 'a swarm of signifiers – conveying quite specified characters' (SXIV: 22/2/67)
35. 'These possibilities or necessities, without which there would be no language, *are themselves not only human*. It is not a question of covering up ruptures and heterogeneities. I would simply contest that they give rise to a single linear, indivisible, oppositional limit, to a binary opposition between the human and the infra-human. And what I am proposing here should allow us to take into account scientific knowledge about the complexity of "animal languages", genetic coding, all forms of marking within which so-called human language, as original as it might be, does not allow us to "cut" once and for all where we would in general like to cut' (EW: 117).
36. The word is indeed Derrida's (SM: 168–9; R: 79), although these passages do date from after Gasché's intervention (1986), which is sometimes thought to be the origin of the term.
37. Agamben has skilfully pointed this out as Derrida's concern: 'What is unnamable [*sic*] is *that there are names*' (Agamben 1999: 211); the 'anonymity of the name' (Agamben 1999: 214); and quoting Heidegger's 'On the way to language', 'there is no word for the word' (ibid.) (cf. Agamben 1995 [1985]: 105–6).
38. Derrida acutely recognises this in Lacan: 'This omnipresence of a condition of possibility, this permanent implication, in every signifier, of the "signifier of signifiers"' (PC: 477, n 56).
39. '[O]ne cannot attempt to deconstruct this transcendence without descending, across the inherited concepts, towards the unnameable' (SP: 77). Deconstruction must 'designate the crevice through which the yet unnameable glimmer beyond the closure can be glimpsed' (OG: 14).

'The unnameable is the play which makes possible nominal effects, the relatively unitary and atomic structures that are called names' (MP: 26). And: 'this unnameable movement of *difference-itself*, that I have strategically nicknamed *trace*, *reserve*, or *différance*, could be called writing only within the *historical* closure, that is to say within the limits of science and philosophy' (OG: 93).

40. 'Determination' has a discreet but persistent presence in Derrida's work. In 'Violence and Metaphysics', Derrida speaks of the question as such being determined as soon as it enters philosophy (WD: 98–9), and we have seen him refer to the fact that 'the positive *sciences* of signification can only describe the *work* and the *fact* of *différance*, the determined differences and the determined presences that they make possible' (OG: 63). Derrida refers his quest to relieve the indeterminate of determinations to Heidegger's notion of a history of *words* for *being*, which effectively, though without the negative teleology and archaeology presumed to dog Heidegger's history, is very close to Derrida's: 'In examining the state just *before all determinations of being*, destroying the securities of onto-theology, such a meditation [as Heidegger's] contributes, quite as much as the most contemporary linguistics, to the dislocation of the unity of the sense of being, that is, in the last instance, the unity of the word' (OG: 22, my italics).
41. If one can never leave a certain order to stand outside of it, how will it ever become a question? Derrida refers to 'the free act of the question, which frees itself from the totality of what precedes it in order to be able to gain access to this totality' (WD: 210).
42. 'The future can only be anticipated in the form of an absolute danger. It is that which breaks absolutely with constituted normality and can only be proclaimed, *presented*, as a sort of monstrosity. [. . .] [T]hat which guides our future anterior' (OG: 5). Later, Derrida even describes the future as the possibility of absolute *evil* (cf. SM: 175).
43. 'Apparently "formalist", this *indifference to the content* has perhaps the value of giving one to think the necessarily *pure* and purely necessary form of the future as such, [. . .] the necessarily formal necessity of its possibility – in short, in its law. [. . .] It is what we are nicknaming the messianic without messianism' (SM: 73, my italics).
44. Perhaps Borch-Jacobsen's critique of the subject of the enunciation also latches onto this *opposition* of the symbolic and the real in Lacan. What we are about to show is that the later Lacan does not persist with such an understanding, thus rendering this critique only partially valid (cf. Borch-Jacobsen 1991: 190–1).
45. This is apparent at least as early as 1964: 'this opposition of nature and institution, of *physis* and *nomos* (which also means, of course, a distribution and division regulated in fact by *law*) which a meditation on writing should disturb' (OG: 44). (The title of Part II of *Of*

Grammatology is precisely 'Nature, Culture, Writing', writing forming a third that could not neatly be distributed between the two terms of the opposition.)

46. '[T]he essence or the energy of the *graphein* as the originary effacement of the proper name' (OG: 108; cf. OG: 109; MP: 243–4; PC: 359).

3

The real and the development of the imaginary

In Chapter 2, we demonstrated that the name-of-the-father issues in an oppositional understanding of the relationship between the real and the symbolic, and that this understanding must be deconstructed. In this chapter, we shall see how the necessity of deconstruction dawned on *Lacan*, and how it took place. We have focused almost exclusively on just two elements of Lacan's thought: the real and the symbolic. But there is a third: the imaginary. The real and the symbolic could have been opposed only if a lesser importance was ascribed to the *imaginary*, for the imaginary could precisely have mediated *between* the two. We shall see that, despite its presence and potential in Lacan's early work, the imaginary was left in abeyance, particularly in the work of his middle period, from the 1950s. And yet later it came to assume an equal status, in the threefold that Lacan writes in the form of three-ringed Borromean knot or 'chain', 'the Borromean knot, which is not a knot [*nœud*] but a chain [*chaîne*]' (SXXIII: 129).[1] In this chapter we shall therefore follow the unfolding of the imaginary, and at the same time, the effect this has on Lacan's understanding of the relationship between the symbolic and the real, and particularly his understanding of the real.

If the name-of-the-father undermines what the phallus implies regarding the functioning of the signifier, might the phallus, freed from the *archē* of the name-of-the-father, allow Lacan to develop his own 'deconstructive' notion of the signifier, and, at the same time, of the real?

Derrida always identifies a 'deconstructive resource' in each text that he reads, a second or 'minor' reading that offers an alternative to the metaphysical relation to the outside of the text presented by the 'major' reading.[2] But Lacan's phallus is not of this order. It is rather a thread which Lacan can seize and follow in order to carry out his own version of deconstruction, his own rethinking of the relation between the real and the symbolic, which is not strictly compatible with Derrida's. The presence of this phallus and indeed of the imaginary from the very beginning of Lacan's work seems to be only a slight twist, and it is – as we shall see – an element which Derrida's reading explicitly dismisses: 'I have never been convinced of the necessity of this conceptual tripartition' (P: 84). We hope to demonstrate why Derrida was forced to adopt this attitude.

At the end of Chapter 1, we made a promise to return to a strand that was left hanging. It was precisely the thread of the phallus and in particular its opening of the symbolic onto the imaginary. The phallus embodied elements of both the symbolic and the imaginary: it was the imaginary form which anticipated the oppositional character of the symbolic. If a third element mediates between the symbolic and the real might this not have troubled in advance any complacent assertion that the real and the symbolic are *simply* opposed by Lacan? However, the phallus does not ameliorate this opposition in the way that Derrida's quasi-transcendentals do, by suggesting the transcendental event of the origin of oppositions; it allows Lacan to ask after another kind of genesis, the *chronological* emergence of the oppositional structure. This is not (just) to think the transcendental event which constantly differentiates the two halves of an opposition, but to think how one could actually have been *produced* by the other. It is by means of the imaginary mediation between the pre-symbolic real and the fully constituted symbolic that this can be achieved. Thus psychoanalytic theory also asks questions about the chronological genesis of the signifier and does not simply pose transcendental questions from the standpoint of a fully-formed and infinite symbolic order in which we are always already trapped.

For Derrida, any finite symbolic order must suture itself against the infinity of signifiers from which it is drawn and upon which it depends. It seems as if this suture occurs simply because man's finite consciousness is unable to comprehend an infinity of signifiers and so mistakes this infinity for a moment of full presence (the transcendental signified) that is then taken to precede and condition that order, to supply a moment at which the reference from signifier to signifier will stop and so finitise a particular symbolic system. For Lacan it seems as if the process by which the suture is made is different, and precisely because it involves the imaginary, and this point of suture *tells us more* about the *past* of the signifier than Derrida believes the archi-trace to reveal. It is as if the imaginary gives us another way out of the symbolic. (Though at the same time, as we shall see, it also installs something like another barrier between ourselves and the real.)

Not only does the imaginary help to explain the moment of finitisation, it also allows us to posit an explanation of the necessarily prior moment of *in*finitisation, the very emergence of the signifying system itself. Thus, by way of the imaginary, Lacan would explain those strange steps which lead up to that supposedly mythical moment of infinitisation, the creation of the novel symbolic order of culture as an infinity of traces. Psychoanalysis would attempt to understand this motion *not* from the perspective of the symbolic, which can only retell its origin mythically in terms of signifiers, but to approach it from the standpoint of the real, to see how the real itself can produce the infinite other that is the signifier. Lacan finds it necessary to invoke the imaginary in order to explain how such a thing as the symbolic could ever have arisen. It is a notion he inherits from the Gestaltist and Uexküllian studies of the *animal*'s relation to its world, which Lacan invokes in order to understand precisely why human beings do *not* enjoy the animal's functional relationship with its environment.

Lacan accepts Derrida's critique of oppositions, but finds another way to exceed the opposition. By means of their animal nature, creatures of language retain a trace of the chronological precedent of the symbolic order and can therefore infer more about the real than the mere fact that it must condition the signifier, that it traces. It is as if for Derrida the animal in man is accessible to him only in a proto-linguistic form: the animal is – for us – just like man, part of the all-encompassing system of the trace. For Lacan, the animal in man tells us something else: that the real must also be capable of forming *images*. Not that this will exhaust the real since we infer the imaginary capacity of the real as a condition of possibility of the *animal*, and thus the inference is still transcendental; but it is, so to speak, *genetically inspired*.

This is all to insist that we do not know where or what we are. We cannot rest content in the belief that our current situation is so exhaustively defined by the linguistic. Psychoanalysis insists that the very nature of the present must be determined at least partly on the basis of its genesis. This means that philosophy is compelled by the insight of psychoanalysis to open itself to the natural sciences which deal with the processes of the non- and pre-human real, sciences of the real (evolutionary biology, animal ethology, palaeoanthropology, ethnology, mathematics).

If the transcendental is understood by electing some element of the conditioned to the place of the condition (as writing is transposed to become *archi*-writing), is it not crucial to understand in full the possibilities of the system from which the election takes place? This is how the genetic approach relates to the transcendental. The genetic approach provides us with a more complete understanding of the nature of the system in which we reside, and from which we must then ask transcendental questions regarding how we are to exceed this system and to access its other, the real. So Lacan's approach is *still transcendental* in that it believes one can reach the real other only subtractively, by abstracting from the system in which the human being currently finds himself. But after attending to this system's *genesis* Lacan finds it necessary to abstract from *more* than just language. It is also necessary to abstract from the imaginary. Without an attention to genesis, *this* aspect of transcendental thought would never have become apparent, as we shall argue that it did not for Derrida, who was in this respect 'too much at home with the philosophers' (R: 56).

Thus the necessity to think transcendentally is not circumvented – after all, it is not as if the name-of-the-father is entirely eradicated by Lacan; only its status and uniqueness are put in question. For Lacan, however, we can infer not only that the real must be able to trace, in order for the signifier to be possible, we can also infer that the real must enjoy certain *imaginary* characteristics, a certain unity and wholeness that are characteristic of the Gestalt, one of the fundamental references in Lacan's understanding of the imaginary.

Thus we do not merely determine the real as the real-of-the-symbolic (the archi-trace) but also as the real-of-the-*imaginary*. Like Derrida, Lacan believes that this determination is inevitable. One cannot see round one's own corner – Nietzsche's metaphor for our being irremediably hemmed in by a certain horizon. Lacan thus insists on a modesty which his earlier work did not betray, confining our attempts to understand the real other to the real that is constitutive for each of the symbolic and the imaginary but *identical with neither*, just as the archi-trace constitutes language for Derrida but is not to be identified with a fully fledged signifier. The real is the otherness which constitutes the symbolic and the imaginary but is irreducible to and exceeds both.

This is why Lacan will propose *two* ways in which we must understand the real, one on the basis of the symbolic and one on the basis of the imaginary: the real-of-the-symbolic is the *letter*, while the real-of-the-imaginary is the *objet petit a*, the object-cause of desire which is encountered in the *fantasy*, the symbolic's mythical yet *imaginary* depiction of its own origins, of that which was lost due to the emergence of the symbolic and which our desire apparently strives to recapture.

This chapter tells the story of the development of the imaginary from Lacan's early work to his late work. At the same time it explains the necessary alteration in his understanding of the relation between the real and symbolic, to which the development of the imaginary is *necessarily* related. It will turn out that the real is nothing besides the lack in the imaginary and the symbolic that necessitates their mutual dependence.

Thus, the chapter will culminate in a description of the way in which the real is understood insofar as we subtract from the *imaginary* and attempt to 'transcend' *that* element of our current situation. This will be the real as the object *a* of the fantasy. In Chapter 4, we shall complement this with an examination of the specifically *Lacanian* understanding of the real-of-the-*symbolic* that we have met already in Derrida. We shall show precisely how Lacan's account of the 'letter' differs from Derrida's account of the archi-trace, to which it nevertheless remains close. Lacan's writing differs from Derrida's in invoking the *imaginary* dimension which will always have promised to open the transcendental approach onto a genetic approach. Lacan's account of archi-writing will demonstrate that the letter is a remnant *within* the symbolic of the proto-symbolic mark which actually preceded the symbolic's constitution and formed part of its chronological genesis.

But to begin with, let us attend to the question of Lacan's own genesis, which Derrida perhaps does not.

The genetic approach

The genetic approach has two aspects, one of which we have addressed above, and both of which are considered redundant by Derrida: it involves an attention to the development of a thinker's thought, and allows for the simple possibility that his or her position might change so radically that a reading which attends exclusively to a text whose position has been surpassed simply cannot do justice to that thinker. It broaches the possibility that a thinker's thought *cannot* be summarised by one isolated text. In this chapter, we shall extend the punctate moment pinpointed by Derrida's deconstruction and envisage the entire length of Lacan's development.

Deconstruction does not address genesis in this sense, it can only take a synchronic snapshot of a thinker's works. Derrida is quite explicit that Lacan's thought changes over time[3] and that by addressing just one of his pieces he is not attempting to state anything about Lacan's thought as a whole beyond the frame of the particular work or works under consideration.[4] This is part of the nature of deconstruction: it opens any one finite text onto an infinite textuality upon which its meaning can be shown to depend.

However, this approach is particularly problematic in Lacan's case, and it is revealing that although Derrida acknowledges the change in Lacan's later thought, he never returns to consider it in any detail, as if it were simply not *safe* to return. This failure to envisage the entirety of Lacan's thought allows Derrida to ignore the development of the notion of the imaginary. The approach that isolates a chronological and logical moment in Lacan's work sees neither the development of the imaginary in a genetic rethinking of the relationship between the symbolic and the real, *nor* the presence of imaginary elements in Lacan's *earlier* work, specifically the imaginary form of the phallic Gestalt. This is the serif responsible for a clinamen that is revealed only in the unfolding of the *entire* trajectory of Lacan's development. It is precisely the imaginary that allows Lacan to surpass the deconstructibility of his thought *and* the deconstructive understanding of the relation between symbolic and real.

Derrida's trajectory intersects Lacan's only at a certain moment. It cannot look left and right to encompass the entire development of that thought and thus cannot see the twist at the beginning and the consequently novel position it arrives at in the end. By charging ahead, blinkered, on its own path, it can only subordinate the deconstructible moment of Lacan's thought to its *own* deconstruction, and ignore or marginalise everything else. It can only deconstruct. Derrida's trajectory, fully formed from the very beginning, remains utterly unchanged by its encounter with Lacan. It ploughs ahead, and indeed churns up his thought, marking it with its trace, rather brutally, indifferent to the relief of its actual terrain and the processes which formed it, trampling over the unnoticed seed that will still flourish in spite of the ravages of the furrowing. But for Derrida, the path is one-way, once travelled he will never return to it. Occasionally, he will be compelled to glance backwards, called by his unflagging honesty to admit that Lacan has changed in a radical way. But he cannot go back. He will have gone too far down the one path which any great thinker is compelled to follow. And perhaps Derrida dimly senses that Lacan has something which is not only not susceptible of deconstruction but which offers a genuine *challenge* to his deconstructive approach. This is something I believe he was capable of intimating, as we shall see in his perturbed response to the proximity of another such thinker, Deleuze.

Here the privilege of our 'scholarly' perspective becomes apparent. From this elevated, somewhat removed eyrie, atop an ivory tower, unable to intervene in the battle of the giants, we can see that to traverse the path as Derrida does is to treat what it finds scattered along its way either as an object or as a traveller who can be travelling in one of only two directions: his own direction or the opposite direction. There is only one path. The limited nature of this traversal can be seen only by one who does not walk *this path alone*, but surveys a larger territory, to map out *other* paths. We have seen Lacan approaching the intersection with Derrida *from another direction*, with a different starting point, bearings, and aim. And he seems to us to carry on, winding up a different track *after* this encounter, emerging into the mountain air, from which vantage point he would survey Derrida's travails: 'I showed him the way . . . (but alas . . .)'

The very fact that Lacan *realises* that his early work is 'deconstructible' should make us feel uneasy about the satisfaction with which deconstructionists have left Lacan behind, assigned to the archives of logocentrism, having defused any threat they might have felt emanating from his hugely influential work.[5] If Lacan realised his work was 'criticisable' in this fashion, is it plausible that his final position would remain equally vulnerable? And even if deconstruction is to confine itself to finite texts, is it not obliged to attend to *all* such texts, and not just those which are so jointed as to be susceptible to the incisions of its scalpel?

We isolated if not a single text, at least a single *moment* of Lacan's work in Chapter 1, to ready it for deconstruction in Chapter 2. In this chapter we shall focus on the way in which Lacan's understanding of the real, symbolic and imaginary *changes*. We shall demonstrate that this alteration necessitates a renewed attention to the role of the *imaginary*, which will have appeared almost entirely *irrelevant* to the deconstructibility we have outlined in the previous two chapters. Indeed, this elision had to be made in order for the deconstruction to be carried out successfully. This is precisely why we suppressed it as far as we could in Chapter 1, to indicate its genuine abeyance in Lacan's earlier work and to demonstrate that this abeyance rendered a deconstruction both possible and necessary.

This chapter falls into two parts:

The first demonstrates the alteration that took place in Lacan's understanding of the relationship between the real and the symbolic. It begins from the period we have so far isolated in his work and shows that Lacan did indeed understand the real and the symbolic to be opposed to one another. This suggests that Lacan believed in the myth of the one unique name-of-the-father. But we shall see just as clearly that this understanding later changed, and it changed in tandem with a rethinking of the transcendental notion of the name-of-the-father, the metalanguage in its distinctness from the object-language. It is as if the monolith here begins to crumble or suffer duplication, and the phallic stones begin their re-erection.

The second part of the chapter demonstrates how the unfolding of the *imaginary* made these changes both possible and necessary. We trace its development from a submissive position in Lacan's early work to a crucial role in the later work, where it assumes the guise of the object *a* of the fantasy, which allows the symbolic order to form a totality.

I. THE REAL AND THE SYMBOLIC

Chiesa opines that one of the reasons for Lacan's shift in his understanding of the relation between the symbolic and the real was 'the necessity finally to thematise the Real in a more direct and convincing way' (Chiesa 2007: 124). Lacan seems to express this in his ventriloquial exclamation: ' "Finally, he is going to speak to us about this famous real which had up to now remained in the shadows" ' (SIV: 31). The lack of profound investigation, which was to be remedied in Seminars IV, V, VI, and VII (1954–60), had allowed Lacan to rest content with a negative, oppositional account of the real. The real was 'the impossible' (cf. SXIV: 10/5/67), 'at the limit of our experience' (SIV: 31). It was acceptable to have spoken for so many years without investigating it for the very simple reason that one *could not* talk about it. One could say no more than that it was 'impossible' to speak about.

However, there were already elements of Lacan's thought which could have been mobilised against this, which seem to acknowledge that the oppositional understanding of the symbolic and the real is a retrospective illusion created by the symbolic and does not give a *true* picture of the real. As we shall see in the second part of this chapter, these elements are ones which refer to the role of the imaginary in the very generation of the symbolic from the real.

The symbolic is not the real

In Lacan's middle period, the real and the symbolic were placed in an *oppositional* relationship by virtue of the transcendence of the name-of-the-father, the prohibition of incest that marked *every* symbolic order as different from any natural order. The dominance of the name-of-the-father forced Lacan to understand the real as a full presence that preceded the differentiality of the symbolic order. To the extent that one believes in the myth of the prohibition of incest one will *oneself* speak of the real only negatively, as that which is *not* symbolic, that which *lacks* its defining trait, differentiality: 'the signifier [. . .] introduces difference as such into the real' (SIX: 6/12/61). And this is precisely how Lacan speaks of the real, early on. *The real is everything that the symbolic is not*: 'the real, or what is perceived as such, is what resists symbolisation absolutely' (SI: 66). And Lacan is quite clear that we have *no way* in which to access any more positive aspect of the real: 'we have no means of apprehending this real – on any level and not only on that of knowledge – except via the go-between of the symbolic' (SII: 97).

If the symbolic is a differential order, in which entities are individuated solely by their differences from other entities, then *real* entities must be those entities which are not individuated with reference to anything other than themselves. They are substances. They do not require anything else in order to be what they are. Everything real is self-identical: in a word, immediately *present*. 'Stars are real, integrally real, in principle, there is absolutely nothing about them pertaining to an alterity with respect to themselves, they are purely and simply what they are' (SII: 238).[6] This real is what Derrida refers to as 'authenticity' or 'propriety', an absolute self-belonging or self-proximity (*chez-soi*), the *para* of *parousia*, the being alongside itself of the *ousia* in presence, uninterrupted by difference. The real is, in other words, the presence which precedes and exceeds the signifier. The real is *presence* or substance.

This explains Lacan's two common locutions for describing the real in his earlier works. First, the real is always in its place: 'Everything that is real is always and obligatorily in its place' (SIV: 38). This is what distinguishes real things from the signifier, rendering real things 'speechless': 'The fact that we always find them [stars] in the same place is one of the reasons why they don't speak' (SII: 238). Lacan sometimes describes this as the real's *returning* to the same place: 'the real is what returns always to the same place' (SIX:

30/5/62). 'What assured [Aristotle], in nature, of the truthfulness of the Other as real were those things that always return to the same place, namely the celestial spheres' (SIII: 65). This notion of the real endures until at least 1959: 'Reality [*réalité*] faces man – and that is what interests him in it – both as being structured [by the signifier] and as being that which presents itself in his experience as that which always returns to the same place' (SVII: 74–5).

The real is always in its place because it is not part of a differential structure in which positive elements can take *different* places because their only relevant value is given by their place in a structure and not by their actual content, which is arbitrary. This returning to its place can be reconciled with the real's remaining in its place if one understands this orbit to be the reflexive loop of selfhood which constitutes propriety, self-sameness without reference to otherness, the propriety of the individual as the state of absolute self-proximity, the very nature of presence as *para-ousia*.

Because real entities are defined in their nature only by themselves, their 'place' is always where they are, and as the loop of their reflexive self-hood returns on itself rather than making any detour through another, so the entity itself may be said to return to its place. Perhaps its place is nothing other than this orbit. This would be exemplified by natural phenomena that exist independently of human culture: the regular circuit of the stars, planets, moon, and sun, reflected on earth in the rising and receding of the tides, the passing of the days, and the changing of the seasons. Nature's place is *in* its cycle, which remains self-same. The identity of the entity *is* its orbit, from which it does not deviate. So the fact that the real is always in its place does not mean that it is immobile, just that wherever it moves it 'should' be there, because it moves only in the cycles of return which characterise it.

Lacan's second common locution regarding the real is that it is without fissure: 'The real is without fissure' (SII: 97). In the real there is no differentiality and no opposition. Without differentiation, there is nothing that could be understood as a gap between entities, the gap across which signification takes place, where one entity is understood as a sign and hence as a signi*fying*, pointing towards another entity and being exhausted in this pointing. There can be space, but it cannot strictly speaking be a fissure, which refers oppositionally to the banks between which the crevice runs, or a lack which implies an oppositional determination with respect to something not lacking, something present. In order to be lacking, the lack must carry the mark of a possible presence. Without the notion of a difference between an entity and its place, nothing can strictly speaking be missing.[7]

The real, therefore, is for the early Lacan a place of presence.

For the symbolic, the real is dead. There can be no possible interaction between symbolic and real. As soon as the real enters the symbolic order it becomes differentially defined and so evacuated of its self-possession, it quite simply loses itself and its realness. And if the symbolic is transposed into the real, it loses its very symbolic quality, since all signifying references are annulled.

Thus the early Lacan understands the real *exclusively* as that which the symbolic is *not*. The real and the symbolic are opposed; once the real thing enters the symbolic it must be left behind: 'the symbol first manifests itself as the killing of the [real] thing' (E: 262).

The paradox of the name-of-the-father

Lacan understands the relationship between the real and the symbolic *symbolically*, from the standpoint of the signifier. He is allowed to do so by his presupposition that there is only one name-of-the-father, that unifies all symbolic orders and so separates *everything* symbolic from the real. A *signifier* controls the border between the symbolic and the real, the very relation is appropriated unto the *symbolic*.

One must believe oneself entirely confined to the symbolic if one ventures to describe the real as 'impossible'. The name-of-the-father is responsible for this confinement. The castration instituted by the name-of-the-father and its '*non*!', the prohibition of immediacy and the institution of the law of re-presentation, absolutely forbids any transgression between the two orders.

How does the name-of-the-father overpower the phallus? Precisely because the name(*nom*)-of-the-father as the '*non*!' of the father amounts to the castration of the imaginary phallus that might have mediated between the real and the symbolic: 'The object is imaginary. The castration of which it is the stake is always of an imaginary object' (SIV: 38). The 'castration' of the child from the mother – for the child is the mother's phallus – is what is enjoined by the name-of-the-father. The name-of-the-father sees to it that, for those properly situated within the symbolic, no traffic with the real takes place, nothing 'incestuous'. The intermediary that might have been, the imaginary, is cut off.

Thanks to the one name-of-the-father, every symbolic order there *could be* is unified and opposed to nature. The symbolic as such is therefore universalised and homogenised. To the extent that we are human we *must* accept the name-of-the-father, and identify with the symbolic father in order to partake of the most minimal communication with others, from other symbolic orders as well as our own. The penalty for doing otherwise is either an impossible and so failed return to the real or the return of the real in psychosis, the leakage of the real as senseless into the supposedly meaningful symbolic order. In both cases this would be due to the failure of the medium of the big Other to provide access to a genuine Other beyond the imaginary relation in which one relates only to one's own image.

The father would thus occupy a paradoxical position: he would create the symbolic as a total system, a 'universe' (of discourse), turned (*versare*) towards the one (*unum*) of the father, and yet the very creation of this total symbolic system would require the exclusion of the creative origin from that which it creates. Thus the very notion of a synchronic whole is premised upon the exception of one element. Lacan would later come to recognise this as a masculine logic, and so it is fitting that it should be god-the-*father* who is exempt from his creation, the uncreated creator.

The father must be both real and yet capable of producing the symbolic, somehow occupying an intermediate position between the two, the place of the mythical 'thing' (cf. SVII: 43ff). The only signifier that is not a signifier but which is pinned unambiguously to the real is the name. It opens the signifying system and yet is not itself a signifier.

Let us establish that Lacan begins in his middle period with a blunt assertion of the genuine exception of the name-of-the-father and see how this crumbles, as Lacan sees the flaw in its logic, a flaw that Derrida well understood. The point is to realise that there is nothing unique about the signifier which is taken to govern the symbolic order; indeed it often signifies the most meagre things of all, like writing and the textile. Lacan will perform his *own* 'deconstruction' and thus come to see that the name is *not* unique. No, the name can be more or less anything.

The history of the other of the Other

Lacan begins, absolutely explicitly, from a position in which 'there *is* an other of the Other', an exception to the symbolic: 'the father qua bearer of a signifier as such, a signifier to the second degree, of a signifier which authorises and founds the whole system of signifiers' (SV: 463). 'Experience demonstrates to us at which point the backdrop [*arrière-plan*] of an Other with respect to the Other [*un Autre par rapport à l'Autre*] is indispensable, without which the universe of language [*langage*] would not know how to articulate itself' (SV: 463).[8] The name is thus a metalanguage, able to totalise the signifier as an object and determine objectively its significance. 'All language implies a metalanguage, it's already a metalanguage of its own register. It's because potentially all language is to be translated that it implies metaphrase and metalanguage, language speaking of language' (SIII: 226–7).

A discourse about language within language. A signifier which signifies the signifier and can yet be *distinguished* from all other signifiers. Metalanguage means that 'one can *extract from language*, specifically, the loci and the points where, as one might say, language speaks of itself' (SXIV: 26/4/67, my italics).

It is this myth that Lacan will soon debunk.

In deliberate and explicit contradiction of his earlier statement, Lacan later states: 'There's no such thing as a metalanguage' (SXX: 118; SXIV: 26/4/67 *et al.*; E: 737). As to Lacan's discourse: 'It is *not* a metalanguage' (SXIV: 26/4/67, my italics). In other words, language is infinite, it has no outside, and so no second language which can independently and unambiguously discourse upon it. Something has caused Lacan to lose faith in the effective suture of the symbolic order. The name-of-the-father must have been rattled. And if the signifier becomes infinite, ineptly sutured, it cannot be opposed to the real, since this presupposes an absolutely clear boundary.

And yet, Lacan does speak of the signifier and how it functions *as if* he were producing a metalanguage. One makes one's words 'serve the function' of a metalanguage: 'Just because I have written things that serve the function of forms of language doesn't mean I assure the being of metalanguage. For I would have to present that being as subsisting by itself, all alone' (SXX: 118). Lacan *performs* his metalanguage in such a way as to make it exist. The words that he uses are not in some way unique, free of the signifying ambiguity which characterises the order of which they speak. There is no name of the name in that sense. And yet Lacan finds a way to make a singularity exist, to behave and deliver his discourse in such a way that it does manage to escape, at least partially, the commonality and ambiguity which infects the language under investigation. It is precisely this singularity that Lacan will attempt to create in his works, grouped under the sign of his own *name*. Thus the name-of-the-father, the metalanguage is in this case nothing other than the surname '*Lacan*'. It is solely in his own idiosyncrasy and idiosyncratic use of language that Lacan *makes* the metalanguage exist. 'We have to show where the shaping of that metalanguage – which is not, and which *I* make ex-sist – is going' (SXX: 119, my italics).[9]

Metalanguage *is* not, and so in order to say anything, Lacan 'makes it ex-sist', he performs in such a way that something like it comes to be. To ex-sist means to 'stand outside', to stand outside that which would be its target language; to make it ex-sist means to elect some signifier to the transcendental position. Lacan tells his audience how he writes down his speeches, 'one must ensure things by writing. The latter certainly is not a metalanguage, nevertheless, though, one can make it fulfil a function that resembles it' (SXX: 121–2).

Thus one might say that Lacan's very discourse becomes, like Derrida's, a discourse on the impossibility and necessity of the transcendental. And yet the manner in which the two thinkers go about presenting it is different. It is as if Derrida is utterly self-effacing in this regard and regards his transcendental narrative as *absolutely* susceptible of usurpation, while Lacan believes that by means of his (discourse's) very *singularity*, his metadiscourse *can* achieve some especial virtue. One can still achieve the miracle of saying something true, even if it is impossible ever to get outside of language, even if such transcendence is always bound to remain anchored in that which one transcends. This is why Lacan's performances *must* have an element of masquerade, in the highly exaggerated idiosyncrasies of his mannerisms and particularly his baroque use of the signifier, which emphasise the ridiculousness, the 'idiocy' of the suggestion that these signifiers would be the only ones that could be used to express the nature of the real. It is not by self-effacement, but by self-aggrandisement that Lacan achieves some externality to the signifier and admits the impossibility of doing so; Derrida achieves this by hiding behind the texts that he reads, wearing each of them as a mask and constantly moving on, changing masks all the time.

Reading Lacan requires an extra subtlety, beyond an understanding of its signification. One must examine not just the enunciated statements but the act of enunciation, the performance of the piece, and understand what effect this has on the status of the signifiers. Lacan's whole thesis has been that signifiers can always be substituted by others as a result of their differentiality, the irrelevance of their positive content and the ultimate importance of their place in a structure. In light of this, what could be more ridiculous than presenting one unique metalanguage *about* this language, in proposing himself as the sole author of 'the truth'? What is important is creating a fantastic image – of 'Lacan' and his teaching – in all its singularity, which binds together a community, that of Lacan's students, his trainees, the psychoanalytic community. Hence the still highly hermetic nature of Lacan's thought and the immense time and devotion required to understand it.[10]

But those outside of this community, studying it as an object rather than a credo, must see it for what it is: a singularity, with a singular signifier and image occupying the place of the transcendental, and they must see that this is the very nature of any attempt to signify the signifier, to speak of the transcendental. It is a question of an each time singular *election*, an act, a performance, a masquerade of uniqueness, or perhaps a masquerade that *is* unique. One can either evacuate one's singularity altogether (Derrida) or one can assert it with the most astonishing idiosyncrasy (Lacan).

It is not as if the signifier of the signifier is simply presented as unique and thus rejected out of hand for deconstructive reasons. Rather, what Lacan comes to see is that it is possible by means of a singular act to promote a signifier to the place of the name. One's response to the impossibility of a signifier of the signifier need not be to ignore it, but to promote one's *own* peculiar name as *one* name-of-the-father. It is avowedly not general, not a universal metalanguage, but *one's own* metalanguage, that is clearly just one name in a series of names(-of-the-father). One is unique, and one can communicate this, if one has the right strategy.

Lacan indicates the impossibility of a single signifier that would represent the whole signifier with his formula, 'S(A barred)'. 'S(A barred), the signifier of the Other insofar as the Other himself in the final analysis can only be formalised, be made significant as himself marked by the signifier, in other words in so far as it imposes on us the renunciation of any metalanguage' (SIX: 21/3/62). This at the same time signifies the impossibility of the signifier's ever forming a perfect whole. This it did thanks to the suture of the name-of-the-father which was precisely a signifier of every signifier there was. S(A barred), the signifier of the *incomplete* Other or the Other's incompleteness indicates precisely the ambiguity of Lacan's position: it signifies the impossibility of itself, and yet it *is* a signifier. This signifier, we are arguing, is precisely, in *Lacan*'s case, the name 'Lacan'.

There is a signifier of the signifier, but it signifies only the impossibility of *completely* signifying it, since this would be to signify itself, and as Lacan has it, 'a signifier cannot signify itself' (SIX: 11/4/62; cf. SXIV: 14/12/66). This is precisely because it is determined differentially, and in order to have a univocal relation with, for instance, the entirety of the signifier, for the signifier as a whole to be able to signify itself, it would have to be able to determine itself, to finitise itself, to become a finite whole with a definite outside: there would need to be one signifier that defined itself. This would be the transcendental signifier.

The question is what one does in the face of the *aporia*: one needs this transcendental signifier and yet the nature of language rules it out. So one pretends. One adopts masks and one masquerades. One puts on a plurality of faces and adopts a sequence of names. The difference is perhaps one of scale. Derrida adopts a never-ending series of masks, never his own. While Lacan adopts just one mask, his own, and leaves it to the scholars to understand that this is just one in a series of obviously impossible attempts to make a unique metalanguage exist. The signifier of the barred Other is the signifier of the *subject*, the proper name, or the subject's absolutely singular symptom.

Just like the subject, the signifier is barred too; indeed, as is indicated by the ambiguity of Lacan's matheme, '$', the two overlap, the subject *is* that which the signifier finds impossible, that which is otherwise than the signifier, which doesn't quite fit in there. And why? Because the subject is the reflexive self, the moment of *self-relation* which the signifier rules out. And the subject is picked out by a name, such as 'Lacan', and this name is what comes temporarily to suture a finite symbolic order, one which we must spend a long time learning to inhabit. The single biunivocal signifier, the name of God, is impossible. There *is* a signifier of the signifier, but it is impossible, it is the subject or his redundant presence within the signifier, which opens it onto the outside, the real. The signifier for the subject is $, and this is precisely what may be superimposed upon the S(A barred) which is the impossible or impossibly unique signifier of the signifier itself.

Because such a signifier does indeed exist, rather than saying 'there is no signifier of the signifier' or 'name-of-the-father', because this signifier comes from nowhere *other* than the signifier and does not constitute an entirely *exterior* metalanguage, Lacan says, 'there is no *other* of the Other': 'there is no Other of the Other[11] [. . .] no signifier exists which might guarantee the concrete consequence of any manifestation of the signifier [in other words, eliminate the ambiguity that is introduced by the infinity of the signifier]' (SVI: 13/5/59); 'there is no Other of the Other, there is nothing that is opposed to the symbolic, site of the Other as such' (SXXIII: 55; cf. SIX: 4/4/62).

Thus, the relation of otherness which the real enjoys with respect to the symbolic must be something *other* than an opposition, the inverse symmetry of the opposition must be replaced by the asymmetry of the relation between same and other. And this other is precisely not an (opposed) other of the Other, but something immanent to the Other which is nevertheless *not* a signifier. The real is not opposed to the symbolic but is *of*-the-symbolic.

The absence of this opposed other of the Other means that there cannot be a single name-of-the-father, because for the uniqueness of the name to be maintained, the name would have to be distinct from the signifier. And the absence of the other of the Other prevents this.

We have said that a unique father could be nothing besides the monotheistic *God*. Lacan identifies the other of the Other as God in the following passage, but then states that when this is realised in its non-existence, it can take on *another name*, that of 'The Woman': 'The whole necessity of the human race being that there should be an Other of the Other. This is what is generally called God, but which analysis unveils as, quite simply, *The* woman' (SXXIII: 128). 'The-woman [*La-femme*] which is at issue is an other name of God, and this is why she doesn't exist' (SXXIII: 14). If there is no outside of the text, no 'Other of the Other', then there is no unique name, no finally proper name. Lacan has evaded the deconstructive assault. Any name that is *promoted* to the transcendental position of the name *must* be susceptible of pluralisation. Thus, God the father is replaced by a perhaps indefinite number of names. The name-of-the-father can be anything, it can even be its very opposite, a *woman*! Indeed, *the* woman.

In the title of his abortive seminar of 20 November 1963, Lacan explicitly replaces the monotheistic name-of-the-father with a plural: 'name*s* of the father'. And as he says later that academic year, this is a consequence of his realisation that it is impossible to name a single origin of the signifier as a whole, a transcendental signifier outside of the Other: 'What I had to say on the names-of-the-father had no other purpose, in fact, than to put in question the origin' (SXI: 12).

Thus Lacan refers to the name-of-the-father as a 'place' (in a signifying structure), a place that can be usurped, occupied by a *sequence* of signifiers. There is no one genuinely transcendent signifier – a proper name – but only a sequence of substitutes:

> The other of the Other exists only as a place. It finds its place even if we cannot find it anywhere in the real, even if *all we can find to occupy this place in the real is simply valid insofar as it occupies this place*, but cannot give it any other guarantee than that it is in its place. (SVII: 66, my italics)

If that which sutures the symbolic is not stable, and not something which can institute a clear border between the symbolic and the real, then the once absolute boundary that separated nature from culture has to be understood as porous. And this in several senses: it means that we are called to understand the processes in the real which produce the symbolic order, and that the 'fully constituted' symbolic is itself full of holes. And it is in these holes that the real exists, the real insofar as it can be accessed by the symbolic. In fact, these holes should be understood as something akin to an abyss, a lack of ground for the signifier, for the trace which constitutes the signifier is infinite, without end. The endless overlapping of real marks in no way provides a grounding for the signifier in some real *presence*, which would be a transcendental signified in the traditional sense. This real is precisely what constitutes the referral of one signifier to another and infinite others. One might say therefore that because the real is *inside* the symbolic, no one piece of signifying material can ever be stable, can ever remain in its place, but can always be replaced by others, since the only thing that defines that signifier is its place.

The hole in the symbolic is never fully corked, as it might have been by a transcendent signifier like the name-of-the-father. The hole retains its status as hole and is only temporarily *masked* by a series of always fleeting signifiers.

Whatever fills the place of the name is thus only temporarily and contingently privileged. However, to retain the reference back to the incorrectly understood transcendental function of the father as monolithic signifier of the signifier, Lacan retains the syntagm 'name-of-the-father' but pluralises it, to indicate the enduring *necessity* of the transcendental and the inadequacy of any *one* transcendental.

There is now *no* sign, except for simulacra, masquerades of signs. The univocal signified remains *permanently* castrated from any signifier in the symbolic. Castration remains the law, despite the name-of-the-father. Thus the insight of the phallus, the imaginary intercessor between the real and the symbolic, is no longer overpowered by the name. Thus Lacan slips the chains of his originally deconstructible position and rethinks the relationship between the real and the symbolic.

The imaginary suture

If there *is* an other of the Other, it cannot be symbolic, it must be real. And this gives a new sense to the real as 'impossible'. It is not the real as abstractly opposed to the symbolic, but the real as the symbolic's inability to totalise itself, both to be finite and to *be* entirely symbolic: 'The real, which is to say impossible, Other of the Other' (SXXIII: 64). The real occupies the symbolic solely as a gap, as that to which the symbolic can never be adequate, as the very *fact* that the symbolic can never be finished. The real is nothing besides the absence of a complete finite totality of the signifier. We shall explicate this in Chapter 4 as the infinity of real traces which go to compose the symbolic order. This infinity, this other, is precisely what the 'real' (of language) is.

As that which refuses to be subordinated to meaning, as that which renders the symbolic infinite, the real trace creates an element of senselessness within language. The real is thus both the necessary condition of meaning (as the necessary condition of the signifier from which meaning is generated) and the excess of meaning, condition of both possibility and impossibility. As Lacan has it, 'the real has, and does not have, a meaning [*sens*]' (SXXIII: 134). And yet, the symbolic *is* in a certain way sutured, it does have a meaning, at least to the level at which some form of intersubjective communication is possible. We have implied that it *is* sutured, but only temporarily and by a series of contingent signifiers. This is not altogether true. And it is precisely here that Lacan begins to depart *fundamentally* from Derrida's notion of 'transcendental (s)election'. What allows the suture to take place is something in the region of the *imaginary*.

The impossibility of a finite totality, and the consequent impossibility of all human beings' sharing a common symbolic order, is compensated for by the *fantasy* (*le fantasme*). The fantasy 'masks' the real in the sense of the infinity of the signifier. Each of the series of signifiers that claim to signify the signifier as a whole is not sufficiently firmly installed unless it is accompanied by a fantasy. The fantasy lets us believe that the master signifier *is* the master, and therefore that the symbolic is a finite entity with a meaning. 'Meaning is the result of an intersection between the imaginary and the symbolic' (SXXIII: 72). Perhaps we might say that it is the *fantasmatic* element of a particular signifier that allows it to occupy a transcendental position for us.

No finite signifier can ever fully plug the gap that infiltrates the symbolic due to its construction by an infinite number of real traces. The last yard needs to be filled in by the fantasy. How can an impossible, infinite number of traces be assimilated by the finite subject? With the assistance of fantasy.

The real-of-the-symbolic as the infinity of traces is domesticated and rendered intelligible *as* the real-of-the-*imaginary*. The real-of-the-imaginary is the object *a*, the cause of desire, depicted in the fantasy, which thus makes the absolutely unreachable infinity seem like something that could one day be attained, and that is *desirable*. The infinity of the trace is given a positive (imaginary) form as the regulative ideal that is the object of *desire*. The infinity of the real is rendered accessible to us as the infinite striving of desire.

It is as if early on Lacan fell victim to the illusion of the fantasy, the illusion of ideology, that there was a permanent suture of the symbolic, and that this suture could be carried out by the signifier *alone*. In truth, the suture was illusory: in a word, imaginary. It is not ahistorical and universal, but historical and contingent upon the particular symbolic order one happens to inhabit. The myth is not a set of signifiers that recount one's origin, it is an image.

The fantasy is Lacanian theory's explicit admission that it does not believe in God any more. It amounts to an acceptance of the empty place of the divine and the impossibility of filling it in with a signifier, the name-of-the-father, along with the necessity of completing this suture with a fantasy. God exists only in the fantasies of the necromancers, living in the shadow of the one God's death. Famously, Lacan states that God is dead but does not know it (SVII: 184), and we might say that it is as well for the existence of community that we do not let him in on the fact.

The role of the phallus in the actual origin of the symbolic order, its imaginary form, which anticipates the signifier itself, is reflected in the signifier's own reflection on its origin, since the only way it can understand this origin is by way of an *image*. God is not a name, a signifier, but a historically and culturally specific fantasy, which is how, individually and collectively, the meaning of the symbolic is finally determined – or determined enough for there to *be* community, which is to say a place in which intersubjective communication can succeed.[12]

Thus Lacan begins to approach the real by way of the fantasy, with Freud's tales from *Totem and Taboo*, the fiat of God, and even the prohibition of incest, the Oedipus complex, understood as mythical *images*.[13] The signifier is given an image of the real, and through this fantastic image, the real presents itself to the signifier in a manageable form, the infinity of the real trace *framed* and thus limited. The myth – perhaps the 'primal scene', always staged later, by means of a '*mise-en-scène*' – is always a myth of the origin of the signifier in its arising *out of* the real.

So the imaginary has two roles: one genetic, and one transcendental. The phallic form *actually does* play a part in the genesis of the signifier; and looking back, an image is used transcendentally by the signifier, or by creatures of language, to *explain* this generation in a myth or fantasy. It was not merely a deconstruction which led Lacan to change his understanding of the transcendental, but also a reflection on the *genesis* of the symbolic order. Hyppolite, the Hegelian, often urges Lacan in his early seminars in the direction of the genesis of the symbolic, in order to ameliorate the appearance that the signifier of the name-of-the-father is simply transcendental.

Factually, chronologically speaking, human culture *has not* always been here, and *did not* arise all at once, as a creation sprung from the mind of god. The mere fact of anthropological, 'evolutionary' evidence compels us to approach the symbolic in another way than in its fully constituted form. It is when Lacan is forced to approach the signifier from this other point of view that the appearance of an absolutely unique name-of-the-father and an oppositional separation between the real and the symbolic is tempered. And it is precisely here that Lacan finds himself compelled to renew his appeal to the imaginary.

II. THE IMAGINARY

The development of the imaginary

We have let it be imagined that, to all (deconstructive) intents and purposes, the imaginary is absent from the middle period of Lacan's work. But it is indeed present, and Lacan is at times forced to say things about it which, if unfolded, would threaten his transcendental understanding of the signifier from within. We indicated this almost as an appendix to Chapter 1, just before it was trampled into the dust by deconstruction.

The imaginary is present in Lacan's earlier work in the guise of the phallus, and the phallus was already recognised as the *hinge* of the real and the symbolic. The phallus can occupy this position precisely because it has both a symbolic and an imaginary aspect. It is a product of the real, but it is an image *of* the symbolic. It was only in the middle of the 1950s in his fourth and fifth Seminars that Lacan would come to substantiate his earlier, marginal comments on the phallus, but it was *always* involved in a *chronological* understanding of the relation between the real and the symbolic.

This position and function of the imaginary persists and develops in light of the rethinking of the name-of-the-father we have chronicled: the collapse of the uniqueness of the father opened up the possibility that the oppositional understanding of the real and the symbolic might be rethought. Thus we shall demonstrate the serif in Lacan's trajectory which, when the time is right, will take it in a direction that leads beyond deconstruction. At the end of this path, in Chapter 4, we shall turn back to survey Derrida's thought from the Lacanian standpoint we will have reached, and thus finally address the most fundamental issues that lie between them.

There are three stages in Lacan's assumption of the mediating role of the imaginary: (a) the phylogenetic dimension of the evolution of the symbolic from out of the real; (b) the ontogenetic dimension of the individual's accession *to* the symbolic order, which involves the imaginary phallus as an image of the symbolic order in the Oedipus complex; and (c) the quasi-imaginary suturing of the symbolic in the fantasy: this is precisely the transcendental moment. Here we can begin to demonstrate that an attention to genesis must cause us to rethink our philosophical – and that is to say, transcendental – outlook. It is the synchronous moment whereby the symbolic domesticates the senseless real that remains within it, limiting the infinite real of the trace.

The imaginary beginning

It is not just that Lacan's early seminars contained the imaginary element in the triad of symbolic, real and imaginary, his very first theoretical intervention of any significance came in the form of the 'mirror stage', the mirror *image*. This formed part of a *pre-philosophical* attempt to explain the genesis of the human being from a natural state. It describes the fault which arises in the human animal that necessitates the cultural-symbolic crutch, which is a failure of the imaginary to ensure the actualisation of man's survival instincts.

Lacan was attempting to explain purely genetically how culture could have arisen from nature. A deficit in the human imagination, a collection of schematic images which relate instincts to the objects in the world that would satisfy them, necessitates the intervention of symbolic culture.

The imaginary in animals

The imaginary is the animal within us. It is that which remains of the animal kingdom and whose corruption explains our differentiation from it. The imaginary, for certain contingent physiological reasons, malfunctions in man. Lacan does not accept a philosophical authorisation for this view – Rousseau, Nietzsche – but bases it on empirical work in the extra-philosophical sciences. Following Jakob von Uexküll and the Gestalt ethologists, Lacan understands the instincts in animals to be governed by certain *images*.[14] The stimulus to which instincts respond is a certain 'meaningful' imaginary form presented by elements of the external world, which appeals to the animal and triggers a response. The instinctual partakes of the realm of the *imaginary*. But what precisely *is* the imaginary?

In the animal ethology of von Uexküll, the world of an animal is understood to be composed of those perceptible elements within it which had some relevance to the survival and reproduction of the animal, triggers that sparked off certain instinctive behaviours.[15] Perceptual capacities in successfully adapted organisms have generally evolved only so far as is necessary for that animal to be able to perceive those elements of its environment which are relevant to the survival of its kind: indeed, the sum-total of these elements *constitute* its 'environment' (*Umwelt*, 'surrounding world' [*Welt*]). These constitute those elements which would inhibit its survival and reproduction (enemy, danger, poison) and those which are necessary for it (mate, food). The sight of an enemy triggers the fleeing cycle, while the sight of a potential mate triggers the mating ritual. Lacan describes these environmental triggers as 'the rails upon which animal behaviour is conducted towards its natural aims' (SIII: 9). Images are the 'guide to life' (SIII: 9). They constitute those points in the real which evoke a pre-given response in the animal. These images populate the animal world, giving to the world of each species its characteristic structure: 'The structuring of the animal world is dominated by a certain number of fundamental images which give this world its lines of *force majeure*' (SII: 165).

These elements are those bits of the real which, due to the nature of the animal's perceptual system, are endowed with a certain '*significance*' for that animal. This is the origin of the elements' 'appeal': 'the actualisations of instinct would not occur without a call from the environment [*un appel environnemental*]' (SII: 86). The animal's 'environment' consists of those elements which 'appeal' to the animal, which constitute a call. This call evokes a single unequivocal response on the part of the animal. There is a one-to-one relation between the 'signifier' in the environment and the 'signified' of the 'signifier', the response: the animal's relation to its environment constitutes 'signs' in the proper Saussurean sense:[16]

> animal psychology [. . .] has emphasised lines of force in the world, in the *Umwelt* of the animal, lines of forces, configurations which are for it preformed points of appeal corresponding to its needs, that is to say to what is also called its *Innenwelt*, the structure linked with the preservation of its form. (SII: 111)

Lacan describes these 'configurations' which 'figure' something for the animal with the German word for 'figures', '*Gestalten*', or quite simply as 'images'. These images are the elementary, indissoluble units that compose the animal's world, the minimal atoms that its perceptual apparatus can apprehend.

It might be asked why these would be described as 'images', since often in the animal world they are not *visual* stimuli, but matters of smell, touch, feel, and so on. The answer might be that to speak of the pre-linguistic animal world we must retroactively import words from the *human* realm, and in man the visual function takes on the primary role, his upright stance relieving olfaction of much of its relevance for survival, certainly for sexual reproduction, whereas smell is primordial in many other mammals (cf. SIX: 29/11/61). 'In man, the imaginary is reduced, specialised, centred on the specular image' (SI: 282). Hence we understand the elements which 'appeal' to all senses as (visual) 'images'.

Another reason for using the word 'image' is the location of the *imagination* and the image in traditional philosophical thought, in a space between the concept and the intuition, representation and immediate presentation, the subject and the object. The images are *schemata*, schemes which map onto certain features of the real that are *susceptible* of being perceived, by that particular organism, and in man's case, ultimately having concepts applied to them. Lacan does indeed refer to Kant's schemata on this point.[17]

The word 'image' is also used to capture the notion that these points of appeal should be understood as non-decomposable wholes.[18] Their stimulating force derives not from any analysable element belonging to them, but from their very totality: they are those elements which the animal's perceptual system must treat as elementary units. This is why Lacan describes them as '*Gestalten*' or 'total forms'. Thus Gestalts are those images which are not taken in successively in terms of their parts but are 'a given unity accessible to what in the end will be an instantaneous, theoretical, contemplative apprehension' (SII: 78).[19]

Gestalts are 'forms', and 'form' is to be taken here also in the Platonic sense of the essence of an entity which appears to us (*eidos*).

The Platonic term also refers to the genus: it is not a particular starling that arouses a female starling, but effectively the species as such, which in truth is ultimately all that concerns the individual animal, since with respect to this species it is in any case always 'already dead' (SV: 464; cf. E: 263; cf. SIII: 179–80). The 'specific image' is necessary if not sufficient to trigger the bird's mating rituals. Thus the images which form the animal's 'imaginary' are all images of species, *kinds* of thing:

> What is the basic mainspring determining the setting into motion of the gigantic sexual mechanism? [. . .] It isn't the existence of the sexual partner, the *particularity* of one individual, but something which has an extremely intimate relation with what I have been calling the *type*, namely an image. (SI: 121–2, my italics)
>
> The imaginary [. . .] includes an intervention from the *Gestalten* predisposing the subject to a certain relation with a *typical* form which *specifically* corresponds to it, it presupposes a biological coupling of the individual with *an image of its own species*, with the images of what is biologically useful for it in a determinate environment. (SII: 107, my italics)

Images are what render an other entity *desirable* to us.[20] 'The essence of the image is to be invested by the libido. What we call libidinal investment is what makes an object become desirable, that is to say how it becomes confused with the more or less structured image which, in diverse ways, we carry with us' (SI: 141; cf. SI: 122). Unless an entity can be schematised by one of our images, it will not be a desirable mate. 'The animal makes a real object coincide with the image within him' (SI: 138).

In the case of the animal, Lacan employs the notion of tessellation, a harmony between inner and outer worlds which the images provide. The images are sufficiently successful to have allowed that animal to adapt to its environment in a way that is sustainable. 'There is a convergence, a crystallisation, here which gives us the feeling, however sceptical we may be, of a pre-established harmony [. . .]. The animal fits into its environment' (SII: 86). Thanks to the image, the inner and outer worlds are adapted to one another: it is not as if there is a preformed environment and a pre-formed interiority, rather the two will have evolved together, becoming mutually adapted to one another, reciprocally acting upon one another.

Thus the imaginary is what allows there to be a perfect link between an animal and its outside, even if this point of perfect fit is mythical and an illusion projected from the point of view of man's evident disharmony. Here, in man, the images do not function as they should, there is a fault in the imaginary schematisation, and the one-to-one signals of the animal imaginary are carried off into the freely expanding realm of the imagin*ation*. There is no longer just one signified for every signifier that appeals to us. We do not know what to do, and what we want is not necessarily what is good for us.

The imaginary in humans

In man, the imaginary link between inner and outer worlds is broken. There is a hitch, preventing a biunivocal relation between stimulus in the outer world and response in the inner world, ruling out even an asymptotic harmony with one's environment. This gap is the origin of the barrier separating signifier from signified, which renders impossible the unequivocal signs which signal to the animal.

There is with man 'a crack, a profound perturbation of the regulation of life' (SII: 37). This 'crack' separates man's instincts from the objects of these instincts, the need from the object of need. Man does not naturally want what he needs. Nothing in the environment speaks to him, or rather everything speaks, but in neutral tones, and he has no idea what is good for him: he *desires*. For him, there are more objects than needs, indeed an almost infinite number of objects: 'The human world isn't at all structurable as an *Umwelt*, fitting inside an *Innenwelt* of needs, it isn't enclosed, but rather open to a crowd of extraordinarily varied neutral objects' (SII: 100).

This gap is precisely the unconscious, need perverted in its aim and become desire. The unconscious is the space of the pleasure principle, not the reality principle of the animal. It separates the interior of man from his exterior environment. This results in the irruption of a *death* drive in the animal realm of the 'struggle for *life*'. The gap in the imaginary thus signals 'the importance of the notion introduced by Freud of the death instinct' (SII: 37).[21] This means at the very least that man's instinct to stay *alive* is not the only thing that motivates his behaviour: it can be and often is overridden. One's relation with one's outer world can become destructive. Simply because man is born without the knowledge of how to live, and is *not* fitted to survive, poorly adapted to his environment, his success in survival cannot be explained by Darwinian evolutionary theory.

In man, the imaginary does not link us univocally to those elements of the world which are relevant for our species' survival. For entirely material reasons, we lack images sufficiently accurate to guarantee the survival of *Homo sapiens*. The imaginary in man is the *imagination* (in Greek, *phantasia*[22]), which can precisely interpose a *fantasy* between man and the real, allowing an entirely fictitious relation between ourselves and the world, opening up the space in which a drive towards death can intervene, one that is anti-natural, which does not strive, like the pleasure principle, after a controlled level of excitation entering the organism from the outside, but which can either close itself off entirely or open itself to excess.

This is what Lacan calls our 'disordered imagination' (SI: 138). 'Imagination' in itself implies disorder, the capacity to synthesise that which does not belong together, extravagantly, in a way detached from reality.

Why we lack an image of ourselves

The basis for the Gestalt as such is *totality*. The animal must have a sense of totality, a certain base unit in its perceptual capacities, an ability to perceptually 'comprehend' rather than merely be affected apprehensively.[23] The animal must have been born with a 'notion' of *wholeness*, a wholeness that is not composed out of prior units. This is what an 'image' or 'Gestalt' means for Lacan.

Lacan suggests that the primal image in the animal's imaginary is the image of its *own* species, which is to say the Gestalt of *itself* (SII: 107). This image is foundational for every other image: 'this image of self is the very framework of his categories, of his apprehension of the world' (SI: 282). But man, unlike the animal, *lacks* such an image in the first place. The reason for this is ultimately our species' natal prematurity: 'The prematurity of birth hasn't been invented by the psychoanalysts. Histologically, the apparatus which in the organism plays the role of nervous system, still a matter for debate, is not complete at birth' (SI: 149). This is the materialistic base of Lacan's thought. Certain biological, natural facts explain the nature and emergence of the imaginary and the symbolic.

> In man, however, this relationship to nature is altered by a certain dehiscence at the very heart of the organism, a primordial Discord betrayed by the signs of malaise and motor uncoordination of the neonatal months. The objective notions of the anatomical incompleteness of the pyramidal tracts and of certain humoral residues of the maternal organism in the newborn confirm my view that we find in man a veritable *specific prematurity of birth*. (E: 78; cf. E: 152; cf. AE: 33–5)

We are born too early.

For the animal, 'the *imaginary* idea of the whole [. . .] is given by the body' (SXVII: 31). But the human being's inability to coordinate his whole body means that he does not yet see himself as a unified individual, a totality. The only perception he can have of himself – and he precisely does not yet *have* a 'self' *stricto sensu* – is a series of momentary fragments, flashes of perception that supply him with images of organs that are not combined into a unitary body, a set of movements and sensations, an uncoordinated cluster of limbs. These experiences are not yet unified so as to become '*my* experience', they do not belong to just one entity who might be called 'I' – there is as yet no 'ego'. There is no centre to this disunity, no 'transcendental unity of apperception', a minimal basis of reflexivity which might synthesise these sensations to form one centred totality.

This situation is described by Lacan as the baby's 'fragmented body' (*le corps morcelé*) (E: 78), a cluster of morsels which need not imply a prior totality. Due to the incomplete coordination of the human body, the baby is not, in its own perception of its own fragments, a totality. And yet the body is in some ways a distinct organism, in terms of its *imaginary* difference from other things and other like bodies. So, the only thing that could give one a (psychic) sense of one's own individuality *is* this body. This bodily unity can neither be felt from the inside nor seen as a whole from the outside (one cannot see one's back).[24] For this reason, one's actual bodily individuation will *not* be matched by any subjective perception of this individuation. Individuation exists for the human only at the level of the image. How can one understand oneself as a totality with clearly defined limits save in the imaginary form of one's total body? What else could license us in defining the boundaries of an individual thing's identity outside of the symbolic order in which a certain *signifier* individuates it?

Given one's lack of self-perception, if one is to achieve such individuation by means of an image of totality, this totality cannot be one's own. While we cannot see ourselves as a whole, we *can* see another, at least from the outside. And this includes a sight of our *own* body *as* another, which is to say, in a *mirror*. This imaginary identification is possible from the moment at which one's sensations are sufficiently accurately perceived and differentiated for one to understand that the moves one is making run parallel to those seen in the mirror. Then, one can begin to achieve a sense of one's own individuality.

Thus the moment at which one's psychic individuation begins to match up with one's bodily individuation is called 'the mirror stage'.

By means of this identification with another, the human being compensates for his lack of an innate image of himself as a totality: 'The function of the mirror stage thus turns out, in my view, to be a particular case of the function of imagos, which is to establish a relationship between an organism and its reality – or, as they say, between the *Innenwelt* and the *Umwelt*' (E: 78).

Since man does not enjoy a sense of his own totality at birth, images take on a different role for him. They are not recognised as totalities on the basis of a primordial cognition of one's own totality, since one lacks any innate sense of the latter. Rather these images *form* the human being's sense of its own totality in the very first place. Certain images take on a *formative* role: '*Imaginary* [Lacan's italics] here refers, in the first instance, to the subject's relation to its *formative* identifications, which is the true meaning of the term "image" in analysis' (SI: 116, my italics). 'Identification' then does not refer primarily to the mimicking of one human being by another, but to the very *achievement* of any identity at all. For this reason, the images with which one identifies are called 'imagos', the Latin word for both image and statue, the frozen image which the statue constitutes, an image of petrifaction, the statue as a *formed* individual. The image thus compensates man for his native lack of totality: 'This image is functionally essential for man, in that it provides him with the orthopaedic complement of that native insufficiency, constitutive confusion or disharmony, that is linked to his prematurity at birth' (SIII: 95)

The external image can form a whole simply because it is external, and it is at least possible to view it in all its aspects:

> the other which we are, is there where we first saw our *ego* – outside us, in the human form. This form is outside of us, not in so far as it is so constructed as to captivate sexual behaviour, but in so far as it is fundamentally linked to the primitive impotence of the human being. The human being only sees his form materialised, whole, the mirage of himself, outside of himself. (SI: 140)

Man has one natural counterbalance to his motor inability: his *sight*. 'It is owing to this delay in development that the early maturation of *visual* perception takes on the role of functional anticipation. This results, on the one hand, in the marked prevalence of visual structure in recognition of the human form' (E: 152, my italics).[25]

Since one is capable of seeing wholes outside oneself, one acquires the *idea* of such a thing as unity, and by means of a certain homology between the other's movements and one's own, one comes to identify the other's wholeness as one's own. However, since one does not yet *feel* oneself as a unity, one posits the unity of the other's body as something one might acquire in the *future*; one *anticipates* that one day one will achieve this wholeness. The sight of another as a coordinated whole allows one to foresee and indeed precipitate the time when one will be able to coordinate one's own body. The image which allows one to anticipate one's own individuality as a conscious, unified ego is an *ideal* apparition, it is an ideal ego:

> The image of the ego – simply because it is an image, the ego is ideal ego [*moi idéal*] – sums up the entire imaginary relation in man. By being produced at a time when the functions are not yet completed, it has a salutary value, expressed well enough in the jubilatory assumption of the mirror phenomenon. (SI: 282)

One's physical disarray and torment is thus ended in 'jubilation' as one connects the image of wholeness presented by another with one's own future, perhaps 'when one is bigger', that time in which our parents continually promise us the things we desire but cannot have according to the law that issues from their mouths. The big Other is also the *Big* other, the other who is imaginarily more 'grown up' than we are.

Thus the ideal I is always ahead of us as the myth we retain of a completed self-identity, an end to individuation in a fully formed individual substance: 'The myth of the ideal I [. . .] whereby at least something is identical to itself' (SXVII: 63). Hence the second meaning of the word 'imaginary': '*Imaginary* here refers [. . .] secondly, to the relation of the subject to the real whose characteristic is that of being illusory, which is the facet of the imaginary most often highlighted. (SI: 116)

The intervention of the symbolic in the gap of the imaginary

This delay is the reason why we do not live happily ever after. Because this wholeness with which we identify is *ideal*, it is not something we can ever actually achieve. We can approximate it in the control we gain over our own limbs and the approximate awareness we achieve of our own body shape, but nothing will ever eliminate the fact that the image of wholeness was always originally the image of *another*: 'He will never be completely unified precisely because this [identification, unification] is brought about in an *alienating* way, in the form of a *foreign* image' (SIII: 95, my italics). The relation of self to self always incorporates a detour to the other. There is always a gap, something is always missing in the subject's self-relation. Individuality always remains in the process of individuation, and hence image after image can be laid over one's developing ego and an individual's identity constantly remoulded, the process of identity-forming never quite completed. The ego is, as Lacan says, like a layered 'onion' in this sense (SI: 171).

Because it forces self-identity to detour through the other, this primal identification is alienating: 'The imaginary relation [. . .] is an essentially alienated relation' (SIV: 12). This means that we cannot construct a perfect imaginary that would lock us in a sort of simulated harmony with our environment. This primary alienation prevents us from ever becoming the animals we would have been. It prevents *ab initio* any return to nature.

There is always a gap between I and myself, which is in truth the space of desire, the desire to return to mythic 'real' wholeness, a lack which is given a positive form by the object *a*, that element which always remains in the possession of an other (*a*utre). One is never an independent, free-standing substance, though one seems to desire it.

It is into this gap in the imagination between inner and outer worlds that a supplementary alienation enters: the signifier, opened up by the failure of the one-to-one relation of the animal signal. The signifier amounts to the possibility of responding to the world in different ways. Because of this always outstanding element in an individual's individuation, consequent upon a faulty imaginary, the symbolic enters human life. Language is the human being's final attempt to acquire a unity which he has failed to achieve in the imaginary. Language comes along to name and thus substantify those lives which remain verbs: 'the imaginary is surely the guide to life for the whole animal domain. While the image equally plays a capital role in our own domain, this role is completely taken up and caught up within, remoulded and reanimated by, the symbolic order' (SIII: 9). The symbolic order, *law*, directs man's instincts so that they reach their natural aim, spanning the abyss which separates man from his environment at the level of the imaginary.

We have reached the stage in our exposition where an imaginary deficit has necessitated a symbolic supplement. But how does the symbolic arise? We have shown only that human beings *need* a symbolic order in order to compensate for their animalic-imaginary deficit. We have not explained how that symbolic arises, in tandem with the survival and ultimate triumph of man over his own nature and indeed nature as a whole.

The deformation at the imaginary level is a necessary condition of the adoption of a symbolic order. A developmental explanation could be given for the way in which, ontogenetically, the individual enters the symbolic order and acquires language. But this approach is infected by the 'transcendentalism' which presupposes this language always already to have existed. Instead, we shall demonstrate just how this symbolic itself first arose, and arose simultaneously with the imaginary corruption of the human species. If every human being as such suffered from the imaginary deficit and yet the human species survived, the symbolic supplement must have arisen concomitantly with their emergence, such that the human species was itself always symbolic and the development of the human being *is* the development of the symbolic order of culture. And indeed, once again, in this regard, some features of the *imaginary* form of the human being engender the symbolic order. So, once again, the mediation between symbolic and real is imaginary. An imaginary defect necessitates the symbolic, and the unique imaginary form of man's body (in terms of erection, the erect form, the erectability of penis, nipple and thumb) is sufficient for its generation.

Since we are speaking here of the arising of human culture as such – the point at which a natural deficit and natural form precipitate this symbolic order – we are speaking in the realm of anthropology.

Structural anthropology: the transcendental and the genetic

It was however in this reference to anthropology that the psychoanalyst remained fatally in thrall to Lévi-Strauss's structuralism and its mythical assertion of the incest taboo. This cut the creature of language off from any access to a nature in which one might trace a genesis of the symbolic order. The very beginnings of the symbolic *in* nature no longer appear, and language seems to have come about by means of a divine *fiat*: in other words, it appears always to have existed and any origin we might propose for it can only be a mythical projection. It is as if the Lacan of the 1950s wins out over the Lacan of the 1930s and '40s, where his attention dwelt in the non-philosophical realm of the development of the child.

Thus, in the later 1950s and beyond, following the travails of the name-of-the-father that we have traced in the first part of this chapter, it became necessary to negotiate between the two insights, the (onto)genetic approach of psychoanalysis as such and the transcendental approach of structuralism. Lacan at first put them together in too abstract a way, and as a result transcendentalism won the day. This is why we have not immediately pursued the ontogenetic assumption of language on the part of the individual child, for this merely accepts the structuralist position in which language is always already a fully formed structure and we must simply accept it, as if the symbolic preexisted the generation of the human and we had only to find our way within it. In fact, we need to see how the symbolic as a whole developed in parallel with the 'evolution' of the human species.

But what could address this question better than anthropology?

One thus finds two contradictory impulses issuing from anthropology, one towards the genesis of the signifier and one towards a transcendentalism of the signifier, which would entirely confine us to synchronic considerations.

We shall now examine how it is once again the *imaginary* form of man and certain elements of nature which are responsible for the generation of the symbolic as such. We shall here justify another aspect of our earlier suggestion that an at least marginal attention to such genesis was present even in Lacan's earliest seminars.

The evolution of the imaginary: natural symbols

> When something comes to light, something which we are forced to consider as new, when another structural order emerges, well then, it creates its own perspective within the past, and we say – *This can never not have been there, this has existed from the beginning*. [. . .]
>
> Think about the origins of language. We imagine that there must have been a time when people on this earth began to speak. So we admit of an emergence. But from the moment that the specific structure of this emergence is grasped, we find it absolutely impossible to speculate on what preceded it other than by symbols which were always applicable. What appears to be new thus always seems to extend itself indefinitely into perpetuity, prior to itself. (SII: 5)

This is just the illusion under which creatures of a fully constituted language labour. This is why the signifier as such is considered by Hyppolite to have 'a transcendental function' for Lacan. This condemns us to understand the origin of the signifier *as* a signifier. And yet, it is insofar as we admit that this can only be a myth and not a real (genetic) explanation that the transcendental approach of itself admits its beyond in real genesis. This is perhaps why Hyppolite describes the transcendental as follows, in all its necessity and insufficiency: 'we can neither remain in it, nor can we get out of it. [. . .] We cannot do without it, and yet we cannot inhabit it either' (SII: 38).

Lacan's response to the charge of transcendentalism, *even in Seminar II*, is to suggest that he has *always* considered the genetic approach which transcendentalism elides. He even identifies Lévi-Strauss himself as deconstructing the opposition between nature and culture, as if he had realised that its only purpose could be to point towards the empty locus of a genetic explanation for culture:

> Lévi-Strauss is in the midst of backtracking as regards the very sharp bipartition which he makes between nature and symbol [. . .] he is afraid that the autonomy of the symbolic register will give rise to a masked transcendentalism once again [. . .]. He doesn't want the symbol, even in the extraordinarily purified form in which he offers us it, to be only a re-apparition, under a mask, of God. (SII: 35)

In other words, he does not want the myth of the name-of-the-father to be mistaken for an actually divine creation of the human, as if anthropology could end up suggesting that no explanation of the emergence of culture were possible and only transcendental myths could be offered.

So what is this genetic account that Lacan claims to have offered? One can find fragments of it even in the early 1950s, in Seminars I, II, and III, although it emerges fully in Seminars IV and V, with their scrupulous rethinking of the Oedipal process of the individual child's accession to language. But Lacan often indicates that his ontogenetic thought can also be applied to phylogenesis: 'I'm speaking of the history of humanity in its entirety' (SIV: 50). In order to indicate that this geneticism will always have troubled a deconstructive reduction of the early Lacan to a certain transcendentalism, we shall focus on the first three seminars.

We have already suggested this genesis in Chapter 1 with respect to the imaginary phallus. The phallus in its very form *resembles* the signifier. Lacan admits that, in the history of man, there is a progressive introduction of such a thing as a signifier, or at least of things that *resemble* signifiers, *proto*-signifiers, *quasi*-signifiers. The symbolic can form itself, gradually, only because there are certain elements of nature, the real, which are in fact *susceptible* of symbolisation, which in hindsight can be understood as inchoate stages *of* the signifier, things that 'will have been' symbols. 'Nature provides – I must use the word – signifiers' (SXI: 20). '[T]here are already in nature certain reservoirs and equally in the signified a certain number of elements, which are given to experience as accidents of the body, but which are reworked [*repris*] in the signifier, and give it, if one can say this, its first armaments [*armes première*]' (SIV: 51). Lacan instances the erectness of the human body and the standing stones which mimic it with a more enduring stability (cf. SIV: 51).

These erectnesses in the real, these proto-oppositions, appeal to *man* and not animals because they *resemble* him – *homo erectus* – who has the power to erect, they are erected in his image and perhaps reflect back to him the complete image which he lacks. Perhaps these forms constitute the ways in which man finds some hook in the real, which his faulty imaginary has otherwise prevented him from discovering. All he is capable of recognising infallibly is erection. This is perhaps his only image of what he should be: he crawls or he prowls and he *could* stand erect. What sets this image apart from the animal's external images is that man has to build it himself. Without setting himself up there in the form of buildings and stones, man, unlike the animal, would find himself nowhere in the world. His imagination is not altogether dysfunctional, and we can presume that he recognises the difference between erection and non-erection: thus, when he compares his prone state and the ambulatory stance of the adults around him, he aspires to erection from the very moment at which he begins to be troubled by his lack of unity.

What is crucial is the contrast. Animals are not interested in alternating rhythms of this kind but only in stable totalities, constant forms. For man what appeals to him in the environment, and what his first built creations respond to in his most primitive stages, are things which anticipate opposition, difference, things which have a periodic character. In light of this alternation, man then creates things which respond to this periodicity: things which *stand* or endure, in opposition to the evanescence of nature.

Lacan stresses that proto-signifiers are real things taken in their *image*, their imaginary form:

> The first symbols, natural symbols, stem from a certain number of prevailing images – the image of the human body, the image of a certain number of obvious objects like the sun, the moon, and some others. And that is what gives human language its weight, its resources, and its emotional vibration. (SII: 306)

From such imaginary rhythms, 'natural symbols', language gets its 'weight', which is to say its real materiality, that about it which is not ideal and diaphanous, its 'resources', which make it possible and sustain it. We are speaking of those elements of the real that *support* the signifier as differential marks taken up into a totality. Lacan is clear that it is the *imaginary form* of the real that is crucial here: 'there is something in the symbolic function of human discourse that cannot be eliminated, and that is the role played in it by the imaginary' (SII: 306).

On the oppositional rhythm of images

The natural-real images which engage man enjoy a certain quasi-oppositional relation with other images. It is this primordial *relationality* that will make possible the strict *differentiality* that characterises the signifier proper. They will be elements of the real that are beginning to stretch out beyond themselves and *refer* to another entity, they will constitute the beginnings of *signification*. Lacan describes this anticipation of the signifier's oppositionality as 'asymmetry', which is a quality of the mirror image:

> we have, of course, to take the formal side of nature into account, in the sense in which I qualified it as possessing *pseudo-significant asymmetry* [*asymétrie pseudo-significative*], because that is what man embraces in order to produce his fundamental symbols. The important thing is what gives the forms of nature symbolic value and function, what makes them function in *relation* to one another. It is man who introduces the notion of asymmetry. Asymmetry in nature is neither symmetrical, nor asymmetrical – it is what it is. (SII: 38, my italics)

Those things which man 'embraces' in order to produce his first symbols are such regular rhythmic processes as the tides of the sea and the passage of the sun: certain real things which 'return to their place', rhythmically. These will later come to form genuinely oppositional couples with the help of a linguistic mark which differentiates the one from the other in the way of presence and absence. First, one experiences a mere 'alternation', and then language seals this as a genuine opposition where one half is defined *exclusively* as the absence of the other. It is this formality and this absoluteness which characterises the fully constituted signifying order.

Lacan defines each term of an oppositionally related couple as follows: 'It is presence in absence and absence in presence' (SII: 38). And he relates this precisely to one of the earliest of man's 'symbols', the natural alternation of the sun, its rising and its setting:

> Day and night are in no way something that can be defined by experience. All experience is able to indicate is a series of modulations and transformations, even a pulsation, an alternation, of light and dark, with all its transitions. *Language* begins at the opposition – day and night. (SIII: 167, my italics)

'Very early on, day and night are signifying codes, not experiences. They are connotations, and the empirical and concrete day only comes forth as an imaginary correlative, originally, very early on' (SIII: 149).

The signifier latches onto this natural phenomenon of the occultation of the sun. By marking one phase as the absence of the other, it makes a signifier of the two states, applying marks to both, one half of the opposition defined as possessing a mark (light, day), the other as lacking it (not-light, night), the one as the absence of the other. The mark of lack is precisely the 'minus' sign, negation, −, which could be described as the trace constitutive of the signifier. Only with the *mark* does an alternation of states become a genuine opposition, but without this alternation, this use of the mark would never have revealed itself.

Lacan's locutions are never arbitrary, and it is significant that he should describe these parts of nature as 'natural *symbols*'. Let us take this not in the Lévi-Straussian sense but in the Saussurean where it denotes a relation of *resemblance* between signifier and signified. The proto-signifier in nature imaginarily *resembles* the signifier, it is a prehistoric 'signifier' *of* the signifier. The signifier as such is the signified, but the relation cannot strictly be one of signifying, since the proto-signifier is not yet a signifier; it can only *resemble*.

Now this symbolism is precisely left behind with the origination of the signifier proper. In the entirely differential system of the signifier there can be *no* iconic relation between signifier and signified. It is in opposition to this iconicism that the sign's arbitrariness is posited. So when we speak of resemblance, we are speaking of a relation that is otherwise than the relations which characterise the signifier. The symbol's relation to the signifier is not *itself* significant (*signifiant*) but imaginary. Thus, imaginarity *precedes* the symbolic order and can therefore partake of a non-circular genetic explanation of the emergence of the symbolic.

This is a materialist approach to the signifier, to what will come to *act* as transcendental in any perspective we adopt on the past: 'the point of view I am trying to maintain before you involves a certain materialism of the elements in question, in the sense that the signifiers are well and truly embodied, materialised' (SIII: 289). A materialism in this regard would explain the origination of the symbolic from out of the non-symbolic. It would not presuppose an ideal meaning as existing at the origin, but would ask the question of its origin in real matter. Thus Lacan is now prepared to speak of the 'mirage' of believing that language has always existed: 'there's a mirage whereby language, namely all your little 0's and 1's, is there from all eternity, independently of us. [. . .] [W]ithin a certain perspective, we can only see them as being there since the beginning of time' (SII: 292).[26] He is even prepared to say, '*error*':

> the error of believing that what science constitutes by the intervention of the symbolic function has always been there, that it is given.
>
> This error exists in all knowledge, in as much as it is only a crystallisation of the symbolic activity, and once constituted there is a dimension of error, which is the forgetting of the creative function of truth in its nascent form. (SII: 19)

And precisely what counters this error of perspective is *psychoanalysis*. For Lacan, as a psychoanalyst, the crucial thing is the genetic dimension, how the symbolic is formed and entered: 'But we analysts, we can't forget it, we who work in the dimension of this truth in its nascent state' (SII: 19; cf. SII: 5).

This then is what psychoanalysis offers philosophy.

The phallus as image of the symbolic

Man himself, along with that natural symbol closest to him, the phallus, embodies the quasi-opposition: recumbent and upstanding, flaccid and erect.

The phallus is an image of every single signifier as such, defined oppositionally as either present in its place or absent from its place. Thus the symbolic is totalised by the imaginary, by a certain *image-like* resemblance among all signifiers. The existence of the phallus and its imaginary resemblance to the signifier is precisely what replaces the lack of a *signifier* of the signifier: 'If we think that there is no Other of the Other, [. . .] it is necessary that we make a stitch [*suture*] between this symbolic which alone extends itself [*s'étend*] there and this imaginary which is here' (SXXIII: 72). 'Suturing' is the word Lacan uses for what stitches together the quilt work of the signifier, recalling the upholstery button that pinned together the signifier and the signified. The stitch creates a centre and thus organises a small portion of the signifier to create pockets of meaningfulness. It is always a question of how the two separate threads of Saussure's wobbly diagram can be woven into a textile with some consistency, how meaning can be fixed sufficiently firmly for communication to take place and autism to be avoided. It is the imaginary phallus that sutures, and – as we shall see – the object *a* is always a representative of the phallus, which is what is missing from the imaginary self-image of the subject. This amounts to 'situating the function of *a* at this point of failure [A barred]' (SIX: 13/6/62).

There is always a signifier missing. The signifier does not fully close the gap in the subject's self-relation opened up by the alienation of the mirror image. The subject can find a place in the signifier only because the signifier fails to signify itself, and thus lacks a signifier that would be appropriate to the subject as self-relation. The signifier does not complete the determination of meaning which would be the proximity to itself of the subject's consciousness. It is this gap in self-relation that the fantasy can cover over. The signifier is totalised by an *image*, and fantasy has a necessary place in the signifying *structure*: 'fantasy [. . .] is structural' (SXIV: 6/12/66).

God, the one father, is dead, but his place is kept warm by fantasy, a mythic projection of a culturally, historically determined god. Thus fantasy is the synchronic, quasi-*transcendental* form of the imaginary, which was revealed to Lacan by his growing attention to the *genetic*: 'the true imaginary function [. . .] insofar as it intervenes at the level of desire, is a privileged relationship with *a*, object of desire, term of the fantasy' (SIX: 13/6/62).

One can clearly see Lacan's approaching this thought in the progression of his Seminars' foci. Seminar VII is an exposition of the real Thing and the problems of accessing it, that moment of the real which is susceptible of becoming a signifier. Then, two years later, a fully genetic account of the signifier is explicitly signalled in Seminar IX, which is precisely concerned with the genetic arising of the signifier and the subject's identification as an individual. And then, once Seminars X and XI have discussed the object *a* in detail, a great deal of time and a number of seminars will be devoted to the fantasy itself.

Object a *as representative of the phallus*

The symbolic order is the institution of a permanent lack of imaginary wholeness in man. It castrates his image of the thing – the 'phallus' – which would have rendered that image complete. This lack is expressed and covered up by the fantasy, which projects an image of the wholeness which the individual lacks. The fantasy projects various objects that might supplement the gap left by the castrated phallus. These objects are called 'objects *a*': 'the object *a*, the object of castration' (SIX: 27/6/62). The object *a* is that which would bind together the morsels of our fragmented body, and which would overcome the split in the subject instituted by castration. The object *a* is thus a 'part-object', the part of us that was lost: '*a* comes to fills the gap [*boucher la béance*] that constitutes the inaugural division of the subject' (SXI: 270).

The object *a* is not the phallus as always already lacking from the point of view of the symbolic, but the manner in which this lack is *positivised* in a series of desired features or objects projected by the desirous symbolic. Our lack is *represented* in the objects *a*. The lack in the symbolic, the real, is given an *imaginary* form, as that which we picture of our *desire*. Object *a* is the cause of desire in the object.

Lacan describes the object *a* as follows:

> the partner of this 'I' that is the subject [. . .] is not the Other, but that which is substituted for it [the representative of its impossible wholeness] in the form of the cause of desire – that I have diversified into four causes, insofar as the cause is constituted diversely, according to the Freudian discovery, on the basis of the object of sucking, the object of excretion, the gaze, and the voice. (SXX: 126; cf. SXI: 194–6)

These constitute 'a certain type of object which, in the last resort, can serve no function. These are the objects *a* – the breasts, the faeces, the gaze, the voice' (SXI: 242). These objects *a* are those parts of ourselves which we (imagine ourselves to have) lost and are now seeking to regain. They are what we desire.

Each object *a* has the same form: it is an image of that which is beyond the image, the real, it is the obscene, which would normally have to be hidden. This is perhaps why shit is privileged among the objects *a*: among other things the '*a*' of 'object *a*' stands for '*anal*', the anal, faecal object. It does not stand for the objects of the scopic, vocal, or oral drives. And yet, the objects of all these, the desirable elements, are precisely what *represent* such objects as were both inside and outside of us, a part of us or a product of ours that we could not fully appropriate, such as the shit, but also the breast (of another), the voice, and the gaze.

Perhaps with all of these objects, it is a case of the impossibility of maintaining two opposed, mutually exclusive states at once. In the case of the anal object, it is impossible to locate the object either inside or outside of the body; the breast is that object which completes us and yet never entirely belongs since it is proffered by the mother; the voice, like the anal object, refuses location in either the interior or exterior of any one subject, since it originates in the interior but immediately projects itself into the exterior, neither subject nor object; the gaze is that element of the eye which cannot be seen. One cannot at the same time view the eyes of the other as an object seen and 'look into their eyes' at a subject seeing. We can see them looking, but we can never see the place from which they look (cf. SXI: 71ff).

The same goes for our own gaze in the mirror. The subjective point of view of the image we see cannot be incorporated into our vision of the mirror since this takes it solely as an *object*: we can never see the *place* from which we *look*. The eyes in the mirror appear the same as ours, but what they lack, what the mirror cannot differentiate, is the position, the subjective position of the *real* looker. That is not revealed in the mirror. The mirror does not differentiate between its image and the real, which is marked solely by the different orientations of reflection and reflected: right becomes left, left becomes right. The object *a* is our unreflectable singularity, the subject of enunciation, the real which escapes specularity. What the mirror image lacks, the object *a*, is precisely the real singularity of our subjectivity. The thing that we really are is always this object that cannot be made part of our conscious egoic self-image.

The object *a* is the very otherness of the other (or of ourselves) which means that, however complete our identification with their image, we shall never be identical with them, and hence our identity will never fully be defined by reference to the other. 'I have given it back the name "object" for this reason, that the object is *ob*, an obstacle to the expansion of the concentric, that is, engulfing [*englobant*], imaginary' (SXXIII: 86). Thus the object is an object in two senses, the true sense of object which is the object over against the subject, and that which remains objectal in the sense of being entirely outside the subject, not at all consciously assimilable by him.

It is perhaps a question of contradiction, and the impossibility of contradiction in any non-symbolic order. The object *a* would thus be that moment of overlap between symbolic and real. In its two guises, as imaginary part-object and symbolic object-cause of desire, the object *a* would represent the signifierisation of the real, its sublation into a structure governed by the law of non-contradiction (which is the theoretical expression of an order constituted by *oppositions*). The object *a* would be the symbolic form of that which precedes and eludes the very possibility of such a thing as contradiction. Or rather, the object *a*, since it enjoys a dual form, would also be the remainder of the sublation, that which the symbolic can never capture in the sense of providing one signifier that would be adequate to it. It is the surplus of the real over the symbolic, and even the surplus of the real over the imaginary, for it has a plurality of imaginary forms, all of which attempt to represent that which is *lost*, the phallus.

Because the subject's conscious thinking remains governed by the principle of non-contradiction and the oppositions consequent upon that, the objects *a* must always remain objectal for the subject in a dual sense: as permanently beyond the subject, non-subjectal, but at the same time as taken up into the subject–object binarity. This indicates the ambiguous status of the object *a*, and the real.

The object *a* is the object of the *other* (*autre*), it is the object-cause of desire, what the other has that we believe would complete us if we possessed it. It is that moment of desire which always *remains* other, which always belongs to another, for once we have it, it no longer becomes desirable, it was not what we truly wanted, for it does not complete us. The object *a*, insofar as it is part of the symbolic, is metonymic, subject to substitution. One simply cannot regain one's imaginary completeness, which was only a myth anyway.

Desire exists, the object *a* exists, as the lack in our imaginary individuation. The object *a* is then the discrepancy that exists between the mirror image and the reality of our own ego, or rather the gap between our ego and our true subjectivity. All the signifier can do is provide a chain of metonymic substitutes which attempt to fill this gap, to *explain* or *express* what is lacking in intelligible terms. The objects *a* are *organs*; that which is lacking is not truly an organ, but this organ, the product of a symbolic anatomisation of the body, is the form in which the symbolic is forced retrospectively to understand its own loss. It is the acceptable imaginary form which the real can be given in the symbolic, thus preventing the gap that the real *is* from *being* a gap for the symbolic. The imaginary form which the real takes in fantasy thus plugs a gap in the signifier's constitution. The object *a* is the form which lack assumes when it is *represented*. In truth, the object of desire is merely lack, void, which must be lacking in both the imaginary and the symbolic: which is to say, the real: '*a* is of the order of the real' (SXIII: 5/1/66).

The object *a* is thus both symbolic and imaginary, because it is an image which symbolises what is lacking in the symbolic, the imaginary univocal signified, the always castrated phallus.

> The object *a* is something from which the subject, in order to constitute itself, has separated itself off as organ. This serves as a *symbol* of the lack [*symbole du manque*], that is to say, of the phallus, not as such, but in so far as it is lacking [*en tant qu'il fait manque*]. It must, therefore, be an object that is, firstly, separable and, secondly, that has some relation to the lack. (SXI: 103, my italics)

The object *a*, representative of the castrated phallus in an order which has cut it off, is a signifier of the missing signified, the missing imaginary element, which the signifier would as *symbol* unequivocally represent. Insofar as it is imaginary, the object *a* is the object of need, but insofar as it is symbolic it is the object(-cause) of desire. It is precisely that part of the real which was lost but which endures in the symbolic by way of its imaginary form and so perpetuates the symbolic's desire for that which it has lost, for the object *a* marks the real and constitutes a memorial or reminder of what has been lost.

It is the lack of coincidence with itself on the part of the individuated subject, the incomplete self-constitution of the imaginary *and* the symbolic, that is the individual's only access to the *real*.

The object *a* is the remainder of the real (cf. SXI: 196–9, 205), in the subjective genitive, in the sense that this remainder, this gap in our self-relation *is* the only real to which we have access. It is that which we *cannot* encompass within the loop of our subjectivity. Objects *a* are the real defined *with reference to* the imaginary, as that which cannot be contained within the imaginary but partake of a relation of exclusion *with* it (cf. SXXIII: 64–5). There is nothing beyond the veil of fantasy: what is real is the veil, and one could easily call it 'the tain of the mirror'.

The object *a* is what is missing from both the symbolic and the imaginary, it is the real, but the moment at which the real of the symbolic and the real of the imaginary overlap. It marks the fact that the lack inherent to both makes the two regions *need* one other. The symbolic order needs the fantasy, the fantasy that the object *a* can in fact be attained.

The object a *and fantasy*

The lack in an individual's totality is sutured by the object *a* as imaginary object-cause of desire; the lack of wholeness of the symbolic order is sutured by the imaginary fantasy, which is precisely expressed as $ ◊ *a*, the subject in relation with the object *a*.[27] The notion of fantasy thus clearly depends on the theory of ontogenesis, whereby an individual's wholeness is seen to be completed by something (the object *a*) that will always belong to another. It was only by means of an attention to the genesis of the human being that the imaginary element of the transcendental conditions of the symbolic order as a whole could have been discerned. If one takes a transcendental approach, from the point of view of the present, and ignores genesis, one can only seek – or deconstruct – a signifier of the signifier; if one takes a genetic approach, one can envisage an *image* of the signifier, which then leads one to see the possibility of a *fantasmatic* suture of the signifier as a whole.

Lacan compares the fantasy to a picture placed over a window, but a picture that depicts what is actually beyond it, what is visible *through* the window (SXIII: 30/3/66; cf. SX: 89).[28] And yet the two are different: the frame of the picture renders the real tolerable by confining it within strict limits. By bordering the real that it pictures, it produces an image of oneness which limits the unboundedness or non-wholeness, the 'not-one' of the real that exists outside the symbolic. Unity, individuation, exists only at the level of the imaginary and the symbolic and hence by definition does not characterise the real.

That which fills in a lack within a totality is precisely the object *a*, and Lacan has precisely identified the object *a* with the *frame* of this painted screen, that which renders the real imaginary in the sense of being pictured *as a complete totality* (SXIII: 30/3/66). What is presented is not the real outside the window but the real depicted by an *image* and framed. And yet, since the imaginary is *genuinely* a way in which the symbolic opens onto the real, the pre-symbolic real, it is clear that the picture does mark a genuine opening of the symbolic house onto the real outside: 'This screen is not simply what hides the real, it surely is that, but at the same time, it indicates it' (SXIII: 18/5/66). Even if it does not and cannot truly adequate the real, it nevertheless indicates the lack that the real *is*.

We address the object *a*, we positivise the lack that is the real, in *fantasy*. One paints over the window that opens onto another in order both to block the outside and to indicate it: 'this little reality [*peu de réalité*] that is the whole substance of fantasy [*toute la substance du fantasme*] but which is also, perhaps, the whole reality to which we can gain access [*toute la réalité à laquelle nous pouvons accéder*]' (SXIII: 8/6/66).

It is precisely the real, which seems to us to spell an end to our alienation and separation from ourselves, that is the object of desire. Therefore by maintaining the presence of the real within the symbolic, the imaginary fantasy is the only thing that can *sustain* desire as desiring and ever unsatisfied: 'the puppets of the fantasy [. . .] are the support, the only possible support for what can be in the proper sense a realisation of desire' (SIX: 4/4/62). The fantasy sustains desire by luring us towards what seems to be real within the symbolic, and yet by presenting it as an object which we might be able to achieve, when in fact the real object of desire is nothing besides a void. Hence the fantasy presents the object *a* as the guide-rail for our desire, replacing the guide-rails Lacan identified in the orderly animal imaginary: 'desire is supported by fantasy' (SXIII: 30/3/66).

Desire dies if *either* the real is closed off altogether *or* its object is achieved, thus in order to sustain itself, the real and the symbolic must be held together *and* held apart. This is carried out by the fantasy, which draws a veil of promise that lures one towards the real and yet keeps one infinitesimally distinct from it. By presenting an image (the object *a*) of what is in truth merely and always a lack (the real itself, the real of the symbolic and the imaginary), it opens us onto the real, but never allows us to attain it.

The fantasy will be that (imaginary) presence which the real has within the symbolic, which allows the real to relate to the symbolic in a way that is not oppositional, that neither excludes it entirely nor appropriates it absolutely. It is a translucent curtain of an image which allows the symbolic to see the fire of the real burning behind it but not to stare directly into the blinding flames, which would burn out one's desire and indeed one's very self (cf. SXXIII: 121).

The object a *and the real as orientation: left and right*

The fantasy provides what is missing in the mirror image, that remainder which alienates us from our exact duplicate. What is the difference between us and our mirror image? Nothing but orientation. What is right for us, is left for the mirror. This is why Lacan identifies this sense of orientation (another meaning of *sens*) with *the real*.

The object *a* is that element which is missing from our image of ourselves: 'the object of the fantasy, *a*, the object of desire has no image' (SIX: 30/5/62). The object *a* is the discrepancy between the image and the real, and this can be captured neither by symbolic descriptions nor by images: it may be understood analogously with the non-symbolic, non-imaginary difference between left and right: '*a* qua object of desire is at once orientable and undoubtedly very oriented, but [. . .] is not, if I can express myself in this way, specularisable' (SIX: 6/6/62):

> the specular image is an error [. . .] the origin of the ego and its fundamental misrecognition [. . .] insofar as the subject is mistaken he believes that he has his own image in front of him; [. . .] if he knew [. . .] there are only the most deformed relationships in any identifiable fashion between his left-hand side and his right-hand side, he would not dream of identifying himself with the image in the mirror. (SIX: 30/5/62)

This is 'the misrecognition of what I called above the most radical asymmetry' (SIX: 30/5/62). It is orientation that cannot be reflected in the mirror, that always remains 'other' in a way that is not imaginary or symbolic, in a way that has no meaning and cannot be signified: 'The orientation [*orientation*] of the real in my own territory, forecloses meaning [*sens*]' (SXXIII: 121). The real is the difference between a right glove inside out and a left glove (cf. SXIV: 19/4/67).[29]

The object *a* is that object which would overcome our imaginary alienation, fantasy is the belief that we could ever possess it and thus flip the mirror image around its vertical axis of symmetry, such that our imaginary ego would be true to our real subjectivity. The gap between ego and subject would be eradicated.

The fantasmatic real

The symbolic is totalised by the presentation of an image of its origination in the real: this is what myth has always signified. This allows one to reject the perhaps ethnocentric notion of Oedipal normalisation and to accept that *all* accessions to a symbolic order of community are specific, contingent, and to some extent peculiar. We each find our own way in, and we each enjoy a certain (sub-)cultural cobelonging with those who share our fantasy of the ultimate meaning of life within this order.

The very nature of the signifier is to be lacking, to have one signifier missing. The name-of-the-father can do nothing about that. It is just another signifier. The only way to allow the infinity of signifiers to achieve some semblance of determinate signification is to suture them with something that is *of another order* to the signifier: the fantasy.

Castration consequent upon the nature of the symbolic order has rendered an unequivocal meaning impossible, and yet in its very form the phallus and its representative symbols provide an *image* of what unambiguous meaningfulness *would be* like. They present this state as attainable and yet futural, to keep us interested, so to speak, to maintain our desire. This is what fantasy is, and this is why it is phallic, it presents on the horizon the image of a fulfilled, univocal meaning, and hence an unambiguous, free and fully successful communication and coexistence with the other, and of course with the sexual partner: it promises *relation* (*rapport*).

The *signifier* of the name-of-the-father would truly have sealed the hole in the symbolic, but the *fantasy* provides a delusive *mask* for it, only contingently and temporarily suturing it, rather than *actually* doing so. At the same time it sutures the symbolic order in a way that differs for each person and each culture, and so does not unify *all* symbolic orders under the name of the one Father: it does not express any implicit belief in God. The fantasy *simulates* a fully autonomous symbolic order, it is the *semblance* of a transcendental, or rather the admission that any transcendental signifier which the symbolic provides, any account it tells of its own origin, *is a myth*.

The non-oppositional real

The real is then presented to the symbolic as the object *a* which the fantasmatic myth represents. The real is the gap that separates us from the image. It is the difference between image and reality, the difference of left and right, a lack in the ability of the symbolic and the imaginary to symbolise and to reflect.

In this way, Lacan ceases to understand the real as a full presence that would be opposed to the differential signifier. He now differentiates the real not just from one realm but from two. It is an inherent lack in the self-constitution of *both* the imaginary and the symbolic.

This is still to understand the real by abstraction, negatively. The object *a* about which we fantasise expresses our being *debarred* from the real. Fantasies are masks of the real. What the masks mask is left indeterminate. All that we can know of it are the masks we are able to project. The ambiguity of the mask is that it is an identity assumed *by* the mask-wearer but at the same time it disguises his identity. It is an identity assumed and concealed. Lacan describes the real as a *cold flame*, the blazing sun of appearance that blinds us when we look at it, the light tamed by its containment in the lantern that we use to light our way. What is hot for us, is not hot for the volcano: 'The fire is the real. The real sets fire to everything. But it is a cold fire. The fire which burns is a mask, so to speak, of the real. The real is to be sought on the other side, on the side of the absolute zero [the temperature at which *cold* burns us?]' (SXXIII: 121).

Perhaps we do not have to substantialise the real at all, as if the real were its own realm as the imaginary and the symbolic are. Perhaps, in the diagram of the Borromean knots, the real is nothing besides the *thread* that ties together the other two links. Why should the stitch between the imaginary and the symbolic, the fantasmatic suture carried out by the object *a*, not itself be the only real that there is? The symbolic and the imaginary, would then, in good materialist fashion, be mere excrescences of the real, which would itself be nothing but the production of two qualitatively distinct orders that need one another due to the lack in both orders, originally consequent upon a material deficit in the nervous system of *homo sapiens*?

In this case, in the diagram of the sign, S/s, the real would be the bar that separates and joins the symbolic signifier and the imaginary signified.

But this is precisely where Derrida placed the real.

The real would be that element of the symbolic which is not taken up into the service of meaning, and that element of the imaginary which is not reflected in the mirror. The real would then be nothing separate from the imaginary and the symbolic, but would be that part of them which eludes their nature. It would be that which would allow them to subsist as independent complete spheres. It is this lack of completeness which necessitates their overlapping with each other: 'to the imaginary and to the symbolic, that is, to things which are quite alien to each other [*étrangères*], the one to the other, the real brings the element which is able to make them hang together [*faire tenir ensemble*]' (SXXIII: 132).

The symbolic needs the imaginary (the fantasy) because it is not complete, and the imaginary needs the symbolic (legal guidance for our disordered instincts) because it is not complete. The symbolic would otherwise be infinite and meaningless, and the imaginary would be so disorderly the human species would die out.

The real is the phallus that *resembles* the signifier but is *not* it. It is the notch which goes to constitute the signifier without yet being one, since it is still a moment of self-sameness, or it is a proto-signifier that precedes a genuine differential system. The only real we can know, and which we access in fantasy, is that element of the real which makes the signifier not only possible but *actual* in a genetic sense. The real can do this because of an image which it bears. The real is the actual process of inscription that writes the imaginary into the symbolic and the symbolic into the imaginary. Its lettering forms the stitch that binds the one to the other and inscribes a real *in* the imaginary and a real *in* the symbolic.

The bar which takes the imaginary form of the notch is the *way* in which the real inhabits the symbolic, it is the real insofar as it is a part of the symbolic *and* the imaginary. It is what will become, or will have become, the signifier proper, but it *is* this only by virtue of its *imaginary* form, its sticklike phallic nature. Thus the real is nothing distinct from the imaginary and the symbolic, and yet it binds all three together: itself and the symbolic, itself and the imaginary, the symbolic and the imaginary. Lacan does indeed describe these links as real, as woven together by a certain kind of writing, which is how one might understand the real (cf. SXIV: 23/11/66). The real writes letters, the meaningless scratches of the signifier, the imaginary marks which, as we shall see, recall the most primitive genetic beginnings of the signifier in the primeval scoremarks of the hunter. The rings of the Borromean knots are indeed letters, they are all O's. This is why Lacan sometimes writes the three rings in the form of 'I S R' or 'R S I', a senseless concatenation of letters, in real ink. It is a sense of this realness that Lacan will always have been trying to convey to his audience.

We must therefore propose that the object *a* is the moment at which the two reals of the imaginary and symbolic overlap. And yet the real of the symbolic is the *letter* (*lettre*).[30] But is not the letter *also* such an overlap? This must be the case if the real is nothing besides a lack in the imaginary and symbolic which necessitates their co-belonging. In this chapter we have investigated the object *a* as the culmination of Lacan's thought of the imaginary, which began with the mirror stage and ended here in the object which escapes specularisation. In the following chapter, we shall finally come to address the real-of-the-symbolic, the letter.

We shall then determine just how close Lacan comes to Derrida. For Lacan, the real is that which takes on an imaginary form that resembles the signifier and thus makes it possible and actual. It is this imaginarity which distinguishes Lacan's understanding of the real-of-the-symbolic from Derrida's understanding of 'archi-writing'. In other words, it is not as if the trace of original writing is merely a transcendental signifier that is elected from the constituted body of the signifier. The real trace *actually* refers the signifier back to its primal generation from out of the primitive hunter's first notch. And the letter does this by virtue of its imaginary, phallic form. The letter, we might say, *is* the object *a*, but seen from the point of view of what is (lacking) in the symbolic. The object *a* is the same real seen from the point of view of what is (lacking) in the imaginary.

Transition

Does Derrida explain how thc empirical signifier becomes *actual*? What processes in the real caused the archi-trace to assume the particular form of empirical human writing? He speaks of the trace as existing at all levels of life and indeed in the inorganic real itself, but is he able to say why in each case it assumes this *particular* empirical form? Why for instance did the system of the empirical signifier or writing in the vulgar sense arise with the ascent of *man*? Perhaps Derrida's belief that a genetic dimension cannot be addressed prevents him from answering such questions, or perhaps he believes that this is not the business of philosophy.

And yet, does Derrida, on the basis of written texts alone, assume that he knows what writing is? It is on the basis of this presumed knowledge that he models his understanding of the transcendental, archi-writing. And yet must we not be *certain* that we know what something is before we infer what its conditions of possibility are?

If man is generated by way of a defect in the imaginary realm, and this animality persists in him, in his very life, when we ask after his transcendental conditions we must take into account this other facet of his actuality. The *zōon logon ekhon* is not just 'having *logos*', it is also *zōē*.

In this chapter, we have seen that the development of the imaginary in Lacan's thought has allowed him to take this into account, and as a result the transcendental moment is for him not merely a signifier, but also an image, the fantasy. Thus while we have reinstalled the necessity for genesis, by charting the development of the imaginary and showing its role in a genetic account of the signifier, there is still transcendentalisation. Consider our description of the real. It is not as if we have made any attempt to describe the real 'in itself'; rather we have described how such a thing as the real must appear to those animals who partake of an imaginary and a symbolic dimension. Effectively, given that it is – perhaps – man alone who exists at the frontier of these two dimensions, we have still only described how the real 'appears' to *him*. We have understood the real only so far as it may be abstracted from the imaginary and the symbolic, or in other words, from the human perspective. We have used a *transcendental* method.

After all, when we speak of the origin of writing we are speaking of the origin *of writing*. And when one understands that which precedes or exceeds oneself *as* one's origin, this is a transcendental deduction. One reaches the real by considering the present moment as we currently understand it, and then one subtracts from it, one removes determinations to reach the real in its indetermination: this is transcendentalism.

What matters is to acknowledge the fact that we *have* a genesis. And Lacan's understanding of the real as a writing-process, while it may describe it on the basis of what it originates – the signifier – and thus amount to a transcendental appropriation, is nevertheless designed to open the synchronic signifier onto a *diachronic* dimension, the axis of its generation. And it does this by virtue of its imaginary form. This allows Lacan a certain insight into the actual genesis of the signifier, and this is what differentiates his archi-writing from Derrida's: its imaginary form.

It is always a question of another way of writing the real origin, or of understanding the origin itself as a form of writing, but in this case it is a writing that refers us back to the chronological origin or prehistory of the signifier, with the help of the non-Derridean element of the imaginary. For a written mark to explain the actuality of the signifier and not just its possibility in a variety of forms, human writing being just one of them, attention must be paid to the *imaginary* form of the letter. The erect or *phallic* form of the archi-trace.

Notes

1. Lacan himself translates '*chaîne*' into English as 'link' (SXXIII: 64), and sometimes writes '*chaînœud*', linknot (cf. SXXIII: 73). '*Chaîne*' is a manner of connecting rings together, and hence a way of 'linking'. To explain an abbreviation Lacan makes of '*le nœud borroméen*', '*nœud bo*' (pronounced 'nuh-bow'), Lacan says this: 'Calling it *nœud bo* makes us think of something which is evoked somewhere in Joyce: "*on Mount Nebo the law was given to us*"' (SXXIII: 144).
2. Derrida is at pains to state that his readings of Lacan 'never claimed' to exhaust him or reduce his corpus to homogeneity: 'I never speak of a philosopher or a corpus in general as if it were a matter of a homogeneous body: I did not do so for Lacan any more than for any other' (R: 48). We shall scrutinise this claim in the final sections of Chapter 4.
3. 'The discourse of Lacan [. . .] continued thereafter to readjust, even recast, sometimes contradict the axioms I have just mentioned' (R: 61).

4. '[M]y reading of the "Seminar on 'The Purloined Letter'" as well as what prefigured it from 1965 to 1971 in *Of Grammatology* and *Positions* did not claim to enclose or exhaust Lacan' (R: 61).
5. It is worth stressing that to my knowledge, none of the authors of the three great deconstructive critiques attended Lacan's seminars: Lacan himself alludes to this in the case of Lacoue-Labarthe and Nancy as a good thing, since it enabled them to avoid the transferential love which tends to affect one's critical faculties (SXX: 65–71). On the other hand, this non-attendance will have increased the lacunae in their reading caused by the disappointing tardiness of the publication of Lacan's seminars, which continues to this day (2008).
6. Lacan speaks of '[t]he polar star of the relation of man to the real' (SVII: 75). The polar star or 'North star' in the Little Bear (*Ursa Minor*) is a star which, for observers in the northern hemisphere of the planet Earth, always remains in the North, never moving from its place in the sky. While the rest of the heavens appears to move, the North star acts as its pivot.
7. As a library book is marked as 'missing' ('*manque à sa place*') (SIV: 38).
8. '[T]he Other of this Other, so to speak, to be understood as that which allows the subject to perceive this Other, the locus of speech [*lieu de la parole*], as being itself symbolised' (SV: 463).
9. Lacan's notion of the '*act*' might be invoked in this context, the act of making metalanguage ex-sist: 'The act then is the only locus where the signifier has the appearance – the function in any case – of signifying itself. Namely to function outside its possibilities' (SXIV: 15/2/67).
10. Borch-Jacobsen seems to suggest that this is *all* that Lacan was trying to achieve, to set up a community, irrespective of the sense of what he said (Borch-Jacobsen 1991: 123–67).
11. The first 'Other' is capitalised presumably to indicate that the other would be another *language*, a metalanguage of a similar order to the Other that is the object-language, but of course, somehow distinct from it. It might also be to indicate that one is speaking of a *radical* heterogeneity, and not the relative otherness of the 'little or imaginary other'.
12. Lacan speaks of 'collective, socially accepted sublimations': 'In forms that are historically and socially specific, the *a* elements, the imaginary elements of the fantasy come to overlay the subject, to delude it, at the very point of *das Ding*' (SVII: 99).
13. '[W]hat we propose is to analyse the Oedipus complex as being Freud's dream' (SXVII: 117).
14. Although Lacan rarely mentions Uexküll by name, the reference is made explicit by his constant use of German, Uexküllian terms in this context, *Innenwelt* and *Umwelt*, among others.
15. Agamben provides a characteristically excellent condensation of Uexküll's thought (2004 [2002]: 39–47).

16. The animal is thus a 'jammed machine' (SII: 31) in that it has only a finite and fixed number of attitudes which it can adopt to *any* object in its environment. Moreover, its perception has developed such that it cannot even perceive certain elements of another animal's world, as the fly cannot perceive the almost diaphanous threads of the spider's web (cf. Agamben 2004 [2002]: 41–2). So strictly speaking there are only so many objects it can have *tout court*.
17. 'The source and storehouse of this preconscious of what we call imaginary is not unfamiliar, it has already been successfully explored in the philosophical tradition, and it may be said that Kant's schema-ideas [*idées-schèmes*] are situated on the border of this domain' (SIII: 165). Lacan also identifies the imaginary with the intuitive realm: 'intuition, in other words the imaginary' (SXIII: 30/3/66), 'the imaginary, or intuitive, plane' (SII: 18). 'Everything intuitive is far closer to the imaginary than to the symbolic' (SII: 316). The imaginary is the realm of comprehension, in the Kantian sense, where one takes things in *as wholes* rather than piecemeal, though this carries the notion of intuition beyond Kant, in light of contemporary science.
18. Lacan speaks at great length on the technical nature of the image in optics, as we shall see in Chapter 4.
19. Lacan discusses Gestaltism and atomism with reference to Merleau-Ponty's lecture, 'Philosophy and Psychoanalysis' (1971 [1948]: 83ff) (SII: 77–8).
20. Strictly, animals have no desire, although Lacan does occasionally use this word: 'the relation of the living organism to the objects that it desires is linked to the conditions of the *Gestalt* which locate the function of the imaginary as such' (SI: 281–2).
21. Lacan tells us that it is precisely this death drive that is responsible for the arising of the signifier itself, which as we shall see is a compensation for this mortal gap at the level of the imaginary (SIV: 48).
22. 'I mean what this term "fantasy" suggests in terms of a relation to *phantasia*, to the imaginary' (SXIV: 16/11/66).
23. Perhaps this defines the *organism*, which of itself enjoys a form of totality not to be found in mere matter, enjoying a certain structure where the organs in their functional relations serve to define what the organism is.
24. Without extremely complicated mirrors, which even then fail to include the subjective point of view, thus depriving the subject of any ability definitively to connect itself with the body it is viewing.
25. Despite Borch-Jacobsen's deconstructive critique of such a prevalence of vision, 'the whole onto-photo-logy of the imaginary', we have shown that this is not a philosophical presupposition, but the consequence of a material fact about the human being (Borch-Jacobsen 1991: 217, cf. 53–61).

26. '[L]anguage [*langage*], which has been functioning there for as long as you can remember [*souvenir*]' (SIV: 50).
27. Although the lozenge has many meanings, explained in Seminar XI in great detail (cf. SXI: 209ff). What joins the barred subject to the remainder of the real is ultimately the drive, which prevents desire from ever settling on one object and thus ceasing to desire. Hence the motion of circulating around the lozenge may be understood as the motion of the drive around the void in the symbolic and the imaginary, the void that is the real.
28. Lacan first discusses the veil (*voile*) or curtain (*rideau*) in this context in Seminar IV (SIV: 155–6).
29. Lacan refers the example to Kant (SXIII: 30/3/66; SXXIII: 83–4), who discusses the matter in ¶13 of his *Prolegomena* (Kant 1997 [1783]).
30. '*Lettre*' is homophonic with '*l'être*', being. Lacan will refer to this and thus suggest that the real is to be understood as 'being', but at the same time that such a notion as 'being' is always associated with *language*.

4

The real writing of Lacan: another writing

A letter from Derrida to Lacan

In the previous chapter we showed the notion of the imaginary to result from a genetic approach to the human being, and that its enduring presence necessitated a different understanding of the transcendental. It demonstrated that the symbolic, in whose order human beings reside, was not constituted in the way that Derrida thought, and this altered the way in which it could transcend itself towards the real. The real needed to be understood in two ways, by subtracting from both the symbolic *and* the imaginary. The real is a part of the signifier that is not a full-blown signifier, and it is a part of the image that is not specular. In truth, both of these ways have to coincide, since the real is nothing besides a lack in both the imaginary and the symbolic which necessitates their dependence on one another.

However, the subtraction can nevertheless be accessed from either of the two different realms. We have so far investigated the real of the imaginary, the object *a*, and the fantasy of its possession. But we have not yet fully examined the real of the *symbolic*. This is the letter, the scoremark or trace, which – when infinitely conglomerated – constitutes the empirical signifier. It is the mark that is needed in order for signifiers in their differentiality to exist. It is precisely the materiality of language itself, the density or 'opacity' of the signifier. If the object *a* is the real *of the imaginary*, then the 'letter' is the real *of the symbolic*, and our account of the latter will constitute the concluding chapter of this book.

'I shall speak, therefore, of a letter' (MP: 3).

This will *simulate* Lacan's proximity to Derrida. For this exposition will bring to light most starkly the contrast between Lacan and Derrida. For the notion of the letter is Lacan's own notion of 'archi-writing'. But to show where it is possible and necessary to exceed Derrida, we shall show how this writing differs from Derrida's in opening onto an imaginary and genetic dimension. It was necessary to trace the development of the imaginary in the previous chapter to bring it to the point at which it became evident that in Lacan's later thought it is just as important as the real and the symbolic.

One cannot distinguish the object *a* from the letter save in terms of perspective: it is the same real viewed from the perspectives of the imaginary and the symbolic respectively. Indeed, let us consider things more graphically: the 'a' of 'object *a*' is nothing besides a *letter*. The letter 'a'. When viewed from the point of view of the symbolic, the real in its imaginary form is (also) a letter. The letter is not just a mark, it also has a certain imaginary form, as it did in the very beginning: this imaginary form is that aspect of the letter which characterised the chronologically earliest of its forms: a certain picture.

By insisting on the second, complementary perspective on the real, that which views it from the standpoint of the symbolic, we shall in this chapter be insisting on the *unity* of the two reals. In truth, the real is nothing besides that which borders the imaginary and the symbolic, a ring which passes through both. This togetherness is precisely what we shall demonstrate here, in the guise of the letter and its relation to Lacan's *diagram*, the diagram being a letter that is used in an explicitly imaginary or pictorial way (*dia-grammē*). It is the lack of sense and the excess of sense belonging to the letter and the diagram respectively that constitutes their object *a*, the cause of their desirability, the motivation behind our desire to find a meaning in the mysterious letters of the matheme and to limit the ever expanding meaningfulness of the diagram.

In demonstrating this object '*a*', this imaginarity in writing – for diagrams are also written – we are demonstrating how Lacan presents, in comparison with Derrida, *another* writing.

There are in fact three aspects to Lacan's writing: the literary, the mathematical, and the diagrammatic. The baroque style of his commentaries, the terse formulae, and the excessive intuitive schemata. In each of these cases, the purpose of writing is to fuse the imaginary and the symbolic in such a way that the real is conveyed to the reader without being betrayed. The question of the real which escapes both imaginarity and symbolicity is hereby raised for the reader or auditor. It is always a question of writing the real, or, as we might say, 'writing: the real'.

We must first examine the archi-writing of Lacan, this real of language towards which the three *forms* of his writing are attempting to direct our attention.

Archi-writing in Derrida and Lacan

For Derrida, archi-writing is the inscription of a mark made by one thing (the 'other') on a certain surface (the 'same'). It is necessary that the mark exist in order for difference to exist, that one thing's absence be marked in an other. Thus, the mark, and the archi-writing which produces it, are necessary conditions of language as a system of differentiated signifiers.

If we were to spatialise this notion, as we cannot avoid doing when we speak about it, we would say that the trace, which constitutes the signifier, runs *between* signifiers since it joins together each signifier with all of the others. It is the reference that each signifier has to all of its kind. But in truth signifiers as a synchronic system are not distributed in space, and the body of the signifier is composed of nothing but these traces, these differences *between* signifiers. The signifier's existence lies outside of itself, *in* this 'between'. The signifier is nothing besides its 'signifyings', its references.

Archi-writing composes a positive signifier by overlaying the traces of all other signifiers. It is the depositing of an infinity of traces, present marks of absent 'things'. Traces are not signifiers, but the signifier is nothing besides trace. The real of the symbolic is not symbolic.

Since language is the prerequisite of sense, the trace makes sense possible, but it also ensures that there is an element of language, its very most fundamental constituent, that remains opaque to sense. The trace is the real of language, and for Derrida, as we have seen, this is the only real that is available to us.

By another route, Lacan also locates the real here. He also deems it 'writing'. And yet the real of language also binds the symbolic to the *imaginary*. For Lacan the real to which we have access is *both* the real of the symbolic and the real of the imaginary. Archi-writing is not just a quasi-transcendental of language, it also retains within language a mark of its *chronological* origin. Archi-writing is also *proto*-writing.[1] It is the imaginary, phallic form of certain elements of the pre-historic, pre-symbolic real that allowed the symbolic to be generated in the first place.

Lacan demonstrates that what today we call 'letters' originated in the score-marks made by the primeval hunter on the bone of a deceased animal or the cave wall. These were the first human marks left upon the surface of the earth in order to depict something beyond themselves, and retrospectively they can be understood as the first moment in the chronological emergence of the signifier. This sticklike form, and indeed the most basic pictograms, endure in many languages even today. Even in the Latin alphabet, scholars recognise an inverted ox head in the capital A, which is significantly the *first* letter (of the alphabet). It is also apparent in the Hebrew *aleph* and other Semitic and Phoenician letters.[2]

The letter by itself retains unchanged something which existed *before* the signifier was structured into an infinite system and sublated towards meaning. It is a meaningless element that not only indicates the transcendental, non-sensical origin of sense, but also the *pre-sensical* chronological origin of sense.

'Lalangue': on not meaning and not understanding[3]

If the traces of archi-writing are the scoremarks at the origin of the signifier, Lacan believes that there are moments in speech at which these traces come to the fore, when the material trace-structure of the signifier actually reveals itself. In symptoms. A symptomatic use of language Lacan calls '*lalangue*', a compaction of the French word '*langue*' and its definite article.

What appears in language in these symptomatic moments is the real written trace. But what is this? It is the bar that primally represses the real subject of enunciation in the symbolic, $. This is, at the same time, the bar which separates S and s, S/s, in the diagram of the sign. It is the prohibition of the sign, of any univocal meaning. The subject does not have a signifier, and yet he is in the signifier, in the place where it is incomplete. He is there because the real in the infinity of its trace holds it open. If the signifier cannot form a (finite) totality then none of its elements can achieve a stable signification. The subject enjoys this moment within language that is responsible for its meaninglessness.

And yet, this senselessness, this material trace, is the condition of possibility for the signifier. Thus the bar makes signification possible, and renders its complete determinacy impossible.

The trace itself, because it is the immanent condition of the signifier but not a fully fledged signifier that could refer to a signified, cannot be understood. But it can become legible, and indeed it does so precisely in those symptomatic moments at which meaning is evacuated from speech. 'The bar, like everything involving what is written, is based only on the following – what is written is not to be understood' (SXX: 34). What is written is not of itself ideal and resists sublimation to meaningfulness in a way that speech (apparently) does not. If one considers *the writing itself*, or rather the writ (*écrit*), one need not understand it. In itself, it is a set of marks that are made by one piece of material impinging on another. But one must read it. Reading: that is to say an attention to the material graphicity of the words, their writtenness, the way the signifier functions in a manner that is not subordinated to the signified, but with its own regularities and quirks. This is what Lacan draws attention to in entitling his book, '*Écrits*'.

One has to *read* what is *written*.

> There is some relationship of being that cannot be known. It is that relationship whose structure I investigate in my teaching, insofar as that knowledge – which, as I just said, is impossible – is prohibited [*interdit*] thereby. This is where I play on an equivocation – that impossible knowledge is censored or forbidden, but it isn't if you write '*inter-dit*' appropriately – it is said between the words, between the lines. We have to expose the kind of real to which it grants us access. (SXX: 119)

In simply placing a bar between '*inter*' and '*dit*', Lacan bespeaks the 'between' that is the archi-written trace: 'excuse me for slipping writing [*l'écrit*] into my speech', says Lacan before essaying another extraordinary neologistic pun (SXX: 40). These places in which writing comes to the fore in an almost inaudible moment of speech are '*lalangue*':

> It is here that *lalangue*, *lalangue* in French must help me out – not, as it sometimes does, by offering me a homonym, [. . .] which must be there to serve some purpose for us – but simply by allowing me to say that one souloves [*âme*]. [. . .] You see here that we can rely only on writing. (SXX: 84)

Such things rely only on *writing*, the two homophones can be distinguished only in a written text. In other words there is no way – or at least very little way, and no way *in speech* to be *certain* – to distinguish between the original word and the pun. But in writing, by reference to the graphic text, one can (quite) clearly distinguish them.

Thus, the syntax of *lalangue* amounts to an explicit incursion of the graphic into the linguistic, as Derrida says of '*différance*' (cf. MP: 3). It is a moment in which archi-writing shows itself in speech.

The failure to communicate: the sinthome

Archi-writing, therefore, is the bar that joins one signifier to another. The bar of the hyphen can also be read as a notch, marking a repetition. In order to be a repetition the second instance must be inscribed with a notch to indicate that it is different from and yet a repetition of the first. Thus, for instance, the second 'la' is marked with a notch ('la-') that counts the preceding, now phonically absent 'la', and however many have gone before: 'la-la-la-la-la'.[4] In these moments of explicit repetition within language ('la-la'), the tracing process that takes place at a level distinct from the signifier, beneath its surface as the signifier's very ground, becomes manifest *within* the signifier, in the sound itself. The trace is displaced from the real into the signifier which it makes possible, it reveals itself.

If one takes the French word for 'language', *la langue*, and highlights the senseless fact that the first two syllables of the syntagm '*la langue*' in fact repeat one another, one writes '*lalangue*'. *Lalangue* is for Lacan a symptomatic moment in the use of language where its real lettricity or trace-structure comes to the fore. It comes to the fore in repetition or similar phenomena in which language is evacuated of meaning.

Previously, the symptom was the moment at which the real of the unconscious subject of enunciation appeared in language *as repressed*. To indicate that he no longer understands the symptom in precisely this way, Lacan rewrites '*symptôme*' as '*sinthome*', using the more idiomatic old French spelling as distinct from the Greek – an almost indistinguishable sound but a different grapheme (SXXIII: 11).

What has changed is precisely Lacan's understanding of the relation between the symbolic and the real. Thanks to the development of the imaginary intercessor, the symbolic is no longer absolutely opposed to the real, ruling out 'full speech'. Now, it is possible that the speech of the subject of enunciation *can* find, not the words, but some way within language to express himself properly. The symptom is not necessarily a symptom of his repression, but the symptom (*sinthome*) of his *presence*. For this reason, such symptoms are not to be eradicated, but fostered to a certain extent, as the only way in which one's real desire can find expression in the symbolic.[5]

If *lalangue* is the incursion of the real, then the real can no longer be opposed to the symbolic. As a result, the aim of analysis can avoid the aporias that haunted 'full speech': it is no longer necessary to choose between a destruction of language in favour of speech and a use of language which would not sully singular speech with generality, both of which were impossible, if only because of Lacan's understanding of the real and symbolic as opposed. Since the real and the symbolic are no longer opposed, it is no longer the case that the aim of analysis should be to indicate the *discrepancy* between our real subjectivity and any signifier that would claim to represent us, and hence to keep our desire constantly dissatisfied with any symbolic object. In that case, the symptom expressed a repressed desire that had become fixated on some object. The patient needed to learn that no one object could ever fully satisfy it, and the aim of the analysis was therefore to unblock desire and allow it to be true to its infinite nature.

If achieving full speech means recognising that the symptom speaks of a desire that has become ensnared in a piece of language that will always be inadequate to this speech, then the aim of analysis would be the destruction of the symptom, its dissolution, for it indicates a blockage of desire. However, if it *is* possible for the real to inhabit the symbolic, then the symptom will no longer be a mark simply of *failure*. Rather it is a mark of success in a certain way. It would be the very *presence* of the real in the symbolic. And since the symbolic is a necessary crutch for man and cannot be eradicated, this presence of the real in the symbolic must be the *aim* of psychoanalytic treatment. Thus, what matters is not to relieve the subject of the symptom, albeit temporarily until a new object of desire comes along and one's desire once again fails to receive adequate expression. In place of this ultimately pessimistic view, psychoanalysis becomes the attempt to *know* the symptom in what it is, and that is the irruption of the subject's singularity *in* language. Desire need no longer be excluded by the symbolic and the ultimate space of enjoyment relegated to some impossible place outside of language. One's enjoyment need no longer be understood as dead on arrival in the symbolic order. There is some enjoyment to be had *in* language, something real *in* the symbolic.

Thus we can see how *lalangue* may be understood as a rewriting of Lacan's earlier notion of full speech as the aim of psychoanalysis. It is crucial that '*parole*' is no longer opposed to '*langue*'. *Lalangue* is precisely that moment at which the bodily tongue of speech is shown to be inherent to language.

Symptomatic moments are those moments at which the real – understood as *writing* – appears in language. They are moments of *lalangue*, of a graphic incursion upon the phonic, when the real lolling (lalalalalal. . .) of the tongue (*la langue*) appears in experience, moments in which the real insinuates itself upon the symbolic reality of experience.

The unconscious structured like lalangue – the unconscious as real

Due to his earlier oppositional understanding of the real and symbolic, Lacan was compelled, despite himself, to identify language and the unconscious. The unconscious had to be composed of *signifiers*. What Lacan was not in a position to see was that signifiers are themselves composed of something that is *not* significant. They are made of something real, and it is this senseless materiality that must remain excluded from consciousness. Now, following the travails of the name-of-the-father and the imaginary, he can see that the real is that which makes possible the very differentiality of language, it is the support of language itself, the material from which it is formed. And it is precisely this materiality that is repressed in conscious experience, which must idealise language and efface its materiality in favour of its signification. The trace effaces itself: '[the unconscious] gives only traces, which not only efface themselves, but which any use of discourse tends to efface, analytic discourse included' (SXXIII: 124). The unconscious is nothing besides the real traces of language: 'the unconscious would be real' (SXI: xxxix).[6] The unconscious is the letter of language.

If *lalangue* is the symptom, a formation of the unconscious subject, then we can understand why Lacan tells us that the unconscious itself *is lalangue*: 'That is what the experience of the unconscious has shown us, insofar as it is made of *lalangue*' (SXX: 138). This reiterates and yet renders more rigorous his earlier slogan, that 'the unconscious is structured like a language' (cf. SXX: 138 *et al.*). We have argued that the oppositional status of the real and the symbolic forced Lacan to mean that the unconscious *was* language in its infinity. But now Lacan is able to say that it is not *la langue* but *lalangue*. It is not language itself, but the real marks from which it is constructed. 'Language is, no doubt, made up of *lalangue*' (SXX: 139). Language itself is not completely linguistic, indeed it is entirely constituted by the real, the archi-written mark, and so effectively, language as *such* does not exist, it is just the way in which we are *conscious* of the infinity of unconscious marks comprising *lalangue*: 'If I have said that language is what the unconscious is structured like, that is because language, first of all, doesn't exist. Language is what we try to know concerning the function of *lalangue*' (SXX: 138).

We cannot *know* what is not conceptually or linguistically structured, signified or signifier. That real must remain unconscious since it can only be betrayed by the dictates of consciousness, that everything should be significant. The unconscious is still language, but language insofar as it is not itself. Insofar as writing imperceptibly impinges upon and creates language, it is the real trace that constitutes language. The signifier fully formed, or rather intuited by consciousness as a *finite* totality, elides the traces of which it is made. Why is the real trace unconscious? Because it is infinite, and it must be to give rise to a positively present signifier. And yet the conscious ego is, as we have established, finite.

And yet, *lalangue*, the unconscious, *appears* in language, in symptoms (*sinthomes*). The real trace comes to the fore. It does so when language no longer functions in the way that consciousness requires, which is to subordinate itself to meaning.

Lacan's notion of '*lalangue*' amounts very broadly to repetitive nonsense. The repetition evacuates of meaning both the repeated and the repeating instances, and the very doubling of the signifier causes us to focus on it in its own archi-written character, its real, non-meaningful composition by an infinity of traces. By refusing to be meaningful, to efface itself before meaning, *lalangue* fails to communicate, and thus we come to focus on the enunciator himself rather than his opaque statement. *Lalangue* is the moment at which, by failing to make sense, language ceases to communicate. But by failing to communicate, to institute an intersubjective event of meaning, it manages to *express* the real subject of enunciation in language. '*Lalangue* serves purposes that are altogether different from that of communication' (SXX: 138).

The only thing one can do with these instances is not to understand them, the only thing one can do is to *read* them.

Writing as symptom of the real unconscious subject

This is the meaning of the *near meaninglessness* of Lacan's *Écrits*. The Seminars are pedagogic, but the *Écrits* are hermetic, intended to express only the singularity of Lacan himself. 'The style is the man himself' (E: 3). They aim to communicate the singular subject of *enunciation*, by dwelling on the limit at which the communication is elided by the communicated, the speaking by the spoken (*énonciation-énoncé, dire-dit, écrire-écrit*). They are near enigmas: 'An enigma, as the name indicates, is an enunciation whose enunciated cannot be found' (SXXIII: 67; cf. SXVII: 36). These enigmatic enunciations have to be read and interpreted, for they do not render themselves transparent to their own signified: 'you are not obliged to understand my writings. If you don't understand them, so much the better – that will give you the opportunity to explain them' (SXX: 34).[7] This is why the difficulty of Lacan's writings is *essential* to what they are attempting to convey: 'I want to lead the reader to a consequence in which he must pay the price with elbow grease' (E: 5).

The reason meaningfulness must be resisted is because meaning always betrays the real, by idealising it: 'The only excuse that I have for telling you something today [. . .] is that it is going to be meaningful [*sensé*]. In exchange for this I will not achieve what I would want, which would be to give you a bit of real [*un bout de réel*]' (SXXIII: 119). Communication requires meaningfulness:

> The only trouble [. . .] is that in this case *the real would be given meaning* [*sens*], whereas [. . .] it appears that the real is founded [*se fonde*] to the extent that it doesn't have any meaning, that it *excludes meaning*, or, more precisely, that it is *deposited in this exclusion* [*se dépose d'en être exclu*]. (SXXIII: 64–5, my italics)

And this is inevitable, since a certain level of communicability must be maintained. Hence Lacan can say, 'the real both has, and does not have, a meaning [*sens*]' (SXXIII: 134).

Lacan's writings 'follow the *trace* of the real', they attempt to depict the marks that are made by the real, and for this they need to evacuate themselves of meaning. To do this is to 'tell the truth about (the real, unconscious) truth':

> what is it, to tell [. . .] the truth about truth [*le vrai sur le vrai*]?
>
> It is to do that which I have effectively done – to follow the trace of the real, the real which only consists [with (*con*) the other rings, imaginary and symbolic] and ex-sists in the knot [*suivre à la trace le réel, qui ne consiste, qui n'ex-siste que dans le nœud*]. (SXXIII: 66)[8]

Each of Lacan's *Écrits* is 'a little bit of real' which Lacan desired to bring to us (cf. SXXIII: 119).

The symptomatic moments of *lalangue* are thus moments at which language ceases to communicate and becomes entirely idiosyncratic, revelatory of itself in its peculiar materiality. Thus one overcomes the absolute alienation of the structuralist understanding of language as a fully formed system into whose machinations one is thrown at birth, which Lacan himself once came close to endorsing. Because one has *grown* into language, because language has *arisen alongside* the development of the human, Lacan can now see that one's immersion in language is *not just an alienation*. It is an alienation only insofar as one considers the system of language to be complete, which is to say a totality that is meaningful, insofar as language is used for *communication*. 'What I put forward, by writing *lalangue* as one word, is that by which I distinguish myself from structuralism, insofar as the latter would like to integrate language into semiology' (SXX: 101).

It is when (archi-)writing comes to the fore that the unconscious is manifest. This is why *lalangue* may be identified with the symptom, which is a formation of the unconscious, a manifestation of the unconscious subject. 'Writing [*L'écriture*] is thus a trace in which an effect of language can be read' (SXX: 121), and what is the unconscious if not an 'effect of language'? What is traced is the real. Writing is precisely a trace of the real, which is not *meant* to be understood.

We have identified the real with the singularity of things, including the singularity of the subject of enunciation, in this case the one named 'Lacan'. In just the same way, any slip or tic of our own reveals *us* as subjects of enunciation, normally elided by successful acts of communication.

To tell the truth about the truth, to tell the truth about the unconscious subject of enunciation is not to produce a meaningful metadiscourse on him. It is to *embody* that subject, to *describe* the real with one's written – and explicitly *written* – words. Writing allows the trace structure of the unconscious, the real density of the unconscious subject, to come to the fore.

Lacan's writings are not a metalanguage *about* the subject and *about* the imaginary, symbolic and real. They are attempting to direct us towards what eludes words, which lies *between* signifiers; the writing which takes place *there*, the real as the interstice, as what is *left out* of any word and any image. The purpose of the baroque filigrees of both is to indicate that no matter how much is written, something is missing, and the deliberate, sometimes ludicrous excess is precisely designed to indicate this lack, this excess (of meaning), which is the real.

If language (and pictures) were used in a *common* way, to communicate, the real would not be indicated. Thus language must be used in a way that is not indifferent to its normal use but which takes the possibilities of this use to their very limit. It must present, in a carefully calculated fashion, a near absolute idiosyncrasy, which will suggest *by means of signifiers* and (imaginary) *signifieds* the real which is neither symbolic nor imaginary.

Lacan's writings are symptoms of his singularity. And we are to *read* symptoms (the only way to distinguish '*symptômes*' from '*sinthomes*') and not understand them, for their very singularity *escapes* meaningfulness.

The subject is *responsible* for holding together a finite totality of language, by means of his finite consciousness of it.[9] He is the missing signifier or sign that would complete the totality of the signifier. *He* is the link between the signifier and the real, that provides the former with its 'polar star' of orientation: 'man [is given] the role of mediator [*médium*] between the real and the signifier' (SVII: 129);[10] 'we must find the subject at the origin of the signifier itself' (SIX: 24/1/62).[11] The very structure of language could not have arisen without the speaking subject, the entity which traced notches on bones and thereby *marked itself in the real*.[12]

Lacan suggests that there are two ways to approach this moment in which speech gets determined by language, one unintentional and one intentional. The first is the unwitting symptomatic expression of *lalangue* displayed by the neurotic patient. The second is that which is consciously achieved by his own work and that of Joyce (for example). We indicate the determination of singular speech by a certain generic language by an absolute (poetic) mastery of the particular *idioms* of the language in which we find ourselves. A poet is absolutely in tune with the idiom of his language and so brings before us the absolutely contingent specificity of that language. Others, such as Lacan and Joyce, use an idiom *so* extremely, approximating a point of *absolute* idiomaticity, to the point of near psychosis, at which one's symbolic order is *exclusively* one's own, *entirely* incommunicable, that they are able to point up the moment at which an absolutely singular and incommunicable speech is determined by a particular language, for the *sake of* communication.

One must have one's own idiomatic *speech*, but it must use and yet twist the idiom of one's *language*. One's manner of manipulating the signifier is crucial in this regard, for it is the trace-structure of the *signifier* that is the real, which is to say the place of our subjective singularity.

One cannot simply jabber; one must communicate, and so one must have a *concern* for meaning, without entirely effacing the materiality of one's signifiers before the ideality of meaning. The fact that others still understand me indicates that my language is still a language, a shared idiom, however small a brotherhood are capable of using it. But by achieving maximal idiosyncrasy, by coming as close to singularity as is possible within language, *and still failing*, Lacan intimates that utterly indeterminate singularity beyond language.

Idiomaticity, then, takes two forms, one individual, one collective: one is the individuality of the *use* of language and the second is the individuality of the 'mother tongue' itself.

Why are we stressing this? Because for the early Lacan, all language is the same, unified by the one transcendental signifier of the name-of-the-father. Now, with the fragmentation of the name, each language is its own, and has its own relation to the real, its own real perhaps, each can be more or less alienated from its own materiality. If one's purpose is to convey a sense of the real, one must *respond* to the *particular* language that is one's own, to its peculiar *idiom*.

The idiom of the mother tongue

Lacan explains that one of the reasons for the spelling '*sinthome*' is the fact that it belongs to a French language unaffected by the later intervention of Greek. It is a word that can be spoken only in the *French* language: the very word exists only in a *determinate* language in an idiomatic form.

'I write [*lalangue*] as one word to designate [*désigner*] what each of us deals with, our so-called mother tongue [*lalangue dite maternelle*], which isn't called that for nothing' (SXX: 138). This means two things: first, that the syntagm can be constructed only in the *French* language, and hence represents a certain untranslatable idiosyncrasy relating to the very materiality of the signifiers, the sonic material which differentiates one language from another;[13] and second, that it refers to the '*lingua*', the meaningless physical tongue, which lolls (lollanguage) or rolls to produce the very syllable with which it begins, '*lal*'.[14] The tongue is the organ which produces significant speech. Thus a signifier refers to the tongue as the real physical organ that is required for its production. It is an organ that also actualises itself as the wholly physical organ of tasting and food-manipulation. To draw attention to the tongue in its physicality is to emphasise the rooting of the signifier in materiality, and ultimately perhaps in infantile or primeval needs, which first stirred us to communicate.

The origin of difference, the source of the individuation of signifiers, is real: it lies in the contortions of the physical lungs, throat, tongue, lips and teeth. These differences are those which run between signifiers, distinguishing them one from the other. *Between* individual signifiers is precisely where Lacan would have placed the *subject*.

Earlier he named the subject as a *signifier* but a *missing* signifier. He had to, because the only thing there was in language was the signifier. Now, the subject can be *in* the signifier and yet *not* a signifier *at the same time*, he can reside between signifiers.

The subject was always understood to dwell in the 'holes in discourse' (E: 253), but now these holes need no longer be understood as a lack of signifier. Rather they can be understood as follows: 'the subject resides in this division which I have represented in its time by the relation of one signifier to another signifier' (SXXIII: 158). Naturally, the subject still cannot be named adequately with a signifier. But the bar of the barred subject is now rethought as the notch of *différance*, the space between signifiers, and '$' may be understood as the subject's taking up its residence in and as these very bars themselves. The real subject is *written*.

'Joyce' the sinthome[15]

The real trace which the subject occupies is the letter. Lacan closely associates this with the name. The subject can appear in the symbolic – symptomatically – by writing his *name*. Contrary to Derrida, as we shall see, the name is no longer ruled out by the signifier.

'Joyce' is a *sinthome*, the name Joyce, the surname. Joyce's father was a 'good for nothing [*Fénian*[16]]' (SXXIII: 15). Assuming his father's name and position did not present an enticing prospect for James. The name-of-the-father did not promise him any place in the symbolic order at all, for his father was nothing in society. So Joyce had to go about using his name, his '*sinthome*', in such a way as to achieve some place in a symbolic order by himself, and this meant something close to creating a symbolic order of his own, though without relinquishing a common, meaningful language altogether.

When the name-of-the-father in the proper sense is foreclosed, one risks attaining no symbolic order at all, and remaining locked at the level of imaginary rivalry with the real father. One risks psychosis, and Joyce certainly came close.

To spite his lack of a surname, Joyce took it upon himself to 'make his name', to create his own highly idiosyncratic symbolic world, which, by being published and read, would allow him to father a certain symbolic universe that others, academics, might come to share in. In order that this be no transitory matter, it was necessary that the books be difficult. If interpretation is needed it is because a text's meaning hovers on the edge of absence or inaccessibility, the text yielding up its meaning only to those who are prepared fully to immerse themselves in it, to share almost absolutely Joyce's way of using the signifier, to partake of his averted psychosis. This is the meaning of Joyce's desire to keep the academics (*universitaires*) busy for three hundred years (SXXIII: 16).

An analogous situation can be seen to exist with the creation of Lacanian discourse; Lacan shares his words only with those who come to follow him, his pupils: many of his writings are intelligible only to those who have followed him from the beginning. Joyce's readership is wider. Perhaps the need for a community was greater in Joyce's case than in Lacan's, due to their respective fathers. So his was not an entirely singular soliloquy, but an extremely idiosyncratic use of a language in which he found himself: English rather than Gaelic. He produced his own symbolic order that was then centred around and named by the word 'Joyce'. This is how he made his name what it is, the name *of a father*. 'Joyce' then came to be that signifier which allowed the man some access to a symbolic order, which his real father had not supplied.

'Joyce-the-*sinthome*' is '"Joyce" the *sinthome*', it is Joyce's very name placed in the position of the name-of-the-father as the mark and organising pole of his very own self-created symbolic order. This order is what made his name famous: his writing did it. He wrote his name, he inscribed it as the author of his own idiosyncratic language. This writing was his legacy to future generations, those whom he wanted to keep busy, intrigued, desirous.

This making of a name, writing one's name into a symbolic order, or organising a new symbolic around the real writing (the archi-writing) of the name, one's name naming the very *structure* that one makes, is precisely what Lacan is doing with his own highly individual style, vocabulary, and exaggerated performance.

Lacan the sinthome. On idiosyncrasy and idiocy: Lacan's bodily presence

It is not at all irrelevant, then, that Lacan's signifier of choice, '*lalangue*', begins with the first two *letters* of his own name. 'Lacan' begins with 'La'. A meaningless repetition renders this '*Lala*': Lacan's language, *la langue de Lacan*.[17] The name *itself* must thus be counted as one instance of *lalangue*, a meaningless blemish on the surface of sensible language, a signifier that does not have any meaning and is hence not properly a signifier at all. It is rather a remnant of something else within the signifier, indeed a remnant of a time when the signifier did not fully signify and so cover over the real and the imaginary. We shall soon see that the name is not unrelated to real writing.

One should always attend to those elements in speech which seem to be mere nonsense, or just plain stupid, such as Lacan's puns: all are symptoms, formations of the unconscious. A joke is always unnecessary from the point of view of meaningful discourse, it is always a distraction. These idiocies, the fact that one uses such baroque excesses of meaningfulness, rather than merely using one's words as vehicles to communicate a meaning to one's audience, are always related to the entirely senseless fact that someone exists, and that they are unique, *real*.

Lacan states that the most important thing about his discourse is the meaningless fact that he is standing before them, *speaking*, in person, physically, a body (*corps*) emitting sounds. Lacan connects this blunt factuality with the *enjoyment* of the audience:

> at stake is the stupidity that conditions what I named my seminar after this year and that is pronounced '*encore*' [homophone of *en corps*, bodily presence, 'in the flesh']. You see the risk involved. I am only telling you that to show you what constitutes the weight of my presence here – it's that you enjoy it. My sole presence – at least I dare believe it – my sole presence in my discourse, my sole presence is my stupidity. (SXX: 12; cf. SXX: 14, 22, 26–7)

Unlike a signifier, real bodily presence, stupidity, can be *enjoyed*. Only the real, the non-significant, can be enjoyed.[18] Perhaps Lacan is here deploying the Kojèvian opposition between the functional world of work and the purposeless world of enjoyment. Signifiers are formal tools for communication, materiality alone can be a substance that we enjoy.

The subject is the dummy (*la mort*) in the system of signifiers in a new sense: he is present there in his realness, his uniqueness, and that means his insensate singularity. Lacan is aware that no signifiers he uses (beyond his name, perhaps, if that is a signifier) will be able to capture his uniqueness, so he *performs* his uniqueness, he demonstrates his unconscious, *deliberately* generating *lalangue* where the neurotic does so involuntarily: 'my sole presence *in* my discourse, my sole presence is my stupidity'.

And yet one cannot choose what to find enjoyable, what jokes make one laugh. But there is a reason why they do: 'In general, I do not amuse myself by chance' (SXIV: 31/5/67). The same goes for each member of an audience finding a joke funny. One's singularity is always an unchosen fact. The very fact of making jokes and laughing at them introduces one's singularity into a discourse – an intersubjective bond, as language always is – in which formality is demanded. If one were simply using propositions to convey a meaning, they would be out of place, mere incidental distractions. Lacan's jokes (*lalangue*) are *crucial* to what he is trying to convey.

What is curious about symptoms is that they are enjoyed, even if this enjoyment is unconscious, masochistic, and we feel it consciously as suffering: 'the symptom is enjoyment [*jouissance*]' (SXIII: 27/4/66). In truth, here, unconsciously, there is enjoyment, or, perhaps more simply, we enjoy the pain, but consciousness cannot handle such a contradiction. If this is a contradiction, it points to a dimension of ourselves which lies beyond the symbolic order, where contradictions are effective, towards the real where they are not (cf. SIX: 21/2/62). Enjoyment then must be our relation to the real, which, perhaps because of its foundational role with respect to the symbolic (and imaginary), Lacan describes, quite literally, as a 'substance'.

The substance of enjoyment

At least, the fact that enjoyment does not depend on anything else for its existence, that it cannot be differentially defined, explains why Lacan calls it 'substance' (SXIV: 31/5/67). This is in effect a reworking of his earlier notion of the real as that which is self-same and does not refer to anything else for its definition. It refers to the Aristotelian notion of *substantia* or *hypokeimenon* as that which depends on nothing beyond itself for its existence, and which supports other existences, accidents or attributes. Enjoyment *is* part of a substantialist metaphysics, but one which confines this substance to the very weave of language, to a oneness at the very *origin* of *difference*. This is the materiality of the perceived physical sound, unique to a certain (mother) tongue.

In the hyphen which marks the repetition characteristic of empirical symptoms – 'compulsive behaviour', tics – the real that is accessed in enjoyment (*jouissance*) is hyphenated with the symbolic. But what is crucial is that the real of language is nothing besides this hyphen, this trace which inscribes one signifier's absence within an other. Thus Lacan hyphenates enjoyment and sense, to form '*jouis-sens*'.

One *hears* (*ouïr*) the *materiality* of the sound uttered. The real trace is senseless – unintelligible to consciousness – because it is infinite: the only way a signifier can come to appear as present is if it is composed of an infinite number of traces. But this means that the symbolic can never form a finite totality – save fantasmatically – and so, what renders meaning possible also renders it impossible. The trace makes signifiers, but it also prevents them from forming a whole

In this case, it can be seen that the written signifier was not first a secondary translation of a phoneme, a verbal sound. Rather, first of all, the vocal signifier must have been composed of writing, of traces, in order to become differential at all. The signifier needs to be differentiated in order *then* to be able to stand for a *distinct* sound or phoneme, which may then be taken as the phonic vehicle of a signified.

We have seen, with Derrida, that the illusion of presence and transparency, of meaning, is created only by the *infinity* of the dense material trace. For this reason, a common trope, in the later Lacan at least, is that in this way the primacy of the phonic and the subordination of the graphic is subverted, if not inverted.

> It is through the intermediary of writing that speech breaks up [*se décompose*] at the moment of imposing itself as such, that is, in a deformation which remains ambiguous if it concerns being freed from the verbal [*parolier*] parasite [. . .], or, on the contrary, of letting oneself be invaded by the properties of the essentially phonemic order of speech. (SXXIII: 97)

It is precisely such pre-phonetic 'letters', syntactical elements, which Lacan invokes in his *mathematical formulae*. With regard to his 'little letters', which go to make up the various mathemes, the a, $, A, Lacan speaks as follows:

> Their very writing constitutes a medium [*support*] that *goes beyond speech*, without going beyond language's actual effects. Its value lies in centring the symbolic [. . .]. To retain a congruous truth – not the truth that claims to be whole, but that of the half-telling [*mi-dire*]. (SXX: 93, my italics)

The real then is the support and the orientation of the symbolic around a point that is real.

The mathematical form of language, (what seems like) 'logic', is the other side of Lacan's baroque quasi-literary writing. It has almost the same effect, but it joins up and constitutes a bridge between this literary writing and Lacan's *diagrams*, in which we shall soon be able to see that an image is *also* a *letter*. Thus, whichever way we look at it, the lack inherent in the imaginary and in the symbolic can in both cases be understood as a form of letter. The letter does not transcend that in which it constitutes a lack, but is immanent to it. Thus the letter, the archi-written and proto-written mark, constitutes a real bridge between the imaginary and the symbolic. It is our task to understand precisely how it can do this. We have already acquired a sense of how an idiomatic use of language, *lalangue*, writing in speech, can manifest symptomatically the singular real of the speaker. Now we must negotiate our way through the mathematical formulae and the diagram, to see how the two extremes of Lacan's work, the apparently pure signifier and the apparently pure signified (or image), in fact require and imply one another, and how *both* imply the *third* form of Lacan's language, his baroque spoken discourse.

The matheme – psychoanalysis on the border of mathematics

One crucial way in which writing literally makes its incursion into Lacanian discourse is in Lacan's use of written formulae, the discourse, supposedly, of science. This discourse attempts to avoid images, significance, and hence the anthropomorphism which forces the real to conform to the comprehension of human consciousness. It is a logical language evacuated of the meaningfulness that ordinary *logos* has for us. For Lacan, science believes that a symbolic logic purified of imaginary elements will give us access to the real beyond the limitations of our egoic and egomorphic consciousness. It seems that science is here purporting to present pure letters, the pure real of language. One avoids the level of meaning and the constraints thereby imposed on language and one just writes the real with these meaningless letters and symbols: this allows it to be 'present' in its very incomprehensibility. The notion is perhaps that by refusing to be involved in the imaginary realm at all, the symbolic is emptied even of its signifying qualities and reduced to its naked *realness*. Thus in their very meaninglessness, the symbols would cease to be symbols, since imaginarity, as the signif*ied*, is an essential part of this, and they would become real.

We must be clear from the very start that this is the view of the mathematical sciences, according to Lacan; it is not the psychoanalyst's own. It is as if the sciences believed that they could sidestep Derrida's insight, which is also Lacan's, that while one must exist at the point of *exhaustion* of meaning, one cannot avoid meaning altogether, the mark can never be altogether removed from its potential (if always incomplete) sublation towards sense.

Mathematics describes this eradication of all imaginary elements as the favouring of 'formalism' over 'intuitionism',[19] the eradication of the imaginary being the eradication of the 'intuitive'.

> Everything intuitive is far closer to the imaginary than to the symbolic. It is very much a present-day concern of mathematical thought to eliminate the intuitive elements as thoroughly as possible. The intuitive element is considered to be an impurity in the development of the mathematical symbolic. (SII: 316)

The formulae of mathematics thus attempt to approximate a meaningless syntax: 'the exact sciences do nothing other than tie the real to a syntax' (SII: 305). Their formulae are pure *writing*: 'the formalisation of mathematical logic [. . .] is based only on writing [*l'écrit*]' (SXX: 93). 'The prestige of this logic was entirely in what we have reduced it to ourselves, namely the usage of letters' (SIX: 20/6/62). And this was how mathematics presumed to reach the real: 'Mathematicisation alone reaches a real – and it is in that respect that it is compatible with our discourse, analytic discourse' (SXX: 131).

Lacan even seems to admit that he was seduced by this notion, in his structuralist moment: 'That is why I thought I could provide a model of [the real] using mathematical formalisation, inasmuch as it is the most advanced elaboration we have by which to produce signifiance [*signifiance*[20]] [. . .]. The mathematical formalisation of signifiance runs counter to meaning' (SXX: 93). Nevertheless, the impetus from the mathematicisation of language is crucial since it indicates *another use* of language than that of rendering it diaphanous before the signified: 'nothing seems to better constitute the horizon of analytic discourse than the use made of the letter by mathematics' (SXX: 44).

Lacan recognised the possibility of emphasising the inadequacy of subordinating ordinary prose to meaning by advocating a certain form of mathematical writing at least as early as 'The Instance of the Letter' (1957), where he states that, '[o]nly mathematical algorithms [. . .] are considered to be devoid of meaning, as they should be' (E: 416). In Seminar I (1953–4), we find: 'Mathematical progress [. . .] comes good the day some man thinks of inventing a sign like this, $\surd$, or like that, $\int$. That's what mathematics is' (SI: 275):

> To extract a natural law is to extract a meaningless formula. The less it signifies anything, the happier we are. [. . .] You would be wrong to think that those little equations of Einstein's that express the relationship of inertial mass to a constant plus some exponents have the slightest meaning. They are pure signifiers. (SIII: 184–5; cf. SII: 299)

But it is precisely in this pretension to do without the imaginary *altogether* that Lacan departs from science. What science does not realise – or perhaps does not need to realise? – is that the imaginary is necessary to an understanding of the real, since the real is from our standpoint *nothing besides* the deficiency of both the imaginary and the symbolic. Its mistake is to think that one need speak only of the real of the symbolic. In truth, the real of the symbolic is the lack within the symbolic which necessitates its entwinement with the imaginary.

This is what Lacan means when he speaks of his discourse as a form of negative theology, a delimitation of what is beyond the limit of our comprehension. It is this beyondness which is denied in the mathematical use of the signifier: 'If my discourse today hadn't been absolutely and entirely negative, I would tremble at having lapsed into philosophical discourse. [. . .] The analytic thing will not be mathematical. That is why the discourse of analysis differs from scientific discourse' (SXX: 117). And this quite simply because mathematics believes it can positively *present* the real beyond the imaginary.[21] Thus Lacan distinguishes his own writings from those of mathematical science: 'Emerging from analytic discourse, the letters I bring out here have a different value from those that can emerge from set theory. The uses one makes of them differ, but nevertheless – and this is what is of interest – they are not without converging in some respect' (SXX: 36).

Lacan borrows the grammatical nature of the formulae of mathematics but uses it in his own non-mathematical way, precisely to indicate that he is *not* attempting to do mathematics. Hence any accusation of mathematical mistakes or misuse seriously misses the mark.

What is different about Lacan's formulae is that they explicitly *invoke* the imaginary character of the signs that they use. The bar of the 'fraction' represents a barrier preventing passage between the 'numerator' and the 'denominator'; the *phi* (φ, Φ) resembles the actual phallus. In other words, Lacan uses a mathematical sign as a *diagram*, as for instance in his formula for the metaphor, where the sign of addition, +, is taken in its pure graphicity to indicate one line, the vertical, piercing a barrier, the horizontal line, which represents the bar separating S from s in Saussure's diagram of the sign.[22]

The letters of the Lacanian matheme are also *images*, *diagrams* of what they wish to convey.

Commentary

Lacan hints at the necessary imaginary form of his symbolic formulae in his insistence that these formulae are *insufficient* on their own. They need *commentary*. They need to *mean* something.

However close Lacan came to this in his final seminars, as speech became difficult and perhaps more inadequate, one *cannot* communicate solely in images, in the physical construction of loops of string or by the inscription of opaque formulae. Lacan insists on the need for oral or written commentary on these images and symbols. This is how the diagrams and formulae are made transmissible. In practical terms, one has to 'speak about' and 'write around' one's maths. On a simplistic level, no-one will understand the mathemes if they are not talked about in a language which all of the group shares (cf. Lacan in Lemaire 1977: vii–viii). One cannot have writing without speech: 'signs that are called mathematical – "mathemes" – [. . .] are not transmitted without the help of language' (SXX: 110).[23]

> Mathematical formalisation consists of what is written, but it only subsists if I employ, in presenting it, the language I make use of. [. . .] [N]o formalisation of language is transmissible without the use of language itself. It is in the very act of speaking that I make this formalisation, this ideal metalanguage, ex-sist. (SXX: 119)

We have already described how Lacan's performative speech makes the impossible metalanguage exist. Here we can explicate this as the return of the pure letter of symbolic logic to the imaginary realm of meaningfulness and communicability.

Ex-sistere means stretching out beyond oneself, and this is precisely what the symbolic does here: it stretches out towards the imaginary. This is how the two relate, and it is this stretching, this *desire* to exceed one's own borders, that *is* the real, and it is in performing this stretching, by speaking around his mathematics, that Lacan *performs* the real for his audience.

Recalling that the intersection of symbolic and imaginary is what produces meaning, Lacan describes the necessity to surround his writings with language as the production of a 'new imaginary', a new set of *meanings*, or a new way of *being* meaningful, of appealing to the 'intuition', perhaps of coining a signifier which is *not* arbitrarily connected with its signified: 'The orientation of the real, in my formula, *forecloses meaning*. [. . .] It is necessary to break through, if I can say this, to *a new imaginary* [*un nouvel imaginaire*] establishing *meaning* [*instaurant le sens*]. This is what I am trying to establish with my language [*langage*]' (SXXIII: 121, my italics).

Diagrams of formulae

If one cannot ever escape the image, should we not understand Lacan's *diagrams* as the same meaningless letters that comprise the mathematical formulae, but ones which more explicitly *acknowledge* their imaginary character? Lacan speaks of the schema as a 'formalisation that is presented in the intuitive realm' (E: 476).

The diagrams attempt to indicate the real as that which stands beyond the imaginary, but in a way that does not *transcend* the imaginary and so constitute something that would be *opposed* to it. The real is indicated here as the internal *limit* of the imaginary. This is demonstrated by what Lacan calls the diagrams' 'excess'.[24] The images take imaginarity so far, they attempt to picture so much, that they draw the viewer of the image to the sublime limit of the image, to the point at which he may become aware of a beyond. The image is taken to the point of being *counter*-intuitive: 'these figures are not something that you legitimately translate by what I am nevertheless forced to represent them to you by, namely, by something that can be intuited' (SXIII: 30/3/66). Such images create a *desire*, a desire to reach beyond the image to the real that it seems to be attempting so profusely to depict. This beyond of the image within the image is the object *a*, object cause of desire.[25]

It is always a question of a picture which leads the viewer beyond the pictorial. For instance, in the 'cross cap' or mitre, the most famous form of the latter being the Moebius strip (SIX: 16/5/62), that which must intuitively have two surfaces turns out to have one.[26] The knots are so counter-intuitive that they seem to exorcise the imaginary of its very imaginarity.

> Disquieting strangeness is incontestably of the order of the imaginary [*L'inquiétante étrangeté relève incontestablement de l'imaginaire*], and the specific original geometry, of the knots, has the effect of exorcising it. But that there should be something which allows it to be exorcised is certainly in itself strange. (SXXIII: 48)[27]

'We are in fact always captivated [*captivés*] from the outset by a geometry [. . .] comparable to the sack, which is to say to the surface [Euclid's geometry]. [. . .] To think of the knot – something which is done more commonly with the eyes shut, you can make the attempt

– is very difficult' (SXXIII: 28). 'Captivation', it should be recalled, is a notion that Lacan often uses to describe the imaginary.[28] Our limited, surface-bound perception compels us to imagine and to see in a Euclidean way. We need to break away from it if we are to reach the real to which the (impasse of the) imaginary gives us access.

It is almost more crucial to be able to explain *diagetically* what is going on in Lacan's diagrams than to intuitively appreciate it. It is the fact that one encounters *obstacles* in trying to imagine the knots that lends these representations their efficacy as representations of that which *exceeds* representation:

> This [the knot] is constituted by a geometry which one could say is *forbidden to the imaginary* [*interdite à l'imaginaire*], because it *can be imagined only across all sorts of resistances*, indeed difficulties. It is this that constitutes the knot in as much as it is Borromean. (SXXIII: 31, my italics)

Thus Lacan understands the Borromean knot as a barrier to the imagination, which means as something which cannot be appropriated by human intuition. 'The Borromean knot does not constitute a model in that it has something in whose vicinity [*près*] the imaginary fails. I mean that which as such resists the imagining of the knot' (SXXIII: 42).

It is in obstructing the imagination that the diagram opens onto the real. And yet this is the moment it also comes to be seen as a *symbol*.

Since the real of the imaginary is that lack which necessitates the symbolic supplement, any image that represents the real will not simply be an image, it will also be symbolic, it will be a letter. For instance, the O's of the Borromean chain are not just images, they are also letters: 'It has all the characteristics of writing – it could be a letter' (SXX: 122).[29] If the real is the limit of both the imaginary and the symbolic, the only way to intimate it in a representation will be by way of an entity in which the symbol and the image coincide such that each one exceeds itself: 'In its standing [*sister*] outside the imaginary and the symbolic, the real bangs them together [*cogne*], it plays precisely in something which is of the order of limitation [. . .] the real has ex-sistence only in the encountering of the limit [*l'ârret*] of the symbolic and the imaginary' (SXXIII: 50).

An image is also a letter: Lacan suggests as much by insisting that his schema are always written on a blackboard, flattened out into two comprehensible dimensions – reduced to *writing*. In other words, the image alone is not enough, it needs to become symbolic in order to be presented to an audience.

Neither writing alone (mathemes) nor images alone (diagrams) are enough to present the real. Each one must be *both*.

The written flattening of the diagram

There is a crucial distinction between the knots themselves and Lacan's representations of them on the blackboard. These representations are *written* upon the blackboard (or the page). The three-dimensional, counter-intuitive *realness* of the knots must be reduced to a flattened *net* when it is inscribed upon the blackboard or the page: 'this writing represents for you the flattening out of a knot' (SXX: 122).

Writing takes place in two dimensions, while the actual knots themselves require *three*. For their very being, the knots require *depth*, as well as length and width. Direction, *orientation*, behind and before, are crucial to the tying of the knot. Perhaps this is what renders them such apt exemplars of the real, which Lacan at times identifies with *orientation*. *Writing* the knots evacuates them of their specific dimensionality: 'there is nothing more dangerous than things on the blackboard – it's always a bit flat' (SI: 77).

> [The drawing of the knot] has all the characteristics of writing – it could be a letter. However, since you write cursively, you never think of stopping a line before it crosses another in order to make it pass underneath, or rather in order to assume that it passes underneath, because in writing something completely different than three-dimensional space is involved. (SXX: 122)

And yet, this disparity between the representation and the real is crucial to the *depiction* of the real, since the real for *us* must be understood solely as a *limit*. So it is *only* in the form of this written 'betrayal' that we can properly gain *access* to the real: 'if there is any chance of grasping something called the real, it is nowhere other than on the blackboard' (SXVII: 151).

This writing allows the knots to be *communicated*: writing is indeed the 'mathematisation' of the image, insofar as a *matheme* is something that can be learned by heart and transmitted, a formula that is memorised and passed on.[30]

The real as impasse of the symbolic and the imaginary

Thus we can see why the real is accessed *only* in the aporia or impasse in which *neither* imaginary *nor* symbolic can *by themselves* provide access to the real. The real is accessed at the limits of both realms, where they find that they need each other. Lacan speaks of this as an impasse of formalisation, as if the real were some substance that eluded form in the sense of either formulae or images: 'The real can only be inscribed on the basis of an *impasse* of formalisation' (SXX: 93, my italics); 'this *impasse* [. . .] this impossibility *by which* a real is defined' (SXX: 144, my italics). The real *for us* is an impasse of both the symbolic and the imaginary.

When Lacan writes his knots, he does not intend first and foremost to be understood, to posit something that would comfortably accommodate itself to the capacities of his audience and reader: 'We haven't the slightest idea what they mean' (SXX: 110); he intends precisely to stretch these capacities to their *limits*, since it is only *at* these limits that the real will reveal itself to us.

For this reason, Lacan's diagrams can only be described as 'sublime', a term which Lacan makes much use of in his seventh Seminar, where he states that sublimation 'raises an object [. . .] to the dignity of the Thing' (SVII: 112).[31] In other words an ordinary object of representation is rendered so as to lead our apprehension on towards the real. The diagrams are objects represented by a subject which stretch this subject's faculties towards a place *beyond* representation, precisely by allowing *ap*prehension to outstrip *com*prehension.

So it is in the way that these mathematical formulae and diagrams *fail to communicate*, in the impossibility of their being *fully* understood or *fully* intuited, that they achieve their goal and present the real. Thus the demand for clarity, the complaints at Lacan's 'baroque style' and the opacity of his formulae and diagrams are misguided in principle. The real cannot directly be presented, it can only be intimated in the impasse. This is why the truth can only be half-told (cf. SXX: 92), because in order to be told, which is to say communicated, the real must be appropriated unto the signifier and the signified, the symbolic and the imaginary, but it is that to which neither of these can be adequate.

Thus Lacan's diagrams are the mirror image of his mathemes. The mathemes take the *symbolic* to its limit, and at this point of meaninglessness their imaginary form comes to the fore; while the diagrams take the *imaginary* to its limit, and here become legible as something like signifiers.

The three rings and the letter

Thus, Lacan understands the Borromean knots as *symbolic images*. But is not *all* writing imaginary? How else is one to distinguish one letter from another save by its imaginary form? The letter insofar as it differs from the barest scoremark must be characterised by *imaginary* differences, if it is to act as the support for different sounds, as it does in alphabetical writing.

Lacan often insists that writing is real, and that writing is inherently related to the knot, which is to say that writing is always at once both symbolic and imaginary, or rather it is the support of both and of their necessary belonging together. It is insofar as the real *writes* or inscribes marks that it can and must bind together the imaginary and the symbolic. 'I have invented what is written [*ce qui s'écrit*] as the real. [. . .] But this real I have written in the form of the Borromean knot' (SXXIII: 129).

The knot is a form of writing which gives us some access to the real: 'my *nœud bo* [. . .] changes the meaning [*sens*] of writing. It shows that there is something to which signifiers can be attached [*accrocher*]' (SXXIII: 144). Here Lacan names writing as the real *support* of the signifier, and that means the *letter*: 'the letter here [the letter *a*] is nothing less than a testimony to the intrusion of a writing as other [*autre*], with a small *a*. [. . .] The writing in question comes from somewhere other than the signifier' (SXXIII: 145).[32] Indeed it precedes it and constitutes its very condition. The letter is the real of language, the trace which supports the signifier, the very material from which any signifier is made: 'The writing of little mathematical letters is that which supports the real' (SXXIII: 68).

And yet Lacan refers to writing as an other (*autre*) with a small *a*, as an *imaginary* other, or perhaps as the object *a* which is that part of the mirror that cannot be reflected. The letter is thus the real of the symbolic *and* the real of the imaginary.

We have by now established that Lacan's excessive diagrams and his impoverished logical symbols are to be taken as intersections of the imaginary and the symbolic that attempt to convey a sense of the real. Lacan is quite clear that the process which produces his knottings – and not simply their two-dimensional representations – is writing, and that writing is real: 'it is through little bits of writing [*petits bouts d'écriture*] that, historically, one has entered the real, which is to say one has ceased to imagine' (SXXIII: 68).

> [W]riting can always have something to do with the way we write the knot.
>
> A knot is commonly written like this. [Lacan writes a diagram of a knot that resembles the $.] This already gives us an S.
>
> It is there something which has, all the same, a lot to do with the instance of the letter such as I maintain it. (SXXIII: 68–9)

Writing is a process that the real itself carries out. The real writes in order to knit together the three letters of I, S, and R, or the circular O, O, and O. These latter amount to unitary marks, single strokes of the pen, which mark out different terrains, each singling out one realm as distinct from another. The letter's original function is that of the scoremark, to count *different* things as different occurrences of a situation which is in some way the *same*. The scoremark ignores certain 'contingent' differences between cases, counting each event as an instance of the same.

The genesis of the letter

The letter, then, is reducible to the mark, the scoremark, which Lacan believes to be the remainder of the pre-symbolic real that continues to endure even in the fully constituted signifier. It is as if for him, the trace has a history, a prehistory, from *before* the beginning of the signifier, which provides the signifier itself with a history, or rather a *genesis*.

It is as if Derrida does not recognise any *oneness* in the archi-written trace. For Lacan, the unified wholeness of the notch is its imaginary or Gestaltic form. For Lacan, it is the genesis of the trace that must be explained. Derrida does not seem to believe in the possibility of this kind of explanation, and we shall argue that this is precisely because he ignores the imaginary as such.

For Lacan, archi-writing is also proto-writing, and for this reason, the transcendental and the genetic converge in the trace. The trace is both the transcendental condition of possibility of the signifier, and the genetic condition of its actuality. The transcendental archi-trace itself has a 'history'. There is a 'history' of the written mark. And Lacan traces such a 'history'. He finds its beginning in the scoremarks of the primeval hunter. The scoremark is something that divides up a surface that was formerly homogeneous. It makes a cut in the real, like a nick in a sheet of paper, torn by the nib of a stylus: 'This is the origin of the unary trait [*le trait unaire*]: a hole' (SXIII: 8/12/65).[33]

The simple scoremark is developed by eradicating the *imaginary* qualities of the drawings of animals that hunters would paint on cave walls. Lacan is quite clear that these 'pictograms' came first: 'These strokes which only appear much later, several thousand years after men knew how to make objects of a realistic exactitude' (SIX: 6/12/61). Lacan's aim is to explain how one moves from an imaginary depiction to a signifier, in which such content is rendered irrelevant.

Lacan concerns himself with the chronology of writing in his ninth Seminar (1961–2), although, as he always insists, he engages with the question of writing throughout his work. Seminar IX is concerned precisely with 'the genesis, the birth, the emergence of the signifier itself' (SIX: 20/12/61) and how this must occur in tandem with the emergence of the subject. The human animal must make its mark on the real in order to become a subject, and for language as such to begin its emergence. In this Seminar, Lacan is concerned precisely with 'the attachment of language to the real' (SIX: 10/1/62).

The unary trait as the first letter of the alphabet

Writing is generated from marks that were originally pictures of animals, the graphics drawn by hunters of a particular hunting adventure, a particular animal they had killed. Each proto-'letter' was constituted by the distinctive imaginary marks belonging to each animal. But with an increasing number of kills, it became harder and harder to find ways to distinguish between the various adventures, and so the marks which recorded them eventually had to relinquish the task of individuating them graphically. The qualitative particularity of each slipped from memory and henceforward the only thing to be recorded was the pure quantity of kills. The pictograms become mere score-marks that notched up the number of adventures and nothing besides. The single stroke is from that moment on 'the I which distinguishes each repetition in its absolute difference' (SIX: 14/3/62).

It is in this guise that the mark could become the support of the signifier as such, the basis of a signifier whose relation with its signified is wholly *arbitrary*.

It is insofar as the imaginary differences became *irrelevant* that the mark could serve as the support of the signifier, where all that matters is the presence or absence of a mark, irrespective of its imaginary nature. So it is insofar as we evacuate the letter of its imaginarity that it functions as a trace that can support the signifier in its fully fledged differential character: 'everything that is properly speaking of the order of writing, and not simply a drawing, is something which always begins with *the combined usage* of these simplified drawings, of these abbreviated drawings, of these *effaced drawings* that are in different ways incorrectly called ideograms' (SIX: 10/1/62, my italics). So, by the time language proper has formed, 'there is no longer any relationship between the signifier and any natural trace [. . .] and very specifically the natural trace *par excellence* which the imaginary of the body constitutes, this is not to say precisely that this imaginary can be radically rejected. But it is separated off from the operation of the signifier' (SIX: 17/1/62)

For Lacan, the signifier could function in the absence of *all* imaginary distinction. Signifiers could be *entirely* replaced by the mere accumulation of marks. The single stroke 'could be substituted for all the elements of what constitute the signifying chain, supports this chain, all by itself and simply by being always the same' (SIX: 22/11/61).

Lacan describes the written mark after it has been evacuated of imaginary content as 'depersonalised', relieved of its individuality (SIX: 22/11/61). It is important to recall that if the trace has lost its imaginary form then it once *had* such a form. The trace exists *as relieved* of its imaginarity. Its very existence involves a subtraction *from* the imaginary. The real trace that composes our signifiers even today thus contains a reference to its primeval imaginary form, as that which it *had* to lose in order to be constituted. This loss and *continuing* irrelevance of imaginary qualities is a *necessary condition* of the signifier.

The mark is a distinguishing mark. It does not institute a qualitative difference between two things but is the simple mark that one thing differs absolutely from another, that one thing's presence is marked by the *absence* of another. This is the purest form of difference. Signifying difference is pure difference because it is absolute difference, opposition, one signifier *absolutely* excluding the presence of the other. 'This I as such [. . .] marks pure difference' (SIX: 6/12/61).

This is why Lacan describes the scoremark as relieved of all qualitative difference: 'the signifying difference is distinct from anything that refers to qualitative difference' (SIX: 6/12/61). But is a lack of qualitative difference not precisely a qualitative *sameness*? Lacan denies this in the following way: the unary trait is 'different because of this difference which would or would not be based on similarity [*ressemblance*], of being something else which is distinct [*d'être autre chose de distinct*]' (SIX: 6/12/61), 'what distinguishes it is not at all an identity of resemblance, it is something else' (SIX: 6/12/61).

For Lacan it is of 'little importance' that the strokes resemble each other (SIX: 13/12/61). This way of writing them is a pedagogical simplification which forces us to confront the paradox of *pure* otherness:

> the paradox of this One is precisely the following: it is that the more it resembles, I mean the more everything which belongs to the diversity of appearances is effaced from it, the more it supports, the more it incarnates I would say, if you will allow me this word, difference as such. (SIX: 21/2/62)

Is this consistent with the irrelevance of imaginary likeness? Lacan seems now to be saying that the *more* the I's *resemble* one another, the more they 'incarnate' difference: in the signifying order, the only thing which truly differentiates is the mark, the notch. '[T]he unary trait plays the role of symbolic reference point, precisely by ruling out [*exclure*] that it should be either similarity or difference which is posited as the principle of differentiation' (SXIV: 15/2/67). For Lacan, imaginary difference and likeness are not crucial since the notch is a notch insofar as it *disregards* imaginary difference and attempts to record *pure* difference, the difference of cases, and tries merely to count, merely to quantify. It thus eradicates any form of relative differences and institutes *absolute* difference. The trait is to become a pure isolated 'one', a I , a unit.

All that remains of the imaginary properties of the original 'ideogram' is the trait of *oneness* itself: 'The foundation of the one which this trait constitutes is grasped nowhere other than in its unicity: as such one can say nothing else about it except that it is what all signifiers have in common by being above all constituted as a trait, by having this trait as a support' (SIX: 22/11/61).

It was this evacuation of the ideogrammatical elements of writing that paved the way for writing to become *phonetic*, to be able to represent the *sound* of the signifier – for Saussure, the image of the sound in the brain – rather than the form of the signified thing. Thus the evacuation of imaginary traits is the origin of *alphabetic* writing, and this is why the written mark is described by Lacan as a 'letter'.

Although the letter *as such* comes to exist only when language has become *phonetic* language and writing has hence become alphabetic, Lacan explicitly identifies the trait itself with the *letter*: 'I am going to try to show you in the letter precisely this essence of the signifier' (SIX: 6/12/61), and 'the essence of the signifier [. . .] [is] the *einziger Zug*' (SIX: 6/12/61). The trait is the support of the signifier, and Lacan identifies the letter with this support: 'the support of the signifier, the letter' (SIX: 6/12/61). Thus the letter *is* the unary trait, the support of the signifier. The letter as composed of a series of strokes forms the real support of the signifier.

The signifier in its most basic form, the real element of language, is derived from an image. What is derived from an image, inherent in the image, and yet *not* an image? It is the object *a*. It is the *letter* 'a'. This is what has been subtracted from the image, as the *real* of the image which acts as that indefinable *je ne sais quoi* which makes the other *different* from us. The letter, the real, marks the discrepancy between me and my image, me and my ideal ego. After all, the term 'single stroke' or 'unary trait' (*einziger Zug*) in Freud refers to an identification with a unique feature, a single trait, which we latch onto in an ideal ego, to give ourselves some imaginary identity or individuality.

The object *a* is the true *name* of the subject of enunciation, with which the subject of the enunciated desires to be reconciled, but from which it is separated by the very symbolicity of the signifier (cf. Safouan 2004: 77–8; cf. SVI: 3/6/59). And yet as that part of the signifier which is not a signifier, the letter is indeed something like a name, which *brands* something as unique, and it is this real singularity that we desire, or even love. We shall soon see that the proper name is precisely to be understood in terms of the brand, the marking of singularity, and that this is analogous to the function of the letter. It is in the guise of the letter, the real of language, that something like a name can still exist in the generality of the signifier, which we had thought to rule out proper names and the singularity to which they attempt to refer.

The letter which brands me as uniquely who I am, my lost name, is the 'a' which, unlike the 'A', cannot be read in the same way in its inverted form: it is not symmetrical, it is lost in the process of mirroring. It is thus what makes the *real* other desirable, since he holds the secret of the self-identity which I lack. This 'a', chronologically speaking the first letter of the alphabet, is the 'unary trait' which renders an object *one* object, which makes of it a unified object, a whole. It was this totality that was lacking in our own ego, our imaginary identity, and this lack took the form of the object *a* that belonged to the other and was not reflected in the image I had of myself by way of him. The 'unary trait' is the distinctive mark that *makes* us an individual, distinguishing us from any other: it is *une*-ary, it *makes* one. It is like the scoremark, it allows us to *count* as one, absolutely different from every other one, but not in qualitative (imaginary) terms, simply indefinably *different*.

In this way, the letter ('a') is the real of language, the support of the signifier, arrived at by the historical subtraction of the 'signifier' from its originally imaginary pictographic form.

The unity of the trace

At the same time, even in the form of the scoremark, can it truly be said that the imaginary has been *altogether* left behind? The mark is defined by its *unity*, its wholeness, its indissolubility. And indissoluble totality is a feature of the *imaginary*.

It is our hypothesis here that this unity – or at least its acknowledgement – is what distinguishes Lacan's trace from Derrida's.

It could hardly be clearer that the function of the unary trait is akin to the function which Derrida gives to the trace: Lacan describes the trait's inscription as 'original writing [*écriture originelle*]' (SIX: 24/1/62), and this trace is precisely a capacity that the *real* must possess or acquire if the signifier is to appear: 'it is necessary and sufficient that this thing called the unary trait should have appeared *in the real*' (SIX: 14/3/62, my italics).

The signifier is made up of traces: 'the effect of the signifier, namely, in the last resort, of the trace' (SXIV: 15/2/67). Lacan also understands the constitution of the signifier in its positivity to involve an *effacement* of the trace. The signifier is attained by the forgetting of the mark that constitutes difference, in favour of things which *are* different: 'the signifier originates from the effacing of the trace' (SXIII: 20/4/66).

Lacan explicitly recognises his kinship with Derrida here, just after the appearance of Derrida's article, 'De la grammatologie', in 1965:

> The question was posed in the first part of an article [. . .] by someone who is very close to some of my listeners and who introduces with a vivacity, a crispness, a vitality which really gives it an inaugural importance, this question of the function of writing in language. He highlights in a fashion which I must say is definitive, irrefutable, that to make of writing an instrument of what would be in speech, of what would be alive in speech [*un instrument, de ce qui serait, vivrait dans la parole*], is absolutely to fail to recognise its true function.
>
> That it must be recognised elsewhere is structural to language because of something that I indicated sufficiently myself, if only in the predominance given to the function of the unary trait in identification so that I do not have to underline my agreement on this point. (SXIII: 15/12/65)

However, Lacan had already, in 1961, departed from Derrida *avant la lettre*, in seeking precisely the *origin* of the trace, the chronological generation of such a thing as a unary trait.

Attention to this pre-history reveals two things: that singularity can exist in the symbolic order, in the form of our proper name. And most crucially, that by attending to this pre-history one can see that there is a moment of *indivisibility* at the base of the signifier. A certain oneness, a wholeness, is required in order for *difference* to exist. Lacan indeed speaks of 'the unary trait in so far as it is as such the support of difference' (SIX: 13/12/61).

The proper name as written

The signifier began life as a mute *brand*, the stamping of a 'letter' upon a thing to identify it as one's own conquest (on the bone of the slaughtered animal and perhaps the prehistoric 'bedpost'): 'this unary trait insofar as it functions as distinctive [. . .] can on occasion play the role of the brand' (SIX: 20/12/61). For Lacan, the proper name can distinguish us absolutely and thus capture our singularity precisely because of its association with *writing* and thus the absolute difference of the unary trait: 'there cannot be a definition of the proper name except in the measure that we are aware of the relationship between the naming utterance [*l'émission nommante*] and [. . .] the order of the letter' (SIX: 20/12/61; cf. Chiesa 2006: 80).

The proper name is closer to the original trace that existed before language proper had arisen, when a plurality of these traces was grouped to form a differential *system*, containing signifiers in the strict sense. Names are thus moments within the signifier that refer back to the prehistory of the signifier and thus allow some singularity to endure in an order which might otherwise have been thought to alienate it altogether. As Schuster puts it: 'In the proper name, one thus rediscovers within the synchronic order of language a signifier in its "pure state", a state represented in diachronic (pre-)history by the primitive hunter's notched bone' (Schuster, unpublished). The proper name, far from being merely another signifier that is swallowed up in the infinite synchronic realm of the signifier, links us back to the pre-symbolic real, to the thing.

Derrida, on the other hand, does not believe in the possibility of the uniqueness of the proper name. It is as if the prehistory of the signifier is irrelevant to the way in which we are to understand its functioning. It teaches us nothing about its nature or its conditions of possibility.[34] For Derrida, it seems that we are utterly entrapped in language and its differentiation, with no way out. This entrapment manifests itself in the fact that, for Derrida, we can *never* reach any form of *unity* that would constitute the *atomic constituent* of the signifier. This relic from prehistory is no longer present to us. The bones of the past and their single strokes, which for Lacan stand at the very basis of the signifier, are for Derrida well and truly buried beneath the weight of the fully constituted, infinite system of the signifier proper.

There is no moment of indivisibility in the signifier, no letter that cannot be torn up.

Derrida and Lacan on imaginary unity

Derrida does not believe we have access to any such thing as a primal unity: any 'origin' to which we have access is not 'simple'. Rather, there is always something that precedes simplicity, even that which might characterise the archi-trace, and that is a *process*, a process of *inscription*. Archi-writ*ing* precedes the archi-trace, Derrida's *écrit*ure precedes Lacan's *écrit*. Indeed, Derrida's own deconstruction of Lacan could be understood as saying that Lacan believes in the primal nature of the writ letter that cannot be further divided, while deconstruction shows that there is a more primordial process of writing or differentiation which *underlies* the letter: 'Writing Before the Letter', the title of Part One of *Of Grammatology*. For Derrida, what remains presupposed by any supposedly unitary trace is the 'undeconstructible duality' of same and other, the surface of inscription and the inscription itself. Any trace will always presuppose this. For this reason the origin is never a unity but a primal difference or a heterogeneity. And naturally, every attempt to identify the unity of either of the different elements must itself be subject to the same division, for identity is constituted by the mark and the mark will always have to have been written, and writing presupposes the duality of same and other, surface and inscription.

There is no indivisible unity or Gestalt: such would be a phonetic prejudice for Derrida, the retrospective projection of a monadic phoneme. From the standpoint of the signifier, difference is all pervasive. This is crucial, for it is the exclusive adoption of the *standpoint of language* that causes Derrida to refuse the notion of a primordial simplicity. Lacan, on the other hand, allows us to ask if there are not *other standpoints*.

Why does *Lacan* believe in this oneness? Ultimately, we believe it to be a consequence of his thesis on the *imaginary*. This is the realm of the indissoluble whole, provably present in animal perceptual systems, which endures in man as the animal that has language. If Derrida does not see the necessity or the possibility of the One, is it because of his own attitude to animals and to the animal that man would be? Does he not reduce the specificity of the animal, and indeed all organic life and inorganic matter – in our human eyes – to the structure of the trace? Does this not fail to distinguish between the different *types* of code that exist for the varying levels of complexity that characterise inorganic and organic structures? Is there not for instance an essential difference between the animal code and the human signifier? This, in a way that is not straightforward, is Lacan's thesis (cf. SIII: 167).

We believe that the *reason* Lacan identifies a oneness at the basis of the signifier is precisely *dependent* upon his understanding of man as some form of animal, of man as participating in the imaginary dimension. This is to say that to posit a unity as the basis of language's differentiality is the consequence of an originally *genetic* understanding of the human being, psychoanalysis in this instance.

Why does man have the ability to institute such a thing as a notch, a unity, a oneness, or even to recognise one kill as *one* kill? Have we not seen that *any* form of unity is dependent upon the atomic unity of an animal's perceptual system? Is it not the case that man's perception also has its atom? And might this notion of an indissoluble, Gestaltic unity not explain how such a thing as 'one' (I) could exist, how man could ever have used a drawing or stroke to represent something as *one*?

The reason for the 'indivisibility of the letter', around which Derrida sees his disagreement with Lacan to revolve, is the letter's *imaginary* form, its unity. And this unity is only revealed to an initially *scientific* approach to the human being that examines the genesis of the signifier and does not presuppose that man is always already consumed by it.

But could one not say that the Lacanian notion of a unity at the basis of difference was therefore a *zoomorphism*? It would appropriate the real unto the imaginary realm of organic life and import a notion of totality that would be foreign to the real in itself. But for Lacan, just as we must see the real transcendentally as akin to the signifier (as archi-writing), it must be necessary to view the real genetically *in terms of our animal nature*. The real can never be seen 'in itself' but only from our perspective as human animals, only on the *horizon* of our vision. Thus, to see the real letter as a unitary totality is to see it as 'the real of the imaginary'. The letter is the letter 'a', the object *a*, that part of the image which is not imaginary. The real as object *a*, the 'letter', is subtracted from the image, causing it to become incomplete. This lack of wholeness appears to afflict man *only* in the comparison he makes between himself and the animal, which seems relatively well-adjusted.

Thus the impression we cannot but have of the animal as enjoying a perfect fit with its environment is a fantasy, a vision of nature as a harmonious totality which does not lack the object *a* that we find missing from our own imaginary.

Derrida wishes precisely to deconstruct this vision of the animal as absolutely opposed to man, for the opposition is a structure which characterises the symbolic and therefore this understanding of the animal views the relation solely from man's point of view. In fact, the generalised trace knits us all together in something like homogeneity. It is as if any presumption that we can know the properties of the animal *beyond* archi-writing can only amount to an oppositional determination.

We can see then, that the difference between Lacan and Derrida with regard to the signifier results from a difference in their respective understandings of the nature of the animal. For Derrida, any attempt to speak of the animal beyond the trace will do it an injustice and oppose it to the human being. To protect it we must remain silent about it.

But this is to relinquish on principle the insights of the natural sciences. It is to rule out the possibility that we might have access to the realm of the *imaginary*.

Does Derrida believe in the imaginary at all? Does he have any notion of the fantasy, which we have seen to be consequent upon the notion of the imaginary?

Once again, this fantasy is the fantasy of regaining animal *wholeness* or *unity*. It is a notion that would occur to us only on the basis of what we perceive ourselves to have lost in leaving the animal realm. And at the same time it is the unitary trace that, in the beginning, formed the basis of the signifier's difference. The two are not unconnected, for if difference is subdivided *ad infinitum* and extends to infinity in every direction, how can meaningfulness ever be fully constituted? By means of the notion of a unitary trace resulting from the limits of man's perceptual system, Lacan can account for the way in which differentiality is limited and a meaningful totality instituted, even if this is grounded on a notion of oneness that is itself a fantasy.

The tain of the mirror

And yet, can we say that Derrida has no notion of the image at all? What of his constant reflection on the *mirror* as the instrument of thought's *speculation*? Derrida is precisely interested in the materiality that underlies a speculation which seems wholly ideal, the materiality that is required by the illusion of full self-reflection, self-relation or presence. His work is, famously, written in ink drawn from the *tain* of the mirror, the mercurial matter that is always hidden from view by the image that it reflects.

Derrida is precisely attempting to demonstrate that part of the image which is *not* imaginary. He is showing that a certain *writing* underlies speculation, a writing which makes its graphic incursion into phonetic language by means of such letters as the '*a*' of *différance*. In other words, he wishes to demonstrate the contamination of the supposedly pure image with the symbol. This seems to be his 'criticism' of Lacan's notion of the imaginary, its rigid separation from the symbolic. For Derrida, the doubling which seems to characterise the imaginary in fact overflows it and binds it to the symbolic:

> if the dual relation between two doubles (which Lacan would reduce to the imaginary) includes and envelops the entire space said to be of the symbolic, overflows and simulates it, ceaselessly ruining and disorganising it, then the opposition of the imaginary and the symbolic, and above all its implicit hierarchy, appears to be of very limited pertinence: that is, if one measures it against the squaring of such a scene of writing. (PC: 491–2)

But this is precisely what Lacan's later understanding of the imaginary involves, right down to the use of the letter 'a'. That image which is lacking from the imaginary marks the point at which the imaginary is tied to the symbolic in the guise of the object *a* of desire, which can also be understood, from the symbolic point of view, as the letter ('a'). The real of the imaginary and the real of the symbolic are superimposed. There is no absolute separation of imaginary and symbolic.

And yet, a difference remains. And it lies in the indivisibility of this letter. Derrida not believe in this indivisibility and Lacan does. Derrida, with his remarkable acuity, identifies this as the most fundamental point of disagreement between them. But does he understand the *reasons* for this divergence? We have attempted to show that the reason for Lacan's belief in this unity lies in his genetic reference to the animal and the imaginary unities of its perceptual system. It is because man retains some remnants of his originally animal nature, even in his language, that a certain unity grounds difference.[35]

So is the disparity of the chiasm constituted by Derrida and Lacan's respective attitudes to the *animal*? Does Derrida, despite everything, genuinely have a notion of the *imaginary*? We have appealed to the tain of the mirror, but the images reflected therein were invoked to describe the self-presence of wordless, conscious thought. Derrida's notion of the image seems to be a notion of *reflection* that, in its ideal character is *wholly* illusory. Lacan, on the other hand, has a highly developed theory of the image, which he gleans from the science of optics. Optics is the science of the imaginary, the science which Lacan uses, together with zoology, to justify his understanding of the *Gestaltic* nature of the imaginary, for the image is produced as a *whole* that cannot be atomised. Optics 'sets itself to produce [. . .] *images*, in contrast to other sciences, which import into nature a cutting up, a dissection, an anatomy' (SI: 76).

In this precise way, by opposing such continuous dissection, does Lacan not stand fast against the abyssal deconstructive descent?

The lens of optics produces images which are of an entirely different substance to the lens itself. Thus can one explain the emergence of a differently constituted realm *without* its being dismissed solely as a *subjective* illusion, without real existence: 'everything which is imaginary, everything which is properly speaking illusory, isn't for all that subjective. [. . .] There are illusions that are perfectly objective, objectifiable' (SII: 49; cf. SI: 76ff). The 'illusions' of optics are like the illusions of mirrors: they are not non-existent but exceed the material nature of the constituents of the mirror from which they result.[36] For Derrida, it seems that the images of the mirror should always be tied back to their material base but are not investigated for their *own* sake and on their *own* terms. It is as if, for us at least, in the beginning was the symbolic. Derrida does not consider that we might be able to explain the very generation of the symbolic *from* the mirroring of the imaginary, *without* presupposing an original ('undeconstructible') duality. Does he confine his attention too rigidly to a history of philosophy that has always taken geometry as its ideal and ignore the hope which Lacan expresses for a future mode of thought that would base itself on *optics*? 'The odd thing is that an entire system of metaphysics has been founded on geometry and mechanics, by looking to them for models of understanding, but up to now it doesn't seem as though optics has been exploited as much as it could have been' (SI: 76).

Thus, while Derrida may demonstrate the intersection of the symbolic and the imaginary in the mirror's tain, he does not see that the trace may be understood as a short-circuit of the transcendental and the *chronological*. He does not see that, genetically speaking, one might understand the symbolic to originate from a deficit in the imaginary. For Derrida, the image must always be considered secondary to the real of language which makes it possible, transcendentally.

Derrida's attitude to the imaginary is reflected in his attitude to the sciences, which for Lacan precisely offer us a relation to the imaginary that does not appropriate it unto the symbolic. For Derrida, science eludes metaphysics only when it comes to recognise the *trace* in nature, and thus perhaps comes to terms with its inherent anthropocentrism. Whenever science goes *beyond* the trace, which can be inferred on the basis of the existence of empirical human language, it becomes metaphysical again, 'positivistic':

> This supposes a kind of *double register* in grammatological practice: it must simultaneously go beyond metaphysical positivism and scientism, and accentuate whatever in the effective work of science contributes to freeing it of the metaphysical bonds that have borne on its definition and its movement since its beginnings. (P: 35)[37]

Our thesis all along has been that Lacan need not take such a 'transcendental' attitude to science, for the simple reason that he *does not begin as a philosopher*. He is thus able to take science more seriously on its own terms, and genuinely to open the very foundations of his thought to determination by the insights of these other sciences.[38]

We shall now establish that Derrida does indeed explicitly reject a consideration of the notion of the imaginary in its specificity as distinct from the symbolic, along with a similar consideration of the animal. Derrida realises that the animal, the *zōon*, as distinct from the *logos*, is precisely what is at stake in Lacan's notion of the imaginary, but he never engages with it in any detail, and this is either the cause or the effect of his general indifference to the genetic, and to the sciences which attempt to address that which is otherwise than discursive. And this is why he does not believe in 'such a thing as One' (cf. SXX: 5).

Derrida on the Lacanian imaginary and the tripartition

When Derrida speaks of the imaginary in Lacan, either he dismisses its *distinctness* from the other two parts of the tripartition, or he dismisses the tripartition altogether, and generally without fully explaining his reasons. It seems to me that it is not something that Derrida ever manages to take seriously and to understand in its necessity, a necessity which has its origins in a genetic consideration of the human being:

> dissemination situates the *more or less* that indefinitely resists [. . .] the effect of subjectivity, of subjectivation, of appropriation [. . .], what Lacan

> calls [. . .] the order of the 'symbolic'. Escapes it and disorganises it, makes it drift, marks its writing, with all the implied risks, but without letting itself be conceived in the categories of the 'imaginary' or the 'real'. I have never been convinced of the necessity of this conceptual tripartition. It is pertinent only *within* the system that I put into question. (P: 84)

Derrida never directly expands on the reasons why he is not convinced, or how such a threefold could come to exist 'within the system that I put into question'. Again and again, his trope runs as follows: 'all of this makes of triangular logic a very limited play within the play' (PC: 491).

What Derrida *is* prepared to admit is that his notion of the signifier may be mapped onto Lacan's notion of the *symbolic*.[39] And yet, because he believes the tripartition in Lacan to be 'strict'[40] – the boundaries of imaginary, symbolic and real to be clearly defined – any specific consideration of the real and the imaginary *apart* from the symbolic exceeds the limits set by deconstruction to any attempt to go beyond the text: 'dissemination designates that which can no more be integrated into the symbolic than it can form the symbolic's *simple* exterior under the heading of its failure or its (imaginary or real) impossibility' (P: 85–6).[41] Derrida thus spells out what deconstruction *would* be when explained in Lacanian terms:

> [D]issemination would be [. . .] not only the force [. . .] which permits it to break what fastens it to the unity of a signified that would not be without it, not only the possibility of bursting from this *clasp*, and of undoing the eider quilt of the 'symbolic' [. . .]. It is also the possibility of deconstruction [. . .], or, if you prefer, of unsewing [. . .] the symbolic order in its general structure *and* in its modifications, in the general *and* determined forms of sociality, the 'family' or culture. (P: 85)

The imaginary animal

Derrida, then, despite his avowed intention to protect that which is beyond the text, refuses to admit the Lacanian real as his own concern simply because he believes it to be oppositionally distinguished from the symbolic and thereby understood – metaphysically – as *presence*. However, if we take seriously his occasional, marginal admission that the real is (in later Lacan) the inherent impossibility of the signifier, the latter's incompletion, then we may say that the symbolic and the real *are* the textual and the non-text which concern him. As a consequence, his criticism of the tripartition *as threefold* must be focused upon the notion of the *imaginary*.

Despite never speaking in detail about his concerns with the Lacanian imaginary, Derrida is more voluminous with regard to the *animal*. Examining Derrida's understanding of the animal, along with his understanding of Lacan's position on the same topic, should give us some clues as to why he does not 'believe' in the imaginary.

Derrida's problem may broadly be stated as follows: Lacan understands the animal to be *opposed* to man, thus following metaphysics and its understanding of a distinction between nature and culture in terms of the opposition between the non-trace and the trace.[42] Derrida deals with Lacan's statements on animality, and the distinction between animal and human language as follows:

> we do not have enough space[43] to verify the essential link between metaphysics [. . .] and humanism in this system. This link is more visible, if not looked upon more highly, in the conglomeration of statements about 'animality', about the distinction between animal and human language, etc. This discourse on the animal (in general) is no doubt consistent with all the categories and oppositions, all the bi- or tri-partitions of the system. And it condenses no less the system's greatest obscurity. The treatment of animality, as of everything that finds itself in *submission* by virtue of a hierarchical opposition, has always, in the history of (humanist and phallogocentric) metaphysics, revealed obscurantist resistance. (PC: 474, n 51)

Derrida then recognises that the 'tri-partition' is related to Lacan's understanding of the animal and that the latter even 'condenses' the unclarified elements of the tripartition. This gives more substance to Derrida's early allusions to his belief that the tripartition is metaphysical. Although it is more easily seen how a discourse which opposes animal and man is metaphysical, it is less clear how this infects the tripartition, since metaphysics is characterised by the *two*fold structure, opposition. Perhaps this slippage and this obscurity is indicated in Derrida's hasty juxtaposition of the 'bi- or tri-partitions' of Lacan's system.

In his last major engagement with Lacan, in 1990, the question of the animal is still troubling Derrida, and not because Lacan's views are *simply* metaphysical or *simply* deconstructible. Perhaps even in 1975 this was the reason for their being 'of capital interest' (PC: 474, n 51), and yet he *never* devotes to this capitally interesting question much more than a footnote: 'the unanswered questions I am still today putting to Lacan, *with* whom it is worth discussing: questions on the subject of what he has to say on, in effect, being, man, animals (especially animals), and thus God – no less' (R: 64–5). The questions continue to perplex because '[t]he remarkable things Lacan says on the animal are also in my view most problematic' (R: 66).

But is it really a matter that Derrida wants to discuss? To be frank, he never does so in public, nor does he adduce more than formal reasons for his disagreement, which he applies in like manner to Heidegger and the whole philosophical tradition insofar as it understands man to be distinguished from animals by the possession of something (reason, language) which they lack.

Derrida never sees that Lacan's statements on the animal and its relation to man are *not* philosophical or metaphysical speculations, but are drawn from *scientific* experiments and insights. From this point of view it is quite clear that the relation between animal and man is *not* one of opposition, nor does it depreciate animals by placing them on a lower rung of a hierarchy. Indeed, man is not the animal + x, but the animal – x, minus a fully functioning imaginary. The notion of man as a lacking animal could be a perfectly respectable evolutionary proposition: a trait arises and dies out, something has a function and then becomes redundant or takes on another function.[44]

At stake is that to which Derrida remains blind, the role of the imaginary in the genesis of the trace, which Derrida does not believe we can speak about. Lacan was pushed in this direction by a genetic approach which he believes psychoanalysis to pursue and philosophy to ignore. He speaks of a 'fundamental dishonesty in the philosophical position itself, if it refuses to acknowledge the degree to which psychoanalysis renews it' (SXIII: 30/3/66). This is perhaps the basis of his 'insurgence' against philosophy: '*I am rebelling*, so to speak, against philosophy' ('Dissolution': 18/3/1980).

Derrida on Lacan

To bring this work to its conclusion, we shall demonstrate the various ways in which Derrida continually evades a *proper* confrontation with the novelty that Lacan's thought presents to philosophy, and yet continues to be troubled by it and indeed perhaps even a little obsessed. We can see this in his three major engagements with Lacan: *Positions* (1971), 'The *facteur* [postman/factor/maker] of truth' (1975), and 'For the love of Lacan' (1990), which constitute something like a thesis, antithesis, and 'synthesis'.

Characteristic of Derrida's later writing is the admission that things have changed in Lacan, that he has 'contradicted' some of his earlier positions (cf. R: 59, 61), but Derrida never admits that his early pronouncements on Lacan were wrong *at the time*, nor does he ever substantially rework his earlier readings of Lacan *in light* of these changes. Derrida evades this critique by referring to the very nature of deconstruction as restricting itself to a finite text, or even a single text, and opening it onto the infinite general text, upon which its meaning depends and which nevertheless takes this meaning beyond its control. He explicitly insists that his earlier work was not a critique or a meta-discourse on Lacan *as a whole*.[45] It is not, however, accidental that it was interpreted this way, since in truth it is hard to view at least his first engagement as anything other than cursory and *formal*. It is after all 'just' a footnote.

I believe Derrida's reading of Lacan from beginning to end is symptomatic of deconstruction's limits, which we will ultimately have been trying to uncover.

Derrida's strategies

If we have revealed something like a genuine encounter between Lacan*ian* and Derrid*ean* thought, then it should be illuminating to contrast this with the actual encounter which Derrida himself stages. It is a relation which he describes as 'love' (R: 42), with all its squalls, bitterness, misunderstanding and cross-purposes. Perhaps, however, it is a Lacanian love in which two people reach out for an object they see ahead of them and miraculously end up clasping hands.

There are two curious strategies in Derrida's explicit engagement with Lacan. The first is the tendency to treat his early suspicions, based on incomplete grounds, as being 'confirmed' by his later readings. It seems as if nothing Lacan ever wrote, no matter how much his thought changed, could ever persuade Derrida that he had been wrong about him, or if it did, it never precipitated a full-scale reappraisal. This bolsters a suspicion we shall see most glaringly confirmed in 1971, that in the case of Lacan, Derrida seems to apply deconstruction as a *formal framework* to Lacan's thought *as a whole*, a set of *theses* against which Lacan is measured and found wanting.

The second strategy, which both undercuts and underscores the first, is the twofold quality of Derrida's attitude to Lacan: Lacan is said to be *both* the most deconstructible figure Derrida has engaged with *and* the one *closest* to him, the most deconstruct*ive*. Again, it is as if they were striving for the same thing, but Lacan was always infected with a metaphysical remainder that caused him to misinterpret the object sought. As a psychoanalyst perhaps, and one who stressed the linguistic nature of the unconscious, Lacan kept to the deconstructive impulse, but insofar as he was a philosopher, a transcendental-metaphysical thinker who retained some notion of 'full speech' or full presence, free of language, he was deconstructible.[46]

And yet, we shall see Derrida admit that it is not the case that Lacan surreptitiously or unbeknownst to himself slips in such metaphysical motifs: he *parades* them. It is as if he is well aware of his deconstructibility and proud of it! Perhaps this is what makes Lacan seem so uncanny to Derrida, so disturbing. And perhaps this explains how one can be both close and distant, deconstructive and deconstructible, a contradiction that perhaps bears witness to the fact that Lacan exceeds Derrida's ken.

It has been a constant if muted refrain of this book that Derrida so often gets things right in his reading of Lacan and yet is unable to understand him fully. Lacan is precisely performing a kind of deconstruction, and yet he does not do it in the same way as Derrida. In Derrida's eyes, this can only mean that Lacan must himself be deconstructible. But we have attempted to show that Lacan deconstructs *otherwise*, and in Derrida's inability to envisage this alternative, he demonstrates that he is unable to answer the questions put to him by Lacan.

I believe that this, above all, exposes a trait inherent to deconstruction, that it cannot wholeheartedly enter a dialogue that would put its entire procedure in question. If someone is not an ally, they are an 'enemy'; if they do not deconstruct, they are to be deconstructed. And anyone who can only be construed as falling outside this binarity must be passed over in silence, those such as Deleuze, with whom Derrida experienced such a similar feeling of uncanniness. The crucial difference is that he spoke of Lacan, and not Deleuze, save to pay his respects. We have been trying to understand why.

One is tempted, given how little effect Lacan's proximity had on Derrida's own, unwavering thought, to view his proximity with Lacan along the lines of Heidegger's Hölderlinian understanding of the poet and the thinker: two adjacent trees, running parallel to one another and so never touching, never interfering with one another's growth, like lovers between whom harsh words have been spoken (Heidegger 1971: 13). Their paths did cross, and perhaps they were reaching for what they saw to be the same fruit, but it was a failed encounter, and they carried on their separate ways.

a) Positions: the general metadiscourse and the confirmed 'suspicions'

In a long – and famous – footnote to *Positions*, written in 1971 (P: 107–13, n 44), Derrida lays out several criticisms of Lacan. They are unique in that they are so *formal*. They do not deal with single texts but indicate general 'motifs' (P: 108, n 44) which Derrida believes to characterise Lacan's thought in its generality. Is this really a deconstruction or even *appropriate* to deconstruction as Derrida understands it? If not, why does he do it? In any case, following this sally, Derrida will, without explanation, undercut these criticisms with the assertion that it is possible that there is a crucial encounter yet to be had between his own thought and Lacan's, Lacan's '*most of all*'.

Derrida's words quite often betray the personal affront caused by Lacan's aggressive 'kettle logic' with regard to his own insights.[47] And he takes this aggression to be a respectable enough reason for not referring to him at length in his own early foundational texts (P: 107, n 44). And yet, at the same time, Derrida admits that his own acquaintance with Lacan's thought at the time was *incomplete* (P: 108, n 44). He had nevertheless decided that for him there were more urgent things to do (P: 111, n 44). One can understand why: it was necessary to deconstruct the more obviously deconstructible texts from the history of metaphysics, to build up a corpus sufficient to impart a new force to words that were formerly wholly magnetised by the discourse of metaphysics.

And yet who was more 'deconstructible' than Lacan? Derrida goes on to lay out the various metaphysical motifs which he had already found in Lacan's work. Here in 1971, Derrida is writing in retrospect of the time of his first publications five or six years earlier, but these are clearly motifs which he discerned at the time, as indicated by the tenses in Derrida's statement: 'I will point out a certain number of major motifs that kept [Lacan's thought] within the critical questions that I was in the process of formulating, and *inside* the logocentric, that is phonologistic field that I undertook to delimit and to shake' (P: 108, n 44).[48]

So Derrida already knew the basic structure of his objections *before* he was fully acquainted with Lacan's continuously evolving text, and without ever having properly deconstructed a single finite text.

Derrida is here speaking of the past, in an attempt to explain, under interrogation, the absence of Lacan. Derrida suggests, quite rightly, that, '[s]uch references would only result in the accumulation of fog in a field already not lacking it. They also risked compromising the possibility of a rigorous juxtaposition that perhaps remained to be constructed' (P: 110, n 44). This is true, even though Derrida had already come to some hasty, albeit provisional conclusions, as he admits, with his usual unimpeachable honesty.

His reasons for being able to speak *now*, albeit in a written footnote and not in improvised conversation, as if an even greater caution and hesitation were required in this hazardous negotiation, are that he has finally had a chance to read ('almost') the whole of the *Écrits* (P: 111, n 44):

> The ensemble of the *Écrits* having been published in the interval [after Derrida's works were first published between 1959 and 1964], I not only had to acquaint myself with it, but also to engage myself, given what I have just said about Lacan's rhetoric, in a labour that announced itself as out of proportion with what my initial readings had led me to expect [. . .]. This certainly is not sufficient to make me give up [. . .] but perhaps to make me prefer to respond for a time [. . .] to demands that I considered more urgent, and, in any event, prerequisite. (P: 111, n 44)

By rights, and by Derrida's own standards, his inadequate acquaintance with Lacan should have ruled out *any response whatsoever*. It is not even as if Derrida isolates a single text and deconstructs it, as he later claims. Rather, he confines himself to the general 'motifs' which he perceives to characterise Lacan's work. In this his first engagement, he lays out some largely unreferenced 'general impressions'. Derrida *does not deconstruct*, he does not refer to particular texts, but refers to Lacan as a whole. He *does* write a 'meta-discourse' that presumes to confine what Lacan says to one set of theses. In this footnote at least, Derrida does not live up to the ideals of deconstruction, precisely by not restricting himself to reading, but *formally* applying a framework of deconstructive 'theses' to a general impression of Lacanian theory. Derrida spends several pages laying out severe 'criticisms' of Lacan's work *in general*. His accusations here are just that, they are not substantiated by extensive readings, and contain only four short quotations and two further citations.

Is this justified by the curious suggestion that Lacan is *more* deconstructible than anyone else, so (obviously) deconstructible that he does not even need to be read? Is that what is taken to license this lapse in deconstructive technique?

And this is not the only thing that is unique to Derrida's encounter with Lacan: in *The Postcard*, we witness a battle over Freud, or perhaps rather his liberation from any purportedly definitive appropriation, any proclamation that claims to deliver his true message.[49] Derrida uses the very rare syntagms, 'No' and '*it is false*' (PC: 490, n 66), as well as 'misconstrual' (P: 112, n 44).

If these remarks on motifs from Lacan were made on the basis of a reading of just two of Lacan's early works and constitute a general metadiscourse or formal application of a deconstructive framework, then later on, when Derrida had had a chance to read 'almost all' of the *Écrits*, his suspicions were confirmed. It is as if his initial reading were a 'hermeneutic pre-understanding' of the text, which can never be radically discarded, only refined. Does this not compromise an open-minded reading, and particularly a deconstructive one which is precisely concerned with the possibility of quite another, 'minor' reading?

'Since then I have reread these two texts, and have read others, almost all of them, I believe, in the *Écrits*. These last few months notably [in 1971]. My first reading of them has been largely confirmed' (P: 111, n 44). And yet, if Derrida's opinion of Lacan as the most (easily) deconstructible writer he had yet come across was confirmed, he does nevertheless open up a certain ambiguity, which is something like a double reading. And yet it is distinct. He suggests not simply that there are deconstructive resources in this metaphysical text as there are in every other, but that *deconstruction itself* must encounter Lacanian psychoanalytic theory in the way of a dialogue with an equal.

This is the strange duality that always marks Derrida's relations with Lacan, and we are proposing that it is just this 'flustering' proximity that will have upset Derrida so much, ruffled him so deeply, that his deconstructive rigour will have lapsed.

Derrida suggests, then, that he is not closed to the possibility that his own work might be *closer* to Lacan's *than to any other*: 'whether or not this work [deconstruction] should encounter Lacan's, and Lacan's – I do not at all reject the idea – more than any other today' (P: 111, n 44).

Lacan's work is in a way 'deconstructive', in the way that *Freud's* is, and indeed Derrida seems to suggest that, despite his phonologism, Lacan is instrumental in saving Freud from something like ego-psychology, retrieving a genuine unconscious that would question the primordiality of conscious presence: Lacan's was 'a discourse whose critical effects seemed to me, despite what I have just recalled, necessary within an entire field' (P: 111, n 44).

Perhaps Derrida had a sense that when he was ready to enter a true dialogue and challenge the foundations of his own thought, much later, it was with Lacan that this should happen. Certainly, if Derrida was 'flustered' here, he was right to be flustered. This has been our hypothesis in the present work. Was it only Deleuze's courtesy that allowed Derrida to admit this in his case but not in the analogous, more 'aggressive', competing case of Lacan?

But Derrida does make good on his promise of an encounter with Lacan, an impressive and now famous encounter, a few years later, in 'The *facteur* of truth'.

What becomes of the duality of Derrida's attitude here? It seems to me that the flustering possibility that Lacanianism might be a kindred threat to the deconstructive process is levelled off and the usual metaphysical duality reinstalled, whereby a text of necessity allows both a metaphysical and a non-metaphysical reading. Thus, it is as if the initial hermeneutic impression is ever more firmly embedded beneath layers of textual evidence. After the delay described in the footnote to *Positions*, where Derrida's suspicions were confirmed, here, after a further four years, they are *re*confirmed. What Derrida will not explain is the *reason* for this twofold 'delayed action' (*Nachträglichkeit*, *après-coup*). We suggest that it is due to something more genuinely troubling in Lacan, an untameability which it will have taken Derrida fifteen years to subdue.

b) 'The facteur of truth': Lacan's metalanguage and the indivisibility of the letter

In 'The *facteur* of truth', in 1975, Derrida revises his earlier opinion that Lacan's 'Seminar on the Purloined Letter' is

> [a]n admirable achievement, [. . .] [and yet] a reading that is ultimately hermeneutic (semantic) *and* formalist [. . .]. Although it is doubtless productive in other respects, this misconstruing seems to me to be determined systematically by the limits I mentioned a moment ago under the rubric of logocentrism. (P: 112, n 44)

Once again then we find the same ambiguity in Derrida's relation to Lacan's reading of Freud: it both tends towards a phonologism which is in fact present in Freud, and yet undercuts this by picking up on another strand of Freud's thought. Does Lacan protect Freud or betray him? In any case, here in 1975, Derrida follows the same procedure as before, opening up the possibility that Lacan properly understands the unconscious in terms of the signifier and yet still, by means of a longer detour this time, returns to the conclusion that Lacan employs the metaphysical notion that the system of signifiers is ultimately centred around a transcendental moment. Perhaps no longer a signified, but a signifier, which in its failure to be substituted acts as if it were real, as if it were a signified.

In 'The *facteur* of truth', Derrida seems to retract his original, very general(ist) view of psychoanalysis that it is a hermeneutics, concerned with determining a repressed signified which in full speech would come to conscious *presence*. Derrida recognises that this cannot be the case with Lacan's psychoanalysis because the latter explicitly criticises such semanticism, at least to all appearances (for this will be the deconstructive double reading: Lacan is both non-semanticist and semanticist). Lacan does not submit the signifier to a transcendental signified, but rather posits the dependence of the signified *upon* the signifier. The unconscious is not a signified awaiting interpretative discovery but a cluster of real traces devoid of sense, a meaningless letter:

> the *general* question of the text is at work unceasingly in his writings, where the logic of the signifier disrupts naive semanticism. And Lacan's 'style' was constructed so as to check almost permanently any access to an isolable content, to an unequivocal, determinable meaning beyond writing [*un sens univoque, déterminable au-delà de l'écriture*]. (PC: 420)

And yet, a certain centring of the signifying structure, a transcendental moment in the traditional sense, is ultimately asserted by Lacan. It amounts to a transcendental *signifier*, but this will itself depend upon something that is *not* subject to the divisions imposed by the signifier and hence on something real, a presence. This will be the indivisible moment of the *letter* that will for Derrida re-orient the signifier towards *meaning*.

First of all, to speak of the transcendental signifier. Derrida finds that Lacan's essay ultimately reads Poe's tale as a story about the nature of the signifier. It is read as a metalinguistic account of the functioning of language. This is what it is *about*: 'The displacement of the signifier, therefore, is analysed as a signified' (PC: 428). The tale is precisely a signifier *of* the signifier, and in this way Lacan's account presupposes the very possibility of such a thing, embodying thereby a certain transcendentalism. Thus the signifier is the transcendental 'signified' of the story. But the signifier is described most basically in terms of the *letter*, the letter which is not torn up but always returns, intact, to the same place, its destination. The *real* letter, in other words.

Here the reappropriation of what seems to be a freeing of the signifier for itself is re-anchored in something *beyond* signifying difference. Remarkably, again Derrida hits upon precisely the point of genuine disagreement between himself and Lacan: that for Lacan, difference is grounded in a unity, the letter. For Derrida, to posit a letter at the basis of the signifier amounts to yet another positing of an opposition between the differential symbolic and the non-differential real, an 'outside-of-the-text'. This real which grounds the symbolic order is something that can no longer be divided by symbolic differences and thus amounts to a substantial real that will ground and centre the signifier. 'Here, first of all, is what solders, beneath the conceptual heading of the *letter* or of the *materiality of the signifier*, the indivisible to the local' (PC: 424). Derrida states in a later interview that the motif of divisibility is 'that on which everything depends' (PC: 512).

The letter cannot be torn up (made into *litter*):[50] the letter in Poe's story here functions as a metaphor for the letter as the real-of-language, which resists differentiation by the divisive powers of the signifier. It is therefore something that links the signifier to the *non*-differential *real*. It is a moment within the signifier that is not subject to the differentiality that for Derrida characterises every possible level of the signifying structure.

Derrida defines the letter as 'the site of the signifier' (PC: 439). Crucially, he relates the letter to the alphabet and hence to the phonetic, as if Lacan were grounding the signifying structure in the sonic substance and ultimately subordinating the whole of the differential signifier to the full presence of the voice. We have seen however that Lacan's use of the word 'letter' is not so straightforward.[51] But for Derrida, this is the metaphysical moment that reinstalls itself at the bottom of Lacan's otherwise promisingly deconstructive 'logic of the signifier'. 'It is a philosopheme, an undemonstrable theorem or matheme, although it remains analysable in its unanalysed interest' (PC: 513).

If the castration of the phallus is the deconstructive moment in Lacan, the letter, by recentring the symbolic structure, betrays this deconstructive insight and allows the signifier to refer for a moment to the real. Derrida defines castration, loss of the phallus, as follows: 'where the signifier (its inadequation with the signified) gets underway' (PC: 439). And the letter betrays this. Derrida continues: 'this [the place of castration] is [also] the site of the signifier, the letter. But this is also where the trial begins, the promise of reappropriation, of return, of readequation' (PC: 439). This means that castration is not genuine, the phallus is *never altogether lost*: 'the signifier must never risk being lost, destroyed, divided, or fragmented without return' (PC: 438). The never-irretrievable loss of the phallus 'implies a theory of the proper place, and the latter implies a theory of the letter as an indivisible locality' (PC: 438).

> In castration, the phallus is indivisible, and therefore indestructible, like the letter which *takes its place* [en tient lieu]. And this is why the motivated, never demonstrated presupposition of the materiality of the letter as *indivisibility* was indispensable for this restricted economy, this circulation of the proper. (PC: 441)

The *deconstructive* character of the phallus is overcome by the *deconstructible* motif of the (indivisible) letter:

> if the lack has its place in this atomistic topology of the signifier, if it occupies a determined place with defined contours, then the existing order will not have been upset: the letter will always refind its proper place, a circumvented lack (certainly not an empirical, but a transcendental one, which is better yet, and more certain), the letter will be where it always will have been, intangible and indestructible via the detour of a *proper*, and properly *circular*, itinerary. (PC: 425)

The fact that a definite, immovable place or trajectory is given to the phallus by the letter makes the phallus the 'transcendental signifier' (PC: 465). The lack of a signified is *localised*, restricted to *one* signifier, the phallus, and not genuinely disseminated to every *other* signifier. Derrida intimates this in stating that the letter gives the lack a *stable* place, and this would explain why the phallus can be described as occupying a transcendental *position*: 'The *transcendental* position of the phallus (in the chain of signifiers to which it belongs, while simultaneously making it possible)' (PC: 477). For Derrida, if one takes the disseminative consequences of the infinity of the signifier to their extremes, 'the lack does *not* have its place [*le manque n'a pas sa place*] in dissemination' (PC: 441, my italics). Every signifier lacks a univocal signified. In Lacan, there is a lack of signified in the signifier, but it is restricted to the phallus, which is given a unique place by the theory of the letter, establishing the signifier at a certain point in the real, and thus the lack of signified is not generalised to *all* the signifiers of the system.

For Derrida, the letter reinstalls the subordination of the signifier to meaning precisely because it implies that writing will always ultimately be *phonetic* writing: 'What does count here [. . .] is the implied equivalence [. . .] between symbolic articulation and phonematicity. The symbolic occurs through the voice, and the law of the signifier takes place only within vocalisable letters' (PC: 463). Thus Derrida returns, and feels justified in returning, to his earlier 'suspicion' regarding full speech: 'what is at issue is an *emphasis*, as could equally be said in English, on the authentic excellence of the spoken [. . .] [Lacan] ceaselessly subordinates the letter, writing, and the text' (PC: 463).

And this return to the voice and the phoneme is dictated by the metaphysical necessity to subordinate the signifier to the signified, that it 'not be disseminated':

> They need speech or the phonetisation of the letter as soon as the phallus has to be *kept*, has to return to its point of departure, has not to be disseminated en route [. . .]. If it were divisible, it could always be lost en route. To protect against this possible loss the statement about the 'materiality of the signifier', that is, about the signifier's indivisible singularity, is constructed. *This 'materiality'* [. . .] *in fact corresponds to an idealisation.* (PC: 464)[52]

This 'idealisation' turns its back on the materiality of difference and towards the guiding presence of a meaning: 'the indestructibility of the letter has to do with its elevation toward the ideality of a meaning' (PC: 466). Thus Lacan 'considers the letter only at the point at which it is determined (no matter what he says) by its content of meaning, by the ideality of the message that it "vehiculates", by the speech whose meaning remains out of the reach of partition' (PC: 464).

Thus, after a long detour, Derrida's 'suspicions are confirmed'. Lacan *is* the most deconstructive, but not quite deconstructive enough.

c) 'For the love of Lacan'

In his final major engagement with Lacan, at a conference entitled 'Lacan *with* the Philosophers' in 1990, the stress of Derrida's discourse falls constantly on the necessity to engage with Lacan. Hence his continual emphasis of the word '*with*'. He now opines that, 'nothing of that which managed to transform the space of thought in the last decades would have been possible without some coming to terms *with* Lacan' (R: 46). Although it might be remembered that at the very start of one of the most important innovations of the last three decades, deconstruction itself, Derrida explicitly excluded the consideration of Lacan. On the other hand, it is quite possible that Derrida is modestly excluding his own thought here.

In any case, here, nine years after Lacan's death, Derrida is at his most positive with regard to Lacan's work; at least he seems to be. And yet the same formal structure once again returns to govern his remarks, that Lacan stands closest to deconstruction but he is still the most deconstructible. 'Lacan is so much more aware as a philosopher than Freud, so much more a philosopher than Freud!' (R: 47). The first part of this exclamation is undercut by the second: if one is more a philosopher than Freud then one is inherently more deconstructible than he is. Lacan was in this regard 'too much at home *with the philosophers*' (R: 56). And yet it is the insight offered by the first half of the sentence that will always have interested us: the thought that Lacan knew full well he was not a deconstructionist and simply did not care.

In any case, this is how Derrida rewrites his earlier opinion that Lacan is both the most deconstructible and the most deconstructive. Indeed, Derrida reiterates this explicitly. At the same time as the deconstructive questioning of philosophy was forming, 'there was an impulse coming from psychoanalysis in general [. . .] to deconstruct the privilege of presence, at least as consciousness and egological consciousness' (R: 55).[53] And yet this also took the form of 'a Lacanian discourse [not necessarily Lacan's, perhaps[54]] that made the most strenuous, and powerfully spectacular, use of all the motifs that were in my view deconstructible' (R: 54). Once again, Derrida uses the term 'motifs', and once again he recognises that it is as if Lacan were deliberately prostituting his deconstructibility, well aware of what he was doing, and what he was doing was not Derridean deconstruction. But in any case, in Derrida's eyes, this means, as ever, that Lacan's discourse was, 'the closest and the most deconstructible, the one that was most to be deconstructed' (R: 55).

And yet here Derrida acknowledges that much has changed in Lacan's work, and much of what caused Derrida, at least in 1971, to consider it *prima facie* metaphysical, has gone. 'The discourse of Lacan [. . .] continued thereafter to readjust, even recast, sometimes contradict the axioms I have just mentioned' (R: 61). And although Derrida may not take this at face value, Lacan even eradicates the phonocentrism that for Derrida resulted from the indivisibility of the letter: 'This explicit and massive phonocentrism will be contradicted by Lacan himself' (R: 59). Perhaps this is why Derrida insists on the continuing need for a discussion with Lacan: 'the ongoing and interminable discussion with Lacan [. . .] the unanswered questions I am still today putting to Lacan, *with* whom it is worth discussing' (R: 64).

And yet, another (published) encounter at the level of 'The *facteur* of truth' never occurred, at least to my knowledge. And that 'encounter' yet to be staged which Derrida referred to in 1971, and reiterated again in 1990, perhaps in light of the alteration of Lacan's thought in the meantime, never occurred. It is as if Derrida could never find a way to do it, to his ultimate satisfaction, as if he never found an adequate protocol for the conversation. In the context of Marx, in the very same interview to which Derrida appended his footnote on Lacan, he speaks of 'not yet having found a protocol' that would allow them to come together.[55]

For essential reasons that concern their respective notions of the transcendental and the genetic, and in particular the lack of a specific thought of the imaginary in Derrida, I have tried to show that Derrida could *never* have found such a protocol. Perhaps this is why ultimately, if Lacan is offering an *alternative* to deconstruction, an alternative transcendental and genetic understanding of *writing*, deconstruction can only treat Lacan as an *object*. It is as if Derrida is unable to admit Lacan to the 'community of the question about the possibility of the question' which he describes in 'Violence and Metaphysics' (WD: 98).[56] It is as if Lacan could only be excluded from such a community of subjects, and addressed by this community in the way of an object, or perhaps solely in terms of the influence his discourse was seen to be having on the intellectual scene.

I believe this to be a necessary exclusion, since deconstruction is a truly great thought, a genuinely exceptional insight into the aporias of transcendental or metaphysical philosophy, and great thinkers think but one thought. This is why for Heidegger they 'shine like stars in the night sky': they enter constellations but never truly interfere with one another's course; they merely shine, proffering their own insights for what they are.

Later on, when Derrida had written enough deconstructive-'critical' works to establish the deconstructive 'force' of certain terms, he *did* engage in many dialogues with his contemporaries (very few of whom, it might be said, understood him): Gadamer, Habermas, Nancy (who did). . . Not that I believe it to be possible that these dialogues could ever have called deconstruction itself into question, for Derrida simply did not believe it to be a thesis that could be subject to the critical modification that a genuine negotiation can bring about. We have tried to demonstrate this inherent monologicality of deconstruction by means of a dialogue with Lacan that we have shown to be unsuccessful, but symptomatically so.

This is the question that was always the most difficult for Derrida to answer, and perhaps the one that embarrassed him the most, if one thinks of his treatment of Deleuze and his precipitate and delayed treatment of Lacan and Marx: how can deconstruction approach a text that cannot obviously be deconstructed?

This is what happens when a text presents its *own* method of 'deconstruction', its own theory of archi-writing and whatever else comprises a theory of the origination of the signifier. Does Derrida take the appropriate attitude to others who partake, or perhaps refuse to partake, in his 'community of the question', those hovering on the margins of philosophy and tugging it in different directions? *Can* deconstruction adopt a proper, ethical attitude to another subject that deconstructs in its own way? Is it *right* to either deconstruct them or pass over them in silence? Normally, Derrida does not engage, as with Deleuze. But with Lacan, and perhaps Lacan alone, he was from very early on precipitated into an engagement. We have tried to show why, and why this engagement had to remain unsatisfactory.

In constantly returning, or gesturing towards a reopening of the dialogue, it was as if Derrida also felt dissatisfied, and was continually harassed by the inkling that here was a discourse which paraded its deconstructibility, that flew in the face of everything that was falling apart around it, that was quite simply an *alternative* to the deconstructive approach itself.

Derrida never wrote on Deleuze, save to express his inability to speak. Derrida describes him as the one to whom he felt closest: 'Deleuze undoubtedly still remains, despite so many dissimilarities, the one among all those of my "generation" to whom I have always considered myself closest' (W: 193). And yet this proximity was *uncomfortable* for him, 'the flustering, really flustering experience of a closeness or of a nearly total affinity concerning the "theses"' (W: 192).

In the case of Lacan, perhaps because relations here were not so amicable as in the case of Deleuze, because of the 'aggression' and perhaps the very 'force' of Lacanian discourse, this closeness became *too* flustering, and Derrida was prompted to speak long before the funeral.

We have in this work tried to diagnose why this is the case. And this is a task that we believe neither Derrida – nor indeed Lacan, perhaps – could have managed. For *every* great thinker – perhaps – treads but a single path. And our purposes have required us to adopt the position of the 'scholar', observing the battle of the giants from without.

To conclude – the betrayal of Zarathustra

One repays a teacher badly if one remains nothing but a pupil.
(*Thus Spoke Zarathustra*: Of the Bestowing Virtue)

In this work we have superimposed Lacan's genetic approach to the transcendental on Derrida's wholly transcendental approach, to indicate the latter's idiosyncrasy and hence its limits. But is this really a criticism of Derrida? Or is this opening of Derrida's thought to critical scrutiny not precisely a way to remain *true* to his most concealed insight? Did Derrida himself not suggest that deconstruction and its determination of the transcendental *had to become* just one signifier in a chain that it should never have been taken to govern?[57] In other words, would we not betray Derrida if we attempted to promote deconstruction as the one master-signifier of the entire symbolic order of theories that we must propose in his wake, the *archē* of a textual canon spawned by Derrida? If we were to become Derrideans would we not precisely fail to be true to *Derrida*?

If we are ultimately to be *true* to Derrida's insights, must we not precisely resist the temptation of making deconstruction itself into some form of transcendental condition, elevating it to a position outside of all textual constellations, a theoretical standpoint from which to criticise others? By enmeshing deconstruction in a chain or network that extends beyond it, do we not open it up to the dialogues and lines of communication which Derrida himself earnestly wished for but often failed to achieve?

Indeed, is it not the case that 'deconstruction' is nothing beyond the readings which it undertakes, each of which is presented in a plural series? If deconstruction itself does not exist, if there is only a series of readings which happen to be signed for the most part by Jacques Derrida, perhaps it is *still* deconstructive to superimpose other readings, if deconstruction is *nothing but* this process of superimposition, which demonstrates the inadequacy of any single text, any single reading. 'Derrida' (or rather 'deconstruction') would be the signature for this process of overlaying. The library of books which are written by Derrida would be nothing besides these readings lain on top of one another to indicate the constant need to remain restless, the demand imposed upon creatures of language to carry on reading and to make sure that no one signifier, no one reading, and no one text, is ever elevated to the genuinely transcendental 'theological' position of *The* Book, that would *not* be vulnerable to usurpation, that would not be swallowed up in a chain of signifiers which it cannot govern.

Is deconstruction's thesis something which is not itself a finite text but which concerns every finite text as such? Is it the attempt to indicate not just that any *finite* text is unable to live up to its own claims, but *also* that any finite reading of a finite text is always an injustice, that there will always be an infinity of other signifiers determining the meaning of what has been said, always a blind-spot, always more books to read? We have always 'read a certain number of texts, but not all. . .' (OG: 162).

It is as if Derrida's constant energy and almost continuous production of texts were a tending towards infinity, the infinity that would be the other, that would be to do justice to a certain work.

Derrida's own finitude meant that his task had to be left unfinished and yet at the same time it allowed his corpus to be finitised, as if his work *had* been done. This is why, with the impending cessation of his publications, we risk today more than ever promoting his work to a position it did not wish to occupy. In order to be faithful to this most honest and upright of thinkers, are we not required to reinscribe Derrida's finite text in a wider economy, to *carry on writing*, and writing over his work? To be true to deconstruction is it not necessary to betray it, to replace it, as we have attempted to do here, to plaster graffiti on Derrida's grave, on the memorial and tombstone tomes that he left behind, to inscribe whole works – Lacan's first of all – in the margins of his books, thus refusing to let them *be* 'Books' in the proper sense? I believe that this vandalised memorial is the only kind that Derrida would have desired.

Thus if one were only to read *Derrida* this would itself be a betrayal *of* Derrida. He often insisted that it was his wish to spur his readers to go back to the original texts, and this would hardly be to say, 'See, it will confirm what I have told you.' Is this the secret *ethical* message of Derrida's plural readings of finite texts? To implore us to read texts more, and simply to *read more*, to strive constantly to adequate this infinite other?

Considered alone, Derrida's own *corpus* cannot *itself* be faithful to deconstruction's insight. It is only by joining him in a plurality, in a community, by following and then working critically upon his work, that one can allow deconstruction its proper voice.

If this is so, then in submitting to this encounter with Lacan, deconstruction would truly have done all it can, and we would have provided the supplement to Derridean deconstruction that allows it to become 'complete', which at the same time means incomplete, open onto another. Every good Zarathustrian betrays his teacher, and it is precisely this betrayal that Derrida must *want*, that his merely finite text and name be only the impetus to an infinity of reading and writing which never rests content, with a good conscience, having 'done enough'.

This book has attempted to write Lacan's thought *over* Derrida's, not to replace it, but to inscribe it as one signifier in a chain that extends beyond it. Lacan's very work, as it is presented here, is another text written on top of Derrida's text: Lacan as an other writing, an other who wrote, and who wrote otherwise, with another writing.

Thus, let the writing of the present book, this 'other writing' *about* Derrida and *about* Lacan not be understood as a *criticism* of Derrida. Let it be a work that attempts to work in his spirit and in the spirit of deconstruction, which always worked only for the sake of the other, for the possibility of the event of the *new*.

At the same time, our image of superimposition should not be taken to suggest that each link in the chain is of the same size or brilliance: it could be the case – perhaps we have suggested it here – that the ink of Lacan's text is more bold than Derrida's, that his grooves cut deeper, that certain elements of his thought *supersede* Derrida's. But the spaces between the inked letters can never be filled in such that there will never be another writing. The eternal scribbling of scholars must see to it that no one palimpsest is ever considered to be final, thus opening up the infinity of reading and writing.

Each text we write as scholars, each comparative study, composes a superimposition such as this. It is the attempt to open a thinker to novelty, in order that the old not be solidified as the final. In it we assert each thinker's text to be a mere mark on the shore, washed over by new tides, rendering the grooves less clear, less permanent, as the Heraclitean child continues to play his game with moist pebbles on a board etched in sand. We are servants of the petulance of the

Heraclitean sea which every now and then must reclaim the pieces and even the board.

Notes

1. Allison's translation of *La Voix et le Phénomène*, one of the earliest, translates '*archi-écriture*' as 'proto-writing'. Incorrectly, but illuminatingly so.
2. '[T]he very name *aleph* is related to the cow, whose head the first form of *aleph* supposedly reproduces. [. . .] [S]omething of it still remains: we can still see in our capital A the shape of a cow's skull upside down with the horns which prolong it' (SIX: 10/1/62). The initial imaginary form of the letter thus explicitly ties us back to the *animal* realm in which as hunters we knew ourselves to exist. It remains in so many ways our bond with the animal and the imaginary.
3. An excellent account of *lalangue*, in a similar vein to my own, may be found in Dolar (2006: ch. 6).
4. '[T]he thing may be presented in the simplest possible way by the single stroke. The first signifier is the notch by which it is indicated, for example, that the subject has killed *one* animal, by means of which he will not become confused in his memory when he has killed ten others. He will not have to remember which is which, and it is by means of this single stroke that he will count them' (SXI: 141).
5. 'There is no radical reduction of the fourth term [the *sinthome*], equally in analysis. Freud was able to state, one does not know by what route, that there is an *Urverdrängung*, a repression [*refoulement*] that cannot be annulled. It is in the very nature of the symbolic to bear this hole' (SXXIII: 41).
6. If in Chapter 1 we may have twisted Lacan's actual words by describing the subject of enunciation as 'real', it is because at the time Lacan did not have the theoretical resources which he now has to state this explicitly. At the same time, our understanding of Lacan's unconscious as the infinity of the signifier's differential trace here receives its retrospective justification.
7. This is why Lacan praises those French deconstructionists who read his work without understanding it in *The Title of the Letter*: 'I have never been so well read' (SXX: 65). Interestingly, Derrida says the converse. Lacoue-Labarthe's and Nancy's texts are 'not readable' by 'most French "Lacanians" ' (R: 60). This opens up an angle of approach that we will hardly have focused on in this study: the question of whether Lacan and Lacanians understand *Derrida*. Hopefully, by the end of this chapter we will have shown implicitly why we believe *Derrida*'s inability to understand is more significant than Lacan's. . . (Perhaps this will excuse our neglecting a detailed engagement with works that may be crucial in this

regard, Lacan's 'Lituraterre' and 'Raison d'un échec', collected in *Autres Écrits*.)

8. This notion of telling the truth about the truth appeared in a dream involving Lacan, dreamt by one of his patients (SIX: 15/11/61).
9. 'One's responsibility goes only as far as one's knowledge [*savoir-faire*]' (SXXIII: 61).
10. In Seminar IX, Lacan is still trying to find a way to situate the subject with respect to the signifier: 'the function of the subject is in the between-the-two, between the idealising effects of the signifying function and this vital immanence' (SIX: 20/12/61).
11. 'What is the meaning of meaning? Meaning is the fact that the human being isn't master of this primordial, primitive language. He has been thrown into it, committed, caught up in its gears. [. . .] Here man isn't master in his own house' (SII: 307).
12. Indeed, Lacan later comes to realise that there could be no subject at all – as for structuralism there was not – if the signifier *could* signify itself: 'it is insofar as the signifier has to redouble its effect by wanting to designate itself that the subject arises as exclusion from the very field that it determines' (SIX: 9/5/62).
13. 'The word can in no way be regarded as a unit of language, even though it constitutes a privileged elementary form. At an even lower level you find the phonematic oppositions or couplings which characterise the ultimate radical element that *distinguishes one language from another*. [. . .] In French for example *boue* and *pou* are opposed to one another, whatever your accent [. . .] because French is a language in which this opposition is valid. In other languages there are oppositions totally unknown in French' (SIII: 225, my italics). According to Dolar, it is the shift from a concern with the actual physical production of phonemes to this oppositionality or relationality that characterises the shift from phonetics to phonology (cf. Dolar 2006: 17–18).
14. One might also hear in '*lalangue*' qua mother tongue a reference to the Mother as the Real thing, as the moment at which we left the real and entered the determinacy of our particular symbolic, our mother's tongue.
15. The title of a contribution by Lacan to Jacques Aubert's collection, *Joyce-le-Sinthome*, reprinted in SXXIII: 161–9.
16. 'Fenian' was an Irish nationalist organisation, but homophonic in French (as indicated by the addition of an acute accent) with *faignant* or *fainéant*, doing nothing, or one who does nothing.
17. Roudinesco asserts that the word is also a pun on the name of André Lalande, author of *Vocabulaire Technique et Critique de la Philosophie* (Paris: PUF, 1976) (Roudinesco 1997 [1993]: 361, 501, n 5).
18. In Seminar VII Lacan tells his audience that his words are attempts to let them 'localise and *feel* [*sentir*]' the limit of the symbolic and the real (SVII: 154, my italics).

19. Lacan often speaks of this procedure as a 'formalisation'. 'When one speaks of mathematical formalisation, we are dealing with a set of conventions from which you can generate a whole series of consequences, of theorems which follow on from one another, and establish certain structural relations, a law, in the strict sense of law, within a set' (SII: 34). And later on: 'Formalisation is nothing other than the substitution of what is called a *letter* for any number of ones' (SXX: 130, my italics).
20. A neologism formed from '*signifiant*', signifier/signifying, referring to the signifier itself freed from the telos of the (imaginary) signified.
21. On the other hand Lacan sometimes acknowledges that even in mathematics itself, the intuitive element *cannot* wholly be eliminated, and this is one of the reasons why Lacan turns to topology in 1961–2. 'M. Poincaré understands very well that it is indeed in topology that one finds the essence of the intuitive element, and that one cannot resolve it and that I would even go further: without intuition one cannot do this science which is called topology' (SIX: 7/3/62).
22. Lacan refers to Laplanche and Leclaire's mistake in reading these formulae for metaphor and metonymy in a mathematical way and equally mistakenly subjecting them to mathematical criticism (cf. Laplanche and Leclaire 1966) (Lacan in Lemaire 1977: xii–xiv).
23. Mathematics as a metalanguage of the real *con*sists by and with itself, it hangs together to form a coherent universe of symbols, but *ex*ists – which is to say exceeds the dimension of the *purely* symbolic – *only* with the support of language: 'There remains in fact the question of the laying out [*la mise à plat*]. In what way is it appropriate? All we can say is that it is demanded by knots, as an artifice [. . .] of representation' (SXXIII: 83).
24. 'This schema no doubt suffers from the excess endemic to any formalisation that is presented in the intuitive realm' (E: 476). They are not designed to make things easier to understand.
25. Recall that Lacan's representations are a *flattening*, and often they perhaps represent shapes which in reality can *not* be represented, the representation thus pointing beyond representation to the real, impossible to comprehend or imagine.
26. Lacan goes to some lengths to criticise Kant's transcendental aesthetic for its foundation in Euclidean geometry, whose axioms have been disproved by other non-intuitive forms of geometry (SIX: 23/5/62). The straight line is *not* always the shortest distance between two points; this is just how it appears to our eyes, due to our limited horizonal perception of the – in truth, curved – surface of the sphere whose uppermost crust we inhabit.
27. 'The form most devoid [*dépourvue*] of meaning, but which is nevertheless imagined, is consistence [*consistance*]. Nothing forces us to imagine consistence. [. . .] What does consistence mean? It means what holds things together [*tient ensemble*]' (SXXIII: 65).

28. Strictly speaking, Lacan uses the verb '*capter*', which signifies both captivation and capture.
29. '[T]he knots are a writing, and the knot is a letter' (Miller in SXXIII: 236). Miller reminds us here – in a note about Lacan and Derrida – that the knot as a form of writing relates back to the unary trait of Seminar IX. Here he is following Lacan's suggestion: 'It's not all the same since yesterday that I have been interested in this business of writing, and I first put it forward when I spoke about the unary trait, the *einziger Zug* in Freud. [. . .] I have given this unary trait another support by making the Borromean knot' (SXXIII: 145).
30. The word 'mathematical' could simply be read as 'matheme-atical', in other words, as an adjective of 'matheme', which derives from the Greek *manthanein*, meaning 'to learn': 'signs [. . .] are called mathematical – "mathemes" – solely because they are integrally transmitted. We haven't the slightest idea what they mean, but they are transmitted' (SXX: 110).
31. Strictly, the thing is the moment at which the real opens onto the symbolic: here already, albeit incipiently, the real is being thought as a limit.
32. The reference is to the object *a*, but it is remarkable that for *Derrida* it is precisely the letter '*a*' of '*différance*' that evinces the incursion of writing upon speech and the dependence of meaning upon the archi-written trace. And it would perhaps have been in Lacan's mind, for this passage is to be found only a few paragraphs after a direct invocation of Derrida's work.
33. Perhaps Lacan is here thinking of his seventh Seminar where the signifier was understood to originate by means of a technically produced hole carved out in the real by man, at least apparently.
34. Derrida begins Chapter 3 of *Of Grammatology* with a meditation on the conditions of possibility of such a (pre)history: 'Where and when does the trace, writing in general, common root of speech and writing, narrow itself down into "writing" in the colloquial sense' (OG: 74). 'Writing being thoroughly historical, it is at once natural and surprising that the scientific interest in writing has always taken the form of a history of writing' (OG: 75), and yet, 'one must know *what* writing *is* in order to ask – knowing what one is talking about and what *the question is* – where and when writing begins' (OG: 74–5). And since Derrida goes on to say that writing evades and makes possible the question of essence, 'what is. . .?', we may infer that a grammatology and hence the form it has usually taken, that of a (pre)history of writing, is impossible. For writing comes *before* history. This is perhaps why Derrida states that 'the phoneticisation of writing must dissimulate its own history as it is produced' (OG: 3), as if it were necessary that phonetic writing should *conceal* its own factual history, the moment at which it was phoneticised, rendering this historical moment inaccessible to empirical research. Phonetic writing is the *precondition* of history and

so cannot be subordinated to and located within history; it is its very opening: 'the enigma of this evolution does not allow itself to be dominated by the concept of history' (OG: 88). And yet Derrida admits something like a *pre*history of the signifier that would not strictly speaking be a 'history': 'To be sure, the latter [history] appears at a determined moment in the phoneticisation of script and it presupposes phoneticisation in an essential way' (OG: 88). History begins at a certain moment. But Derrida never seems to acknowledge that insight into this prehistory could ever fundamentally alter the way in which we understand the *present* nature of the empirical signifier. This is precisely the originality of Lacan.

35. But might this be Derrida's critical point? That in the attempt to reach the real we must erase anthropomorphisms *and* zoomorphisms, such as this notion of a unity? But this will be our point: if this is the case, then it is necessary to erase the imaginary appropriation of the real just as much as it is to erase the symbolic, and Derrida seems to spend no time on the former. Lacan, on the other hand – this is our hypothesis – *is* able to recognise the need to extract the real from both the symbolic *and* the imaginary.
36. '[T]he agencies that Freud constructs should not be taken to be substantial, nor epiphenomenal in relation to the modification of the apparatus itself. Hence the agencies should be interpreted by means of an optical schema' (SI: 123). Lacan thus discusses a materialist – a genetic – theory of consciousness in this regard, the real's ability to produce something of a nature distinct from its own. He instances the image reflected in the lake of an uninhabited planet (SII: 46–9). What is crucial is that the image is not just *subjective*, merely 'epiphenomenal', *nor* can it be *reduced* to some event in the *brain*. The image, while of material origin, has its own ontological realm with its own characteristics and 'laws'.
37. On Derrida's *qualified* praise of mathematics as resisting the reduction of writing to phonetic writing see (OG: 3–4) and (P: 34).
38. As Derrida recognises, Lacan's thought is and 'should be' porous to all kinds of other 'discourses', which is to say in this instance, the sciences (R: 62).
39. Despite this being 'a word whose choice has always perplexed me' (P: 85). Derrida does not seem satisfied with the explanation that its provenance is more Lévi-Straussian than Saussurean.
40. However, Derrida will soon admit, but do *no more than* admit, that this separation is troubled in the later Lacan: 'the strictness of this tripartition, to which, as you know, Lacan was also obliged to return much later' (R: 59).
41. Truly curious in this passage is an insight that Derrida *never* discusses, that the imaginary and the real should both be understood as

impossibilities of the symbolic. An unfolding of this remark would have taken him far, perhaps beyond himself, where he, like all great thinkers, could not venture.

42. Derrida discusses this in the context of Heidegger's supposedly equally oppositional understanding of the relation between man and animal (cf. Derrida 1987 [1985]: 173–4; cf. Derrida 1989 [1987]: 11–12).
43. Will Derrida ever find this space? In 1990 he refuses to publicise his answer to this question once again: 'I can't say more about this here; these things are happening elsewhere, in recent seminars' (R: 66). In 1997, Derrida will speak on 'the animal' at a conference on his work, entitled by him 'The Autobiographical Animal', at Cerisy-la-Salle. His words have recently been collected and translated as *The Animal That Therefore I Am* (Derrida 2008).
44. We should not however suggest that Lacan's approach to the animal wishes *entirely* to avoid the transcendental appropriation: + and − are after all symbolic determinations. There *is* some such mechanism as the imaginary in animals, and we have seen that such a thing as a *quasi*-oppositional alternation takes place in nature, but to posit a fully constituted, marked *opposition* between the imaginary in animals and the imaginary in man (+ and − always form an opposition, whichever way round one puts them) is to appropriate the relation to the symbolic and thus to transcendentalise the relation.

    To understand the animal as confined to the imaginary restricts what it might *really* be on the basis of the fact that the only three spheres man has anything to do with are the symbolic, imaginary and real. We *posit* the animal as having a perfect imaginary or instinctual relation with its world in order to *contrast* it with our own, to explain how such a thing as the novel symbolic order could have arisen, genetically speaking. It is the absoluteness of the division that is transcendental and a consequence of the oppositional symbolic framework in which our thinking for the most part operates.

    One is compelled from the standpoint of our dysfunctional imagination and its immediate symbolic supplement to see the animal as enjoying a pre-established *harmony* with its environment *which in truth, in itself, it may not*: 'There is a convergence, a crystallisation, here which *gives us the feeling*, however sceptical we may be, of a pre-established harmony [. . .] an animal recognises its brother, its fellow being, its sexual partner. [. . .] The animal fits into its environment' (SII: 86, my italics). Later, Lacan becomes quite explicit: 'Once the human being is speaking, it's stuffed, it's the end of this perfection, this harmony, in copulation – *which in any case is impossible to find anywhere in nature*' (SXVII: 33, my italics). It is the fact that the imaginary is already symbolised in man that forces us to understand our relation to the animal other as an opposition.

45. '[N]ot only was I not criticising Lacan, but I was not even writing a sort of overseeing or objectifying metadiscourse *on* Lacan or *on* a text of Lacan's' (R: 63); 'my reading [. . .] did not claim to enclose or exhaust Lacan' (R: 61).
46. This is the very earliest sign of Derrida's wariness of Lacan, and perhaps the first thing that made him prick up his deconstructive ears. In the very *exergue* of *Of Grammatology*, we read, 'the debasement of writing, and its repression outside "full" speech' [*la parole "pleine"*]' (OG: 3), and in his first text on Freud (from 1966, the year of *Écrits*), in a manner that will often be repeated, he plays two Freuds off against each other, one metaphysical, one not, and he is perhaps suggesting that the *Lacanian* interpretation seizes upon the metaphysical: 'Freud invokes signs which do not transcribe living, full speech [*une parole vive et pleine*], master of itself and self-present' (WD: 249). And who else but Lacan could Derrida have had in mind with the following? 'If the Freudian break-through has an historical originality, this originality is not due to its peaceful coexistence or theoretical complicity with this linguistics, at least its congenital phonologism' (WD: 249). He reinforces this reading in 1990: 'Freud, whom I was trying as well to read in my own, not very Lacanian way, in "Freud and the Scene of Writing" ' (R: 55). Derrida admits to having read two – and only two – works of Lacan before writing his articles, 'Of Grammatology' and 'Freud and the Scene of Writing' (P: 108, n 44), so the inferences contained in this footnote are perhaps not unwarranted.
47. Roudinesco refers to an incident in Baltimore in which Lacan claimed in person to have beaten Derrida to the mark in regard to certain theses (Roudinesco 1990 [1986]: 410). Derrida says the following: 'the absence of references to Lacan, in effect, is almost total. This is justified not only by the aggressions in the form of, or with the aim of, reappropriation, that Lacan, since the appearance of "De la grammatologie" in *Critique* (1965) (and even earlier, I am told) has proliferated [. . .]. This is the so called "kettle" argument' (P: 107, n 44). For Derrida, on the whole this amounted to a simple misunderstanding of deconstruction anyway, and the all too common reversal of the hierarchy of speech and writing, without displacement or generalisation (cf. R: 61). Derrida refers to this much later when he says that ' "Of Grammatology" was first the title of an article published some five years before Lacan's new introduction [to the two-volume edition of *Écrits* published in 1970] and – this is one of the numerous mistakes or misrecognitions made by Lacan and so many others – it never proposed a grammatology, some positive science or discipline bearing that name; [it] went to great lengths to demonstrate the impossibility, the conditions of impossibility, the absurdity, in principle of any science or any philosophy bearing the name "grammatology". The book that treated *of grammatology* was anything but a grammatology' (R: 52).

As for Lacan's side of the story, he 'devoured' 'De la grammatologie' (Roudinesco 1990 [1986]: 409), and refers to it approvingly in his thirteenth Seminar, without admitting that it contains an essential advance on his own work (SXIII: 15/12/65).

48. These comprise (let us list them as itemistically as Derrida does):
1) the telos of full speech and the recourse to truth (P: 108, n 44; cf. WD: 249, 276–7);
2) the (allegedly) unthematised or unthought recourse to Hegelian, Heideggerian, Husserlian terminology (P: 108–9, n 44);
3) the authority of phonology, and writing's ultimate derivation from the system of hearing and understanding oneself speak, the immediate self-presence of non-linguistic speech (P: 109, n 44). Already we can hear the indivisibility of the letter which will prove to be the final bone of contention;
4) 'An attention to the letter and to the written according to Freud, certainly, but without any specific investigation concerning the concept of writing, such as I was then attempting to delineate it' (P: 109, n 44).
This last item is particularly revealing of the extent of Derrida's acquaintance. We have already examined at length Lacan's thoughts on writing from *1961*. If Derrida had not read all of Lacan, it is surely unjust of him to assume that certain elements had been left 'unthematised' or 'unthought'. Injustice is *certainly* uncharacteristic of Derrida, to say the least, which makes it all the more remarkable.
49. '[T]he return of Freud's text to its proper place' (PC: 450; cf. PC: 451, n 24). Lacan counters, with his own understanding of the text's 'letter' as *unconscious*: 'Marx and Lenin, Freud and Lacan are not coupled in being. It is via the letter they found in the Other that, as beings of knowledge, they proceed two by two, in a supposed Other. What is new about their knowledge is that it doesn't presume the Other knows anything about it – certainly not the being who constituted the letter there' (SXX: 97–8).
50. Lacan makes this connection, after Joyce (AE: 11).
51. At almost exactly the same time, Lacan will say, '[a] letter and a phonological symbol are already worlds apart' (SXXIII: 131).
52. In fact, Lacan is very explicit that the process of differentiation continues to split, even at the level of the letter, for otherwise one would reach a moment of pure self-reference, self-signifying, which we have taken to characterise, and which Derrida takes to characterise, the real in its oppositional formulation: 'no signifier – even if it is, and very precisely when it is, reduced to its minimal form, the one that we call the letter – can signify itself' (SXIV: 23/11/66).
53. From the very outset, psychoanalysis was identified, along with linguistics, as an *especial* ally of deconstruction. 'Outside of linguistics, it is in

psychoanalytic research that this breakthrough seems at present to have the greatest likelihood of being expanded' (OG: 21).

54. Johnson suggests, in an exceptionally thorough reading, that Lacan's influence, Lacanian*ism*, was Derrida's target in 'The *facteur* of truth' (Johnson 1988: 227–8). Derrida himself suggests as much in conversation with Roudinesco: '"When I spoke of Saussure or of Lacan", Derrida emphasised, "I was criticising less their texts than the role those texts were playing on the French intellectual scene"' (Roudinesco 1990 [1986]: 385). One is reminded that Derrida hardly ever speaks of Hegel when he criticises 'sublation', and rather uses the word 'Hegelian' or 'quasi-Hegelian'. The use of '-ian' or '-ism' always indicates that Derrida tends more generally to consider a thinker in terms of the field of discourse which he opens up and which discourse then places *his work* and *his name* in the place of the (transcendental) principle (*archē*) of their own.
55. 'Reading is transformational. I believe that this would be confirmed by certain of Althusser's propositions. But this transformation cannot be executed however one wishes. It requires protocols of reading. Why not say it bluntly: I have not yet found any that satisfy me' (P: 63). In 1990, Derrida in fact lays out three 'protocols' for 'this history to come of the *being-with* of Lacan and the philosophers, a history which I am quite sure has never been written and which I am not sure ever can be written' (R: 53). Referring back to the diagram we have placed at the head of the present work, the first of these is entitled 'Chiasmus', and refers precisely to this strange paradox of Lacan's deconstructivity and deconstructibility, which we have attempted to understand in a different way to Derrida.
56. Derrida does speak of the variety of deconstructive discourses and their possibilities of engaging with each other (cf. WD: 355–6).
57. What else is the meaning of the following? '[T]he enterprise of deconstruction always in a certain way falls prey to its own work' (OG: 24), and 'what we call production is necessarily a text, the system of a writing and of a reading which we know is ordered around *its own* blind spot' (OG: 164, my italics).

Bibliography

Works are listed in their original order of publication. Translations have sometimes been modified.

Lacan's seminars in various transcriptions are freely available to consult at http://gaogoa.free.fr/, and other texts at http://www.ecole-lacanienne.net – some of my own references to the French are taken from these versions – while certain English translations by Cormac Gallagher may be found, at a price, at http://www.karnacbooks.com

Agamben, Giorgio (1995 [1985]) *Idea of Prose*. Trans. by Michael Sullivan and Sam Whitsitt. Albany, NY: State University of New York Press.

—— (1999) *Potentialities: Collected Essays in Philosophy*. Edited and trans., with an introduction, by Daniel Heller-Roazen. Stanford, CA: Stanford University Press.

—— (2004 [2002]) *The Open: Man and Animal*. Trans. by Kevin Attell. Stanford, CA: Stanford University Press.

Allouch, Jean (1983) 'La conjecture de Lacan sur l'origine de l'écriture', in *Littoral* 7/8: 5–26.

Benveniste, Emile (1971 [1966]) *Problems in General Linguistics*. Miami: University of Miami Press.

Borch-Jacobsen, Mikkel (1991) *Lacan: the Absolute Master*. Trans. by Douglas Brick. Stanford, CA: Stanford University Press.

Chiesa, Lorenzo (2006) 'Count-as-one, Forming-into-one, Unary Trait, S1', *Cosmos and History: The Journal of Natural and Social Philosophy*, 'The Praxis of Alain Badiou', Vol. 2, Nos 1–2: 68–93.

—— (2007) *Subjectivity and Otherness: A Philosophical Reading of Lacan*. Cambridge, MA: MIT Press.

Critchley, Simon (1992) *The Ethics of Deconstruction: Derrida and Levinas*. Oxford: Blackwell.

Deleuze, Gilles (1994 [1968]) *Difference and Repetition*. Trans. by Paul Patton. London: Athlone Press.

Deleuze, Gilles, and Guattari, Félix (1994 [1991]) *What is Philosophy?* Trans. by Hugh Tomlinson and Graham Burchill. London and New York: Verso.

Derrida, Jacques (2003 [1953–4, published 1990]) *The Problem of Genesis in Husserl's Philosophy*. Trans. by Marian Hobson. Chicago: University of Chicago Press.

—— (1989 [1962]) *Edmund Husserl's* Origin of Geometry: *An Introduction*. Trans. by John P. Leavey, Jr. Lincoln, NE, and London: University of Nebraska Press (first publication in English: Stony Brook, NY: N. Hays, 1978).

—— (1973 [1967]) *Speech and Phenomena and Other Essays on Husserl's Theory of Signs*. Trans. by David B. Allison. Evanston, IL: Northwestern University Press.

—— (1974 [1967]) *Of Grammatology*. Trans. by Gayatri Chakravorty Spivak. Baltimore and London: The Johns Hopkins University Press.

—— (2001 [1967]) *Writing and Difference*. Trans. by Alan Bass. London and New York: Routledge.

—— (1982 [1972]) *Margins: of Philosophy*. Trans. by Alan Bass. New York, London: Harvester Wheatsheaf.

—— (1981[1972]) *Dissemination*. Trans. by Barbara Johnson. London: Athlone Press.

—— (2002 [1972]) *Positions*. Trans. by Alan Bass. London and New York: Continuum.

—— (1979 [1978]) *Spurs: Nietzsche's Styles*. Trans. by Barbara Harlow. Chicago and London: University of Chicago Press.

—— (1987 [1980]) *The Postcard: From Socrates to Freud and Beyond*. Trans. by Alan Bass. Chicago and London: University of Chicago Press.

—— (1987 [1985]) 'Geschlecht II: Heidegger's Hand'. Trans. by John P. Leavey, Jr. in John Sallis (ed.) *Deconstruction and Philosophy: the Texts of Jacques Derrida*. Chicago and London: University of Chicago Press.

—— (1989 [1987]) *Of Spirit: Heidegger and the Question*. Trans. by Geoffrey Bennington and Rachel Bowlby. Chicago and London: University of Chicago Press.

—— (1991 [1987]) 'At this very moment in this work here I am', in Peggy Kamuf (ed.) *A Derrida Reader: Between the Blinds*. New York and London: Harvester Wheatsheaf.

—— (1991 [1988]) '"Eating well", or the calculation of the subject: An interview with Jacques Derrida'. Trans. by Peter Connor and Avital Ronell in Eduardo Cadava, Peter Connor, and Jean-Luc Nancy (eds) *Who Comes After the Subject?* London and New York: Routledge.

—— (1992 [1989–90]) 'Force of Law: The "mystical foundation of authority"'. Trans. by Mary Quaintance in Gil Anidjar (ed.) *Acts of Religion*. London: Routledge.

—— (1995 [1990]) *The Gift of Death*. Trans. by David Wills. Chicago: University of Chicago Press.

—— (1994 [1993]) *Spectres of Marx: The State of the Debt, the Work of Mourning, and the New International*. Trans. by Peggy Kamuf. New York and London: Routledge.

—— (1997 [1994]) *Politics of Friendship*. Trans. by George Collins. London: Verso.

—— (1998 [1996]) *Resistances: Of Psychoanalysis*. Trans. by Peggy Kamuf, Pascale-Anne Brault, and Michael Naas. Stanford, CA: Stanford University Press.

—— (2001 [1995]) 'I'll have to wander all alone'. Trans. by Leonard Lawler in Pascale-Anne Brault and Michael Naas (eds) *The Work of Mourning*. Chicago and London: University of Chicago Press.

—— (2008 [1997/2006]) *The Animal That Therefore I Am*. Trans. by David Wills. Edited by Marie-Louise Mallet. New York: Fordham University Press.

Dolar, Mladen (2006) *A Voice and Nothing More*. Cambridge, MA: MIT Press.

Forrester, John (1991) *The Seductions of Psychoanalysis: Freud, Lacan, and Derrida*. Cambridge: Cambridge University Press.

Freud, Anna (1993 [1936]) *The Ego and the Mechanisms of Defence*. London: Karnac.

Freud, Sigmund and Breuer, Josef (1955) *The Standard Edition of the Complete Psychological Works of Sigmund Freud* (hereafter: SE), Volume 2 (1893–95), *Studies on Hysteria*. Edited by James Strachey, in collaboration with Anna Freud. London: Hogarth Press and the Institute of Psycho-analysis.

Freud, Sigmund (1953 [1900]) SE 5, *The Interpretation of Dreams*. London: Hogarth Press and the Institute of Psycho-analysis.

—— (2002 [1901]) *The Psychopathology of Everyday Life: On Forgetfulness, Slips of the Tongue, Inadvertent Actions, Superstitions and Mistakes*. Trans. by Anthea Bell. London: Penguin.

—— (1960 [1905]) SE 8, *Jokes and their Relation to the Unconscious*. London: Hogarth Press and the Institute of Psycho-analysis.

—— (2002 [1911]) *The Schreber Case*. Trans. by Andrew Webber. London: Penguin.

—— (1955 [1913–14]) SE 13, *Totem and Taboo, and Other Works*. London: Hogarth Press and the Institute of Psycho-analysis.

—— (1957 [1914]) 'On Narcissism: An Introduction' in SE 14 (1914–16). London: Hogarth Press and the Institute of Psycho-analysis.

—— (1955 [1921]) 'Group Psychology and the Analysis of the Ego' in SE 18 (1920–22). London: Hogarth Press and the Institute of Psycho-analysis.

—— (1964 [1938]) SE 23 (1937–39), *Splitting of the Ego in the Process of Defence*. London: Hogarth Press and the Institute of Psycho-analysis.

Gasché, Rodolphe (1987 [1985]) 'Infrastructures and Systematicity', in John Sallis (ed.) *Deconstruction and Philosophy: The Texts of Jacques Derrida*. Chicago and London: University of Chicago Press.

—— (1986) *The Tain of the Mirror: Derrida and the Philosophy of Reflection*. Cambridge, MA, and London: Harvard University Press.

Hegel, G. W. F (1977 [1807]) *The Phenomenology of Spirit*. Trans. by Arnold Vincent Miller. Oxford: Oxford University Press.

—— (1975) *Aesthetics. Volume 1*. Trans. by T. M. Knox. Oxford: Oxford University Press.

Heidegger, Martin (1971) *Poetry, Language, Thought*. Trans. by Albert Hofstadter. New York: Harper and Row.

Houlgate, Stephen (ed.) (1998) *The Hegel Reader*. Blackwell: Oxford.

—— (2006) *The Opening of Hegel's Logic: From Being to Infinity*. West Lafayette, IN: Purdue University Press.

Johnson, Barbara (1988) 'Poe, Lacan, Derrida: The Question of the Frame', in John P. Muller and William J. Richardson (eds) *The Purloined Poe: Lacan, Derrida, and Psychoanalytic Reading*. Baltimore and London: The Johns Hopkins University Press.

Julien, Philippe (1983) 'Le nom propre et la lettre', in *Littoral* 7/8: 33–48.

Juranville, Alain (1984) *Lacan et la Philosophie*. Paris: Presses Universitaires de France.

Kant, Immanuel (1997 [1783]) *Prolegomena to any Future Metaphysics that will be able to come forward as Science*. Trans. and edited by Gary Hatfield. Cambridge: Cambridge University Press.

—— (1929 [1787]) *Critique of Pure Reason*. Trans. by Norman Kemp-Smith. Basingstoke: Macmillan.

Kearney, Richard (1995) *States of Mind: Dialogues with Contemporary Thinkers*. New York: New York University Press.

Kojève, Alexandre (1980) *Introduction to the Reading of Hegel: Lectures on the* Phenomenology of Spirit. Assembled by Raymond Queneau. Edited by Allan Bloom. Trans. by James H. Nichols, Jr. Ithaca, NY: Cornell University Press.

Lacan, Jacques (1988) *Seminar Book I: Freud's Papers on Technique, 1953–1954* (All published seminars are edited by Jacques-Alain Miller.) Trans. by John Forrester. Cambridge: Cambridge University Press.

—— (1988) *Seminar Book II: The Ego in Freud's Theory and in the Technique of Psychoanalysis, 1954–1955*. Trans. by Sylvana Tomaselli. Cambridge: Cambridge University Press.

—— (1993) *Seminar Book III: The Psychoses, 1955–1956*. Trans. by Russell Grigg. London: Routledge.

—— (1994) *Le Séminaire livre IV: La Relation d'Objet, 1956–1957*. Paris: Seuil.

—— (1998) *Le Séminaire livre V: Les Formations de l'Inconscient, 1957–1958*. Paris: Seuil.

—— (1958–9) 'Le Séminaire livre VI. Désir et son interpretation, 1958–1959'. Unpublished manuscript (references to unpublished seminars are given by the date of the session).
—— (1992) *Seminar Book VII: The Ethics of Psychoanalysis, 1959–1960*. Trans. by Dennis Porter. London: Routledge.
—— (1991) *Le Séminaire livre VIII: Le Transfert, 1960–1961*. Paris: Seuil.
—— (1961–2) 'Le Séminaire livre IX. L'identification, 1961–1962'. Unpublished manuscript.
—— (2004) *Le Séminaire livre X: L'Angoisse, 1962–1963*. Paris: Seuil.
—— (1963) 'Les Noms Du Père', Seminar of 20 November 1963.
—— (1998 [1964]) [*Seminar Book XI:*] *The Four Fundamental Concepts of Psychoanalysis*. Trans. by Alan Sheridan. London: Vintage.
—— (1965–6) 'Le Séminaire livre XIII. L'Objet du psychanalyse, 1965–1966'. Unpublished manuscript.
—— (2006 [1966]) *Écrits*. Trans. by Bruce Fink with Heloïse Fink and Russell Grigg. New York and London: W. W. Norton.
—— (1966–7) 'Le Séminaire livre XIV. Logique du fantasme, 1966–1967'. Unpublished manuscript.
—— (2007 [1969–70]) *Seminar Book XVII: The Other Side of Psychoanalysis*. Trans. by Russell Grigg. New York and London: W. W. Norton.
—— (1999) *Seminar Book XX: Encore, 1972–1973*. Trans. by Bruce Fink. New York and London: W. W. Norton. (The English translation is entitled '*On Feminine Sexuality, The Limits of Love and Knowledge*'. N.B. All Lacan's seminars in English are now published, with the same pagination, by W. W. Norton.)
—— (2005) *Le Séminaire livre XXIII: Le Sinthome, 1975–1976*. Paris: Seuil.
—— (1980) 'Dissolution', Seminar of 18 March 1980.
—— (2001) *Autres Écrits*. Edited by Jacques-Alain Miller. Paris: Seuil.
Lacoue-Labarthe, Philippe (1998) *Typography: Mimesis, Philosophy, Politics*. Edited by Christopher Fynsk. Stanford, CA: Stanford University Press. (Originally published, Cambridge, MA: Harvard University Press, 1989.)
Lacoue-Labarthe, Philippe and Nancy, Jean-Luc (1992 [1973]) *The Title of the Letter: A Reading of Lacan*. Trans. by François Raffoul and David Pettigrew. Albany, NY: State University of New York Press.
Laplanche, Jean and Leclaire, Serge (1966) 'L'Inconscient, une étude psychanalytique', in *L'Inconscient*. Paris: Desclée de Brouwer.
Lemaire, Anika (1977) *Jacques Lacan*. Trans. by David Macey. Preface by Jacques Lacan. London and New York: Routledge and Kegan Paul.
Levinas, Emmanuel (1978 [1947]) *Existence and Existents*. Trans. by Alphonso Lingis. The Hague: Martinus Nijhoff.
—— (1987 [1947]) 'Time and the Other' in *Time and the Other and Additional Essays*. Trans. by Richard A. Cohen. Pittsburgh: Duquesne University Press.

—— (1981 [1974]) *Otherwise than Being or Beyond Essence*. Trans. by Alphonso Lingis. The Hague: Martinus Nijhoff.

Lévi-Strauss, Claude (1970 [1949]) *The Elementary Structures of Kinship*. Trans. by James Harle Bell, John Richard von Sturmer, and Rodney Needham. London: Tavistock in association with Eyre and Spottiswoode.

—— (1987 [1950]) *Introduction to the Work of Marcel Mauss*. Trans. by Felicity Baker. London: Routledge and Kegan Paul.

—— (1968 [1958]) *Structural Anthropology*. Trans. by Claire Jacobsen and Brooke Grundfest Schoepf. London: Allen Lane, the Penguin Press.

Lewis, Michael (2005) *Heidegger and the Place of Ethics: Being-with in the Crossing of Heidegger's Thought*. London and New York: Continuum.

—— (2007) *Heidegger Beyond Deconstruction: On Nature*. London and New York: Continuum.

Lyotard, Jean-François (1989) 'The Dreamwork does not think'. Trans. by Mary Lydon in Andrew Benjamin (ed.) *The Lyotard Reader*. Oxford: Basil Blackwell.

—— (1990) *Heidegger and 'the jews'*. Trans. by Andreas Michel and Mark S. Roberts. Foreword by David Carroll. Minneapolis, MN: University of Minnesota Press.

Merleau-Ponty, Maurice (1971 [1948]) *Sense and Non-sense*. Trans. by Hubert L. Dreyfus and Patricia Allen Dreyfus. Evanston, IL: Northwestern University Press.

—— (1964 [1960]) *Signs*. Trans. by Richard C. McCleary. Evanston, IL: Northwestern University Press.

Miller, Jacques-Alain (2005) 'Notice de fil en aiguille', in Jacques Lacan, *Le Séminaire livre XXIII: Le Sinthome, 1975–1976*. Paris: Seuil.

Nietzsche, Friedrich (1961) *Thus Spoke Zarathustra: A Book for Everyone and No One*. Trans. by R. J. Hollingdale. London: Penguin.

—— (1990) *Beyond Good and Evil*. Trans. by R. J. Hollingdale. London: Penguin.

Richardson, William J. and Muller, John P. (eds) (1987) *The Purloined Poe: Lacan, Derrida, and Psychoanalytic Reading*. Baltimore: The Johns Hopkins University Press.

Roudinesco, Elisabeth (1990 [1986]) *Jacques Lacan & Co. The History of Psychoanalysis in France: 1925–1985*. Trans. by Jeffrey Mehlman. Chicago: University of Chicago Press.

—— (1997 [1993]) *Jacques Lacan*. Trans. by Barbara Bray. Oxford: Polity Press.

Safouan, Moustafa (2004) *Four Lessons of Psychoanalysis*. Edited by Anna Shane. New York: Other Press.

Saussure, Ferdinand de (1966) *Course in General Linguistics*. Edited by Charles Bally and Albert Sechehaye with Albert Riedlinger. Trans. by Wade Baskin. New York: McGraw-Hill Book Company.

Schuster, Aaron. 'Commentary on Lacan, Seminar IX *L'Identification*, 20 December 1961'. Unpublished manuscript.
Wood, David (2002) 'The Actualisation of philosophy: Heidegger and Adorno', in *Thinking after Heidegger*. Cambridge: Polity Press.
Žižek, Slavoj (1989) *The Sublime Object of Ideology*. London: Verso.
—— (1991) *For They Know Not What They Do: Enjoyment as a Political Factor*. London: Verso.
—— (1991) *Looking Awry: An Introduction to Jacques Lacan through Popular Culture*. Cambridge, MA: MIT Press.
—— (1993) *Tarrying with the Negative: Kant, Hegel, and the Critique of Ideology*. Durham, NC: Duke University Press.
—— (1999) *The Ticklish Subject: The Absent Centre of Political Ontology*. London and New York: Verso.
—— (2000) *The Fragile Absolute, or, Why is the Christian legacy worth fighting for?* London and New York: Verso.
—— (2001) *On Belief*. London and New York: Routledge.
—— (2004) with Glyn Daly, *Conversations with Žižek*. Oxford: Polity Press.
—— (2006) *The Parallax View*. Cambridge, MA: MIT Press.

Index